CATHERINE THE GREAT
AND THE
RUSSIAN NOBILITY

CATHERINE THE GREAT
AND THE
RUSSIAN NOBILITY

A STUDY BASED ON THE
MATERIALS OF THE LEGISLATIVE
COMMISSION OF 1767

BY

PAUL DUKES

Lecturer in Russian History, University of Aberdeen

CAMBRIDGE
AT THE UNIVERSITY PRESS
1967

Published by the Syndics of the Cambridge University Press
Bentley House, 200 Euston Road, London, N.W. 1
American Branch: 32 East 57th Street, New York, N.Y. 10022

© Cambridge University Press

Library of Congress Catalogue Card Number: 67–13802

Printed in Great Britain
at the University Printing House, Cambridge
(Brooke Crutchley, University Printer)

To my Mother and Father

78192

CONTENTS

PREFACE

This work does not pretend to be an exhaustive history of the reign of Catherine the Great. A full biography of the Empress, doing justice to her as ruler and diplomat, lover and correspondent, would take several volumes. Here, I have been primarily concerned with Catherine as legislator, with an attempt to show the limitations placed upon her domestic policy by the prejudices and desires of the nobility. Even this aim has not been thoroughly carried out. For example, at least twenty members of the nobility found their way to her bed, and these favourites, particularly Orlov and Potemkin, exercised an influence on the Empress much greater than most of their fellows. Rather than examining the views of such individuals, I have tried to show the class attitudes of the nobility, which Orlov, Potemkin and the others would to varying extents share.

The principal source material for this study has been the documents concerning the Legislative Commission of 1767 published by the Imperial Russian Historical Society. The focus of attention has been on the statements of noble opinion in the instructions and by the deputies and has only touched on the participation of other classes in the Commission. The activity of the sub-committees, which remained in session after the closure of the General Assembly of the Commission, has been little investigated.

The main body of the work is preceded by an examination of crown and nobility in the years before Catherine's accession, and followed by an analysis of the most important legislation of her reign in the years following the closure of the Commission, with an estimate of the extent to which this was influenced by the attitudes of the nobility. All dates in the book are Old Style, that is eleven days behind the New Style calendar throughout the eighteenth century.

Catherine the Great and the Russian Nobility is a revision and enlargement of a London University Ph.D. thesis, which was produced with the sympathetic encouragement and guidance of Professor G. H. N. Seton-Watson and Dr J. L. H. Keep of the School of Slavonic and East European Studies. Although the subject is one which has not received much detailed attention from Western European or overseas students of Russian history, their pre-Revolutionary and Soviet counterparts have given various aspects of it

Preface

extensive consideration, and I have drawn heavily on the information and ideas supplied by such men as Bochkarev, Bogoslovskii, Chechulin, Florovskii and Got'e, not to mention Solov'ev and Kliuchevskii, of older generations; and Beliavskii and Druzhinin of the newer. Among non-Russian historians, an increasing number of whom have shown interest in eighteenth-century Russian history, Marc Raeff has produced the work of most value to me, and I must also express my thanks to him for the bibliographical and more general advice that he gave me when my researches were just beginning. Allen McConnell kindly read the entire manuscript and made several suggestions for its improvement. Finally, I would like to record my gratitude to E. N. Williams, who in one of his own recent works gave thanks to his pupils 'for the education I receive'. In my case at least, principally more than fifteen years ago but not a little since, the teaching has been in the other direction. Of course, the responsibility for errors and misunderstandings in this book is entirely mine.

King's College, Old Aberdeen   P.D.

ABBREVIATIONS

M.   Moscow.

SPB.   St Petersburg.

L.   Leningrad.

PSZ   *Polnoe sobranie zakonov.*

RA   *Russkii arhiv.*

RS   *Russkaia starina.*

RV   *Russkii vestnik.*

SEER *Slavonic and East European Review.*

SIRIO *Sbornik imperatorskogo russkogo istoricheskogo obshchestva.*

TVEO *Trudy vol'nogo ekonomicheskogo obshchestva.*

VE   *Vestnik Evropy.*

ZMNP *Zhurnal ministerstva narodnogo prosveshcheniia.*

CROWN AND NOBILITY IN RUSSIA
BEFORE 1762

The Russian imperial autocracy could not have survived the eighteenth century without the support of the dvorianstvo, or nobility. Even the more capable and diligent among the rulers at this time, Peter I and Catherine II, needed to foster this class to maintain and exercise their power, and during the other two long reigns of the century, those of Anna and Elizabeth, the business of government was almost entirely handled by favourites and members of the nobility. Both these Empresses, it is true, made their peculiar impact on the statute book, but neither deserves the attention that their illustrious predecessor and successor merit in the field of legislation. Anna liked hunting, and so issued personal decrees prohibiting the pursuit of certain animals and birds in regions which she chose to reserve for her own pleasure. She was upset by the sight of a funeral procession passing her window, and forbade the transport of corpses past her palace. Elizabeth was very fond of clothes, which prompted her to require merchants to show her the fine materials they imported before putting them on the open market. She shared Anna's aversion to unpleasant reminders of mortality, and required the graves in cemeteries on the road to one of her residences to be more firmly sealed to stop any odour emanating from them.[1]

In general, setting aside the personalities of the monarchs, the Russian autocracy in the eighteenth century was moving into a new imperial phase. Giving up neither Muscovite absolutism nor its religious foundation, the crown sought to acquire a more secular basis in keeping with the spirit of the age, which revealed itself, for example, in the many references made in the laws of the period to such concepts as 'the general good',[2] and to adapt its institutions to keep pace with its theory. Such a development was to have far-reaching implications for the dvorianstvo.

Evidence for this can be clearly seen in the Table of Ranks,

---

[1] N. I. Pavlenko, 'Idei absoliutizma v zakonodatel'stve xviii v.', in N. M. Druzhinin, etc. (eds.), *Absoliutizm v Rossii*, pp. 411–12.
[2] *Ibid.* pp. 398–9.

promulgated on 24 January 1722, and expounding a bureaucratic conception of nobility with a whole new set of ranks, mostly of Prussian and Danish origin,[1] arranged in three principal parallel columns, military, civil and court, with the first receiving precedence.[2] Although the Table of Ranks declared that those who occupied the wrong places at church ceremonies and official court functions would be fined, and although princes, barons and counts[3] would be given precedence at such assemblies, section 8 of the Table made it completely clear that nobody would receive rank who had not demonstrated his services to the sovereign and the fatherland. However, section 16 suggested that a nobleman need not necessarily earn his distinction by strict progression from one rung of the service ladder to the next, but could also receive it by direct grant of the monarch.[4] In whatever manner he achieved his eminence, the dvorianin would be expected to obey detailed regulations concerning the dress, equipage and livery suitable for his station.

The Table of Ranks comprehensively described the framework of a hierarchy for the bureaucratic state that had been evolving in seventeenth-century Russia, a state that was to blossom in the eighteenth century, and to survive in its essentials to the Revolution of 1917, and, in a sense, perhaps beyond. Powerful prejudices, the opposition of old families to the promotion of upstarts, the influence of wealth and connection, all worked against the successful operation of the prescribed system, but its essential principle, the pre-eminence of rank achieved by state service over birth, proved durable.[5] The nobility, then, particularly in 1722, was a political institution: all

[1] *PSZ*, VI, 486–93, no. 3,890; V. A. Evreinov, *Grazhdanskoe chinoproizvodstvo v Rossii*, pp. 26–7.

[2] See *PSZ*, no. 3,890, sections 11, 15.

[3] There were essentially two categories of *kniaz'*, or prince, in Russia: descendants of medieval Russian and Lithuanian princes; and those whose ancestors had been created princes by Moscow tsars, or who had been confirmed as such by virtue of creation as princes by foreign sovereigns. *Graf*, or count, was perhaps introduced as a title into Russia because that of prince had sunk into low esteem through overmultiplication. Peter the Great was the first to create Russian counts, and barons, too, perhaps for similar reasons to those for the creation of counts. Counts and barons created by foreign sovereigns, or living in the Baltic provinces, were recognized in the same way as princes of foreign origin (E. P. Karnovich, *Rodovye prozvaniia i tituly v Rossii*, pp. 167, 192–4, 217).

[4] Catherine I was the first sovereign to use section 16 of the Table of Ranks to confer dvorianstvo, the recipient being N. D. Demidov, the industrialist. Elizabeth made particular use of conferment, making several guardsmen dvoriane in 1741, for example (A. Romanovich-Slavatinskii, *Dvorianstvo v Rossii*, pp. 28–9).

[5] Michael T. Florinsky, *Russia, A History and an Interpretation*, p. 421; B. H. Sumner, *Peter the Great and the Emergence of Russia*, p. 156.

2

dvoriane were expected to serve the state, and they received land, and, to an increasing extent, money as rewards for their services, together with honour and status.[1] Thus, the crown and the dvorianstvo stood together.

SERVICES AND PRIVILEGES

The rank of dvorianin gave its possessor certain privileges in return for certain services. Both of these were more clearly formulated during the reign of Peter the Great than ever before, and both were then significantly amended during the reigns of his successors.

The services had always been predominantly military: they remained so under Peter, but on a different basis, for he transformed what had been a locally based militia into a regular army. This reform brought about three key changes in the service of the nobility. First, military and civil service, previously hardly distinguishable, became completely differentiated. Secondly, both military and civil service were now to be compulsorily preceded by a suitable educational preparation. Thirdly, and, according to Kliuchevskii, perhaps most influentially on later Russian development, the new regular army lost its local allegiance.[2]

The segregation of the nobility into military and civil service was the concern of a newly appointed Heraldmaster. In 1722 this official was instructed to make sure that 'no more than one third of a family be allowed to join the civil service, lest the land and sea forces suffer'. Another reason for separating the branches of service was educational. Up to this time there had been almost no professional training for administration, and so the Heraldmaster was now commanded to set up a school with a basic course of study 'in economics and civics' for those entering the civil branch.[3] Similarly, specialized training was to be given also to those entering military service, either in the Guards or military and naval schools. A further consequence of Peter's creation of a regular army was the diminution of the local allegiance of the dvoriane. Now:

---

[1] Romanovich-Slavatinskii, *Dvorianstvo*, pp. 156–74.

[2] V. O. Klyuchevsky, *Peter the Great*, trans. Liliana Archibald, pp. 102–3. Klyuchevsky goes on to point out how the 'exchange of local for regimental or barrack ties could result in the Guards becoming a blind instrument of force in the hands of a powerful sovereign, or Praetorians or Janissaries under a weak ruler'.

[3] Klyuchevsky, *Peter the Great*, pp. 99–100. This school was not in fact created.

3

a man from Ryazan, absent for a long time or forever from his native Pehlets or Zimarov, forgot that he was from Ryazan, and knew only that he was a dragoon in the fusilier regiment commanded by Colonel Famandine. The barracks successfully extinguished any territorial allegiance.[1]

To ensure complete obedience to his service orders, Peter subjected the nobles to a strict inspection system controlled by the Heraldmaster. Between his death in 1725 and the accession of Anna in 1730, this system was allowed to lapse: under Anna it was revived, with some modifications which were announced in 1736 and 1737, and which were probably influenced by the desires of the nobles themselves.

The imperial manifesto of 31 December 1736 made several provisions expressly aimed at the scandalous conditions of the estates of the absentee landlords, and provincial lawlessness and chaos in general. One male member of each family containing two or more males could now stay at home to run the family estates. He would have to learn to read and write, however, to be fit for civil service. The others were to be able to leave service after twenty-five years if they chose. For those staying at home or leaving service, recruits were to be sent to the army at the rate of one recruit for every hundred serfs on each estate.[2] Supplementary decrees of 1737 announced exacting regulations for the training of young nobles. At the age of seven, they were to register for service: at twelve, they would undergo a reading and writing examination. If they passed this, they could then be kept at home to learn arithmetic and geometry and elementary theology, with languages as optional additional subjects, provided that their fathers possessed more than a hundred serfs, or had sufficient alternative means. If the young dvoriane failed the examination, or if their parents failed the means test, they would have to go to school. When they reached the age of sixteen, they would have to go to Moscow or St Petersburg to be examined before the Senate or one of its ancillary departments. If their geometry and arithmetic were satisfactory, they could then go home again till the age of twenty to study geography, 'fortification' and history: that some of those who failed this examination were to be enrolled in the navy as ordinary seamen was an incentive to passing it. Finally, at the age of twenty, a further trip to Moscow or St Petersburg would determine what kind of service the young

---

[1] Klyuchevsky, *Peter the Great*, p. 102. [2] *PSZ*, IX, 1022, no. 7,142.

nobles who had managed to stay the course would enter. During the whole of their training period, the young nobles were to carry pass-ports showing what examinations they had taken. The choice of the dvorianin who was to look after the family estates would be made at the third stage when he was sixteen.[1]

Execution of the regulations of 31 December 1736 was delayed until 1739 because of the war with Turkey, and then, 'requests for dismissal from service were so numerous that the government found it necessary to give the law an interpretation that amounted to partial repeal'.[2] In the second half of the reign of Elizabeth, 1741–62, members of the government were contemplating further emancipa-tion of the dvorianstvo from service,[3] but, in the first half of her reign, laws had been passed reversing the tendency which the 1736 manifesto appeared to introduce. For example, in 1749 all dvoriane who had retired from military or civil service were to register with the Heralds, and present themselves at the Senate for assignment to further duties.[4]

However, the period between the death of Peter the Great and the accession of Peter III can be called, with some reservations, a period of gradual emancipation for the dvorianstvo as far as the law was concerned. Furthermore, the letter of such decrees as those of 1736, 1737 and 1749 could never be strictly enforced by the bureau-crats, and the opportunity for reluctant dvoriane to avoid service illegally was probably greater during the reigns of Anna and Eliza-beth than during the time of Peter the Great.

Certain privileges were awarded in return for the services of the dvorianstvo demanded by Peter the Great and his successors. Most of them were never definitely formulated until the Charter of the Nobles in 1785. This listed six main privileges: freedom from oblig-atory service; freedom from corporal punishment; the right to landed and other property; the right to manufacture and trade; freedom from personal taxes and impositions; and the inviolability of the dignity of the dvorianstvo, protected by the courts and the Supreme Power.[5]

Some of the steps towards freedom from obligatory service, as well as some of those in the opposite direction, have already been

---

[1] *PSZ*, x, 43–5, no. 7,171, 9 February 1737; x, 54–5, no. 7,182, 19 February 1737.
[2] Florinsky, *Russia*, p. 483.   [3] Romanovich-Slavatinskii, *Dvorianstvo*, p. 196.
[4] *PSZ*, xiii, 1, no. 9,569, 17 January 1749.
[5] The main points of the following description of the privileges of the nobility taken from Romanovich-Slavatinskii, *Dvorianstvo*, pp. 214–78.

mentioned. Before 1762 it was not officially possible for dvoriane to avoid service obligations completely, but money, favour, influence and cunning could all circumvent these irksome requirements or alleviate them. One stratagem frequently resorted to was to enlist minors, which would bring early advancement in rank and a curtailment of the period of service: at least one young dvorianin received promotion before he was born.[1]

Immunity from corporal punishment was not guaranteed to the dvorianstvo until 1785, although such a privilege had been considered more than a century before during the reign of Aleksei Mihailovich. In the seventeenth century, there was some class distinction with regard to punishments, but of an arbitrary, rather than legal, nature. While a lower rank would get the knout for a certain offence, a higher might receive punishment by the whip or rods, but if a noble were privileged in this manner, it would be because of the tsar's will rather than the stipulation of the law. The Code of 1649 said that, for certain offences, the boyars could be subjected to 'a cruel punishment as indicated by the tsar'. A contemporary of this Code, Kotoshihin, wrote that everybody suffered the same punishment for brigandage, 'whatever his rank: prince, or boyar, or ordinary person'. This situation did not improve very much during the reign of Peter the Great and his immediate successors, no distinction being made between nobles and others, for instance, in punishments administered by the new regular army. However, Peter, like his predecessors, took some notice of rank in individual cases, and his successors were often more lenient as influential members of the dvorianstvo began to look upon corporal punishment as degrading to their class. Although Prince Shcherbatov wrote that he had known people who had suffered corporal punishment under Peter the Great and were not ashamed of it, and although there was talk in 1730 of treating the dvorianstvo with as much respect as in other European countries, nothing was said specifically about exemptions from corporal punishment, twenty years later (in 1750) I. I. Shuvalov was thinking of such exemptions as he projected fundamental laws for Russia, and thoughts of this kind became more widespread by the early years of the reign of Catherine II.[2]

The third privilege listed in the Charter of the Nobles was the

---

[1] See *RS*, cxxxii, 438.   [2] Romanovich-Slavatinskii, *Dvorianstvo*, pp. 233–40.

right to landed and other property. This is inextricably connected with the problem of serfdom, and will be discussed later. For the moment, it is worth pointing out that the dvoriane did not possess full legal rights to their immovable property: their rights of use and disposition were curtailed by the state, which owned the primary legal right to all Russian land. The principal limitations on the use of the land that Peter introduced were four in number and concerned the 'bowels of the earth', forests growing on its surface, certain appurtenances, and mills. With regard to the first of these, Peter allowed private mining and industry in 1713, but with very restricting conditions, and under the close supervision of the College of Mines; the situation remained legally the same up to the accession of Catherine II. Secondly, Peter clamped down very severely on the use of the forests. There was some relaxation of her husband's severity under Catherine I, but the governments of Peter II, Anna and Elizabeth applied tight restrictions again. Peter controlled the rights of the dvorianstvo to fishing, bee-keeping and mill-owning, but his controls were relaxed under his successors, particularly Elizabeth.

As far as the right of disposition was concerned, Peter's most important piece of legislation was the decree of 23 March 1714. This was much influenced by Western ideas of primogeniture and entail, hitherto foreign to Russia, where equal division of property among all children had long been a practice looked upon as a principle of divine justice. The long preamble to the decree of 1714 criticized traditional Russian practice as harmful to the state, the peasants and the nobles themselves. The subdivision of estates made if difficult to collect taxes, and disinclined the nobles from service or other occupation; a son, with an estate much reduced in size from that of his parents, wanted to enjoy the same standard of living as his parents, and forced his peasants to work harder; subdivision of estates meant general impoverishment and loss of social standing for the dvoriane. The main divisions of the decree stated that all immovable property was to remain in the family; immovable property was to be willed to one heir only, and movables were to be distributed as the testator wished among other children; and, in cases of intestacy, immovable property was to go to the eldest son, or, failing sons, daughter, and movables were to be distributed equally among the remaining children.[1]

---

[1] *PSZ*, v, 91–4, no. 2,789.

Some of the higher dvorianstvo welcomed Peter's adoption of the German *maiorat*. They realized the truth of what Tocqueville was later to point out, that the laws of inheritance were important to any state, and that this system of hereditary tenure would uphold the predominance of their families. However, most of the dvoriane were opposed to it, and pressed for the repeal of the decree of 1714, which was finally achieved in 1730. The preamble to the decree of repeal stated that the introduction of entail and the other hereditary restrictions had produced economic disaster, since many parents, forced to give one child their landed property, had given their cattle, horses and stocks of grain to their other children; sales of land, which Peter had hoped to curtail, had in fact increased; many nobles were engaged in legal and actual battle among themselves; and the disinherited sons, whom Peter had hoped to encourage to enter commerce and industry, could not do so, since they were continually drafted into service. Although the *maiorat* was abolished in 1730, the dvoriane who had been in favour of it pressed for its reintroduction, without success, at least up to 1762.[1]

The fourth of the six principal privileges listed in 1785 was the right to trade and manufacture. To Peter the Great, trade was incompatible with service, and so serving dvoriane were forbidden to participate in it. By trade, however, Peter meant the re-sale of bought goods, and so the sale of domestically produced goods was allowed to all dvoriane in their landowning capacity. In 1711 dvoriane not in service and some other ranks were permitted 'to engage freely in commerce anywhere'. With the abolition of the *maiorat* in 1730, however, dvoriane could no longer become merchants. All classes were allowed manufacturing rights by Peter the Great, but under the supervision of the College of Manufactures. This remained the official policy of successive governments up to the

---

[1] Abolition of *maiorat*: *PSZ*, VIII, 345–7, no. 5,653, 9 December 1730. M. V. Danilov, a noble born in the early 1720s, described how the 1714 law made it necessary for many young dvoriane to fend for themselves. However, Danilov went on to say: 'This inequality between the children moved affectionate parental hearts...there was no other way for a dvorianin's son to seek a living for himself, except from the immovable estate left by his father: nobody was very keen to go into military service, and young dvoriane had to be enlisted by force; the sciences and arts were still known in few houses, and many young dvoriane were barely literate...Such an impossible state of affairs for the young dvoriane forced them to ask persistently for it to be allowed that immovable estates be divided up into equal parts; with these persistent requests, a decree of Anna Ivanovna finally settled the question' (Danilov, *Zapiski*, pp. 14–15). The landed and other property rights of the dvorianstvo are described in Romanovich-Slavatinskii, *Dvorianstvo*, pp. 244–60.

accession of Catherine II. The manufacture of alcoholic drinks was guaranteed as a right of the dvorianstvo in 1716; in 1754, this right was made a monopoly, to include the sale of such drinks to the state contractors, although merchants were also to sell them until the nobles were in a position to manage all the trade.[1]

The other two privileges in the 1785 list were freedom from personal taxes and impositions, and the inviolability of the dignity of the dvorianstvo. Serving dvoriane were excused personal taxes, although it was decreed in 1710 that those not suitable for service would be taxed. Dvoriane were further cut off from the rest of the population by the introduction of the poll tax in 1718. Similarly, dvoriane were not recruited into the rank and file because of their obligations to lead the army. Before 1762 the dignity of the nobility can hardly be said to have been inviolable, although some dvoriane pressed for it to be so in 1730, with a request that a dvorianin be stripped of his rank only after a trial.[2]

Having completed this survey of the services and privileges of the nobility as regulated by the Supreme Power in the first half of the eighteenth century, I shall now discuss the part played by this class and by the government in various aspects of the country's life.

SERFDOM AND THE ECONOMY

The legal niceties of serfdom meant very little before the nineteenth century. As discussion of emancipation became more widespread, many complicated questions concerning the triangular relationship between the state, the dvoriane and the serfs arose, for example to whom and how completely did the serfs belong? But the term *sobstvennost'*, or property, was unknown in Russia before the time of Peter the Great,[3] and such points were elementary in the seventeenth century, and, up to 1762 at least, hardly more subtle in the eighteenth century.

The serf usually accepted the lot that fate had accorded to him with resignation: our body belongs to the sovereign, our soul to God and our back to the master, says one of his many proverbs. The only legal redress for the grievances of the serfs was obtained by

[1] Romanovich-Slavatinskii, *Dvorianstvo*, pp. 248–9, 264–8; Florinsky, *Russia*, p. 392. The 1754 decree, *PSZ*, xiv, 184–6, no. 10,261, 19 July 1754.
[2] Romanovich-Slavatinskii, *Dvorianstvo*, pp. 272–7.
[3] A. Miller, *Essai sur l'Histoire des Institutions Agraires*, p. 71.

petition, and such a step would normally be beyond them. When things got too much even for the elemental patience of the serfs, they would often take more positive action. Just how desperate life could be for the serfs was well described by several observers in the 1720s. In 1723, for example, an official reported from the province of Orel that the local inhabitants 'are completely impoverished, do not eat for two or three days on end, and, leaving their homes, wander about and feed on grass and nuts mixed with chaff, and thus become ill, and many die of hunger'. At about the same time, peasants were threatened with banishment to the galleys for failure to conform to certain regulations. So great was their hunger that many of them volunteered for such banishment. The threat of famine was never far away from the majority of Russian peasants, and this, as well as extortions or cruelties from their landlords, army units or governmental officials, would often drive them to flight, suicide, murder or revolt.[1]

The relationship of the noble landlords to their serfs would be largely governed by their own personal attitude. Each estate was a small autocracy as absolute as that to which the dvoriane were themselves subject, and such government regulations of serfdom as there were stood little chance of exact execution when local administration was in an elementary and malfunctioning condition, and barely able to carry out its principal tasks of collecting state revenues and maintaining law and order. Undoubtedly, there was a degree of paternal concern in the attitude of some landlords to their serfs—a peasant proverb bears witness to this: if there is no grain, the master will provide. On the other hand, the goodwill alone of the master was a poor guarantee of the serf's general welfare.

The services that the peasants carried out for their lords were of two main types, the direct *barshchina*, or compulsory labour, and the indirect *obrok*, which consisted of payments in money or kind in commutation of the *barshchina*, or for the use of land allotments which the peasants farmed on their own account. The relative distribution of *barshchina* and *obrok* was influenced by such factors as soil fertility, estate size and opportunities for employment away from the estate of the landlord. Using the opportunities for trade and manufacture that were increasingly presenting themselves, some serfs prospered

[1] M. M. Bogoslovskii, *Oblastnaia reforma Petra Velikogo*, pp. 463–4; Romanovich-Slavatinskii, *Dvorianstvo*, pp. 364–78.

considerably, and thus accelerated the process of the stratification of the peasantry.[1]

The serfs of the dvorianstvo accounted for about $3\frac{1}{2}$ million or just over half the total of Russian male peasants at the middle of the eighteenth century. A noble's economic status was measured by the number of male serfs, or 'souls', that he possessed. On this basis, three main classes can be distinguished among the dvorianstvo. About three-fifths of the landlords owned less than twenty serfs each, and about 5 per cent of the total serf population; rather more than a fifth owned between twenty and one hundred serfs each, about 15 per cent of the total; and rather less than a fifth owned over one hundred serfs each, approximately 80 per cent of the total. So, from an economic point of view, there were among the nobility a lower, a middle and an upper class, the third of these being the smallest in number but in possession of most of the serfs, and the first of them by far the largest numerically but so insignificant in other ways that their lives are often difficult to distinguish from those of their human chattels.[2]

The estates of the 40,000–50,000 noble landowners were spread around the old capital, Moscow, in a pattern mostly determined by historical circumstances. Thus, the area to the south of Moscow, comprising the later provinces of Kaluga, Tula, Riazan and much of Orel, which had formed the principal line of defence against Tartar incursions in the sixteenth century, was *par excellence* the region for the estates of the lower and middle landlords. To the north-west of Moscow, the area around Smolensk, Pskov and St Petersburg had been developed in the sixteenth and seventeenth centuries as ramparts against the Poles and the Swedes, and therefore also contained many estates of the lower and middle strata of nobles. To the north-east of Moscow, Iaroslavl', Nizhnii Novgorod and Kostroma were surrounded by many of the tsar's lands and the old boyar estates. The centre of the circle, around Moscow, Vladimir and Tver', contained the large domains of the upper-class dvoriane, and large ecclesiastical holdings. Beyond this inner circle around Moscow was another, where the estates of the dvorianstvo

[1] A. I. Baranovich, etc. (eds.), *Ocherki istorii SSSR, Period feodalizma, Rossiia vo vtoroi chetverti XVIII v.*, pp. 66–9, 72–3.
[2] Miller, *Essai*, pp. 255–6. Compiled from post-1750 censuses, these figures must be considered as approximations only for the first half of the eighteenth century.

were more thinly spread. The diminution was quicker to the north than to the south, partly for historical reasons, partly because the land was of a better quality to the south. Kursk and Tambov were in more or less a continuation of Orel and Riazan, and the environs of Voronezh, Penza, Simbirsk and Saratov contained much large-scale property of eighteenth-century origin. State and ecclesiastical peasants predominated in the northern outer circle around Novgorod, Vologda, Kazan' and Perm', although some of the estates of the nobility set up by Ivan the Terrible were to be found in Novgorod province and to the west of Vologda. Finally, to the far north and east, around Olonets, Archangel, Viatka and Siberia, only a few noble estates were to be found.[1]

Estates obviously varied tremendously in size: the largest would have required a considerable administrative staff, and the land-lords of the smaller holdings often had at least a bailiff or steward to look after things for them while they were away. A considerable number of serfs, many more than were necessary to observers such as Shcherbatov, were household servants, and serf orchestras, choirs and companies of actors were not unknown. (One noble opera-lover forbade his servants to communicate with him or among themselves in anything but recitative.) Estates often had their own craftsmen and tradesmen, too.[2] Because of estate mis-management, or over-expanded domestic establishments, basic costs or expenses incurred in improvements, dvoriane often found them-selves in debt. They could raise money after 1754 by loan from the State Nobility Bank, or by selling some land and serfs. Serf sales were encouraged by the fact that replacements could be substituted for those summoned to the colours by recruit levies.[3]

Serfdom was firmly entrenched by the decree of 9 January 1723 which made all 'souls' liable to the poll tax, putting serfs and other classes of bondmen into one group: however, the institution was well established long before this.[4] Possession of serfs was not at first limited to the dvorianstvo, but laws of 1730, 1743 and 1746 curtailed the possession of serfs by other classes, and laws of 1754 and 1758 aimed at the complete prohibition of such possession.[5]

---

[1] Miller, *Essai*, pp. 250–4.
[2] Romanovich-Slavatinskii, *Dvorianstvo*, pp. 335–6.
[3] *PSZ*, XIV, 87–94, no. 10,235, 13 May 1754; Romanovich-Slavatinskii, *Dvorianstvo*, pp. 343–4.   [4] *PSZ*, VII, 2–6, no. 4,139.
[5] Romanovich-Slavatinskii, *Dvorianstvo*, pp. 287–9.

Serfdom and the economy

The power of the landlords over their serfs was legally extended by various pieces of legislation throughout the period from the death of Peter the Great to the accession of Peter III, and, at the same time, the rights of the serfs were legally reduced.[1] Groups equivalent to the dvorianstvo in the Ukraine and the Baltic provinces were similarly acquiring a strong, monopolistic power over the local peasants, and there, as in Great Russia, a large part of the relations between the peasants and their masters were ungoverned by law, which gave completely free rein to the masters, particularly since those laws in existence were rarely strictly applied. Of course, the relations between the landlords and the central government were of a similar nature. Confiscation of their estates for non-fulfilment of orders or decrees, or at the arbitrary whim of the government, was a persistent threat hanging over the heads of individual landlords in all provinces of the Russian Empire throughout the first half of the eighteenth century.[2]

Because of the nature of their property, the members of the nobility were principally concerned with agriculture, and only a few displayed much interest in trade, industry or any other branch of the economy. While agriculture in Russia had largely been unregulated before the reign of Peter the Great, the Emperor was largely interested in it as a supplier of provisions for the armed forces, and as a producer of raw materials for Russia's developing industry. He therefore attempted to promote the cultivation of hemp, flax, jute, sugar beet, tobacco and grapes in addition to that of the more traditional crops, as well as encouraging the exploitation of mineral resources. Horses and wool were necessary for the army, so Peter was anxious to improve horse and sheep breeding: the navy needed timber, so Peter made many provisions for the conservation of forests. There is little evidence that these comprehensive decrees made any great impact on the rural economy, or that his immediate successors demonstrated anything like Peter's solicitude, although members of the government and the nobility continued to believe in the supreme importance of agriculture, and made some attempt to improve its condition on their estates.[3]

[1] *Ibid.* p. 294; Florinsky, *Russia*, pp. 484–6.

[2] Got'e, *Ocherk*, pp. 135–8, 199–200. K. V. Sivkov, *Materialy...hoziaistva*, pp. 372–81, gives a list of landlords whose estates had been confiscated.

[3] Florinsky, *Russia*, pp. 391–2; E. V. Spiridonova, *Ekonomicheskaia politika i ekonomicheskie vzgliady Petra I*, pp. 183–9; P. K. Alefirenko, 'Russkia obshchestvennaia mysl'

Under the influence of mercantilist theory, Peter tried to make Russia export goods manufactured under the shelter of a protective tariff in her own ships. By the middle of the eighteenth century, after several fluctuations in the tariff rate, and further legislation of a mercantilist nature, Russia's exports were still to a considerable degree raw materials; she was still importing a significant amount of manufactures; and her merchants were still very dependent on foreign intermediaries.[1] Internal trade was given a boost by the abolition of internal tariffs in the 1750s,[2] and there is considerable evidence of a national market growing in certain branches of trade during the first half of the eighteenth century, but the wide persistence of an undeveloped natural economy is indicated by the disconnection of separate internal markets, the predominance of trade at fairs, the chaotic variation in prices in neighbouring regions, and wild fluctuations in prices from year to year.[3]

In a country without capital, technicians, industrial labour and *entrepreneurs*, Peter the Great was anxious to promote industry in any way possible, and encouraged members of the dvorianstvo and merchant class alike with financial privileges, loans and facilities for recruiting labour. He also pushed the state further into this field in his efforts to modernize Russia. Such state interventionism was relaxed later on in the century as general conditions became more favourable to industrial development.[4]

The greatest leap forward in the growth of the textile and other manufacturing enterprises seems to have been from the 1760s onwards, but, before then, a growing internal market in some commodities, formed both by the state and private consumers, and

pervoi poloviny XVIII v. o znachenii sel'skogo hoziaistva', *Akademiku B. D. Grekovu, Sbornik statei*, pp. 261–5; P. K. Alefirenko, 'Russkaia obshchestvennaia mysl' pervoi poloviny XVIII stoletiia o sel'skom hoziaistve', *Materialy po istorii zemledeliia SSSR*, 1, 517–44.

[1] Florinsky, *Russia*, pp. 393, 489–90; Baranovich, etc. (eds.), *Ocherki istorii SSSR, Period feodalizma, Rossiia vo vtoroi chetverti XVIII v.*, pp. 166–9.

[2] M. Ia. Volkov, 'Otmena vnutrennyh tamozhen v Rossii', *Istoriia SSSR*, 1957, no. 2; M. Ia. Volkov, 'Tamozhennaia reforma 1753–1757 gg.', *Istoricheskie zapiski* (1962), LXXI. Volkov argues that P. I. Shuvalov and others sought to free peasant trade in the interest of the dvorianstvo through the tariff reform, but, because of 'objective' elements in the situation, they rather assisted the development of the bourgeoisie.

[3] B. B. Kafengauz, *Ocherki vnutrennego rynka Rossii pervoi poloviny XVIII veka*, argues the case for the development of the 'all-Russian market' in the first half of the eighteenth century. For assertions of the wide persistence of a natural economy, it is necessary to look at earlier, and non-specialized, works such as A. A. Kizevetter, *Mestnoe samoupravlenie v Rossii*, pp. 118–20; Lyashchenko, *History*, p. 278.

[4] Roger Portal, 'Manufactures et classes sociales en Russie au XVIII⁰ siècle', *Revue Historique*, CCI, 167–70.

expanding opportunities for export, had already launched Russia on a persistent, if rather modest, industrial revolution. It is difficult to establish the contribution of the nobility to this revolution, partly because available statistics are unreliable, partly because of difficulties of definition. (For example, at what point does a flourishing domestic handicraft enterprise on an estate become a factory? Should such a factory be considered the enterprise of the landlord or the serfs?) Estimates of noble factories in central Russia made by Soviet historians have fluctuated between 10 and 16 per cent of the total: such estimates are not likely to exaggerate the part played by the nobility.[1]

Metallurgical industry, increasingly important, particularly in the Urals, was encouraged by the dvorianstvo in two ways: they owned a considerable number of establishments; and hired out their serfs to the owners of others. The second process was to mean considerable social changes in the ranks of the serfs, although only a small minority of the mass of the Russian population before 1762 was involved in it.[2] To the north-west and south-west as well, nobles were participating in the promotion of local industry.[3]

GOVERNMENT AND SOCIETY

Many of Peter the Great's reforms of local administration got no further than the paper stage. To have set up efficient government where before there was none would have required the close attention of the state's officials and the support of the leaders of provincial society, the dvoriane. The nobles at this time were principally interested in strengthening their ownership of land and serfs, reducing their burdens of obligatory service and limiting arbitrary confiscation of their estates. The detailed plans for a bureaucratic organization of local government, the threat of an additional form of obligatory service, and concentration of all real power at the centre, entailed in the reforms, opposed rather than furthered the chief concerns of the nobility. As for Peter and his assistants, while their heads were full of ideas snatched from the West such as rational government, the separation of powers, and so on, they had

---

[1] Portal, *Revue Historique*, ccii, 9.
[2] *Ibid.* pp. 13–15; Portal, *L'Oural au XVIIIe siècle*, p. 262.
[3] Baranovich, etc. (eds.), *Ocherki istorii SSSR, Period feodalizma, Rossiia vo vtoroi chetverti XVIII v.*, pp. 532, 657, 668–9.

no clear motive for the improvement of local government beyond the encouragement of military and fiscal efficiency. For this reason, a new administrative unit, the regimental district, was superimposed upon the new institutions. As before, but now on the basis of the poll tax, the taxpayers were to provide for the maintenance of the troops quartered in their locality. Army officers were given extensive police, as well as tax-collecting, powers, and carried on their work without the slightest regard for the civil administrators, in conjunction with whom they were supposed to be working.

According to Kliuchevskii, the resulting situation amounted to an invasion of the countryside by the military, a situation unparalleled in Russian history since the early days of the Mongol rule. Not only this:

Bands of pillagers, commanded by deserters, joined together in well-organized and well-armed cavalry groups, and attacked in regular formation, destroying well-populated villages, impeding the collection of taxes, and even penetrating into towns...The civil servant in the capital, the general on a mission, the dvorianin on his distant estates, all ignored the Tsar's terrible ukazes; neither they, nor the brigands in the forests, cared what the semi-autocratic Senate, and...Swedish-type colleges, with their carefully defined jurisdictions, achieved in the capital. An imposing legislative façade merely concealed the general disorder which prevailed throughout the country.[1]

At Peter's death in 1725, it was thought that such troubles stemmed from the fact that his reforms were never completed. Soon, however, the reforms themselves were criticized, and the old Muscovite local order praised and idealized and largely restored. Government by the officials known as *voevody* was recognized as such a panacea for Russia's internal troubles that the very title seemed to have effectiveness. Thus, discussing the introduction of new administrators, the newly created Supreme Privy Council ruled that they be given this title, 'because the rank of *voevoda* can be more awesome for people running all affairs in the provinces'.[2] By a decree of 12 September 1728 the *voevoda* became again the financial, administrative and legal agent of government in a simple, straightforward way, and, by this time, the whole structure of seventeenth-century provincial government had been reintroduced with very few changes, some of which were left over from the reforms of Peter the Great.[3]

---

[1] Klyuchevsky, *Peter the Great*, p. 246; Florinsky, *Russia*, pp. 377–8; Bogoslovskii, *Oblastnaia reforma*, pp. 507–17.　　　　[2] *SIRIO*, LV, 406.

[3] *PSZ*, VIII, 94–112, no. 5,333. There were other simplifications of provincial administration in 1726 and 1727 (Florinsky, *Russia*, p. 378).

Government and society

The new governors and *voevody*, working in a three-tier system of administration comprising province, county and district, were not concerned with the prosperity and general welfare of the population to the extent that Peter's later reforms envisaged for local officials. The creators of the reforms of 1725–8 were wisely less ambitious and were rather looking for simplicity and cheapness. Elementary institutions with a small number of functionaries, costing the state very little, could have been capable of the demands made upon them if the functionaries had been adequate to their task. But the people working in these institutions were poorly prepared for broad administrative activity, and, weighed down by ancient tradition, were servile before the strong and overbearing before the weak. The best of them followed the interests of their class, the nobility, and rarely achieved an understanding of the interests of the community or the state. The vast majority of them looked upon the office that they filled as a means of providing for themselves from state and private sources. The standard of the governors changed a little for the better in the 1750s, perhaps, but the *voevody* remained the same up to 1762 and beyond, partly because their cultural and moral level did not rise, partly because their job was simply too much for them. Various governments between the death of Peter the Great and the accession of Catherine II realized the inadequacy of local institutions, and tried to help matters in various ways. They introduced supervisory officials and bodies; they developed on a large scale the system of special commissions, supplying extraordinary agents where provincial government was breaking down. Finally, the failure of all such piecemeal attempts at the correction of the inadequacies of the existing order led to the conviction that the fundamental reconstruction of the whole system of local government was necessary. But this conviction did not become widespread until after 1762.[1]

The participation of the nobility in local government grew rather than diminished after the death of Peter. Just before the introduction of the 1728 machinery, two-thirds of the nobles in the army were sent home on extended leave. Their service was considered unnecessary and costly at that particular time, and it was intended that they should personally supervise the collection of the poll tax, the management of their estates, and the welfare of their serfs.

[1] Iu. V. Got'e, *Istoriia oblastnogo upravleniia v Rossii ot Petra I do Ekateriny II*, i, 465–7.

The army was to cease collection of the poll tax, although it was to remain distributed among the provinces and receive its upkeep from the landlords or bailiffs via the local government officials. This process was completed by 1731.[1] The period from 1725 to 1762, it has been pointed out, can with some reservations generally be called a period of gradual emancipation from service, and this tendency was reflected in the development in some provinces of a close link between the nobility and the provincial administration, particularly the all-important *voevoda*.[2] Moreover, there is evidence of a change in attitude on the part of the nobility before 1762 towards local elective duties.[3]

In the early centuries of the evolution of the service class, there had been little lasting connection between the noble family and any particular locality.[4] However, by the eighteenth century, such a connection can be observed in some parts of Great Russia, and it had long been established in the Baltic provinces.[5] Whether or not dvoriane became less itinerant, their estates possessed little of the magnificence with which some of them were to be endowed in later years. For example, an inventory of the estate of Prince D. M. Golitsyn made in 1737 showed that the manor house consisted of two rooms only. There were some icons and pictures on the walls, but little evidence of the luxury that Shcherbatov and others were soon to complain of. The homes of lesser nobles were similarly modest, usually consisting of a lower set of two or three living rooms and a storeroom. Hunting and the various cares of estate management occupied the lives of most nobles living in the provinces. Hospitality was informally and lavishly, but rarely, given, for distances were great and travel often difficult.[6]

Perhaps the greatest influence on the lives of provincial landlords was serfdom. Each estate, with its own craftsmen, household servants and administrative officials, was a complete kingdom over which

---

[1] *PSZ*, VII, 734–6, 743–4, 750–1, 758–61, nos. 5,010, 5,016, 5,018, 5,033, 9, 24, 28 February, 15 March 1727; Florinsky, *Russia*, pp. 483–4.

[2] Got'e, *Istoriia*, I, 154–61, describes how this link developed in the Klin region.

[3] Got'e, *Istoriia*, II, 120–56.   [4] Karnovich, *Rododvye prozvaniia i tituly*, p. 27.

[5] See, for example, Baranovich, etc. (eds.), *Ocherki istorii SSSR, Period feodalizma, Rossiia vo vtoroi chetverti XVIII v.*, pp. 659–60; Romanovich-Slavatinskii, *Dvorianstvo*, pp. 170–1. Too much should not be made of this point, for, as Romanovich-Slavatinskii says, estates still rarely stayed in the same family's hands for more than three or four generations.

[6] M. M. Bogoslovskii, *Byt i nravy russkogo dvorianstva v pervoi polovine XVIIIogo veka*, pp. 30–3.

the landlord or his bailiff ruled as absolute monarch or regent plenipotentiary. Questions of foreign policy towards other kingdoms often arose, particularly boundary disputes, and these could be very tricky, since there was no properly instituted survey. Lengthy and costly lawsuits were common, therefore, and the landlords, for want of very much else to do, showed great interest in them. The bolder and more fiery nobles, whose principal calling was, after all, war, did not have the patience to await the results of drawn-out lawsuits, and preferred to settle their disagreements in a more direct manner. So neighbouring kingdoms were sometimes at war with each other. Thus, in 1742, a wealthy landlord of Viaz'ma in Smolensk province called Griboedov, at the head of a band of retainers, drove a female landowner from her estate by night, and occupied it. In 1754 the brothers L'vov marched on their neighbour in the Orel region, a Lieutenant Safonov. An army of about six hundred, spiritually encouraged by a priest and vodka and urged on by their leaders, took their enemies, who were busy haymaking, by surprise, and a bloody scrap ensued, in which eleven persons were killed, and forty-five heavily wounded. In 1755 a female landowner named Pobedinskaia led her followers against two of her neighbours allied together, and killed them both. On several estates, there were trained bands of serfs with arms and uniforms ready to wage small-scale war against their masters' neighbours and to provide opposition to roaming brigands. The war between the classes was more important than that between individual members of the dvorianstvo, and the lackeys of the ruling class often found themselves called upon to fight against their revolting fellow commoners.[1]

The Russian central administrative system as reformed by Peter the Great remained roughly the same up to the accession of Catherine II; the Senate, the colleges and the office of Procurator-General were never abolished, although they suffered several attacks on their authority, for example, from the Cabinet set up during Anna's reign. The two most long-lasting of Peter's successors before 1762, Anna and Elizabeth, both expressed their wish to maintain the traditions of their illustrious uncle and father, and they carried

[1] Bogoslovskii, *Byt i nravy*, pp. 34–5; N. D. Chechulin, *Russkoe provintsial'noe obshchestvo vo vtoroi polovine XVIIIogo veka*, pp. 31–3.

this intention out in more ways than they would themselves have been prepared to confess. Count Nikita Panin said of Russia in the reign of Elizabeth that it was governed, not by 'the authority of state institutions', but by 'the power of persons'. This statement would be equally applicable to Russian government under Peter and Anna.[1]

'The power of persons' resided in the upper ranks of the dvorianstvo, although the class as a whole remained in subservience to the all-powerful state. The somewhat paradoxical nature of this situation needs to be seen in historical perspective. Had the members of the nobility been able to unite as the class was being formed, they might have lost their corporate chains long before they were firmly clamped on: they might have made their class a real political force long before the eighteenth century. However, although there were strong feelings of discontent among servicemen as the dvorianstvo was being developed from the fifteenth to the seventeenth centuries, there was never sufficient *esprit de corps* for a concerted march against the tsar and his establishment, which included a favoured group of nobles. Some of the reason for the continued disunity of the dvorianstvo no doubt lay in the political cunning of various tsars and their advisers, but that was transitory, and some lay in the complex recesses of the Slavic soul, but they are elusive. More demonstrably and less temporarily, the service class was composed of several different groups of men who had come to Moscow at various times for both positive and negative reasons, through attraction or assimilation to Russia, or rejection of former allegiance. According to an analysis made by Zagoskin, the largest group of families in the top ranks of the Moscow service class towards the end of the seventeenth century was of Polish-Lithuanian origin, which accounted for just under 25 per cent of the total. Just over 25 per cent of top-ranking families were of Western European origin of various kinds, with Germans showing a considerable preponderance, and a few stemming from Italian and Greek forebears, with a handful only from Hungarian, French, Jewish, British and Serbian beginnings. About 18 per cent of the prominent service families stemmed from immigrant Scandinavians, and approximately 13 per cent were

[1] Florinsky, *Russia*, pp. 436–7, 446–7, 454–6; Baranovich, etc. (eds.), *Ocherki istorii SSSR, Period feodalizma, Rossiia vo vtoroi chetverti XVIII v.*, pp. 268–96, including a diagram of the central administration on p. 272.

originally Tartars. Allowing for about 4 per cent of miscellaneous Oriental extraction, and others of unknown ancestry, less than 10 per cent could have been of indigenous Russian stock.[1]

The struggle between these families for place and influence had brought about the evolution of a system of hierarchy called *mestnichestvo* (from *mesto*—a place). After the introduction of the Table of Ranks by Peter the Great, a post, in theory at least, bestowed honour on its holder: according to *mestnichestvo*, which might be said to have comprised a 'Table of Families', the idea was that the holder would bestow honour on his post. Genealogical and government department registers were necessary to assist in the 'complicated arithmetic' of *mestnichestvo*, as Kliuchevskii called it, but the destruction of these was ordered at the same time as the abolition of *mestnichestvo* itself in 1682. A single comprehensive register was to be composed as a replacement, with the service class inscribed in it in five different degrees. According to Kliuchevskii, *mestnichestvo* had a defensive character, and was used by the service class to protect itself from above, i.e. the caprices of the tsar and his entourage, and from below, i.e. the ambitions and intrigues of individuals. The system, therefore, had two grave faults. It restricted the government's selection of its servants, and impeded the development of a class or public spirit through putting excessive emphasis on the sentiment of family honour.[2]

Mestnichestvo's complex legalities were often ignored in favour of a naked struggle for power during the Moscow period: similarly, the bureaucratic gradations of the Table of Ranks did little to heal internal rivalries within the higher dvorianstvo during the first half of the eighteenth century. To describe these rivalries most simply, there were 'ins' and 'outs' at court. At the death of Peter the Great, Menshikov was in control with his chief supporters grouped together in the Supreme Privy Council. Menshikov fell in 1727, and

[1] Zagoskin, *Ocherki*, pp. 176–9. Foreigners, Moldavians, Hungarians, Macedonians, Serbs and others continued to enter the dvorianstvo through service in the eighteenth century. See the remarks of V. Mihal'ch, *SIRIO*, IV, 194–5. The nobilities of the Baltic provinces, the Ukraine and the new regions to the south were in a somewhat ambiguous position which will be examined in chapter 4.

[2] Kliuchevskii, *Sochineniia*, II, 145–56. A comprehensive genealogy called the Velvet Book and composed at the direction of Ivan III had been destroyed at some unknown earlier date (Romanovich-Slavatinskii, *Dvorianstvo*, pp. 44–5). S. O. Shmidt, in his contribution to N. M. Druzhinin, etc. (eds.), *Absoliutizm v Rossii*, argues that the view of *mestnichestvo* put forward by Kliuchevskii has been too readily accepted by later historians, and that the system may well have made a more positive contribution to the development of the Russian state, in the sixteenth, if not seventeenth, century.

was soon replaced by the brothers Dolgorukii, some of the Council members changing sides. A member of this group, Prince D. M. Golitsyn, led the movement to place limits on the power of the new Empress Anna in 1730. Anna managed to repel this attack, and Golitsyn and his associates were broken. Then followed the rule of the favourite, Ernst Johan Biron, with several German supporters and some Russian 'outs' returned to power, such as Iaguzhinskii, Menshikov's great rival, who was reappointed to the position of Procurator-General that he had held under Peter the Great, and A. P. Volynskii, who enjoyed a brief period of prominence from 1738 to 1740. At Elizabeth's accession, the German influence was quickly removed, and a succession of favourites ruled the Russian Empire until the death of the Empress in 1762.[1]

The main rule in the game of 'ins' and 'outs' played by the upper-class dvoriane between 1725 and 1762 was that control of the Guards meant everything. Anna, Elizabeth and Catherine II all gained power through the support of the Guards. Under Peter the Great, the Guards consisted of three regiments, the Semenovskii and the Preobrazhenskii, formed about 1690, and the regiment of dragoons, later Horse Guards, established in 1719. Anna added the Izmailovskii regiment, who were to be drawn, at least to begin with, from the Baltic nobility.[2] To maintain its authority, the Supreme Power was obliged to pursue a policy agreeable to at least a large group of the upper-class dvoriane, many of whom were officers or rankers in the Guards: to establish their authority, the Empresses Anna, Elizabeth and Catherine II had to acquire the support of such a group.

Analysing the confusion at the accession of the first of these Empresses, Anna, some observers have discerned a split between Golitsyn and his associates and the rank and file nobility which might perhaps be called a division between a court and country party.[3] Volynskii has been quoted as a spokesman of the latter group, writing from Kazan':

God forbid that it turn out that, instead of one autocratic sovereign, we have tens of absolute and powerful families, and thus we, the nobility will

---

[1] Florinsky, *Russia*, pp. 436–56. Besides the split between 'ins' and 'outs', there was tension between old and new families of nobles, but this did not always reveal itself in a clear-cut division between the two groups.

[2] I. Pushkarev, *Istoriia imperatorskoi gvardii*, I, 8–9, 149–51.

[3] See, for example, A. A. Kizevetter in *Nauchnye trudy russkogo narodnogo universiteta v Prage*, II, 77–88.

Government and society

decline completely and we will be forced more painfully than before to make obeisance and seek favours from everybody—and this will not be easy, because however much they are in agreement now, there will undoubtedly be arguments among them soon.[1]

Some reservations must be expressed to this idea of court and country parties within the dvorianstvo: the parties were not as clearly distinguished as suggested by Volynskii; Volynskii himself was an upper-class 'out'; and there is generally more evidence of cohesion than disunity between the lower and higher dvorianstvo.[2]

Before a closer look is taken at the cohesion of the nobility, it is necessary to glance at a further divisive influence on the class, the distinction between military and civil dvoriane. Peter the Great's Table of Ranks accentuated a split between the Russian *noblesse d'épée* and *noblesse de robe* which had already been clearly discernible in the seventeenth century. As far as social evaluation was concerned, the sword had always been mightier than the pen in Russia. Civil service was actually more welcome to many dvoriane under Peter the Great, when army service could be extremely arduous, but between the death of Peter and the accession of Catherine II, as army life became more comfortable, successive governments had to make a considerable effort to attract nobles into the government departments. There was a certain amount of transfer of nobles from one branch of service to the other, but this did little to reduce the haughty attitude of military men towards civil servants.[3]

Although there may have been differences of interest between civil and military, court and country, and 'in' and 'out' members of the nobility, all dvoriane showed some fellow-feeling for each other during the first half of the eighteenth century. This was noticeable, for example, in the attitude of the class as a whole towards serfdom, and as a result of the noble's common exposure to military and other training as prescribed by Peter the Great and his successors. Their memoirs show that the dvoriane of the period were immensely proud of the service traditions of their families and the social distinctions that they had gained. Thus, Danilov was pleased to point out that his ancestors had been mentioned in earlier genealogical registers and

[1] Quoted in Romanovich-Slavatinskii, *Dvorianstvo*, p. 70.
[2] While Volynskii did not come from an old family, he had been raised to considerable prominence by Peter the Great and was to rise to power again at the end of the 1730s. See D. A. Korsakov, 'A. P. Volynskii i ego konfidenty', *RS*, xlviii, 17–19.
[3] Romanovich-Slavatinskii, *Dvorianstvo*, pp. 140–4.

had been in military service for several generations. Tuchkov was keen to impart the information that his forefathers had settled in Russia with noble rank in the thirteenth century and had all been in the army since then. Aksakov's grandfather prized his seven-hundred-year-old nobility far beyond all riches and other honours.[1] This personal and family pride was to some extent a class pride.

A more material cohesive influence on the dvorianstvo was the patron–client relationship that existed between the higher and lower members of the class. Some good illustrations of this relationship occur in the memoirs of A. T. Bolotov, a middle-class dvorianin. In 1746, Bolotov's father used his influence with higher ranking officers to get his son-in-law transferred and promoted. Two years later, Bolotov senior managed to get his son, still a minor, enrolled in the army. This was not so easy as it later became, wrote the younger Bolotov in his memoirs in 1789, but was made possible by the fact that it happened outside Russia and that his father knew a field-marshal. Bolotov senior died in 1750. Bolotov junior later wrote about the situation then confronting him:

the circumstances of those times were completely different to today's: then there were not such puppet-plays and children's games as there are now: then it was difficult even for the most important people to do something special on their behalf.

Nevertheless, five years after selecting the first of the three career choices that he considered feasible in 1750—the local army, the court or the guards—Bolotov managed to persuade a patron of his to use his influence to have himself made an officer.[2] (Danilov showed that the patron–client relationship was developed before the eighteenth century, pointing out that young nobles 'considered it fortunate (up to the time of Peter the Great) to be in the service of the great boyars of that time...')[3]

Unlike their Western European peers, Russian nobles rarely entered the church as a career. As Romanovich-Slavatinskii put it:

in Western Europe there was a solid family link between the priesthood and the nobility, hence the clericalism of the aristocracy and the aristocracy of the priesthood. The class privileges, the pretensions of the nobility were blessed by the church. With us, on the contrary, the priest-

[1] S. A. Tuchkov, *Zapiski*, p. 1; Danilov, *Zapiski*, pp. 1–3, 7; Aksakov, *Chronicles*, pp. 7–8.
[2] Bolotov, *Zhizn'*, I, 25, 68–9, 112–14, 291.   [3] Danilov, *Zapiski*, pp. 14–15.

hood was always nearer to the people in its spirit: the dvorianstvo treated the priesthood haughtily.[1]

In his advice to his son, V. N. Tatishchev wrote, 'Nobles have three careers before them: the civil, the military, and the ecclesiastical. They rarely embrace the latter...'[2] Thus, young nobles were more or less obliged to enter the civil or military branch of state service. In doing so, they could hardly avoid getting involved in one of the networks of patronage with which both branches of service were richly endowed.

EDUCATION AND CULTURE

At the accession of Peter the Great, Russia had no educational institutions except the theological Kiev Academy, founded in the second quarter of the seventeenth century, the Moscow Slavono-Greek-Latin Academy, founded in 1687, and a few scattered church schools. Peter's modernization of the army and of the administration, the creation of a navy and of new industrial enterprises, demanded men of a type that Russia desperately lacked. To bridge this gap, many young Russians were sent abroad, and many foreign experts were invited to come to Russia.[3] The results obtained by these methods did not always justify the considerable financial outlay necessary. In any case, the long-term solution of Russia's educational problems would obviously depend on her ability to build up an adequate indigenous school system. Peter's approach, here as elsewhere, was a mixture of the piecemeal and the comprehensive, with the accent on the needs of the state, particularly on the preparation for war. By his death, there had been created a Naval Academy, an engineering school and an artillery school. An almost completely unsuccessful attempt had been made also to establish a network of 'cipher' or mathematical schools throughout the provinces: these schools prospered less than some others set up by the church.[4]

Towards the end of his reign, Peter had developed a desire to promote knowledge for its own sake and to follow the lead of en-

---

[1] Romanovich-Slavatinskii, *Dvorianstvo*, p. 153.
[2] *The Testament of Basil Tatistcheff*, trans. J. Martinof, p. 31.
[3] Florinsky, *Russia*, pp. 288, 299, 404.
[4] *Ibid.* pp. 404–8. The decrees setting up the 'cipher' schools to be found in *PSZ*, v, 78, no. 2,762, 20 January 1714; v, 86, no. 2,778, 28 February 1714. At the beginning of 1716, young nobles were excluded from the 'cipher' schools, which were thenceforth to cater for young commoners exclusively (Florinsky, *Russia*, p. 407).

lightened nations in setting up an Academy of Sciences. This was opened in St Petersburg soon after his death, with a university and a gymnasium attached. Professors and students were imported from Germany for lack of sufficient numbers of natives with the relevant qualifications, and the professors were sometimes obliged to attend each other's lectures because of the scarcity of students. The gymnasium was at first more successful than the university: in 1726, its inaugural year, 120 students were enrolled. This number quickly dwindled to fifty-eight in 1727 and twenty-six in 1728, rising again to seventy-four in 1729. The rise did not continue, and, in any case, a considerable number of the children of foreign residents in St Petersburg rather than Russians were to be found among the gymnasium's students. To increase the Russian enrolment, twenty state stipends were set up in 1735, and some students were forcibly transferred from the Slavono-Greek-Latin Academy in Moscow to make use of them, among whom was Lomonosov, later famous as scientist, philologist, poet and historian. However, this move made no great impact on the number of students at the gymnasium, the total dwindling to nineteen in 1737 and thirteen in 1738. A similar policy of subsidy was adopted in 1747 for the university, when thirty state studentships were instituted, and church seminaries obliged to send students to take them up. Twenty-four students kept the professors busy for a time, but after an examination administered to twenty students in 1753, lectures temporarily ceased. Apart from Lomonosov, who became Professor of Chemistry at the Academy, there were few outstanding graduates, although Barsov and Popovskii later became professors at Moscow University, and a few others contributed to the advancement of Russian learning in various ways, for example, through submission of articles to periodicals in the later years of Elizabeth's reign.[1]

Education in Russia began to take on a more definite caste character after the accession of Anna. Whereas Peter's institutions tended to cater for nobles rather than others because of the character of their service functions, a decree of 29 July 1731 set up a more exclusive Noble Military Academy, or *korpus*. The cadets were to receive army commissions on graduation, being thus exempted from beginning

[1] P. N. Miliukov, *Ocherki po istorii russkoi kul'tury*, II, 745–7; Florinsky, *Russia*, pp. 408–9; N. D. Chechulin, 'Vospitanie i domashnee obuchenie v Rossii v XVIIIom veke', *Dela i dni*, I, 97–8.

their career in the ranks, a requirement that the dvoriane had long been opposing. The number of cadets that the corps could originally accommodate was 200, of whom a quarter were to be children of the Baltic nobility. The corps quota was raised to 360 in 1732, when the Academy actually opened. In spite of the name that it bore, the Military Academy offered a comprehensive curriculum and was expected to prepare its pupils not only for the army but also for civil service. The aversion of the cadets for civil service was demonstrated by the fact that, of the 245 young nobles in residence in 1733, only eleven were studying jurisprudence. Some of them were sent to the administrative colleges for practical training, but they showed no inclination for working together with 'pettifoggers', and were sent back to the corps. The education of other ranks was catered for by the increased institution in 1732 of 'garrison' schools, which were financed by regimental funds, and staffed by officers teaching reading, writing, military drill, arithmetic, artillery and engineering. Three of the largest 'cipher' schools still in existence were amalgamated with the 'garrison' schools, and the other five were abolished in 1744.[1]

The growing class character of Russian education, as well as a development of the non-service element originated by the St Petersburg Academy of Sciences, was demonstrated in the arrangement and curriculum of Moscow University and two subordinate gymnasia. These were set up by a decree of 24 January 1755 and opened in April of the same year with Ivan Shuvalov, one of the sponsors of the whole project, as curator. One gymnasium was to be for the nobles, and the other for the lower classes. The commoners were to study the arts, music, singing, drawing and technical subjects, and then transfer to an Academy of Arts, which was to be kept separate from the university. The nobles, on the other hand, were offered a choice of four three-year courses: the Russian language; Latin; first foundations of service (arithmetic, geometry, geography, and philosophy); and foreign languages. The university was given three faculties: law; medicine; and philosophy. The lectures were to be delivered in Latin and Russian. Although a decree of 18 May 1756 attempted to promote attendance by promising the graduates of the university privileges in both military and civil service, the dvoriane at first made a poor response, and places had to be filled yet again by theological

[1] *PSZ*, VIII, 519, no. 5,811, 29 July 1731; Miliukov, *Ocherki*, II, 735–6; Florinsky, *Russia*, p. 482.

students. The gymnasia were a little more successful, but the hopes held out for the whole project, based on its central position and the growing number of domestic teachers in and around Moscow, went largely unrealized.[1]

Shuvalov conceived in 1760 a more ambitious plan for a network of educational institutions covering all Russia, with an elementary school in every town, a gymnasium in each large town, and centres of higher learning in Moscow and St Petersburg. Shuvalov was advised to develop this plan gradually, starting in Kazan', where, conveniently enough, two gymnasia, one for the dvorianstvo and one for the other classes, had already been set up in 1758. Shuvalov's scheme got no further than this.[2]

This concludes the survey of official educational institutions in Russia in the first half of the eighteenth century, but most young dvoriane, if they learnt anything at all during this period, did so elsewhere, from tutors or in private schools. Some of the first tutors in Russia were Ostermann, a German, and Rambour, a Frenchman, hired to teach the three daughters of Ivan V by his widow. The higher dvorianstvo copied the practice of the court, and the rank and file became influenced by the fashion, too.[3] Of course, some dvoriane were educated by tutors or at private schools simply because there was no other means of education available to them. Such a young noble was A. T. Bolotov.

Bolotov started to go to school in 1744 at Pskov, where his father was helping to conduct the second census. The schools in the provinces at this time were not often staffed by Great Russians, and this school was run by an old Little Russian. Bolotov's parents were very pleased with him when he learned an Epistle of Paul to the Corinthians almost off by heart, and encouraged him to look at some theological works owned by the local bishop. In 1746 his father finished his census work, and went off to join his regiment in Estonia, Bolotov returning with his mother to the family estates 120 versts the other side of Moscow, where he continued to learn to read and write Russian, and to study the Russian Psalter under the supervision of a serf tutor. Soon, the son and the mother went off to join the father in

---

[1] *PSZ*, xiv, 284–94, no. 10,346; xiv, 571–3, no. 10,558; Florinsky, *Russia*, p. 491; Miliukov, *Ocherki*, ii, 747–9. The growing class character of Russian schools in the 1750s was also indicated by the arrangement of the Naval Academy, the engineering and artillery schools as exclusively noble institutions (Baranovich, etc. (eds.), *Ocherki istorii SSSR, Period feodalizma, Rossiia vo vtoroi chetverti XVIII v.*, p. 442).

[2] Miliukov, *Ocherki*, ii, 748.   [3] Bogoslovskii, *Byt i nravy*, pp. 6–7.

Education and culture

Estonia. In 1747, after Bolotov had begun to learn to paint, as well as continuing his studies at home, his father decided to remove him from the care of his mother, and get him to learn something besides his native language. The elder Bolotov wanted his son to know German, which he himself knew and had found very useful, and mathematics. Teachers were not so numerous as they later became, and Bolotov senior could not afford to hire one, so he engaged a German-speaking N.C.O. Bolotov junior found the rote teaching system used by his tutor very tedious, and was even more upset by the frequent beatings that the N.C.O. administered to him.

In 1748 the family moved to Courland. By this time, the nine-year-old boy knew thousands of German words, but could not speak the language. His father, noticing that the local nobles were very careful about their children's education, sent Bolotov to a school kept up by one of them, where he learned French, German, drawing and some geography, and spent, according to his own account, the happiest days of his childhood. Soon, however, he was transferred to a boarding school in St Petersburg where there were about a dozen other pupils, all of them less advanced in their education than Bolotov himself. History was now added to his curriculum.

Bolotov senior died in 1750. His son managed to get leave from the Heralds to continue his education. After two years at home, with some desultory studies only, Bolotov went to another school in St Petersburg, where a Frenchman, Monsieur Lapis, who knew no Russian and very little German, tortured his pupils by making them copy out huge chunks from a large French dictionary and learn them by heart. Bolotov finished his formal education at this school, and, after another three years in the provinces, joined his regiment in Livonia in 1755 at the age of seventeen.[1]

Rather less fortunate than Bolotov was M. V. Danilov, born near Moscow in or about 1722. Danilov went with two cousins to be taught by a minor church official named Brudastoi, who lived with his wife in a small hut. Of his early education, Danilov later wrote:

I used to come to school at Brudastoi's at daybreak, and he would open the doors without any greeting...and he would not smile...I was often beaten with a stick. I cannot honestly admit that I was lazy then or obstinate, I studied hard for my years, and my teacher would give me a lesson easy enough for my talents to study, and I would complete it

---

[1] Bolotov, *Zhizn'*, I, 15–17, 25–6, 29–30, 38–9, 53, 72–6, 89–92, 97, 174–5, 251.

quickly. But since Brudastoi would not allow us a moment's leave, except for dinner, we would sit continuously on the benches, and would suffer great torment during the days of high summer. I weakened so much from sitting down every day, that my head lost its memory.

Danilov later moved to another 'school' kept by an illiterate widow, who had two books, the Orthodox Psalter and Book of Hours, one of which she would open before her and recite passages from it that she knew by heart. (Danilov later went to the Artillery School in Moscow, and then to its other branch in St Petersburg. In both institutions, there was great confusion. In St Petersburg, there was no order or supervision, and many students went off into actual service without the permission of the school authorities. The teachers were most inadequate, one of them, Alabushev, was a drunkard who had been arrested three times for murder.)[1]

Private schools such as Bolotov attended numbered just over twenty in St Petersburg and just under twenty in Moscow in the 1780s, and were fewer, probably, in the first half of the eighteenth century.[2] Since Bolotov, Danilov and the other writers of memoirs were obviously among the more literate members of the dvorianstvo, it is difficult to make an assessment of the general spread of education among the class as a whole. However, the fact that schools were so few in number and of such poor quality, coupled with the impression given by writers of memories of both schools and tutors, makes it seem probable that, as Sergei Aksakov pointed out, most of the dvoriane at this time were very badly educated, if educated at all.[3]

That the education of the dvorianstvo was rudimentary in the first half of the eighteenth century was not solely due to the lack of good schools and adequate teachers: additional reasons for the persistence of ignorance were the paucity of books, particularly textbooks; the confused nature of the schools' curricula; the wide application of over-rigorous discipline; the over-stressed accent on education for service purposes; and, most important of all, the attitude of the Russians themselves—a mixture of religious obscurantism and ancient superstition, and a converse belief in the omnipotence of secular enlightenment.

First of all, there was a powerful tradition in Russia that love of

[1] Danilov, *Zapiski*, pp. 38–42, 29–31.　　[2] Chechulin, *Dela i dni*, I, 98–9.
[3] Aksakov, *Chronicles*, p. 6.

secular reading was temptation of the devil.[1] This revealed itself in a seventeenth-century decree forbidding the circulation of books in the provinces. Between 1550 and 1700 only 134 books were translated into Russian, most of them in the second half of the seventeenth century.[2] Such books of an indigenous origin that there were closely followed for the most part the dictates of the church. For example, in the first printed Russian grammar, published in 1648, it was pointed out that teachers had always started the education of their pupils with the Church Slavonic print, and then with church books. This practice remained unchallenged until the 1760s, and can be considered to have been harmful from the point of view of the students' general education, since Church Slavonic was far removed from the language of business and the everyday speech of the people.[3]

Secondly, as far as the curricula of the schools were concerned, the new secular education under Peter the Great laid excessive emphasis on a few practical subjects, particularly mathematics. After Peter's death, there was a tendency towards more diversification, but without much rhyme or reason. In 1747, for instance, a manual for the Academy's university offered the following subjects for study: French, Latin, German, geometry and other parts of mathematics, geography, general history, heraldry, logic and metaphysics, theoretical and experimental physics, antiquities and literary history, natural law, and practical and moral philosophy. Russians in the first half of the eighteenth century, therefore, tended to look on education as something which affected those who were exposed to it with a beneficial photo-synthesis, irrespective of the focus and depth of light that it shed. It was commonly held that education consisted solely of the assimilation of completely shallow, narrow and separate pieces of information, and that to achieve this and become an educated man was simple.[4]

A third reason for the failure of Russian education up to the 1760s was the widespread belief in the efficacy of severe discipline as an aid to the inculcation of knowledge. This belief stemmed partly from the military nature of much of Russian education, and partly, too, from the over-concentration of many teachers on the maintenance of

[1] P. N. Miliukov, *Outlines of Russian Culture*, trans. E. Davis and V. Ughet, I, 5.
[2] Ernest J. Simmons, *English Literature and Culture in Russia, 1553–1840*, pp. 38–9, 43.
[3] Chechulin, *Dela i dni*, I, 99–100. Sumner, *Peter the Great*, p. 207, points out that, of the 374 books published in Russia in the whole of the seventeenth century, only nineteen were secular in content.   [4] Chechulin, *Dela i dni*, I, 105–6.

dumb obedience. It was also, however, a consequence of the religious theory, developed in several seventeenth-century teaching manuals, that the child's nature was essentially wicked and had to be purged before its mind was ready for learning. While teachers were probably no more vindictive and cruel in the eighteenth century than in later periods of history, their generally accepted policy of severe discipline was a considerable handicap to the success of Russian education. This would be particularly so in the common case of a pupil subjected to it at a boarding school after an infancy of self-willed indiscipline at home in the charge of powerless serf nurses and tutors.[1]

Peter the Great secularized education only to nationalize it: in other words, the purpose of education was for Peter the preparation of the young of all classes for their various services to the state. This idea permeated the dvorianstvo, which tended to look on education as a means to advancement in service. This narrow view hampered the free flowering of education in Russia.[2]

More important than all of these contributors to the failure of Russian education in the first half of the eighteenth century, and intimately connected with all of them, was the persistent influence of a traditional culture peculiar to Russia and composed of a mixture of ancient, Slavic superstition and folk-lore, and a simple, but very powerful, Orthodox Christian faith. An enlightened secular culture, which had taken its first faltering steps at the time of Ivan the Terrible or even before, and had developed with the encouragement of Boris Godunov and Aleksei Mihailovich, entered a somewhat unsteady adolescence under the guardianship of Peter the Great and with the increased assistance of older European cultures, German, Swedish, Dutch, English and increasingly French.[3] Russian enlightened secular culture, however, still had to struggle hard against the weight of the older culture even in the second half of the eighteenth century.

Three main trends can be discerned in Western-influenced,

[1] Chechulin, *Dela i dni*, III, 40–1; Marc Raeff, 'Home, School and Service in the Life of the 18th-century Nobleman', *SEER*, XL, no. 95, 298–9.

[2] Raeff, *SEER*, XL, no. 95, 299.

[3] Simmons, *English Culture*, chapters I–III; E. Haumont, *La Culture Française en Russie, 1700–1900*, livres I–II; A. G. Brikner, *Die Europaiserung Russlands. Land und Volk*, pp. 345–61. The part played by Poland, the Ukraine and the Baltic provinces as percolators of Western culture and as cultural influences was also very significant. See, for example, Marc Raeff, 'Staatsdienst, Aussenpolitik, Ideologien', *Jahrbücher für Geschichte Osteuropas*, Band 7, Heft 2 (1959), 165–72.

secular thought about 1750, 'Voltairism', humanism and freemasonry. The name of Voltaire became a watchword for many rejecting
the old ways. Some of these passionately longed to confess some new
faith in place of the old which they had lost, and entered whole-
heartedly into the world of Western culture symbolized by Voltaire,
while others adopted a 'cheap scepticism' or even a 'nihilistic' outlook. 'Voltairism' became a fashionable theme for light conversation
among the dandies of Russian *salons*, while more serious thinkers
studied the works of Rousseau, Montesquieu, Diderot and the Encyclopaedists, as well as those of the master. The radical break with
traditional culture that occurred in the minds of Russian Voltairians
encouraged a tendency towards day-dreaming, towards the construction of utopias, of which a popular imported example was
Fénelon's *Les Aventures de Télémaque*.[1] The development of Russian
humanism showed itself, for example, in attempts to find a basis for
the Russian state outside Orthodoxy. Tatishchev was perhaps a
prime, if rather hesitant, mover in this attempt. Discussing the situation at the accession of Anna in 1730, Tatishchev argued that natural
law demanded the assent of all subjects to government, either personally, or through trustees. Anna had been accepted by the people,
asserted Tatishchev, but a law was necessary to avoid future disorder, and such a law could be introduced only by a general agreement of either category.[2] Freemasonry, which was to satisfy the
religious and philosophical needs of some Russians after they had left
the Church, did not really blossom in Russia before the reign of
Catherine II.[3]

Taking advantage of the increasing opportunities for education
and travel that were presenting themselves in the first half of the
eighteenth century, several members of the dvorianstvo were becoming conscious of Russia's backwardness, and a few of them were
putting forward suggestions to help their country accelerate its progress. Of these nobles, it can generally be said that their acquaintance
with Muscovite practice led them to believe that reform must be
achieved through the agencies of a *dirigiste* state; and the predomin-

[1] V. V. Zenkovsky, *A History of Russian Philosophy*, pp. 72–8; Miliukov, *Ocherki*, III,
297–8.
[2] Zenkovsky, *History*, 78–81; Miliukov, *Ocherki*, III, 249–58; V. N. Tatishchev in *Utro.
Literaturnyi sbornik*, pp. 369–71.
[3] Zenkovsky, *History*, pp. 81–3; A. N. Pypin, *Russkoe masonstvo XVIII i pervaia chetvert'
XIX vv.*, p. 84.

ance of military service in the empire helped to bring about the idea that the new order must be strictly regimented, with all provinces subjected to uniform regulations and drilled into an efficient unit without regard for local variations in law, culture and race. Permeating and, on the whole, reinforcing these attitudes were gleanings from current Western European theory and administrative procedure.[1]

All this, of course, does not mean that political writings of Russian intellectuals at this time were blueprints for revolution: such leaps of the imagination as these would take time to mature. None of them wanted to change the institution of serfdom very much, or, indeed, to jeopardize the interests of their class in any other vital way. Moreover, while it would be rash to draw firm conclusions from a few accessible examples of their work, it is difficult to see that these thinkers penetrated to the roots of Russia's problems, or to agree with P. P. Epifanov that 'already in the first decades of the eighteenth century Russia was one of the world centres of the formation of enlightenment and...Russian thinkers brought their own original important creative contributions to its progressive movement'.[2]

Epifanov wrote this of a group which included V. N. Tatishchev, whose project, composed on behalf of a group of nobles at the time of Anna's accession, can be taken as a sample of their thought. Starting off with the point about the general consent of the governed to their sovereign, Tatishchev went on to consider three forms of government, autocracy, aristocracy and democracy, and the particular suitability of the first of these for the Russian situation. Autocracy was necessary, argued Tatishchev, in large states controlling many neighbouring, smaller states, particularly where the people were uneducated and obeyed the law through fear, not from knowledge of good or evil, and not through good behaviour. Tatishchev went on to concede that three questions arose concerning autocracy: one man, the autocrat, could have grave faults; one man could create powerful favourites of base or foreign origin who would cause the outstanding worthies of the state much trouble; and the secret service, deemed necessary by autocrats, brought shame, dishonour and ruin, since it tortured and executed because of a carelessly

[1] Marc Raeff, 'L'État, le gouvernement et la tradition politique en Russie impériale avant 1861', *Revue d'histoire moderne et contemporaine*, IX, 295–9, 302–3.

[2] P. P. Epifanov, '"Uchenaia druzhina" i prosvetitel'stvo XVIII veka', *Voprosy istorii* (1963), no. 3, 53.

spoken word, and deprived innocent children of their estates. To these questions, Tatishchev answered that one man would have good advisers and paternal concern for his charges, and that a reckless bad man would be punished by God, and should be subject also to some earthly control; that there had been more favourites in the Greek and Roman republics than in Russia; and that the secret service was of very old ancestry, being inaugurated by Tiberius, if not Augustus, did not harm good men, and got rid of bad and dishonourable men.

Tatishchev went on to say that he had full confidence in the wisdom and good government of Anna in Courland, but, since she was a woman, she might find herself in difficulties, and, moreover, she could not be sufficiently acquainted with Russia's laws. He therefore submitted the following suggestions, to be implemented until a man succeeded to the throne. A Senate of twenty-one members should head Her Majesty's government, with another body of one hundred persons relieving the Senate of the burden of the affairs of the internal economy, and the chief posts in the administration being filled by ballot of these two 'houses'. (The top three names in each ballot would be submitted to the Empress for her choice of one of them.) To avoid confusion, difficulties or trouble, laws were to be scrutinized before publication by members of the colleges. To avoid irregularities in government, Tatishchev thought that only one member of a family should serve in each of its departments. Two senators would watch fair play in the secret service, and some outstanding person should keep a check on the state seizure of property. In order that the dvorianstvo should function better in military and civil service, Tatishchev considered that schools should be set up in all towns with arrangements made for their upkeep and housing; that service should not be obligatory below the age of eighteen or for more than twenty years; that nobles should not be assigned to the navy or to trade; and that a national list should be made of all dvoriane, excluding those who, even if they possessed villages, did not have documentary proof of their nobility or authority to possess villages. Not forgetting other classes, Tatishchev wanted the material and educational welfare of the priests and their children to be taken care of, and restrictions and quartering impositions to be removed from the merchants, who should be encouraged to develop manufactures and trade. Finally, Tatishchev said that the 1714 law introducing the *maiorat* should be rescinded, and an adequate replacement brought in on the basis of the Code of 1649.[1]

While Tatishchev's project was one of the more sophisticated groups of suggestions to emerge from the discussions of the dvorianstvo at the accession of Anna, A. P. Volynskii's 'Project for the Correction of State Affairs' was composed towards the end of her reign as the hopes held out in 1730 were coming to naught. Apart from wanting to increase the power of the Senate, decrease that of the Cabinet, and abolish the office of Procurator-General, Volynskii made six recommendations for the amelioration of Russia's position. Although the army should be reduced in numbers, the frontiers of the Empire should be strengthened. On justice, Volynskii thought that confusion resulted from the rapid rotation in office of *voevody*, and that greater order would ensue if these and other officials were to come from the ranks of the educated dvorianstvo. On the economy, Volynskii suggested the reduction of state income and expenditure, a reform in the tariff, the abolition of small taverns on main roads and in small villages, and an increase in the number of factories. Volynskii's attitude towards priests, merchants and nobles was similar to that of Tatishchev. The material and educational level of the priests should be raised, and merchants should be freed from restrictions on their trade and interference from government officials. Regarding the nobility, Volynskii considered that nobles alone should serve in the government and the church; that they should be exposed to a better system of education, including trips abroad; that they should all be enrolled in genealogical registers, to keep the order pure; and that the expenditure of the poorer dvoriane on clothes and their general waste of money should be restricted. Volynskii also believed that the dvorianstvo should have the exclusive right to the manufacture of alcoholic drink and to horse breeding. Iu. V. Got'e, who carried out the difficult task of the reconstruction of Volynskii's project from the fragmentary evidence available, said that it must be considered 'an organic link, connecting the 1730 dreams of the nobility with the ideas of the dvorianstvo's instructions in 1767'.[2]

Another such link was P. I. Shuvalov's 'Of Various Means to the State Advantage', submitted to the Senate on 7 October 1754.

[1] Tatishchev, 'Proizvol'noe i soglasnoe rassuzhdenie i mnenie sobravshegosia shliahetstva russkogo o pravlenii gosudarstvennom', *Utro. Literaturnyi sbornik*, pp. 369–71.

[2] Iu. V. Got'e, '"Proekt o popravlenii gosudarstvennyh del" Artemiia Petrovicha Volynskogo', *Dela i dni*, III, 21–4, 31.

Shuvalov argued that harm came to the Empire from six main sources: flight across the borders; waste of a great number of soldiers' children; collection of forage for the army from the people; insults and exactions caused by regiments on the move; poor harvests, or low prices in case of abundant harvest; and the poor quality of officials, and therefore justice, at all provincial levels of government. Shuvalov's remedies for these six ills were: more efficient frontier control posts; special sections in towns for military families; stores for the army financed by the profits from the sales of alcoholic drinks; commissars elected by dvoriane 'from worthy and honest people of the best local dvorianstvo' at all provincial levels of government to manage the army's stores and supervise its movements; an Office of the State Economy to collect and disseminate information, fix prices, help with the army's stores, etc.; and the payment of adequate salaries to all local government officials, with young dvoriane receiving training in departments of local government.[1]

Tatishchev, Volynskii and Shuvalov, all well-educated, experienced in government service, and leading members of the dvorianstvo, worked out fairly comprehensive plans for the rectification of Russia's problems, including the extension of the influence of their own class in the administration. At a somewhat lower level of society, there were some nobles like Bolotov, apparently little acquainted with political theory and practice and the larger problems confronting the Russian Empire, but reading widely and in several languages, economic books, religious books, historical books, French and German novels, and Russian plays.[2] Folk-lore and superstition, mingled with a great respect for the faith of their fathers, if not its practitioners, dominated the thinking of many dvoriane, and the attitude of the vast majority of the members of other classes in the eighteenth century, as in the seventeenth, remained stolidly conservative towards most questions.[3]

[1] S. O. Shmidt (intro. and ed.), 'Proekt P. I. Shuvalova 1754g. "O raznyh gosudarstvennoi pol'zy sposobah"', *Istoricheskii arhiv* (1962), no. 6, 105–18.

[2] Bolotov, *Zhizn'*, I, 25, 90, 97, 172, 196, 286, 443, 488–9.

[3] A. N. Pypin, 'Do-petrovskoe predanie v XVIII-om veke', *VE*, III (1886), 682–3. M. M. Shtrange, *Demokraticheskaia intelligentsiia Rossii v XVIII veke*, describes the development of a sizable enlightened group of commoners from the middle of the eighteenth century onwards.

PETER III, CATHERINE II
AND THE NOBILITY

PETER III'S EMANCIPATION MANIFESTO

The year 1762 was important in the history of the nobility for two principal reasons: first, it saw the brief reign of Peter III, during which the class was emancipated from the burdens of obligatory service placed upon it by Peter the Great; secondly, Catherine II, whose relations with the dvorianstvo were to be of great importance, became Empress of Russia in June of that year.

Peter III, Catherine's husband, was usually represented by the Empress and her entourage as an imbecile totally incapable of the greatness which fate had attempted to thrust upon him, as 'a permanent patch upon a very beautiful face'.[1] Later critics have been kinder, and probably more accurate. As one of them has written, 'Peter was notoriously unfit for ruling an Empire, but he would have made a good average eighteenth-century *junker* or squire'.[2] Not much more can be said for most of the other Romanovs.

Peter's ideal was Frederick the Great, and 'by this fact alone can be explained the origin of several of the reforms of the strange sovereign who tried to imitate Frederick in everything', according to S. S. Shashkov.[3] A Prussian influence is certainly detectable in some of Peter's internal reforms, but he was also subject to domestic pressures applied by his advisers. During Peter's short reign, the secret police was abolished, and it was proclaimed that nobody should be considered a political suspect or arrested on political charges until his case had been considered by the Senate.[4] Refugees from religious persecutions of the previous reign were offered repatriation and freedom of worship.[5] In the economic field, restrictions were removed from the export of grain, and the prohibition of the purchase of serfs for employment in industrial enterprises was reiterated.[6] A large step

[1] Catherine II, *Memoirs*, p. 264.   [2] R. Nisbet Bain, *Peter III, Emperor of Russia*, p. vii.
[3] S. S. Shashkov, *Istoricheskie etiudy*, I, 59.
[4] *PSZ*, xv, 915–18, no. 11,445, 21 February 1762.
[5] *PSZ*, xv, 894–5, no. 11,420, 29 January 1762.
[6] *PSZ*, xv, 959–66, no. 11,489, 28 March 1762; 966, no. 11,490, 29 March 1762.

was taken towards the secularization of church estates.[1] Such measures as these would more likely secure the approval than arouse the censure of most of the nobility, which, of course, provided Peter with advisers.

This was certainly the case with the manifesto of 18 February 1762, which granted the freedom from service for which the class had long been pressing. The origins of this celebrated manifesto are uncertain: according to Shcherbatov, the reason for its composition was Peter's desire for a good excuse to give to his mistress, Elizabeth Vorontsova, for a night which he actually intended to spend with Elena Kurakina. D. V. Volkov, who was secretary to Peter, described the affair to Shcherbatov in the following manner, according to the latter's account. In the presence of Vorontsova, Peter told Volkov that he wanted to work through the night with him on some important state business. Shcherbatov continued:

Night came, and the Sovereign went off to enjoy himself with Kurakina, telling Volkov to write some important piece of legislation before the next morning, and locking him up in an empty room with a Great Dane. Volkov did not know what to write about, but write he had to. Since he was a quick-witted man, he remembered the frequent statements to the Sovereign by Count Roman Lariunovich Vorontsov about the freedom of the dvorianstvo; he sat down and wrote a manifesto about this. Towards morning he was released from his confinement, and the manifesto was approved and promulgated by the Sovereign.[2]

While it can readily be believed that Peter was more interested in his personal emancipation from the jealous attentions of Vorontsova than the more general emancipation of the nobility from service, this anecdotal account of the origin of the manifesto of 18 February is probably inaccurate, and perhaps influenced by Volkov's desire to lessen his responsibility in the affair, or Shcherbatov's aristocratic wish to pour scorn on the service nobility. In fact, the composition of the manifesto can be more certainly ascribed to A. I. Glebov, the Procurator-General. Volkov's alleged assertion that Roman Vorontsov had discussed emancipation from service with Peter, however, does seem to be correct. Vorontsov and his brother Mihail, Volkov himself, and A. P. Mel'gunov were all members of a group close to Peter and keen to continue the policy of I. I. Shuvalov, who had been

[1] *PSZ*, xv, 910, no. 11,441, 16 February 1762; 948–53, no. 11,481, 21 March 1762.
[2] M. M. Shcherbatov, *O povrezhdenii nravov v Rossii*, p. 77.

contemplating some diminution of service requirements ten years or so previously. Also, Peter's tutor, Shtelin, wrote that the Emperor himself had been considering emancipation for some time before his accession. There was probably a connection, too, between the publication of the manifesto and the continuance in session of the Legislative Commission first convened in 1754.[1]

Whatever its immediate origins, the manifesto of 18 February 1762 appears to have been the culmination of the irregular movement towards emancipation evident in the reigns of Anna and Elizabeth. Its significance was rated highly both by contemporaries and later historians.

Immediately after the proclamation of the manifesto, the Senate asked if it could erect a statue in gold as an expression of its feeling for the Emperor, and the Moscow dvorianstvo requested and received permission to declare publicly its most humble and slavish gratitude.[2] The poet Rzhevskii composed an ode as a token of thanks for the 'unprecedented and gracious grant of freedom to the Russian nobles', declaiming that Peter III 'has given Russia freedom and bestowed prosperity on her'. Dedicating one of his translations to the Sovereign, P. I. Rychkov proffered the opinion that:

Even if the most noble and most honourable Russian dvorianstvo set up not only a gold, but also a diamond statue of your Imperial Highness on a pedestal of pearl, as an immortal testimony of their abject thanks, the undying memory in the hearts of successive generations of the Russian dvorianstvo will be greater and stronger than all statues.[3]

An impression of the reception given to the Manifesto by the rank and file of the dvorianstvo was recorded by the less literary A. T. Bolotov. Wrote he:

I cannot describe what unimaginable joy that document produced in the hearts of all the dvoriane of our beloved fatherland. All very nearly jumped with joy, and, thanking the Sovereign, blessed the moment at which he was pleased to sign the decree. There was good reason for this joy: up to this time, the Russian dvorianstvo had been inextricably bound to serve, and their children, entering service while still in their infancy, had been forced to remain there all their lives right up to their old age.[4]

[1] Romanovich-Slavatinskii, *Dvorianstvo*, p. 196; G. V. Vernadskii, 'Manifest Petra III o vol'nosti dvorianskoi i zakonodatel'naia komissiia 1754–1766 gg.', *Istoricheskoe obozrenie*, xx, 53–8. [2] K.N.V., 'Dvorianskaia gramota', *Istoricheskii vestnik*, xix, 628–9.
[3] Quoted in Romanovich-Slavatinskii, *Dvorianstvo*, pp. 200–1.
[4] Bolotov, 'Zhizn'', *Russkaia starina*, iii, 131–2. It is not perhaps unimportant to note that Bolotov, so often quoted in support of the contention that the emancipation manifesto

It can be argued that some of these contemporaries had no alternative but to welcome with enthusiasm any legislation devised by the Supreme Power, and that their ecstasy is therefore suspect. It could also be said, perhaps, that an observer such as Bolotov might not be able to distinguish the wood from his particular tree. Such restrictions would not oppress later historians, however, and some of them have waxed only slightly less lyrical on the theme of the importance to the nobility of the manifesto of 18 February. For example, Romanovich-Slavatinskii has written:

> The manifesto was an epoch-making event in the history of the class: indeed, it can be compared with the manifesto of 19 February 1861, in the history of the serfs. Similarly to the latter, which freed the peasants from their servile dependence on the landlords, the manifesto of 18 February 1762, freed the dvorianstvo from the burden incumbent upon it, obligatory service to the state, which had placed it, too, in the position of a servile class. It was a revolutionary point in the history of this class when it changed from the *servile service* basis it had possessed throughout its whole existence to that of a *privileged landowning* class spread out in provincial societies.[1]

Another nineteenth-century historian of the emancipation of the dvorianstvo devoted an article to the argument that 1762 was a much more important year in the history of the class than 1785, the year of the publication of the Charter of the Nobility, and, more recently, Richard Pipes has put forward the opinion that, 'Altogether, it is difficult to exaggerate the importance of the edict of 1762 for Russia's social and cultural history. With this single act the monarchy created a large, privileged, Westernized leisure class, such as Russia had never known before'.[2]

Although it would be most incorrect to attribute no significance at all to the emancipation manifesto, there is a considerable case for thinking that both contemporaries and later historians have gone too far in the other direction, and have overestimated the importance of this decree to the development of the nobility. In the first place, the law itself was guilty of sins of omission and commission: it said

was of great significance, had his facts wrong. Since the 1736 decree, a twenty-five year period of service had been the norm, and nobles had been able to retire some years before they could be said to have reached their old age, particularly if they had entered service during infancy.

[1] Romanovich-Slavatinskii, *Dvorianstvo*, p. 198.
[2] Richard Pipes, *Karamzin's Memoir on Ancient and Modern Russia. A translation and analysis*, p. 15.

41

nothing about three important desires of the dvorianstvo, freedom from corporal punishment, guarantee of serf possession, and immunity of estates from confiscation; there were some fairly strong reservations attached to the grant of freedom from service.

To illustrate the second point, the manifesto itself must be examined in some detail. The preamble observed that Peter III's grandfather, Peter the Great, had been forced to institute obligatory service and education for the nobility at the beginning of the eighteenth century because of Russia's moral and cultural backwardness. Now, however, ignorance had been replaced by sound reason, and individual coarseness by a sensitivity to the general welfare. The preamble continued:

Useful knowledge and devotion to service have increased the number of skilful and courageous generals in military affairs, and produced experienced and suitable people in civil and political affairs; noble thoughts have taken root in all Russian patriots, and therefore We do not find necessary that compulsion in service in effect up to this time.[1]

In other words, dvoriane would no longer be forced to serve, but would be expected to do so voluntarily.

After the preamble, the manifesto went on to make the following stipulations. Dvoriane already in service were to have the option of retiring. Military nobles, however, were not to retire during wartime, and civil nobles would need the approval of the Sovereign, if they were in the top eight classes, or of their superiors, if they were of lower rank. Dvoriane could acquire a passport to travel abroad, but would forfeit their estates if they failed to return when summoned. Those dvoriane who chose to retire would have to elect from their midst fifty men, thirty of whom were to be attached to the Senate, and twenty to the Senate's secretariat. As far as the education of young noblemen was concerned, parents were to report locally or to the Heraldmaster the level of their children's education at the age of twelve. The parents could then choose how their children were to continue their education, with the exception of those who possessed less than 1,000 souls. (This would amount to something over 90 per cent of the dvorianstvo.) In order that 'nobody would dare to bring up his children without their instruction in those subjects befitting the noble dvorianstvo', these parents were to send their children to the Military Academy, where they would receive the appropriate

[1] *PSZ*, xv, 912, no. 11,444, 18 February 1762.

education, and be better fitted for advancement in service.[1] The impracticability of this command, or the cynicism behind its announcement, was soon demonstrated by an edict ordering some young nobles to go directly into service because of their illiteracy.[2]

Two further restrictions were placed upon the liberty of the dvorianstvo. First, those dvoriane in service who had not reached commissioned rank could retire only if they had served twelve years with the colours. Secondly, and more generally, the hope was expressed that the nobility would continue to look on service almost as before, and it was inferred that they would incur the imperial displeasure if they did not. The manifesto concluded:

We hope that the whole noble Russian dvorianstvo, appreciative of our generosity to them and their descendants, will be inspired by their most dutiful loyalty to Us and their zeal, not to absent or hide themselves from service, but to enter it with pride and enthusiasm, and continue it in an honourable and decent manner to the extent of their ability, and none the less teaching their children suitable subjects with diligence and application, because all those who have not been in service anywhere, but spend all their time in sloth and idleness, and do not subject their children to any useful education for the benefit of the fatherland, these We, as they are negligent of the common good, command all Our obedient and true sons to despise and scorn, and they will not be allowed to appear at Our Court, or at public meetings and celebrations.[3]

Apart from what the manifesto itself said and did not say, the background to its publication shows that its importance to the nobility has been exaggerated. First of all, Korf and others have argued that, while the provincial life of the dvorianstvo was very undeveloped before 1762, immediately after the manifesto great numbers of nobles took advantage of the new opportunities and flocked to their estates. Arriving in the provinces, they were able to begin to form new communal interests, runs the argument, and take a greater interest in provincial administration. Korf wrote, 'the publication of the 1762 manifesto was the first moment in the history of the corporate government of the dvorianstvo'.[4] It can be argued, if not positively demonstrated, that Korf and his like have underestimated the extent to which the provinces were developed before

---

[1] *PSZ*, xv, 912–14.　　　　[2] *PSZ*, xv, 1000, no. 11,531, 10 May 1762.
[3] *PSZ*, xv, 914–15. Kliuchevskii, *Sochineniia*, viii, 277, wrote, 'The law said: be so good, serve and teach your children and, nevertheless, he who does neither the one nor the other will be driven from society'.
[4] S. A. Korf, *Dvorianstvo i ego soslovnoe upravlenie*, p. 13.

1762, and overestimated the rate at which they came to life after 1762, that, in fact, provincial growth was a more gradual process than that described in Korf's rather cataclysmic view. Iu. V. Got'e, for instance, whose researches have been considerably more detailed than those of Korf, would support such an argument, observing that:

As early as the desire to correct and improve the poor provincial institutions of 1727 appeared the thought of introducing into them an elective noble element. Clearly expressing itself already in the projects of the dvorianstvo in 1730, it steadily developed all the time, and had already achieved great clarity and exactness at the end of the reign of Elizabeth in the project of the Legislative Commission. The beginnings of these desires must not be placed in the Catherinian epoch, to which the development of the desires of the dvorianstvo in the field of local government is generally tied, but rather the commencement of construction on an already old and lasting foundation.[1]

To have shown an interest in local government before 1762, the dvorianstvo must have been developing provincial interests before the emancipation manifesto: with Russia's withdrawal from the Seven Years War in this year, the rate of retirement from service into the provinces would have been likely to rise, irrespective of edicts passed during it.[2]

A second reservation to the importance of the Manifesto is that 'service to the state in some form continued to be the normal practice among Russian noblemen',[3] and this was apparently true even apart from the coercion and encouragement contained in the provisions of the edict. The dramatist Kniazhnin, in his play, *The Boaster*, first produced in 1786, well described, albeit with some exaggeration, what seems to have been a pronounced trait in Russian life at this time. Polist, one of the dramatis personae, complains, 'People have all gone wild about ranks. Tailors, carpenters, are all the same, merchants, cobblers, all dream of becoming officers. And he who passes his dark life without rank does not seem to us a complete man.'[4] As far as the nobles in particular were concerned, contemporary memoirs, such as those of Bolotov, Vinskii, Tuchkov and Derzhavin, give a clear picture of the allure of rank. (It is true that

[1] Got'e, *Istoriia*, II, 155–6.
[2] The question of the rate of retirement could perhaps be more finally settled by an examination of the Heralds' records. Such an examination has not been carried out, and may be impossible.
[3] Max Beloff, in Goodwin (ed.), *The European Nobility in the Eighteenth Century*, p. 181.
[4] A. V. Kokor'ev, *Hrestomatiia po russkoi literature XVIII veka*, p. 464.

the dvorianstvo had been complaining of the burdens of service throughout the eighteenth century, and expressing a strong desire to have them mitigated. Such complaints, however, have been strong among servicemen everywhere at all times, and the reception given to the redress of these grievances, namely the option of retirement, has often entailed a cessation of the complaints and continuance in service. As Korf so aptly put it:

We have here a very interesting psychological fact. The dvorianstvo made very little use of this right not to serve. For nearly a whole century after the 1762 Manifesto the dvoriane continued to stay *in corpore* in state service. It is still the ideal job for a dvorianin. However, the dvorianstvo has never let slip an opportunity to affirm its *right not to serve*. So it normally happens in life, and particularly when dealing with the understanding of freedom. It is repellent to man to do what he is compelled to do.)[1]

While an act that included references to freedom was certainly of great significance in eighteenth-century Russia,[2] a further detraction from the importance of the 1762 manifesto lies in the circumstance that Catherine II, who came to power in June of that year, had a different attitude to the emancipation of the nobility from that of her husband and his advisers. Although the manifesto had stated that freedom from service would be instituted 'for all the noble dvorianstvo for all time as a fundamental and certain rule', it had also said that the continuance of this freedom would depend on the 'unshakable affirmation' of the Emperor's lawful successors.[3] Catherine, who liked to think of herself as the first of these, appeared to confirm the manifesto in decrees of 1766 and 1768, but omitted any reference to her 'unshakable affirmation' from them.[4] Before these decrees, she had noted in a letter to Panin that there was considerable murmuring among the dvorianstvo about the non-confirmation of its freedom,[5] and had set up a special committee to examine this question.[6] Nothing much came of it, and the decrees of 1766 and 1768 notwith-

---

[1] Korf, *Dvorianstvo*, pp. 65–6.

[2] Kliuchevskii, *Sochineniia*, VIII, 276–7, argued that these references to freedom were misunderstood by many contemporaries accustomed to think in a manner less sophisticated than those producing the decree. The decree did nothing more than abolish the obligatory *length* of service, declared the great historian.

[3] *PSZ*, XV, 914–15.

[4] *PSZ*, XVII, 631–2, 948–9, nos. 12,610, 12,731, 31 March, 24 August 1766; XVIII, 489, no. 13,087, 24 March 1768.

[5] Korf, *Dvorianstvo*, p. 8.

[6] *PSZ*, XVI, 157, no. 11,751, 11 February 1763.

standing, the situation with regard to the freedom of the nobility and its relationship to the Supreme Power was still ambiguous at the time of the Legislative Commission.

CATHERINE II AND HER POLICY

Unfortunately for later historians, but necessarily for Catherine, she had developed over the years the habit of covering her tracks and disguising her intentions, and she closely applied these political talents to what was perhaps one of the most important aspects of her internal policy, the management of the nobility. In attempting to understand Catherine, and to cast light on the obscurities of her policy, it is necessary to examine her background and early experiences.

Christian Augustus, one of the several German princelings in the service of the Prussian king, was Governor of Stettin in 1729, when his daughter, originally christened Sophia Augusta Frederika, was born. Northern Germany was at this time full of failing feudal families, forced to look locally and abroad for a livelihood, and the future Catherine's mother, also a retainer of Frederick of Prussia, possessed notable talents in this direction and had considerable family connections to draw on. She might well have been not at all surprised or flattered when an old canon from Brunswick had said to her, 'I see at least three crowns on your daughter's brow'.[1]

As a child, Sophia was something of a tomboy and enjoyed playing tricks, but these early traits had almost left her and she was coming to realize the family predicament when she set off with her mother for St Petersburg at the invitation of the Empress Elizabeth in 1744. Ekaterina Alekseevna, as she was now called after her reception into the Orthodox faith, was married a year later to the designated heir to the throne, the Grand Duke Peter. According to her own testimony, she did not look upon this match with any enthusiasm and on the eve of her wedding, as she later wrote, 'ambition alone supported me; I had at the bottom of my heart I know not what that prevented me from doubting for a moment that sooner or later I should become Empress of Russia in my own right'.[2] At first a great favourite at court, Catherine later became an object of the Empress Elizabeth's

[1] Kliuchevskii, *Sochineniia*, v, 6–8.
[2] Quoted in Florinsky, *Russia*, p. 500.

suspicion, and was kept like a bird in a gilded cage. Catherine took to private diversions, particularly reading. She later wrote in her *Memoirs*:

At that time, it could have been said of me that I was never without a book and never without sorrow, but also never without amusement. My disposition, cheerful by nature, did not in the meantime suffer under these circumstances; the hope of the prospect, if not of a heavenly, at least of an earthly crown, kept my spirit and my courage firm.[1]

During the last years of Elizabeth's reign, Catherine acquired a considerable knowledge of her adopted land and of classical and contemporary political theory and practice.[2]

However, while her outward deportment was modest and retiring, and while she appeared to adhere strictly to the rules of her new confession and the Elizabethan Court, behind the scenes Catherine was already collecting the first of her long line of lovers and scheming for power. Her correspondence with Sir Charles Hanbury-Williams, British Ambassador at St Petersburg, reveals that in 1757 Catherine participated in a plot aimed at maintaining the right of succession of her son Paul, even if Elizabeth disinherited the Grand Duke Peter.[3] Williams secured subsidies from England for the furtherance of this plan, and Catherine herself later calculated that she got through half a million roubles at this time, 'a terrible sum, which I paid out in instalments solely for my elevation to the throne'.[4] The fact that Catherine was in a position to pay out half a million roubles, albeit with assistance from abroad and by instalments, suggests that her lot at Elizabeth's court was not such an unhappy one as she herself claimed in her *Memoirs*, and these reminiscences, which contain more than the usual amount of retrospective wisdom and self-justification, must generally be treated with caution as a source of information concerning Catherine's life in Russia before her accession. Certainly, however, Catherine's relations with Elizabeth and Peter were not very happy, and she was anxious to get to the top.

The occasion actually used by Catherine to achieve her long-maturing ambition and to seize power was the proposed departure of her husband to lead his troops in an unpopular war against Den-

---

[1] Catherine II, *Memoirs*, p. 124.
[2] Kliuchevskii, *Sochineniia*, v, 19–20.
[3] N. D. Chechulin, *Ekaterina II v bor'be za prestol*, *passim*.
[4] Quoted in Kliuchevskii, *Sochineniia*, v, 18.

mark. Peter had alienated quite a large number of his subjects by his personal conduct and some ill-advised policies: more fatally, he had forgotten, or never learned, the cardinal rule for the maintenance of power in eighteenth-century Russia, and neglected to keep the support of the Guards. Peter's treatment of his wife had deteriorated after his accession, and the rumour circulated that he was thinking of divorcing or imprisoning her. (Catherine or her adherents may themselves have fomented the rumour and exaggerated the degree of Peter's lack of uxoriousness.) Catherine had won over to her cause several of the members of her husband's government, and secured the necessary support of many of the Guards through the agencies of her current lover, Gregory Orlov, and his four brothers, who enjoyed wide popularity among both officers and men. The revolt occurred a little prematurely, owing to the imminence of its discovery, but its aim was soon achieved.

Uneasy usually lay the head that wore the Russian crown, and the new Empress had no cause for exceptional equanimity. If she had a conscience, which is doubtful since she had been brought up in a very hard school, there were several grounds disturbing it. The assassination of her husband, Peter III, if not actually instigated by Catherine, met with her approval: Ivan VI, who had been deposed by Elizabeth, was murdered at Catherine's express instruction. The Grand Duke Paul, the fruit of Catherine's obedience to the order of Elizabeth that she should provide an heir, if not beyond all doubt of her marriage to Peter, presented a more difficult problem, which was more tortuously solved. Nikita I. Panin, one of the protagonists in the revolt against Peter, was far from alone in thinking that the Grand Duke should accede to power on achieving his majority, with his mother concluding her regency and retiring to the background. This idea held no appeal for the Empress, who kept her son out of the public eye as much as possible, and maintained a close watch on underground agitation on behalf of the boy, which expressed itself in several minor plots, all nipped quickly in the bud. So well known were the royal family's difficulties that the authorities deemed it wise to suppress the representation on the St Petersburg stage of another royal family's similar difficulties, the production of Shakespeare's *Hamlet*.[1]

William Richardson, visiting Russia towards the end of the 1760s,

[1] Florinsky, *Russia*, pp. 500–5.

clearly described the awkward position in which Catherine and her friends found themselves, writing:

Rumours of conspiracies are secretly propagated; several persons, I have heard, either guilty or suspected of treason, have disappeared: but these things are not noised abroad, they are only mentioned in confidential whispers. The people are prohibited from speaking or writing about politics. The Empress tells them, that as her maternal care for her dear people keeps her sleepless by night, and busy by day;—and I really believe that her nights are as sleepless as her days are busy:—they have no occasion to give themselves any further trouble about public affairs, than to act implicitly as she directs; and, in order the more effectually to save her dear people from unnecessary labour, she not only exhorts, but actually forbids them to speak, write, or think politics. The spies are busy: the suspected great men are closely watched.

However, her early ambition achieved, Catherine now aimed at more than the maintenance of power alone, as Richardson, albeit somewhat unkindly, hinted. Various interpretations have been made of her motives as Empress, ranging from sheer self-advertisement to altruistic devotion to her adopted country's cause, with the truth, as usual, somewhere in between. Undoubtedly, she worked extremely hard at her job. According to Richardson, the Countess Rumiantseva told him that Catherine worked from five till ten in the morning. She then breakfasted, and went to prayers, dined at two, and withdrew to her own apartment soon after dinner. The Empress drank tea at five, received company, played cards, or attended a play, opera, or masquerade, till supper, and retired for the night at ten. By her regular and judicious distribution of time, she was able to transact a great deal of business. The great number of surviving documents written in Catherine's own hand indicate that Richardson was not essentially misinformed.[1]

Moreover, not only was Catherine industrious, she was also not without intelligence, understanding and resolution. Had she been a mere figurehead, a pawn disguised as a queen, her early experiences would have been of no more than incidental or anecdotal interest, but in fact it was the Empress herself who made the important decisions for her administration, who animated the personnel of the Senate and the colleges during bouts of what she called her *zakono-besie*, or 'legimania'. As Empress, Catherine aimed at being executive

---

[1] William Richardson, *Anecdotes of the Russian Empire*, pp. 103–4, 23–5. A great number of the documents written by Catherine were published in *SIRIO*.

and judicial as well as legislative head of her Empire, and saw herself as the sole person in Russia above the spirit of party and bent on
the common good.[1]

Her life before her accession to power had made Catherine cunning: moreover, cosmopolitan as she was, she had developed an
extreme and rather muddled eclecticism, which makes doubly difficult any attempt to form a clear picture of her policy. She herself
confessed to Voltaire that, although her device was the bee, flitting
from flower to flower to collect honey for its hive, her store of political
ideas was less like a hive than an antheap.[2] Apart from this, her
application of political ideas was sometimes as complicated as their
collection. 'Believe me,' she wrote to the British Ambassador, Sir
Robert Gunning, 'I have not based my hopes for success on any *one*
mode of action. There are moments when it is not necessary to be too
precise.'[3] Such moments were many.

More confusingly still, it is possible to go so far as to say that, far
from concealing the basic principles of her policy, swamping them
under a deluge of ideas, or applying them in many different ways,
Catherine did not have any such principles. Kliuchevskii wrote
that she possessed one of those minds 'which do not understand what
conviction is, and why it is necessary in deliberation'.[4] Every ruler
of a country has to change the tack of his ship of state according to
the altering breezes, and concentrate on running repairs or even
complete overhaul when necessary, but he should perhaps have a
clear chart of the general course, too, and steer to it as much as
possible. If Catherine had such a chart, or steered such a course, she
left no sure guide to either.

A considerable number of attempts have been made to work out
exactly what was Catherine's domestic policy in various spheres,
and, understandably enough, interpretations have varied widely.
For example, while some historians have adhered to the traditional
idea of the reign of Catherine as the Golden Age of the Nobility, with
her most important legislation calculated to make sure that this was
so, others have maintained that the dvorianstvo was already on the
decline by the time of her accession, with several key laws aimed at
the promotion of the bourgeoisie.[5]

[1] Miliukov, *Ocherki*, III, 344.　　[2] Kliuchevskii, *Sochineniia*, v, 75.
[3] Quoted in Miliukov, *Ocherki*, III, 370.　[4] Kliuchevskii, *Sochineniia*, v, 75.
[5] For example, Kizevetter of the first, and Sacke of the second, school.

Catherine II and her policy

As Professor Beloff has pointed out, 'The argument as to Catherine's policy turns largely on the interpretation given to the Legislative Commission of 1767–1768 and to the document presented by Catherine to that body and known as the Instruction'.[1] The Empress herself was more active than any of her collaborators in all aspects of the preparation of the Commission, and held out very high hopes for its success. An examination of the Commission and the Instruction, therefore, can certainly provide considerable insight into Catherine's policy. Moreover, it can also allow an evaluation of the outlook and ambitions of Russia's social classes. First of all, however, what were the official reasons for the summons of the Commission?

These are contained in the preamble to the manifesto of 14 December 1766, which announced that five years had elapsed from the accession of the Empress to the Russian throne, during which time she had asked God day and night to help her observe the law of the Orthodox Church, strengthen and defend the beloved fatherland, preserve justice, eradicate evil and all lies and impositions, and, finally, to set up state institutions, by means of which the government would work within set limits, and each government department have a defined sphere of action in the maintenance of general good order. For these purposes, too, she had investigated every case that had come to her attention to find out what inadequacies existed, and how best to achieve the desired results. In the first years of her reign, the Empress had noticed the general confusion and inadequacy existing in the arrangement and application of the imperial laws. Peter the Great, the preamble pointed out, had twice tried to recodify Russia's laws, in 1700 and 1714, and similar attempts had been made by his successors, particularly Elizabeth. None of these had achieved the desired success, however, and for two years Catherine had been preparing instructions for those who could now tackle this great legislative problem once again. To find out the needs and wants of the Russian people in this direction, deputies were to be sent to Moscow from government departments and all districts and towns, and they were to bring with them relevant information. These deputies would also participate in the Commission, which was to prepare the new law code for the confirmation of the Empress.[2]

[1] Beloff, in Goodwin (ed.), *The European Nobility*, p. 187.
[2] *PSZ*, xvii, 1092–4, no. 12,801, 14 December 1766. For the eighteenth-century precedents to Catherine's Legislative Commission, see V. N. Latkin, *Zakonodatel'nye komissii v. Rossii v XVIII st.*, pp. 1–184.

So the official reasons for the summons of the Legislative Commission of 1767 were the recodification of Russia's laws, which would facilitate administrative and other reforms, the collection of information and the convocation of deputies to assist in this great work. In carrying out these tasks, the Commission, far from being a 'bracing precedent',[1] had several roots in Russian tradition, and, therefore, in summoning the Commission, Catherine was acting according to an old Russian spirit, not as an extreme Voltairian innovator. Although there were some representative assemblies in Kievan Russia and during the early Moscow period, the antecedents most comparable to the commissions of the eighteenth century culminating in that of 1767 were the series of *zemskie sobory* in the seventeenth century. The *zemskii sobor*, or national advisory assembly, had first been summoned by Ivan the Terrible, but had not become either elective or representative until the Time of Troubles round about the beginning of the seventeenth century, and, even then, the degree of popular representation was very small. The *zemskii sobor* most resembled the later commissions when it was summoned in 1648–9 to discuss the new law code, or *ulozhenie*. The higher clergy, the boyar council and elected representatives from the nobility, merchant and tradesman classes were to help to put state and local affairs in order, and it was hoped, vainly of course, that all ranks of people would then enjoy equal justice in all cases.[2]

Catherine's approach differed from that of her predecessors in the thoroughness of her preparation and her allowance of a wider representation of the views of various classes. Certainly, the degree of the influence of foreign ideas was greater in Catherine's work towards a new law code, too, although such ideas had by no means been absent from the earlier assemblies and commissions. However, some observers have not been completely satisfied with her officially stated reason for the summons of the Legislative Commission, to complete an old job with refurbished tools, and have considered that Catherine had aims other than the common good. Several of the contemporary European diplomatic representatives in Russia pointed out at the time that Catherine's position on the throne was by no means secure, and that the commission was intended to strengthen

---

[1] G. P. Gooch, *Catherine the Great and Other Studies*, p. 94.

[2] Florinsky, *Russia*, pp. 266–7; V. I. Sergeevich, 'Otkuda neudachi ekaterininskoi komissii?', *VE*, I (1878), 189. See generally, J. L. H. Keep, 'The Decline of the Zemsky Sobor', *SEER*, xxxvi, no. 86, 100–22.

her title to it.[1] Two actual plots at least had already taken place,[2] and various sections of the nobility were not at all happy with the Empress and her Orlov-dominated clique.

In a letter to her newly appointed Procurator-General A. A. Viazemskii in 1764, Catherine had noted the existence of two parties in the Senate, one grouped around the Orlovs, and the other following Panin. The first, she had written, was composed of people with good morals, but sometimes without perspicacious intellects. The vision of the second group, in the opinion of the Empress, was longer sighted, but of doubtful value. Some of its members thought that, because they had spent a lot of time in this or that country, everything must be arranged in Russia as it was abroad, and everything else without exception was criticized by them, in spite of the fact that the internal order of any country should be founded on its own peculiar character. While counselling Viazemskii to avoid entangling alliances with both parties, Catherine made clear in her letter that she favoured the Orlovs.[3] At the same time, the facts that Panin remained a member of Catherine's government and was retained as tutor to the Grand Duke Paul suggest that Panin himself was never looked on by the Empress as a serious danger to herself or her throne, and that the differences between the two groups in the Senate were intellectual, or, at least, not bitterly personal.

Certainly, other members of the higher dvorianstvo would have been more firmly resolved than Panin to guarantee the accuracy of his statement, 'Madame Orlova will never be Empress of all the Russias'.[4] Undercurrents of dissatisfaction with Catherine were noticeable at lower levels among the nobility, too. Rumiantsev noted that 'false and...uncharacteristic republican ideas' had permeated the Guards,[5] and rumours that the Empress intended some mitigation of serfdom were worrying the dvorianstvo in general.[6] Thoughts for the preservation of her power, and, indeed, her life, must certainly have been occurring to Catherine as she prepared for the assembly of her Legislative Commission, particularly at the time

[1] N. N. Knorring, in *Sbornik statei Miliukovu*, pp. 330–1.
[2] Mirovich plotted to replace Catherine by Ivan VI in 1764 (Florinsky, *Russia*, p. 504) and Hitrovo was involved in a conspiracy against the Orlovs in 1763 (*SIRIO*, vii, 289–94).
[3] N. D. Chechulin (ed.), *Istoriia senata*, ii, Appendix xvi, 793–6.
[4] Quoted by Knorring in *Sbornik statei Miliukovu*, pp. 330–1.
[5] S. M. Solov'ev, 'Rasskazy iz russkoi istorii', *RV*, xxxv, 328. It is possible that, in this case, in the Ukraine, 'republican' meant 'independent'.
[6] Knorring, in *Sbornik statei Miliukovu*, p. 333.

described by the French diplomat Rossignol. 'Three weeks ago,' he reported on 6 November 1766, 'a madman dared to throw a stone through the windows of the Empress and the Count Orlov. The terror of the Empress was so great that she almost fainted.'[1]

Catherine was no coward, however, and decided to convene her Commission in Moscow, the stronghold of the old nobility, rather than St Petersburg, the official capital. It was probably true, of course, that she wished to placate the Russian national prejudice that all important laws could issue from the ancient capital,[2] but it seems quite possible, too, as Rossignol suggested, that the idea appealed to Catherine of appearing in Moscow, and forcing her will upon that disobedient city. Wrote Rossignol:

The most ancient dvorianstvo, living there in great numbers, has little respect for the Empress apparently, and expresses itself on this subject quite freely. It despises also the lords who are attached to her, and looks upon them as inferior beings forced to cringe at the will of the Sovereign, whereas it considers itself in its aloof position too powerful to be at all apprehensive about its feelings.[3]

To forestall any dangerous expression of dissatisfaction, 35,000–40,000 troops were deployed in the environs of the city as Catherine, her entourage, her Senate and the Holy Synod moved to Moscow for the opening of the Commission.[4]

At the Commission itself, the influence of the dvorianstvo was perhaps to be restricted by keeping it in a minority in relation to the town deputies. Of course, the Commission was at no time intended to resemble closely a parliament: on the other hand, votes were to be taken, and a noble majority might have solidified into a troublesome 'opposition party'. It seems probable that, as Lipinskii thought, 'Numerical superiority was important for the dvoriane in the Commission',[5] although only one voice is known to have risen in complaint when it became apparent that such a superiority was not to be. This was Shcherbatov, the upholder of the rights of the ancient nobility, who, during the course of an argument against the use of the secret ballot at the Commission wrote; 'As it seems to me, the

[1] *SIRIO*, cxli, 185.
[2] Hans Rogger well describes this prejudice in his *National Consciousness in Eighteenth Century Russia*, pp. 9–20.
[3] *SIRIO*, cxli, 79.   [4] *SIRIO*, cxli, 233.
[5] M. A. Lipinskii, 'Novye dannye dlia istorii ekaterininskoi komissii', *ŽMNP*, ccli, 245.

number of gentleman deputies of other ranks apart from the dvoriane is larger than the number of noble deputies.' He continued:

So it will not be the corps of the dvorianstvo, the most enlightened about the true advantages of the fatherland, who will decide, so much as, because of the preponderance of their number, the merchants, heathen tribes, state peasants, and similar people, who for the most part have never been honoured with such a great task, and are without an understanding of each aspect of the general situation of the Empire.[1]

Connected with the minority situation of the dvorianstvo is the question of the preponderance of the deputies from the towns over noble deputies. This probably stemmed as much from Catherine's desire to develop a middle class in Russia, as her desire to stop the dvorianstvo from becoming over-powerful. The Empress had for some time regretted the undeveloped condition of the Russian bourgeoisie. In April 1766 she had written to Madame Geoffrin that this class must be instituted in Russia, and that 'this motive will make me resolve and act with assurance, since I count it as an essential duty of my position'.[2] Catherine had been working on her Instruction for two years before the publication of the manifesto of 14 December 1766, and included in this work a vigorous assertion of the benefits which would accrue to Russia from the expansion of the bourgeoisie.[3] In giving to the towns the largest group of deputies, Catherine could increase the cohesion and strength of the class that she wished to foster.

Another possible reason for the assembly of the Legislative Commission was the desire to reduce the centrifugal tendencies of the outlying provinces of the Russian Empire, and to incorporate them fully in the main imperial body. Catherine had written to Viazemskii in 1764 that, while Little Russia and the Baltic Provinces had their own privileges, which it would be unseemly to destroy immediately, to continue to consider these provinces as foreign would be an even greater and more stupid mistake. 'These provinces...should be gently reduced to a condition where they can be russified and no longer, like wolves, look to the woods', wrote Catherine. 'This can be achieved without effort if responsible men are put in charge.'[4] One

[1] D. Shahovskoi, 'Russkii deputat xviii veka', *Minuvshie gody*, November 1908, pp. 285–6.
[2] *SIRIO*, I, 285–6.
[3] W. F. Reddaway, *Documents of Catherine the Great*, pp. 275–8.
[4] Chechulin (ed.), *Istoriia senata*, II, Appendix xvi, 793–6.

of these sensible men, it was hoped, would turn out to be P. A. Rumiantsev, installed as Governor of Little Russia after the abolition of the local hetmanship in 1764. Catherine's instructions to Rumiantsev on taking up his difficult new post were similar to those to Viazemskii in some respects. Her representatives must know, she wrote, how to carry on their job, not always with the full power of the authority entrusted to them, but sometimes rather by the devious means of kindness and condescension. According to the circumstances, the time and the man, they must have both the teeth of the wolf and the tail of the fox.[1] The tail of the fox was wagging as the summons went out for deputies from all provinces of the Empire to come to Moscow to help recodify Russia's laws. It probably seemed to Catherine, as it did later to Sergeevich, that the Commission 'could be an excellent way of uniting the various parts of our wide and not everywhere uniformly peopled Empire'.[2]

Finally, her Legislative Commission was convened with the aim of helping Catherine to cut a fine enlightened figure before the eyes of contemporary Western Europe. Her Instruction incorporated many of the ideas of Montesquieu and Beccaria, and some of the ideas of the cameralists and physiocrats—to such an extent that Catherine wrote to Frederick II of Prussia that 'I have acted like the crow of the fable who made itself a garment of peacock's feathers'.[3] The Empress hoped that this Instruction would show Western Europe that she was in touch with its latest ideas and help the members of her Commission to devise a code of laws that would make the Russian people the happiest in the world,[4] and thus gain for its author the further acclaim of the standard-bearers of the Enlightenment. Kliuchevskii, considering the Instruction, or *Nakaz*, some sixty years ago, did not think it capable of carrying out the second aim, although conceding it some success in the first. He wrote:

The *Nakaz* occupies but a modest place alike in our literature and in our legislation. As a literary memorial, it does no more than head a long series of compilations which merely snipped off the topmost leaves of Western civilization, and skimmed the surface of Western thought, and inaugurated the custom (one which we suffer to this day) of seeking an answer to each problem of Russian actuality in theories which non-Russian minds have evolved from non-Russian life experiences. And in

[1] *SIRIO*, VII, 382.   [2] Sergeevich, *VE*, I (1878), 214.
[3] Quoted in Florinsky, *Russia*, p. 511. See N. D. Chechulin, 'Ob istochnikah "nakaza"', *ŽMNP*, CCCXXX, 292, 296, 299.   [4] Reddaway, *Documents*, p. 293.

any case the *Nakaz* remained practically unknown to the public, for the Senate ordered that even in the chancellories secretaries should keep the document under lock and key, rather than that it should be read by inquisitive clerks. Which goes to show that the Government regarded it as so much 'forbidden fruit' of its author's brain. Neither new principles nor new articles did the *Nakaz* introduce. That which Catherine achieved in the legislative sphere less developed from the *Nakaz* than confirmed and continued certain old-established factors in our history. Interest further attaches to the *Nakaz*, because it shows that for at least once in Russia's history Russia's Supreme Power became smitten with dissatisfaction at Russia's legislative system, even though that Power had to recognize its incompetency for the system's reform.

In short, we see in the *Nakaz*, not an historical stage of our legislative progress, but a purely pathological phase; not a factor in our country's record, but a feature in the biography of the document's composer.[1]

Western Europe was made fully aware of the existence of the Instruction and the convocation of the Legislative Commission. Whatever shortcomings they were to reveal later, their initial impact was to increase the fame of their creator as a ruler determined to modernize her adopted country according to the prescriptions of recent Western thinkers, and to place her alongside Frederick II and Maria Teresa as a monarch determined to reform her country's laws. Not only this, and *pace* Kliuchevskii, full of plagiarism though it might be, the Instruction does constitute a worthy attempt to adapt new, foreign ideas to an old Russian setting, and also gives a clear indication of what Catherine officially hoped to achieve in all major spheres of her internal policy.

THE ELECTIONS TO THE LEGISLATIVE COMMISSION

As well as working for two years on her Instruction, Catherine spent a considerable amount of time on the production of the manifesto of 14 December 1766 which was to set the Commission in motion. This preparatory work must now be examined, particularly for the further light that it sheds on the motives governing Catherine's policy and her relationship with the dvorianstvo.

There were at least seven preliminary drafts to the manifesto of 14 December 1766, in all of which Catherine had a hand, particularly the first two and the last two.[2] The first of the seven, the only draft to

[1] C. J. Hogarth (trans.), Klyuchevsky, *A History of Russia*, v, 43.
[2] A. V. Florovskii, *Sostav zakonodatel'noi komissii*, p. 8.

57

propose St Petersburg rather than Moscow as the site for the con-
vention of the Commission, suggested the election of government
officials, both central and local, and representatives from the nobility
and the merchant class. These would form an assembly, which would
elect a five-man committee to work out a new law code with secret
instructions from the Empress. When the code was prepared, the
assembly would approve it, and send it to the Empress for her confirmation.[1] The second draft put forward ideas for representation of
the nobility and town property-owners, on a somewhat different
basis from that suggested in the first draft, without any discussion of
the function of the Commission after it had assembled, or any mention
of government representation.[2]

The third of the seven drafts, referred to by its editor, A. I. Markevich, as the preliminary suggestions, was largely the work of
Viazemskii, the Procurator-General, or A. I. Bibikov, later Marshal
of the Legislative Commission.[3] It is rather more detailed than the
first two drafts, considering at some length the questions, which
social groups and which regions should be represented and by how
many deputies, how much should be given to the various groups of
deputies for their upkeep, and what form the elections and oaths of
the deputies should take.[4]

The fourth draft, edited by M. A. Lipinskii, was concerned with
the number of deputies from each group, and the amount necessary
for their upkeep.[5] The fifth, which had a wider frame of reference,
was the work of a special committee set up with Viazemskii as its
chairman and instructions from Catherine.[6] The sixth and seventh
drafts were largely the work of Catherine herself, using the materials
already collected, which included the preceding drafts and the instructions for setting up previous legislative commissions, the advice
of her government officials, and the collaboration of her secretaries,
particularly G. V. Kozitskii. They concerned all aspects of the preparation of the new Legislative Commission.[7]

In all these preliminary sketches for the final picture as it emerged
on 14 December 1766, there appeared as a leitmotiv the question of

[1] A. V. Florovskii, *Sostav zakonodatel'noi komissii*, pp. 8–12. [2] *Ibid.* pp. 12–15.

[3] A. I. Markevich, 'Predlozhenie o sozyve komissii dlia sostavleniia proekta novogo
ulozheniia', *Zapiski imperatorskogo odesskogo obshchestva istorii i drevnostei*, xx, 3–4, attributes
the draft to Viazemskii and others, while Florovskii, *Sostav*, pp. 17–33, argues that Bibikov
was the principal author.

[4] Markevich, *Zap. imp. od. ob.*, xx, 17–27. [5] Lipinskii, *ZMNP*, ccli, 290–3.

[6] Sergeevich, *VE*, 1 (1878), 200. [7] Florovskii, *Sostav*, pp. 40–4.

representation, which arose over two issues, region and class. The first of these was not discussed as much as the second, even though it was probably of equal importance in Catherine's general scheme. The reason for this might have been to some degree her awareness of the delicacy necessary in handling the outlying regions of her Empire, as expressed in her letters to Viazemskii and Rumiantsev, although precedent could well have been of greater influence here, since previous commissions had not contained representatives from these regions, although some were tacked on to the Elizabethan commission.[1]

In the first two drafts of the Catherinian manifesto, representatives from north-west and south-west Russia were not mentioned. In the preliminary suggestions, regions with separate rights and privileges, i.e. Little Russia, including the Zaporozhian Cossacks, and the Baltic provinces, were to be allowed to send representatives if they so desired.[2] A note appended to the plan published by Lipinskii, on the other hand, pointed out that:

From New and Little Russia and the Baltic Provinces, deputies are to be arranged according to the general rule now adopted, since they too have the good fortune to exist under an equal power, and because their laws are not less, but even more confused and involved than the Great Russian.[3]

The Viazemskii committee reverted to the position taken in the preliminary suggestions, after receiving an instruction from Catherine that, 'Little Russia, Livonia, Estonia and Finland are to be given the option of sending deputies. If they do not send them, they are to stay on the same basis as now, until they petition for equality.'[4] The sixth and the seventh drafts, however, led on to the final manifesto which united all sections of the Empire without exception under the same regulations.

In the preliminary drafts to the 1766 manifesto, there was more discussion of the question of representation on the basis of class than region, and considerable variation in the answers to it before the final decision was made. The manifesto made provision for the representation of the central government institutions, and seven social groups: the nobles; town inhabitants; a class of quasi-free peasants, the *odnodvortsy*; soldier-farmers and allied classes forming the army

[1] *PSZ*, xv, 862–3, no. 11,378, 8 December 1761.
[2] Markevich, *Zap. imp. od. ob.* xx, 7.
[3] Lipinskii, *ZMNP*, ccli, 290–3. [4] Sergeevich, *VE*, i (1878), 213.

reserves; state peasants; tribesmen; and the Cossacks. Excluded from representation in both manifesto and preliminary drafts were: the priesthood; the serfs of the noble landlords; the peasants living on the church lands recently taken over by the state; the state peasants assigned to the factories and the mines; and other peasant groups, such as those responsible for the upkeep of post-horses. Before discussing the classes provided for in the manifesto, I should mention those that were excluded from representation.

Representatives from the priesthood, who had been necessary and constant participants in assemblies of former centuries, had not been included in any of the legislative commissions of the eighteenth century. Their exclusion in 1766, therefore, was not so much due to the influence of Voltaire on Catherine as to Russian tradition. Contributory factors might have been the feeling that the voice of the clergy would be sufficiently heard from the deputy of the Holy Synod, or that a large body of clerical deputies would cause trouble about the nationalization of the church lands in 1764.[1] The serfs were to be represented, if at all, by their lords, and other peasants by the appropriate government department, such as the Economy, Mining or Manufacturing College. The state peasants assigned to the factories and mines also had some deputies among those officially elected by other groups.[2]

Using the figures compiled by V. I. Semevskii, it can be calculated that less than a quarter of the peasants could have a hand in electing deputies to the Catherinian Commission, and that some 77 per cent of the poll taxpaying population were represented indirectly or not at all.[3] Even this, however, was an improvement on the previous commissions of the eighteenth century, to which representatives from the nobility and the townspeople only had been invited. Only these two classes were mentioned in the first two drafts of the 1766 manifesto, but the other five mentioned above were introduced in the preliminary suggestions, and included in all other drafts. (A sole minor exception was the exclusion of the soldier-farmers from the sixth draft.) After some variation, the representation of these five classes was ordered to be on the basis of one deputy per county,

---

[1] Florovskii, *Sostav*, pp. 55–75.

[2] See M. Longinov (ed.), 'Spisok gospodam deputatam', *RV*, xxxvi, Appendix, nos. 249, 250, 251, 252, 295, 546.

[3] V. I. Semevskii, *Krest'iane v tsarstvovanie Ekateriny IIoi*, i, vii-viii.

except for the Cossack representation, which was to be decided by the local 'high authorities'. The elections were to be indirect, in three stages—subdistrict, district and county.[1]

Government representatives had participated in previous legislative commissions of the eighteenth century, but with particular functions ascribed to them, not on a more general basis as in 1767. They received a mention only in the first and last drafts of the manifesto, however, in both of which the Senate, Synod, Colleges and other government offices were to send one deputy each. It was finally decided that all these deputies were to be appointed by the Senate.[2]

The manifesto of 1766 arranged the representation of the bourgeoisie on the basis of one deputy per town. There had been some breakdown of the class in the preliminary drafts into merchants, burghers, and guildsmen. That these divisions were ignored in the final draft was perhaps a reflection of Catherine's desire to develop the solidarity of the middle class. (Of course, there was a great gap between the wish of the Empress and the reality of town life in eighteenth-century Russia, a long way to go before the target was reached. Discussing this question, V. G. Avseenko wrote:

It is difficult to know what is more astonishing, the great enthusiasm with which the government tried to introduce Western institutions in Russia in the eighteenth century, or the ease with which such institutions were destroyed in a *milieu* ill-prepared for them, or the incredibly low level of the actual state of town society, or, finally, the general chaos prevailing under the disguise of an external uniformity of regimentation and bureaucracy.)[3]

While elected representatives from the bourgeoisie had first been summoned to a legislative commission in 1730,[4] the dvorianstvo had been ordered in 1728 'to send to Moscow from the officers and nobles good and learned men from every province, except Livonia, Estonia and Siberia, five men each by election from the nobility'.[5] These delegates were of inferior quality, or insufficient quantity, for a year later the provincial governors were ordered to arrange fresh elections of outstanding and good men, from each province, satisfying the governors as well as the nobles.[6] At the Elizabethan commission in

---

[1] Florovskii, *Sostav*, pp. 92–3, diagram.   [2] *Ibid.* pp. 93–100.
[3] V. G. Avseenko, *Malorossiia v 1767 godu*, p. 60.
[4] *PSZ*, VIII, 284–5, no. 5,567, 1 June 1730.
[5] *PSZ*, VIII, 53–4, no. 5,287, 14 June 1728.
[6] *PSZ*, VIII, 198, no. 5,412, 16 May 1729.

1761, two dvoriane per county were to appear, although an earlier draft had suggested one per county.[1] Representation from the dvorianstvo was increasing, then, at legislative commissions throughout the eighteenth century, and the 1766 formula was a step in the normal direction, with one deputy now to come from each district.

The early drafts of the manifesto, however, sometimes suggested a different basis for the representation of the dvorianstvo. The first draft, for example, proposed the province as an electoral unit, and the Viazemskii committee, although using the district as their electoral unit, wanted to decide the number of deputies from it according to the number of local serfs. Whatever the stipulation for the representation of the nobility, it is noticeable that the grand total of its deputies would always be smaller than that of the bourgeoisie. This reversed the situation of all previous legislative commissions: the inference is strong, therefore, that there was a deliberate intention on the part of the Empress to keep the noble deputies in a minority in relation to the town delegates.[2]

An examination of the preliminary drafts to the 1766 manifesto, and of some aspects of that document itself, thus provides supporting evidence for two of the underlying motives attributed to Catherine in her convocation of the Legislative Commission, as well as bearing witness to the care of her preparatory work and her adherence to precedent. The instructions to the governors for carrying out the elections, the other subject connected with the manifesto most in need of amplification, finally reached the following form.

The governors were ordered to have the manifesto read for three concurrent Sundays in every district of the province under their jurisdiction, and then to arrange the time and place for the elections of each class, making sure that these elections did not clash with each other. A supervisor was to be appointed by the governor to manage the preliminary stages of each election, i.e. in the case of the dvorianstvo, until a marshal was elected, and the governors themselves were to attend as many elections as they thought necessary for the successful outcome of the meetings, solemnly warning all those who caused trouble that they did so under the threat of 'the inevitable burden of lawful punishment'. The governors were also to make sure

[1] Florovskii, *Sostav*, p. 111.
[2] This thesis developed by G. Sacke, 'Adel und Burgertum in Der Gesetzgebenden Kommission Katharinas II von Russland', *Jahrbücher für Geschichte Osteuropas* (1938), pp. 408–17.

that all the deputies were sent off to Moscow as quickly as possible, and they themselves were to attend the Legislative Commission when they were in the old capital, bringing with them, or alternatively sending, a report on the local needs and defects. The other principal duty of the governors was to make decisions on problems arising in the execution of the regulations for completing the elections.[1]

These regulations provided many loopholes, and many questions were bound to arise. As far as the elections of the dvorianstvo were concerned, qualified voters were to be dvoriane actually possessing an estate in the appropriate district. To be eligible for marshal, or deputy, a dvorianin had to possess a local estate and a clean moral and criminal record, and could actually be serving or retired with any rank or title. The marshal was to be elected for a term of two years, and had to be over thirty years of age, while the deputy had to be over twenty-five. Once elected, the marshal was to supervise the election of a five-man committee for the compilation of the local instruction, at the same time making sure that this committee was addressing itself to general needs, without any mention of particular cases which could be decided by the local courts. The marshal would also supervise the election of the deputy, for which position he himself could be a candidate. If the marshal were elected deputy, another marshal would have to be elected. Those dvoriane unable to attend elections because of the calls of service were to send postal testimony of the nobles they favoured most for the elective functions.[2]

As far as the preliminaries to the elections and the elections themselves were concerned, three basic conditions were influential: the attitude of the local administration and population to the points of the electoral law; the correspondence of these points of the 14 December manifesto to the actual situation of the community; and the interest of the local administration in the execution of the elections. As far as the elections of the dvorianstvo in particular were concerned, as I have mentioned, the law made the following three stipulations: the electoral unit was to be the district, or regional approximation to it; the voters were to be dvoriane; and in order to vote in an election, a noble would have to possess an estate in the relevant district.

The first of these stipulations was sometimes varied if the local administration considered that local peculiarities demanded it. The vast capital district of Novgorod province was divided on the basis

[1] *PSZ*, xvii, 1095–100, no. 12,801.   [2] *PSZ*, no. 12,801. See also *SIRIO*, iv, 2–6.

of a local administrative unit, Governor Sivers considering that, with such an arrangement, 'it will be more possible to find out the needs and feelings of the people'. In support of his decision, which was confirmed by the Supreme Power, Sivers pointed out that such a division had been made at the time of the 1648 *zemskii sobor*.[1] Without imperial approval, some districts, grouped together under the same local authority, submitted a joint instruction and elected a joint deputy. Three such groups in Moscow province were Peremyshl' and Vorotynsk; Sudislavl' and Bui; and Kaluga and Medyn'. Similar arrangements were made in Novgorod province by the Gdovsk and Kobyl'sk, and Toropets and Holm districts, and by Poltava and Topol'sk in Belgorod province. Serpuhov, Obolensk and Tarusa, grouped together under one *voevoda* in a Moscow county, attempted at first to work separately, but combined later on.[2] The question of the electoral unit arose in the Baltic states, too, with Estonia and Livonia receiving somewhat different treatment even though their problems were very similar.[3]

The other two points of the electoral law requiring the electors to be dvoriane and landlords also needed interpretation, and were misapplied in some cases. This was to some extent the fault of the law itself. As Florovskii pointed out:

The dvorianstvo at the time of the convocation of the Legislative Commission did not constitute a completely united group, but was divided into separate composite elements depending on their origin and the circumstances of their connection to the general mass of the Russian nobility, as well as the extent among them of the rights of the latter. The process of unification was far from complete, and the heterogeneity of the composite elements was evident in the minutiae of the general situation of their local lives, the spheres in which they were active, and in their very titles, which had not yet lost their local significance or fallen into disuse. And so, on coming across such elements, very close to the dvorianstvo but not yet joined to it by title or full enjoyment of its privileges, the administration was obliged to invite them to the elections or to leave them out of the assemblies being called together. Clearly, it would be difficult to expect complete uniformity in this, because each region had its own peculiarities as far as the social composition of the population was concerned, and required a separate interpretation fitting in with the facts of local life.[4]

The extremely general terms in which the composition of the electoral societies was described in the manifesto, with no reference at

[1] Florovskii, *Sostav*, pp. 233-4.   [2] *Ibid*. pp. 234-5.
[3] *Ibid*. pp. 235-7.   [4] *Ibid*. pp. 239-40.

all to the local variations described above, presented the opportunity of a wide variation in the law's application to the local administrators.

Problems should not have occurred in Great Russia or other old parts of the Empire, however, where there were in fact several cases of deliberate misapplication, or at least crass misunderstanding of the electoral law requiring the voters to be nobles and local landlords. For example, the governor of Kazan' province, Kvashnin-Samarin, tried to limit the local voters to those possessing ancient estates, and, in other places, only staff and commissioned officers were invited to the elections.[1] These instances appear to indicate the influence on local government officials of rivalry between older and newer noble families, and between military and civil dvoriane. However, on the other hand, there is little evidence of disputes concerning the credentials of individual noble electors in the heart of the Empire.

In fact, while a considerable number of intending electors might have been turned away and not pushed their claim, only one case is known of a disappointed reject trying to seek redress for his grievances. M. T. Holiapin, of the Peremyshl', Moscow, district, went on the appointed date to the local assembly of the dvorianstvo, and expressed his desire to participate in the elections, since, as he put it, 'my ancestors, and from them myself, have been in possession of immovable property...granted by the predecessors of the Empress in the town Peremyshl''. The local *voevoda* rejected Holiapin's claim with the explanation that it would not be fitting for him to be together with the dvorianstvo at the elections, and he would not be held guilty of any misdemeanour if he failed to attend. Pushing his claims further, Holiapin was told that dvoriane only would be at the election, and he was not one of them, even though he possessed commissioned rank. He should join the local soldier-farmers, because he possessed his estate in common with them. The case finally reached the Senate, which rejected Holiapin's suit on the grounds that he had not provided sufficient evidence, nor given the names of offenders against the law.[2]

There was no election exclusive to the nobility in Siberia, probably because of the absence from that province of noble estates. The needs and wishes of groups comparable to the dvorianstvo were expressed at the Legislative Commission by the deputy from the town Eniseisk.[3]

---

[1] *Ibid.* pp. 238–9.   [2] *Ibid.* pp. 238–9, 240–1.
[3] *SIRIO*, IV, 155–8. See also P. Golovachev, *Sibir' v ekaterininskoi komissii*, pp. 49–55.

To the south, in Slobodsko-Ukraina, there was no native dvorianstvo, but many landowners from Great Russia, who participated in the elections along with the Cossack chieftains, who were unwillingly allowed inclusion by the local governor, E. A. Shcherbinin.[1] A comparable situation would exist in the province of New Russia.

In Little Russia, or the Ukraine proper, Governor Rumiantsev sent out a circular on 26 February 1767, setting the dates for the elections, and asking for general, not particular, information on lasting rather than temporary grievances, such as the slow work of the courts, and troubles in agriculture, trade and industry. The Little Russian College distributed many copies of the manifesto of 14 December 1766, and detailed instructions in the same spirit as Rumiantsev's circular.[2] News of the Legislative Commission, wrote V. G. Avseenko, was received with enthusiasm everywhere, particularly by the nobility.[3] This opinion cannot be supported by the report on the local reception of the news sent by Rumiantsev to Catherine. The Governor wrote on 2 March 1767:

Many have truly reached such a degree of wilfulness that every law and state decree seems to them to be a violation of their rights and freedoms, all their assertions are the same: why should we be there? Our laws are excellent, and if we have to have deputies, surely they will only seek confirmation of these rights and privileges... The towns alone and the simple people publicly recognize the graciousness of Your Imperial Highness, and the usefulness for them of some measures introduced by me, but here they complain that their superiors, and even more the nobility spread around here, impede them with all their might.

Similarly, Rumiantsev later wrote:

The great lords, chieftains, and imaginary nobility have everywhere been talking differently about the Manifesto. Some have said that all this does not apply to them; others, blinded by their love for their own country, that they have been summoned as learned and upright people only for consultation and the composition of a new law code for Great Russians; they, who have been transformed from nothing, and for the most part by means of money snatched from the lands of others, or by their wives, into nobles, have not wanted even to sit with the burghers, considering this to be derogatory to their honour, and always calling the townspeople peasants; in fact, they have tried to destroy the name of the latter entirely, having already destroyed all their rights and privileges and assuming for themselves limitless power and great possessions in the towns.[4]

---

[1] D. I. Bagalei, *Ocherki iz russkoi istorii*, II, 104–9. [2] Avseenko, *Malorossiia*, pp. 1–3.
[3] *Ibid.* pp. 3–5. [4] Solov'ev, *RV*, xxxv, 324–8.

Elections to the Legislative Commission

To the north-west, too, in the Baltic state of Livonia, difficulties arose soon after the publication of the manifesto. For twenty years or more before the summons of the Legislative Commission, there had been two distinct groups among the local equivalent to the dvorianstvo: the *Ritterschaft*, or *rytsarstvo*, whose genealogy was recorded in a special register, and the *Landschaft*, or *zemstvo*, who were non-registered landowners. After the composition of the register in 1747, the members of the *Ritterschaft*, who possessed great influence in local government, had banded together in exclusive corporations, or *Mitbruderschaften*, which nobody could join without proof of the antiquity of his family's landholdings in the appropriate district. They disputed with the *Landsassen* of the *Landschaft* the interpretation of the clause in the official translation of the 14 December manifesto which stated that, 'Jeder Edelmann, der in dem Districte eigen güter besitzet, hat das Recht einen Deputirten des Adels zu wählen'. The argument that only a member of a *Mitbruderschaft* could be called an *Edelmann* met with the determined opposition of the *landsassen*. Before the affair was settled, Governor Iu. Broun, the Senate and the Empress herself were all involved in it. First of all, the governor tried to break the stubbornness of the *Ritterschaft* by pointing out that the Empress did not have in mind the personal prerogatives of the individual, but rather the *jura realia* connected with land possession. The Senate then said that not too much time must be spent delaying the execution of the imperial will, and that all must participate in the elections who possessed the rank of dvorianin and a local estate, irrespective of their origins. Catherine herself was more explicit in a letter to Broun, in which she clearly expressed her belief that the pretensions of the *Ritterschaft* were without foundation. There was no mention of genealogical registers in the 14 December manifesto, and no such register in Russia itself, where the electoral law was the same as in Livonia, she declared. Commenting on the position taken up by the *Ritterschaft*, Catherine stressed the fact that they were undermining the authority of the Supreme Power in their requirement of a separate standard of recognition or non-recognition of a group of people upon which the Empress had conferred the dignity of dvorianstvo. She supported the views of the Senate, ordering the *Ritterschaft* to combine with the *Landschaft* at the Livonian elections.[1]

The preliminaries to the elections of the nobility in the other Baltic

---

[1] Florovskii, *Sostav*, pp. 242–8.

states appear to have been accomplished rather more quietly, although there were some irregularities of a more individual nature in Estonia.[1] Generally speaking, it has been pointed out that the regulations of the manifesto of 14 December 1766 could be executed in a straightforward manner in Great Russia only, and that even there some unforeseen problems arose.

The further development of the business of the assembly of the Legislative Commission, as far as the dvorianstvo was concerned, depended on the attitude of the nobles and the local authorities to the local elections. Before discussing those dvoriane who attended the elections, however, it must be noted that the attitude of the bulk of the class was one of disinterest. Although there were over 300 districts or their equivalents in the Russian Empire in 1766, elections were held in less than 170 of them.[2] This does not mean that nobles in 130 districts failed to send deputies and to submit instructions, for some districts contained no noble estates. Three provinces, Astrahan', Irkutsk and Siberia, containing a total of some twenty-five districts, were almost completely devoid of them.[3] Some districts in other provinces, such as Viatka in Kazan' and Zapozhok in Moscow, were without noble landlords, and the Empress herself referred to a group of fifteen districts, mostly in outlying provinces, which contained less than ten noble estates each. To all of these can probably be added about another ten districts, so that the number of them not holding elections, although in a position to do so, can be reduced to about eighty. There were thus a great number of defaulters from the elections, and, probably, in an average district holding an election, no more than a quarter of the nobles owning estates locally voted.[4]

It is impossible to give with any assurance the reasons for this state of affairs, and to estimate the relative importance of absence through service, indigence, malingering, hostility, indifference or sheer ignorance. It is also very difficult to make any general observation about the attitude of the local administration. In several districts, where the situation was not favourable for elections, the administration made considerable, but for the most part futile, efforts to

[1] See R. Hasselblatt, 'Die Instructionen der Baltischen Ritterschaften', *Baltische Monatsschrift*, xxxvii, 668–93; I. M. Pokrovskii, *Ekaterininskaia komissiia i tserhovnye voprosy v nei*, p. 19.
[2] K. Arsen'ev, *Statisticheskie ocherki Rossii*, pp. 92–102.
[3] Semevskii, *Krest'iane*, i, 20, points out that these provinces contained no serfs of the nobles according to the third census of 1766.
[4] Florovskii, *Sostav*, pp. 251–3, 267.

carry out the letter of their instructions properly. (In Gorohovets, Moscow province, only seven of the sixty-three dvoriane possessing estates in the district actually lived there. Six came to the election, and four others sent postal votes. The Moscow Governor told the local *voevoda* that he should be able to get at least fifteen voters, and should arrange a new date for the Gorohovets election. At this second meeting, only five dvoriane participated, electing as deputy one of those who had sent a postal vote, and whose whereabouts were unknown.[1] In the Unzha district of Archangel province, 260 dvoriane possessed estates according to the third census, but not one lived there as a landlord. Nineteen postal votes were sent in, however, and so the *voevoda* tried to choose a deputy without holding an election. In other districts, *voevody* delayed the elections for a few months in an effort to collect as many participants as possible.)[2] On the other hand, some local authorities seem to have found the most plausible excuse as quickly as possible for doing nothing at all in execution of the wishes of the Empress, and knowledge of the inefficiency, corruption, lack of initiative and idleness of local government officials forces the conclusion that such *voevody* would be a sizeable minority.

Now for a more detailed look at the actual elections in the various regions of the Russian Empire, and, first of all, at those in Great Russia. As far as these central provinces are concerned, the opinion of the British diplomat, Henry Shirley, that Catherine tried to compose her Legislative Commission of deputies who would be completely submissive to her instructions, appears to have been erroneous.[3] While it is true that some zealous local officials tried to secure a full attendance at the elections, there is very little evidence that they tried to advance the claims of certain candidates for the position of marshal or deputy, or to influence the composition of the instructions.[4] Most of the official interference in the actual elections stemmed from complaints based upon technical infringements of the electoral law, some of these cases being decided locally, and others reaching the Senate. For example, the property qualification of F. V. Goremykin, elected for the Sviazhsk district of Kazan' province, was disputed, but finally upheld by the Senate. In Briansk, Belgorod, and Odoev, Moscow, complaints were made about S. Miasoedov and N. Botvin'ev, the charges being made that the former was under investigation for the destruction of the property of one L'vov, and

[1] Lipinskii, *ŽMNP*, ccli, 246.   [2] Florovskii, *Sostav*, pp. 251–3, 267–71.
[3] *SIRIO*, xii, 330.   [4] See, however, pp. 71, 73 below.

that the latter had been guilty of several crimes. When these cases reached the Senate, Miasoedov was declared fit to serve on the grounds that L'vov objected to his candidature without support from other local nobles, and Botvin'ev was declared unworthy of the honour, since, even though his mother, one of the chief sufferers from her son's criminal activity, had forgiven him, a considerable number of the Odoev dvorianstvo had persisted in their objections to him.[1]

Very little is known of the internal workings of the assemblies of the central Russian nobility. There were, however, more interesting and significant incidents than the 'exceptional fireworks' on which some *voevody* reported, and not all elections went as smoothly as those attended by Viazemskii and Bibikov in the Dmitrov and Kostroma districts of Moscow province. A considerable dispute developed, for example, in the Zaraisk district of the same province, where four nobles complained about the activities of the local marshal. They asserted that the marshal, retired Captain M. Kondyrov, instructed the very poor dvoriane, and asked the others, to elect him deputy, pointing out that, since he was not a rich man, he could not carry on without pay. (While the marshals were to receive no pay, the deputies would receive an annual salary of 400 roubles.) Many of the Zaraisk dvorianstvo, the complaint continued, wanted to vote for *general-poruchik* A. P. Mel'gunov, or some other high-ranking candidate, but the marshal insisted that 'He Kondyrov did not wish to be adjutant to such a great gentleman, and was himself worthy to be deputy', and continued to ask many illiterate, non-serving nobles with small estates to vote for him. The four complainers claimed that Mel'gunov received a majority in the ballot for deputy, but that Kondyrov prejudiced his supporters against the imperial manifesto and claimed that he had received the majority, coarsely pointing out that he was no worse than the aforesaid Mel'gunov. The case against Kondyrov was concluded with the assertion that many dvoriane would not attend the election because of his behaviour, which was completely unacceptable to the noble dvorianstvo. Kondyrov was asked to explain himself to the local *voevoda*, and his version of the story was apparently accepted for he retained the post of Zaraisk deputy.[2]

Whether they were true or not, the allegations against Kondyrov demonstrated that internal tensions within the dvorianstvo did exist

---

[1] Florovskii, *Sostav*, pp. 288–93.
[2] Lipinskii, *ŽMNP*, CCLI, 240, 271–8, 280–3.

at the time of the elections to the Legislative Commission in central Russia, in particular that there was a considerable feeling of resentment from some dvoriane against their poorer comrades, and vice versa. However, the resentment of the lower nobility against their high-rank peers appears rarely to have come out into the open, and more usually inferiors respected their superiors. An example of the respect paid to rank was given, perhaps unwittingly, by the savant P. I. Rychkov, who described to a friend the election in his Orenburg district, and wrote of the dvorianin elected deputy that:

He is a favourite of the Governor's...however much the other nobles wanted me elected deputy, the Governor's party was more powerful. They say that he received two more votes than me. This did not put me to shame, because among those voted for were two major-generals and several colonels.[1]

If an enlightened man like Rychkov could console himself for his failure to be elected thus, how much more conscious of rank were likely to be the less educated dvoriane.

Another kind of dispute occurred at the Moscow district election, where several of those attending, including Shcherbatov, refused to sign the instruction, Shcherbatov trying to insist on the explicit inclusion in it of the prohibition of the sale of serfs to all non-nobles.[2] The French diplomat Rossignol noted that some members of the upper nobility were unhappy at the election held in St Petersburg, too. He reported on 3 February 1767:

This operation has caused a great deal of discontent among a great number of seigneurs, but, although unhappy, they have not been able to refuse on this occasion to subscribe to the expenses suggested to them for the erection of public monuments of their satisfaction and gratitude in honour of Catherine II. This has upset the major part of those who have been present at this assembly, and who, far from expecting anything from the bounty of their sovereign, impute to her, on the contrary, the motive of looking for ways of impoverishing the seigneurs, instead of helping them by giving frequent tokens of her generosity like the late Empress.[3]

More disturbance than at the elections in Great Russia was caused at those to the south and south-west, in the Slobodsko-Ukraina, New Russia and Little Russia. All was relatively quiet in

[1] Quoted in P. Pekarskii, *Zhizn'...P. I. Rychkova*, p. 55.
[2] Florovskii, *Sostav*, p. 262.　　　　　　[3] *SIRIO*, CXLI, 243.

71

the Slobodsko-Ukraina, where Governor Shcherbinin supervised the elections of five deputies from the dvorianstvo. One of the electors, a certain Cherniak, had to be thrown out of the assembly in Har'kov after causing trouble, but this was because he was drunk. A more rational basis for argument was the desire for a return to the arrangement of the Cossacks as it was before the reforms of the early 1760s, but this was less strongly expressed in the Slobodsko-Ukraina than in New Russia, even though, or perhaps because, four of the five deputies of the dvorianstvo elected there were former Cossack elders.[1] From New Russia, Governor F. M. Voeikov wrote to Catherine that the Cossacks in the newly organized Hussar regiments objected to their recent rearrangement, although he gave no example of a protest being made at the local noble elections.[2]

Disagreement between the local government and the nobility over the implementation of the instructions for the assembly of the Legislative Commission appears to have been greatest in Little Russia, where Governor Rumiantsev was kept very busy in seeing the elections through to an acceptable conclusion. Some of the nobles in that province demonstrated their opposition passively, by failing to turn up, and pleading illness, lack of time or calls of service, and two of them were perhaps defaulting in offering the excuse that they had vowed to go to Kiev and Ahtyrka on a pilgrimage.[3] On the other hand, enough opponents of the government's plans appeared at the Chernigov, Starodub, Gluhov, and Nezhin and Baturin elections to cause a considerable amount of trouble before the business was successfully accomplished. Rumiantsev wrote that not one meeting passed without somebody standing up at the beginning and reproaching somebody else for not being a true noble, and having ready a genealogy of the most outstanding lords, who had usually begun their line with a merchant or a Jew. It was proved that some of them had several times changed their names through necessity, observed the governor, and often murder and other crimes were involved. Not only did Rumiantsev have to quell all these disturbances, as soon as the election of a deputy and the composition of an instruction began, many of them started shouting that their rights and privileges must be confirmed, all requisitions from them be stopped, soldiers billeted on them removed, and no further taxes

---

[1] Bagalei, *Ocherki*, II, 106–9.   [2] Florovskii, *Sostav*, pp. 512–13.
[3] Avseenko, *Malorossiia*, pp. 5–7.

72

levied on the nobility. Some of them, who had been members of the hetman's administration, called for the revival of the hetmanship.[1]

Although Rumiantsev did not interfere directly, he supported the marshals A. Bezborodko in Chernigov and P. Iskritskii in Starodub in their attempts to quell the tumult of the local nobility, remarking that the rights of the class had in fact been better protected since 1764 than before, and producing several other arguments. Finally, both Bezborodko and Iskritskii were able to gain sufficient support for instructions which toned down the demands of the local nobility.[2] When Bezborodko went to Gluhov, he was insulted and accused of malevolence towards his native land, but the situation there was less serious than at the meeting of the nobility of Nezhin and Baturin. This assembly demanded the revival of the hetmanship, and put forward many complaints, and their deputy, Selitskii, resigned in protest, declaring that the Chernigov instruction was far superior to that composed locally. Rumiantsev declared the election of a new deputy, Dolinskii, null and void, and asked the marshal, Tarnaviot, for a report on those guilty of the demand for the revival of the hetmanship. The electors at first refused to give Tarnaviot any information, and then a large group of them declared that they had thought of the idea simultaneously. Rumiantsev considered that, if the leaders of this group were removed, those not infected with the disease of independent thinking would be won over by the kindness of the Empress, and would busy themselves with state service, and that those who had a great desire for promotion would quickly change their minds. Some of the troublemakers were in fact brought to trial, and there, for the moment, the matter ended.[3]

As far as the Empress was concerned, her primary recommendation to Rumiantsev in his dealings with the recalcitrant Little Russian nobility was to solve this local problem by degrees. She viewed the obstacles to the smooth execution of the rules for the elections as completely unimportant, and as nothing more than a hangover of the state of mind of former times which would soon disappear. While the instructions of some districts contained requests that were hopeless as far as she was concerned, she hoped that their deputies would be ashamed to speak such thoughts before the Legislative Commission, where they would be ridiculed. However, there were some instruc-

---

[1] Solov'ev, *RV*, xxxv, 325–8.　　　　　　[2] *Ibid.* pp. 326–8.
[3] *Ibid.* p. 330; A. Lazarevskii, *Opisanie staroi Malorossii*, ii, 37–42.

tions, like that from the Chernigov district, which Catherine thought to be moderate in tone and a credit to their compilers.[1] The Ukrainian nobility was active in the town elections in Little Russia as well as in those of their own class. What a contemporary observer, Kochubei, said of the town election in Poltava, that the interests of the burghers were completely antipathetic to those of the military, and that it would be difficult for these two kinds of people to co-operate in the production of a joint instruction, could be applied to the elections in many Ukrainian towns. Thus, in Starodub, the merchants sought confirmation of old privileges giving them exclusive rights to the town amenities, and the nobility was naturally opposed to this. The nobles refused to vote in the Priluki election, and there were further troubles at Lubny and Pogara, in the second of which towns the nobility opposed the idea of a Legislative Commission altogether as an unnecessary innovation.[2]

Some months after the opening of the Commission, Rumiantsev wrote to Catherine that the Little Russian deputies were boasting that those from Livonia agreed with them about the necessity of the maintenance of their former rights and privileges.[3] While this may have been generally true, the internal differences between the groups composing the Livonian nobility prevented them from presenting a solid front at the commission. It had proved impossible for the government's order combining the *Ritterschaft* and *Landschaft* at the election to be carried out. The Senate had been obliged to take this problem up again after a report from the Letskii district that the fourteen members of the *Landschaft* present at the local election would not co-operate with those of the *Ritterschaft*, who wanted to include their exclusivist ideas in the Letskii instruction. As a solution, the Senate suggested to Governor Broun that he should persuade the two sides to produce a joint instruction with each of them being given the right to include criticisms of points put forward by the other which did not seem reconcilable to the general rights and privileges of the local nobility. The Empress did not continue this policy, seeing the difficulties in establishing a balance between the two sides, and finally decided to let the *Landschaft* have completely separate representation.[4] Generally speaking, these differences notwithstanding, the noble deputies from Livonia, Estonia and Finland all considered that they

---

[1] Solov'ev, *RV*, xxxv, 330–1. [2] Avseenko, *Malorossiia*, pp. 13–24.
[3] Solov'ev, *RV*, xxxv, 330. [4] Florovskii, *Sostav*, pp. 249–50.

had been chosen to work on the composition of a new law code which was unnecessary for their region, although they were at first less vociferous in expressing their distaste for the whole business than the deputies from Little Russia.[1]

While a description of the elections of the nobility is circumscribed by the information available on the subject, there is a reasonable certainty that some information would have leaked through had any further problems developed of the magnitude of those arising in Little Russia and Livonia. Problems solved locally by the *voevody* without consulting the Senate or the Empress could not have been very serious. This is not to say, of course, that more knowledge of these problems would not help to build up a more detailed picture than the rough sketch that is possible at the moment.[2]

Some further points of significance are revealed by an examination of the signatures to the instructions and of the men who were chosen as deputies and marshals. In the central Russian provinces, the bulk of the signatories were military men: out of a total of some 4,500 signatures, over 80 per cent were of a military type, and only one of the 122 districts in these provinces, Parfen'ev, Archangel, produced no military signature at all. Civil service signatures accounted for just over 5 per cent of the total, and the rest are unidentifiable. To the south, an even greater majority of the signatures to the instructions from the Slobodsko-Ukrainian, New Russian and Little Russian provinces were of a military character, with only a handful of civil service or unidentifiable signatories. The signatures from the Baltic nobilities, unfortunately, provide no information on type of service.

Most of the military electors came from the middle ranks—*sekund-maiory, kapitany, poruchiki, podporuchiki,* and *praporshchiki.* In the southern provinces, there was an unequal split between the regular army ranks and special regimental ranks from the newly formed Hussars and others, with the latter greatly predominating in Little Russia, the former in the Slobodsko-Ukraina, and the two achieving a more equal balance in New Russia. It is difficult to estimate the percentage of retired military men, but it would appear to be something less than 50 per cent in all regions.[3]

[1] *Ibid.* pp. 509–10.
[2] Florovskii examined the Senate records for this period, and would therefore have brought light to any other serious difficulty arising from the execution of the orders for the assembly of the Legislative Commission.
[3] Florovskii, *Sostav,* pp. 277–9.

The correlation of the social status of the signatories of the instructions with that of the deputies elected to represent them at the Commission is much as to be expected. Although Sergeevich was not strictly correct in saying that the nobles always chose a senior rank as deputy,[1] it is undeniable than high-ranking deputies were proportionately more numerous than high-ranking electors. Although it is not possible to tell in all cases, it can be said that about 45 per cent of the deputies were serving military, something over 20 per cent were bureaucrats, mostly from the central government offices, and something over 10 per cent were retired from service. Military deputies included *general-fel'dtseihmeister* A. Vil'boa, Admiral B. V. Golitsyn, four *general-poruchiki*, six major-generals, nine colonels, and twenty-two majors. Civil service deputies included fifteen senators, the presidents of two colleges and vice-presidents of two others. Local government was represented by Governor Shcherbinin of the Slobodsko-Ukraina, elected as deputy for the Pskov district of Novgorod province, one governor's *tovarishch*, a *voevoda*, and other lesser officials.[2]

Military personnel tended to predominate among the marshals as well as among the deputies, almost a hundred of them having military rank. For the most part, however, the marshals were of lower rank than the deputies, which seems to indicate that the marshal's was a less sought after office than the deputy's.[3]

THE OPENING AND AGENDA

The manifesto of 14 December 1766 stipulated that each district should send a deputy to Moscow six months after the local reception of the news of the Legislative Commission. In the rules of procedure, published on 30 July 1767,[4] the six months became a year, perhaps indicating that things were not going as smoothly as at first hoped. Whenever the deputies arrived in Moscow, they were to report to the Senate, which, in its turn, was to inform the Empress when a sufficient number of deputies had appeared. At this point, the Com-

---

[1] Sergeevich, *VE*, 1 (1878), 207.
[2] Florovskii, *Sostav*, pp. 305–9.
[3] *Ibid.* pp. 309–10. This analysis would be applicable to the situation at the commencement of the Commission only, for over 50 per cent of the deputies of the nobility were changed later, and there might well have been some turnover of marshals, too.
[4] *PSZ*, xviii, 182–92, no. 12,948.

mission was to be convened, and an oath taken by the deputies in a sequence arranged according to province and social origin. Then followed the election of a Marshal who was to read out Catherine's Instruction and the rules of procedure. The Commission was then to pass on to the election of a five-man direction committee, whose members would have to be officially approved, and this committee was to arrange the elections of several sub-committees, to supervise their work and to see that it was in accordance with the Instruction, and to make suggestions where the Instruction was not clear. An expedition committee, also consisting of five elected members, was to correct errors, poor phraseology, and ambiguities in documents prepared by the various sub-committees, and a similar group was to prepare a digest of the instructions brought with them to Moscow by the deputies.

The Procurator-General and Marshal were to supervise the general assembly of the Commission between them, and one of them would have to be present on every occasion that the assembly was in session. The first task of the general assembly, according to the rules of procedure, was the examination of those laws most in need of revision, and the general opinion on this was to be passed on as a guide to the relevant sub-committees. The general opinion of the assembly was to be reached in the following manner. First of all, an existing law would be read out. Then, those deputies who desired to speak would indicate their wishes to the Marshal, who was to allow no more than half an hour per person and no interruption. Votes were to be taken on controversial points, and the majority would indicate 'the opinion of the assembly'. The sub-committees, it was hoped, would produce drafts of a new code of laws in the areas of jurisdiction assigned to them, and these drafts were to be returned to the assembly, which would then express its opinions about them. The whole project would be reviewed on completion by the Senate and the colleges, and then passed on to the Empress for her confirmation. The proceedings of the general assembly and the sub-committees were to be recorded in daily journals, and the three committees were also to keep notes on their activities. The director of the assembly's journal, A. P. Shuvalov, was given a secret instruction to supervise the records of the committees and sub-committees as well as those of the assembly, and was to be directly responsible to the Empress, independently from the Marshal and the Procurator-General, with whom he was to form a *troika* management of the Commission.[1] The rules of procedure were not distinguished by clarity or exactness, and divergences from them were hardly to be avoided when the Commission convened. Nevertheless, the rules could not be blamed for the extent of these divergences.

When 460 deputies had arrived in Moscow, the Senate informed the Empress, who issued an order on 24 July 1767, ordering the commission to start work on 30 July.[2] The Procurator-General carried out the arrangements for the opening of the Commission, and the inaugural ceremonies duly took place on the appointed day. A church service was held, the deputies took an oath, and then joined in a formal parade to the Kremlin, where the metropolitan of Novgorod Dmitrii delivered a flowery address comparing Catherine to Justinian, and Vice-Chancellor Alexander Golitsyn read out a speech from the throne.[3]

The first business session of the Commission took place on 31 July. Four hundred and twenty-eight deputies, under the supervision of the Procurator-General, assembled in the Granovitaia palace of the Kremlin, first listened to a recital of the rules of procedure, and then carried on to the election of the Marshal. The journal pointed out that, during the nominations for the office of Marshal, 'there was no favouritism. Everybody chose whom he pleased, basing his choice on the provisions of the rules of procedure. . . The vote of the majority of the deputies nominated Counts Ivan and Gregory Orlov.' Happy the land where the people's choice coincided with that of their ruler! Unfortunately, the only information vouched to posterity on the election for Marshal, apart from the results of the voting, is that, while the votes were being counted, Gregory Orlov sat calmly talking to N. E. Murav'ev about the interior architecture of the Granovitaia Palace. Both affirmative and negative votes were to be cast on the various candidates by the deputies, most popular of whom turned out to be the Orlov brothers, with Ivan, a little surprisingly, receiving fifty affirmative votes more than Gregory. Third in the poll was Z. G. Chernyshev, President of the War College, and fourth, A. I. Bibikov. Bottom of the list was M. M. Shcherbatov, receiving only ninety affirmative votes to 338 negatives. Gregory Orlov requested that his

[1] *PSZ*, no. 12,948; *SIRIO*, iv, 46–7.
[2] *PSZ*, xviii, 181–2, no. 12,945. The rules of procedure, although not published until 30 July 1767, were presumably already completed.
[3] *SIRIO*, iv, 34–40.

name be removed from the list to be offered to the Empress, owing to pressure of work, and this was agreed to: Chernyshev made a similar request, and this was refused. The list was to contain three names, and Bibikov who had been nominated by the Procurator-General was included with Ivan Orlov and Chernyshev. A report was prepared for Catherine, and read out to the assembly before being sent on to her. In her reply, Catherine excused Orlov and Chernyshev, and declared that Bibikov would be Marshal.[1] A dark shadow is cast upon the genuineness of this 'election' by the fact that the French diplomat Rossignol was already aware six months previously that Bibikov would be the man selected to fill the position. Bibikov, reported Rossignol, would be opposed by the nobility, who wanted to choose their own candidate. The luckless Shcherbatov was certainly the choice of a group of the dvorianstvo, although it seems unlikely that he would have emerged the victor even from a more open election.[2]

Rossignol thought that although devoted to the Empress, Bibikov had little intellect or decisiveness. This opinion was shared by the historian, V. I. Sergeevich. Bibikov had no special training for the post, his background was mainly military, and his inclination was away from the job rather than towards it, as Sergeevich pointed out. A letter to Bibikov from his friend Filosofov, Ambassador to Denmark, clearly indicated the marshal's apprehensive attitude towards his new task. 'You certainly speak the truth, that you are getting into the depths and gulfs of an ocean in your affairs', wrote Filosofov: 'My soul has become sick imagining the chasms surrounding you.' Declared Sergeevich scornfully:

This was the state of mind of the president of the Catherinian Commission. Those unacquainted with the affair might think that Filosofov's answers were written to the president of some revolutionary meeting, shaking the foundations of the state. However, the correspondence was being carried on with our Marshal, who had to manage the representatives of the people of whom Peter the Great had said that it was 'the most obedient people in the world', and whose deputies did not in fact stir up the waters at all. This brave military leader and pacifier of factory peasants, who had received for his successful termination of a revolt the Order of Saint Alexander Nevskii, turned out to be susceptible to a feeling of fear, and showed timidity, before the peaceful legislative work going on around him. Here,

---

[1] *SIRIO*, IV, 53-5.
[2] *SIRIO*, CXLI, 219.

of course, was necessary another kind of courage that was even beyond the power of the Seven Years War to arouse.[1]

However, fortified by the encouragement of the Empress, and enlightened, or perhaps mystified, by her gift to him of a copy of the journals of the House of Commons, and the rules of procedure for the Commission, Bibikov now had to tackle the task for which he had been chosen. (Viazemskii, the Procurator-General, who was to be Bibikov's chief co-operator in the management of the Commission, was probably rather more capable than the marshal. As far as his supervisory functions were concerned, Viazemskii was particularly instructed to see that the Commission made no suggestion contrary to the laws of God, the church, nature, the people, the state, and the family. Four experts of jurisprudence were to assist him, and, where they disagreed, the university, the Academy of Sciences, and that impressive group of savants the law class of the Military Academy, were to give an opinion. Viazemskii was to make the final decision about any point at issue on the basis of what would be advantageous to the state.)[2]

After the selection of Bibikov as marshal, the Commission began to listen to a reading from Catherine's Instruction, first of all by Gregory Orlov, and then by I. Elagin and D. Volkov. A panegyric to the Instruction was recorded in the journal. The deputies next heard Bibikov's inaugural address, and the remainder of the Instruction. Four deputies were then chosen to express the general thanks to the Empress for her summons of the Commission. The metropolitan Dmitrii, one of the four, reported to the assembly on the gracious reception accorded to him and his three companions, which led on to a discussion of what title should be given to Catherine for her great magnanimity. The deputies were then told that they had all been invited to an audience with the Empress on the following Sunday, and were each given a gold medal and chain as a badge of office. Meanwhile, the preliminaries to the election of the direction committee had been completed, and the results of the first ballot were announced. The metropolitan Dmitrii, who was deputy of the Holy Synod, had displaced the Orlov brothers at the top of the poll. In fourth place was M. Volkonskii, the Senate's deputy, and he was

---

[1] Sergeevich, *VE*, i (1878), 226–8. See also A. A. Bibikov, *Zapiski o zhizni i sluzhbe A. I. Bibikova*, p. 103.

[2] Sergeevich, *VE*, i (1878), 229; *SIRIO*, iv, 48–9.

followed by three deputies from the dvorianstvo, F. Orlov, Z. Chernyshev, and M. Glazov. Eighth came Alexander Golitsyn, the deputy of Moscow town. This was the first time that a town deputy had attracted any support, and a prince and a vice-chancellor could hardly be said to have been a member of the middle class.[1]

This brought the general assembly to the conclusion of its fifth session. After their Sunday meeting with the Empress, who modestly rejected the title finally offered her, Great and All-Wise Mother of the Fatherland, the deputies returned on 13 August to the question of the direction committee. They agreed by a vote of 225 to 199 that three candidates should be put forward for each of the five places on the committee, and therefore added five names to the original list of ten, including P. I. Panin, the representative of the Moscow district, and four town deputies. It is possible that the Empress herself, with her hopes of encouraging the growth of the Third Estate, recommended the inclusion of the town deputies: she is known to have made such a recommendation with regard to the list of candidates for one of the sub-committees.[2] It was either this development or something arising in the ensuing preliminaries to the election of the instruction analysis committee that caused several disgruntled deputies from the dvorianstvo to get up from their benches and turn their backs on the rest of the assembly, talking in loud voices. Unfortunately, identification of these nobles and the exact reason for their annoyance appears to be impossible.[3]

In its seventh session, the assembly elected three dvoriane, A. Stroganov, R. Vorontsov, and P. Orlov, and two town deputies, I. Piskarev, and I. Meshchaninov, to the instruction analysis committee. In the next session, almost a week later, the members of the direction committee were announced, apparently without a final vote. These were the Metropolitan Dmitrii and four nobles, Z. Chernyshev, I. Orlov, D. Volkov and N. Murav'ev, the last two of whom were not on the original list, but put forward by Viazemskii and Bibikov.[4] The question arises, if Catherine was responsible for advancing the candidature of the four town deputies, why was none of them finally included in the committee? It can be conjectured, although probably too fancifully, that having put them forward as a straw in the wind, so to speak, and observing that the resentment of

[1] *SIRIO*, IV, 55–63.
[2] Sergeevich, *VE*, I (1878), 222; *SIRIO*, IV, 63–7.
[3] *SIRIO*, IV, 67.
[4] *SIRIO*, IV, 67–9.

dvoriane was aroused, Catherine diplomatically refrained from
asing this resentment by the inclusion of town deputies in what
o be the most important committee of the Commission.

During this eighth session of 20 August, some preliminaries to the
election of the expedition committee were carried out, and then the
reading out of the instructions of the deputies began, and then continued with no detectable shape or form until the twenty-first session.
Twelve instructions were read out in their entirety during this period,
with deputies making comments, but in no organized manner, and
the discussion of instructions was suddenly dropped, never to be
brought up again. During session 21, Marshal Bibikov announced
that, since the sub-committee on the Examination of the Kinds of
State Inhabitants had been set up, a reading of the extant laws
concerning the dvorianstvo would commence, with the deputies
giving verbal and written opinions on them. This phase of the work
of the general assembly continued until session 31 on 2 October,
when Bibikov said that the laws and opinions on the nobility should
be given to the direction committee for transference to the sub-committee, and the attention of the assembly was now turned to the
consideration of laws concerning the merchant class. Up to this
point, the Marshal had not once asked for a vote or consensus of
opinion, and, according to Sergeevich, 'The sessions of the general
assembly had completely transformed it into a completely aimless
reading room and parlour.' In session 29 on 27 September, at least,
the assembly managed to break away from this routine to join with
the committees and sub-committees of the Commission in declaring
formally that Catherine was the Great and All-Wise Mother of the
Fatherland, averse to accepting such a title though she had earlier
claimed to be.[1]

For over forty sessions, the assembly talked about the rights of the
merchant class in its usual discursive manner, and gave some of its
attention, too, to the rights of the Baltic nobility, partly, at least, at
the insistence of some of the deputies of this nobility. Then, abruptly,
and giving no reason, Marshal Bibikov informed the assembly
during session 77 on 14 December 1767 that it would temporarily
cease its deliberations, transfer to St Petersburg and start work there
on 18 February. It may have been more than coincidental that Bibikov made this announcement when discussion of the rights of the

[1] Sergeevich, *VE*, I (1878), 233; *SIRIO*, IV, xix–xxvi, 137, 208–9, 219.

Opening and agenda

Baltic nobility was coming to something of a head. At the opening session in St Petersburg, Bibikov said that the assembly would now take a look at laws relating to justice, and make comments on them. This phase of the assembly's activities began and continued as before, without prior warning or preparation, without any voting or attempt at a consensus of opinion. On 10 July 1768 Bibikov announced that a draft for the rights of the nobility had been worked out in committee, and should now be examined by the general assembly, which had not yet read one instruction from the nobility, or made one joint suggestion about the status of this class. The marshal wanted voting to take place on the separate items of this draft without any preliminary debate. Many deputies did not care for this, and, after the first four items had been accepted, an argument broke out over the fifth, which concerned the manner in which nobles would begin service. This outbreak persuaded Bibikov to allow a restricted amount of discussion on the draft, and thirteen sessions went by, with many arguments first advanced in the original discussion of the rights of the dvorianstvo being repeated, and no regular voting. To extricate the Marshal from the mess in which he appeared to have landed himself, the Empress instructed the assembly to organize its proceedings more tightly, but this instruction made no real impact, and the draft was returned to the direction committee on 6 October 1768 without any joint constructive suggestion whatsoever. Sessions of the assembly now became less frequent, with laws relating to landed estates forming the main theme for a meandering debate until the adjournment of the assembly *sine die* on 18 December.[1]

Undoubtedly, the Commission did not work smoothly. This was as true of the committees as of the general assembly. The direction committee, for example, intended to be the general co-ordinator, functioned in a very ragged manner, although composed of experienced and high-ranking government personnel. For its first three sessions, it listened to Catherine's Instruction, and gave it approval. At the fourth session, the Procurator-General posed the following question to the committee: 'Since the Russian state, as far as its laws are concerned, is split up into three parts: Great Russia, Little Russia, and Livonia, and each governs with its own laws, will these be necessary in the future?' Surprisingly, perhaps, the committee gave the answer that the Empress would not welcome, that these laws would be

[1] Sergeevich, *VE*, I (1878), 237–41; *SIRIO*, IV, xix–xxvi; VIII, 382; XXXVI, 145–8.

necessary, and then passed on to the organization of the sub-committees. Next, in their twelfth session, the directors examined Catherine's Instruction once again, and began to read the instructions from the government departments, which took them up to their twentieth session. One of the sub-committees, concerned with the Examination of the Kinds of State Inhabitants, was set up on 6 September 1767, and was told by the direction committee to work out a draft version of the rights of the various classes, and of legislation on the classes. For example, as far as the nobility was concerned, it should try to answer the questions, what is the dvorianstvo, what different degrees does it possess, who is a dvorianin, what are his rights? So this sub-committee was to work on the details of its sphere of activity before receiving any indication of general principles to be observed in this sphere of legislation from the direction commitee or the general assembly. Moreover, the situation soon arose of the assembly and the sub-committee discussing the nobility simultaneously, without any attempt at liaison by the direction committee.[1]

The Empress, whose rules of procedure were at least partly responsible for the malfunctioning of the various departments of the Legislative Commission, attempted to oil the machinery with some additional instructions, particularly 'The description of the means of completion...of the Commission', issued on 8 April 1768, which recommended a division of agenda under two main headings, public law and private law, and reorganized the sub-committees on this basis.[2]

Although the Commission did not realize the high hopes held out for it, the deputies considerably added to the body of information and opinion provided by the instructions before they were dispersed and the Commission dissolved. I shall now examine how much light the materials of the Commission shed on the attitudes of the nobility and the Empress towards the economic, socio-political and cultural questions facing the Russian Empire in the second half of the eighteenth century. This examination might well benefit from a wider application of Catherine's advice to her readers at the end of the Instruction:

Perhaps some Persons may object, after perusing these Instructions, that they will not be intelligible to every one. To this it may be answered: It is true, they will not be readily understood by every Person, after one

---

[1] Sergeevich, *VE*, I (1878), 233–6. [2] *SIRIO*, IV, 49–51.

slight Perusal only; but every Person may comprehend these Instructions, if he reads them with Care and Attention, and selects occasionally such Articles as may serve to direct him, as a Rule, in whatever he undertakes. These Instructions ought to be frequently perused, to render them more familiar: And every one may be firmly assured, that they will certainly be understood; because, *Assiduity* and *Care* will conquer every Difficulty; as, on the Contrary, *Indolence* and *Carelessness* will *deter* from every laudable attempt.[1]

[1] Reddaway, *Documents*, pp. 293-4.

3

SERFDOM AND THE ECONOMY

THE ECONOMIC CONTENT OF THE INSTRUCTION

Both Catherine II and several members of the governing class looked on Russia as an underdeveloped country, and wanted to do something about changing this situation for the better. Sweden, Denmark, Prussia, most German states, Switzerland, England and France, all demonstrated economic development to such an extent that the eighteenth might be called the economic century; this is the view expressed in the foreword to the first number of the *Works of the Free Economic Society for the Encouragement of Agriculture and Good Husbandry*, published under imperial patronage in 1765. To help Russia catch up with the other countries, the Society was to take careful note of what went on in them, and transmit useful information to the Russian public. Some members, continued the foreword, would combine their knowledge with practical experiments, others, who knew foreign languages, would make relevant translations. Governors and other administrators in the provinces were particularly called upon to send in economic information concerning the localities under their supervision. All citizens, of whatever rank or name, were called upon to render assistance.[1]

As in many other fields, the first citizen was prominent in this. While she carried out no practical experiment of any importance, she certainly used her knowledge of languages, incorporating in her Instruction, for example, much that she considered relevant to the Russian environment from the works of foreign writers. The Instruction contains the most comprehensive statement of the views of the Empress on economic matters, although its published version toned down or omitted some of the ideas that she had advanced in earlier drafts.[2]

For Catherine showed the Instruction or parts of it to several of her subjects before its publication, and they suggested that certain points be left out from the final text, or at least altered.

[1] *TVEO*, I, i, iii, vi, ix–x.
[2] See N. D. Chechulin (ed.), *Nakaz Imperatritsy Ekateriny IIoi*, the introduction.

Economic content of the Instruction

Catherine herself later described how this censorship was carried out, writing:

After I had prepared the manifesto for the convocation of deputies from the whole empire in order to become better acquainted with the situation of each region, they came to Moscow in 1767, where I, now staying at the Kolomenskii Palace, appointed several persons of widely differing views to listen to the Instruction prepared for the Codificatory Commission. Debates then ensued on every item. I gave them permission to strike out and erase everything that they wanted to. They erased more than half of that which I had written, and the Codificatory Instruction as published remained.[1]

If this censorship committee were genuinely composed of deputies assembling in Moscow, as several historians have considered to be the case, it is understandable that the politically skilful Empress would not want to persist with ideas which would be unacceptable to influential groups among her people.[2]

The commitee took particular exception to Catherine's remarks on serfdom and cut out from the Instruction all references to serf freedom, amending those to mitigation of serfdom.[3] In the very much curtailed chapter XI of the published version of the Instruction, it was pointed out that, in any society, 'There ought to be *some to govern*, and *others to obey*'. While it was conceded that it was the duty of the government to look after the people, and to increase the number of serfs only when the utmost necessity should oblige it to do so for reasons of state, the sole positive suggestion concerning the welfare of the serfs in chapter XI was that 'A Law may be productive of public Benefit, which gives some *private* Property to a Slave'.[4]

In another section of the published Instruction, Catherine observed that, where taxes were too high, and the people lacked property rights:

Lands, which might feed a whole People, can scarce yield Food for a single Family. The common People in those Parts have no *Share* even in that, which is the *Cause* of their Misery; that is, the Lands which lie *fallow* and *uncultivated*, with which the Country abounds; either some of the principal Citizens, or the Sovereign, insensibly ingross the *whole Extent* of these desert Countries. The ruined Families have *left* their Oppressors the *whole* for *Pastures*, and the laborious Man has nothing.[5]

---

[1] *Sochineniia Imperatritsy Ekateriny IIoi*, XII, 524. The Instruction was also shown to such individuals as V. Baskakov and A. Sumarokov. For their remarks, see *SIRIO*, x, 75–87.

[2] See A. V. Florovskii, *Iz istorii ekaterininskoi komissii 1767 goda, Vopros o krepostnom prave*, pp. 10–11.

[3] Chechulin (ed.), *Nakaz*, cvii, cxxi; Chechulin, 'Ob istochnikah Nakaza', *ZMNP*, cccxxxx, 287.

[4] Reddaway, *Documents*, pp. 256–7.   [5] *Ibid.* pp. 259–60.

The result of such a situation would be particularly harmful for a country like Russia, since, wrote Catherine:

Here *Agriculture* claims the *first* Place; for as *it alone* nourishes the People; if duly improved, it may bring them into such a happy Situation, that they will soon be Possessors of *all other* Conveniences. Without Agriculture there will be *none of the first Materials* for the Use of the Manufacturer, or handicraft Tradesman.[1]

Catherine, then, stressed the importance of agriculture, and the necessity for its improvement, the lack of which she attributed to the stupid cupidity of a part of the nobility and, if her remarks were not a veiled confession, of some of her predecessors.

Elsewhere in the Instruction, Catherine attacked another manifestation of the greed of the landlords, the heavy *obrok* rates levied by them. It seems, wrote the Empress:

That the Method of exacting their Revenues, *newly* invented by the Lords, diminishes both the *Inhabitants*, and the *Spirit of Agriculture* in Russia. Almost all the Villages are *heavily* taxed. The Lords, who seldom or never *reside* in their Villages, lay an Impost on every Head of one, two or even five Rubles, without the least Regard to the *Means* by which their Peasants may be able to *raise* this Money.[2]

Obrok was generally discouraged in the Instruction. Wrote Catherine:

It is highly necessary, that the Law should prescribe a Rule to the Lords, for a more judicious Method of raising the Revenues; and oblige them to levy *such* a Tax, as *tends least* to separate the Peasant from his House and Family; this would be the Means by which Agriculture would become more extensive, and Population be more increased in the Empire.[3]

Elsewhere in the Instruction, too, Catherine spoke more forcibly on the subject of peasant property, arguing that 'Agriculture can never flourish there, where no Persons have any Property of their own'. This proposition, considered the Empress, was based on the very simple law that 'Every Man will take more Care of his own Property, than of that which belongs to another; and will not exert his utmost Endeavours upon that, which he has Reason to fear another may deprive him of'.[4]

While 'Agriculture is the first and principal Labour, which ought to be encouraged in the People', according to the final draft of the

[1] Reddaway, *Documents*, pp. 303–4.
[2] *Ibid.* p. 258.   [3] *Ibid.*
[4] *Ibid.* p. 262. With a certain amount of equivocation, the instruction later considered the possible effects on an heir of his father's legacy to him of property, suggesting that it 'might only serve to make him idle and lazy' (*ibid.* p. 278).

Instruction, 'The next is, the manufacturing our own Produce.' As far as the latter was concerned, the Instruction said:

Machines, which serve to shorten Labour in the mechanick Arts, are not always useful. If a Piece of Work, wrought with the Hands, can be afforded at a Price, equally advantageous to the Merchant and the Manufacturer; in this Case, Machines which shorten Labour, that is, which diminish the Number of Workmen, will be greatly prejudicial to a populous Country.[1]

The Empress developed this point in some notes that she wrote on a report given to the College of Manufactures, in which she described in some detail the advantages of household manufacturing as opposed to that carried on in factories. In these notes, Catherine expressed her antipathy towards 'the multiplication of large heaps, at which the tillers of the soil work in their hundreds to the great detriment of agriculture', and went on to say that, 'as the purchase of villages for factories exhausts agriculture, it must be forbidden'. Evidence for the harm caused by the factory was, in the eyes of the Empress, exemplified by France, where, she considered, the population had decreased from 25 to 16 millions between 1717 and 1757, and much land lay fallow. In Russia, everybody should be encouraged to go in for manufacturing on a small scale. 'Do not take the loom away from the *muzhik*', urged Catherine.

However, the government should not interfere too much in the development of industry. Concentrated or factory industry, dispersed or household, had both developed naturally, and could continue to do so, the first specializing in products which could not be manufactured on the household handicraft basis, and the second occupying the peasants when they could not be working in the fields. The government's function should be to supervise generally without going into details, the College of Manufactures being, after all, 'not a school for manufacturers'. The government could encourage those branches of industry in particular need of development by offering prizes for the best examples of the relevant products; by publicizing the best manufacturing processes; by protecting the industrialists from 'indirect oppressions'; and perhaps by giving monthly information on the prices of various products.[2]

[1] *Ibid.* p. 264.
[2] A. V. Florovskii, 'K istorii ekonomicheskih idei v Rossii v xviiiom veke', *Nauchnye trudy russkogo narodnogo universiteta v Prage*, 1 (1928), 81–93, particularly 88–91. Catherine's view of the French population was, of course, incorrect.

Serfdom and the economy

A similar spirit of freedom was to be encouraged in trade as well as industry, although government supervision was to be rather closer in this instance. For, said the Instruction:

The Liberty of Trading does not consist in a Permission to Merchants of doing whatever they please; this would be rather the *Slavery* of Commerce: what *cramps* the Trader, does not *cramp* the Trade. In free Countries the Merchant meets with innumerable Obstacles; but in despotic Governments he is not near so much thwarted by the Laws. England...*cramps* the Merchant; but it is for the *Benefit* of Commerce.[1]

Before a consideration of the 'cramps' suggested for Russian trade by Catherine, it is necessary to note that, according to her, 'The inland, or Home Trade, cannot be properly called Commerce; it is nothing more, than a *simple Circulation in the same Spot*'. As far as the Empress was concerned, 'True Commerce, *emphatically* so called, is *that*, by the *Means of which* a State procures from foreign Countries whatever Things are necessary, which it does not produce itself, and sends out *in Return* its *own Superfluities*'.[2]

'True Commerce', the Instruction suggested, was to be encouraged by suppression of monopoly; concentration on exports; careful thought about with which countries trade should be encouraged; and exclusion of the nobility from trade. First of all, as well as obliquely asserting that monarchy itself should not attempt to become monopolist in any commercial sense, Catherine also recommended that it 'be constantly observed as a general Rule, *Never to allow of a Monopoly on any Pretence whatever*; that is, never to grant the Privilege of any particular Trade to any one, *exclusive of every other Person*'.[3] Secondly, when discussing the relative merits of machines and handicrafts in the pursuance of industrial progress, the Empress pointed out that too much use could not be made of machines which produced those manufactures which were exported to other nations.[4] (On the other hand, Catherine elsewhere asked whether or not deficiencies in the revenues occurred 'because the Exportation of their Superfluities becomes burdensome' on the people.)[5] Thirdly, while holding England up as an example of how trade should be carried on, Catherine also suggested that this was the kind of nation with which Russia should trade, for, among other considerations, it was better to trade with a people 'who are *pacifick* from *Principle*; who aim at *Profit*, but

[1] Reddaway, *Documents*, p. 265.　　　　　　　　　　[2] *Ibid.* p. 304.
[3] *Ibid.* pp. 267, 302.　　　　[4] *Ibid.* p. 264.　　　　[5] *Ibid.* p. 302.

not at *Conquests*'.[1] Fourthly, Catherine noted with approval that Montesquieu had considered it 'repugnant to the true Spirit of Trade, that the Nobility should engage in it under a monarchical Government', although she conceded that there were others 'who judge, that such Noblemen may be permitted to Trade, as are not actually in the Service of the Government; but still with this Restriction, *that they conform themselves, in every Thing, to the Laws of Commerce*.[2]

In making the distinction between a nation's natural and acquired riches, Catherine included under the latter heading, first of all, manufactures, and then, as well as foreign commerce, 'the convenient inland Navigation through *Canals*... the *Improvement* of Land Carriage, both as to Facility and Safety, by *constructing*, *rebuilding*, and keeping in *good* and *solid Repair*, publick Roads, Bridges, and Ferries'.[3] It was the duty of the state to pay for 'making Roads and Drains' and 'scouring Rivers'. As far as the state's finances were concerned, Catherine wanted to know why deficiencies occurred, but also considered that state debts could serve a useful purpose by building up the public confidence in the government's credit.[4] The greatest of the nation's natural riches, the genius of its inhabitants, was in need of growth as well as those acquired, for, wrote the Empress:

Russia is not only *greatly* deficient in the *number* of her Inhabitants; but at the same Time, extends her Dominion over *immense* Tracts of Land; which are neither peopled nor improved. And therefore, in a Country so circumstanced, *too much* Encouragement can never be given to the *Propagation* of the human Species.[5]

CONTEMPORARY IDEAS ON THE ECONOMY

During the first five years of Catherine's reign, and to some extent with her encouragement, the vital question of serfdom was considered more widely than at any previous point in Russian history. Several members of the nobility, familiar with western European theory and practice, and conscious of the outdated nature of serfdom from both

---

[1] *Ibid.* pp. 265-6.
[2] *Ibid.* p. 267.
[3] *Ibid.* p. 305.
[4] *Ibid.* pp. 301-3, 307.
[5] *Ibid.* pp. 257, 305. For Catherine's economic ideas, see also Basil Dmytryshyn, 'The economic content of the 1767 *Nakaz* of Catherine II', *The American Slavic and East European Review*, XIX, 1-9; A. A. Kizevetter in *Sbornik statei Miliukovu*, pp. 319-20. For a hostile Soviet view of Catherine's views on the serf question, see M. T. Beliavskii, 'Vopros o krepostnom prave i polozhenie krest'ian v "nakaze" Ekateriny II', *Vestnik moskovskogo universiteta*, *Seriia IX, Istoriia* (1963), no. 6, 44-63.

points of view, were anxious to help bring their country into the second half of the eighteenth century.

√ One such progressive thinker was D. A. Golitsyn, who, spending much of his life abroad as a diplomat, was a member of several European academies, a friend of many of the great men of the day, and an intermediary between them and Catherine.[1] Golitsyn argued that, because of the forced labour of the peasants and their lack of property rights, initiative was sapped, and the development of trade and industry was retarded. Because of serfdom, too, the nobility did not prosper, and a middle class hardly existed in Russia. 'While serfdom survives, the Russian Empire and our nobility, intended to be the richest in Europe, will remain poor', wrote Golitsyn. Without radical change, he asked, 'How otherwise can we form the Third Estate, without which one cannot flatter oneself with the hope to create arts, learning, trade, etc.?' Golitsyn was therefore in favour of gradual emancipation, with the serfs at first receiving rights to movable property only, and the court peasants on the imperial estates being endowed in this manner to begin the process and provide an example to the noble landlords. Later, Golitsyn suggested, peasants should be able to buy land.[2]

Catherine was doubtful about the feasibility of Golitsyn's plan: perhaps she also took exception to his idea of serfdom starting to go out of existence on her own estates. Wrote the Empress:

Sincere love for humanity, zeal and goodwill are not enough for the realization of grand suggestions. It is easy for Golitsyn and his like and costs little to be magnanimous. It does not cost them anything to give their peasants the right to landed property, but the rich landowners, who may have thousands of peasants, will think and talk otherwise.[3]

Nevertheless, under the influence of Golitsyn and others, and no doubt with the hope of approval from enlightened western Europe, Catherine suggested to the Free Economic Society in 1765 a prize essay competition concerned with Russia's peculiar institution, and its alteration. 'What is more beneficial to society,' the entrants to the Competition were asked to consider, 'that the peasant should have

[1] I. A. Pashkov (ed.), *Istoriia russkoi ekonomicheskoi mysli*, I, 519–20. [2] *Ibid.* I, 525.
[3] Quoted in Pashkov, *Istoriia*, I, 527. Among the rich landowners referred to by the Empress may well have been herself. She appears to have rejected a project for the transfer of some court lands to the peasants. For the project, see I. P. Elagin, 'Proekt...ob opredelenii v neotchemlemoe vladenie dvortsovym krest'ianam zemli i o razdache kazennyh dereven', za izvestnuiu platu, na vremennoe i opredelennoe vladenie vol'nym soderzhateliam', *Sbornik Kniazia Obolenskogo*, XII.

land as property, or only movable property, and how far should his rights to this or that property be widened?'[1]

Over a hundred and sixty entries were received for the competition, some of them from western Europe in German, French and Latin, as well as several essays of indigenous origin. The prize of a thousand crowns was won by Beardé de l'Abaye, a Doctor of Laws at Aachen University. His proposal was the gradual introduction of landed property ownership for the serfs on a scale so small that it would not suffice even for subsistence purposes, the serfs therefore being forced to rent land at a high price from their landlords. If these innovations were realized, wrote de l'Abaye, the serfs would never think of running away, so quickly would they be attracted even by the thought of a little property. 'The rich, not being troubled by constant super-vision, receive their income punctually and in considerable amounts', wrote de l'Abaye, describing the situation that would obtain were his proposals carried out, 'It is a pleasure to see your dog following you everywhere...can it be compared with the burdensome labour of leading a bear?'[2] By awarding the top prize for ideas such as these, the Free Economic Society was obviously not putting much weight behind the forces of progress and enlightenment.

A second prize in the competition was won by a Russian, A. Ia. Polenov, and for this reason his essay must be studied more closely than that of de l'Abaye. Polenov was born in Moscow in 1738, the son of a military noble. He had studied at the gymnasium and university of the Russian Academy of Sciences, and, in 1762, had been sent by the Academy to study law at Strasbourg University. He submitted his entry to the competition after his return to St Petersburg, having made obvious use of his knowledge of the ideas of western European thinkers. Polenov's work, entitled 'On the serf condition of the peasants in Russia', is divided into two principal parts, the first examining the origins of Russian slavery, the second considering ways of improving the unhappy lot of the slaves.[3]

---

[1] Pashkov, *Istoriia*, I, 532. Romanovich-Slavatinskii, *Dvorianstvo*, p. 383, attributes the inspiration of this competition to Gregory Orlov. V. V. Oreshkin, *Vol'noe ekonomicheskoe obshchestvo v Rossii, 1765–1917*, pp. 59–63, considers that Catherine had little genuine enthusiasm for the prize essay competition. For evidence to the contrary, see A. I. Hodnev, *Istoriia imperatorskogo vol'nogo ekonomicheskogo obshchestva*, pp. 26–30.

[2] *TVEO*, VIII, 51–2.

[3] For this essay and a brief biography by the author's grandson, the historian and jurist, D. V. Polenov, entitled 'A. Ia. Polenov, russkii zakonoved XVIIIogo veka', see *RA* (1865), pp. 509–41, 558–614.

In the first part, Polenov expressed the opinion that serfdom had been brought about, not by a social contract, but by force, particularly war, and could in no way be reconciled with the tenets of natural law. He found it:

impossible to believe that people would voluntarily agree to this and would subject themselves to such a cruel sacrifice, reasoning particularly according to man's inherent inclination towards the acquisition of happiness and the irresistible striving for freedom.

Polenov could think of no people as poor as Russian peasants, who, he asserted, 'having not the slightest defence from the laws, are subjected to all kinds of offences, not only in respect of property, but in life itself, and suffer relentless insolence, torture and violence'. Citing the examples of ancient Greece and Rome and contemporary Poland, Polenov declared that 'oppression is not only harmful for society, but dangerous as well', for: 'A man, who has no advantages, which would stimulate him to the preservation of such a society, where he comprises nothing and is always suffering, must have little ardour for it; he knows, that whatever change occurs in it, he has nothing to lose.'

Moving on to consider ways of improving the situation of the serfs, Polenov put forward as a first step the spread of enlightenment among them. Industriousness, a high level of morals and virtue should be inculcated into the peasants, said Polenov, who thought that it was almost incredible how much education contributed to the welfare of every society, and for this reason, he wanted it to have top priority in Russia.

But education would not be enough without human rights, one of the most important of which was to property. 'From a peasantry possessing its own property,' Polenov claimed, 'the whole state will feel a great relief; its own income will grow incomparably.' Population and towns would multiply as well as income. Like de l'Abaye, Polenov argued that property should be given to the serfs conditionally and gradually. The nobility would retain rights to hunting and fishing areas, and to the forests, for all time, for example. The peasant would not be allowed to sell, give away, or mortgage his land, and he would continue both to make payments and perform services for his lord. However, Polenov went further than de l'Abaye in requiring that: 'Each peasant must have enough land for the sowing of seed and the grazing of cattle, and possess it in an hereditary manner so that the landlord would not have the least authority to be oppressive in any way at all, or to take it away completely.' If the peasant abused his rights, then the landlord would be able to dispossess him, but only by due process of law in the courts.

Polenov wanted taxes to be generally lightened to a tithe or some other part of all agricultural produce. With taxes levied in this manner, peasant industry would be encouraged, and perhaps the move to the towns, too. While believing that agriculture was the basis of all prosperity, Polenov also lamented the fact that Russia had no middle class, and that great shortcomings could result from the expulsion of the peasants from the towns. He resolved this apparent contradiction by proposing to allow rich peasants to join one of the urban classes 'not simply, but with several contracts, so as to prohibit the final emptying of all the villages'.

For all its moderation, Polenov's entry for the competition was thought unfit for publication by the Free Economic Society, which objected to its content and style, 'finding in it many inordinately strong statements unsuitable for this condition', i.e. serfdom.[1]

Also not published by the Society, although probably for different reasons, was an entry taking the opposite point of view to that of de l'Abaye and Polenov. Concealing his identity under the modest *nom de plume*, 'A man who is ungrammatical and has not read any history since birth', the author expressed the opinion that the serfs could not have immovable property: all lands and peasant houses were the hereditary, granted or purchased property of the landlords. Good landlords, the author continued, did not deprive the peasants of their movable property, and even lent some to them when they were too poor to acquire it by themselves, but freedom could not be given to the peasants, as it had been in foreign countries, because this could result only in even more peasant idleness and migration than there was in Russia at the time of writing. If the peasants were on this foreign free basis, the result would be:

endless lawsuits and Their Excellencies the Field Marshals...who command the glorious Russian army would be compelled to petition the commissars for their brave lads but we in Russia have more brave lads than in foreign parts because the peasants are literate there and in Russia, with God's care, even the priests are not all that literate. The landlords teach their serfs not only folk-dancing, but also carpentry and part-singing.

[1] Romanovich-Slavatinskii, *Dvorianstvo*, p. 384.

If the peasants were independent of their lords, moreover, the nobles would have nobody to do their cooking for them. The ungrammatical non-historian was not a complete opponent of the abolition of serfdom, although the conditions that he considered necessary for it made the prospect rather remote. Abolition would be possible, he wrote, when:

> Russia becomes as populous as the kingdom of Holland, when our priests are as literate as foreign priests, the nobles such sharp-witted fellows as the English and the French, the peasants know their ABC and are consequently honest and obey more the wrath of God and go to church more often than to the drinking houses, do not stave in the barges on the Volga, and our rabble has a better understanding of foreign crafts, and becomes more intelligent.

While a Russian historian has considered this entry to be an expression of the typically naïve attitude towards serfdom of most of the nobles in favour of its retention, so ludicrous are some of its assertions that the temptation is strong to consider it an ironic 'defence' of serfdom by somebody actually opposed to it.[1]

Certainly, there were several grammatical nobles who had read a considerable amount of history, and who were able to excuse serfdom more coherently. For example, A. P. Sumarokov, one of the first playwrights to emerge from the ranks of the nobility, who put his argument in the following manner. All classes should be remembered when questions concerned with the abolition of serfdom were posed, and, obviously, there would be some difference between the points of view of the serfs and the noble landlords. What would be more beneficial for the canary who provided him with much amusement, freedom or the cage, and was the chain necessary for the dog guarding his house? It might be better for the canary without the cage, and for the dog without the chain. However, the bird would fly away, and the animal would bite people. In such a manner, the peasant would benefit from the abolition of serfdom, the noble would lose. But what would be better for society as a whole? To this, claimed Sumarokov, 'all sons of society will say, even the slaves of society themselves, that of the two evils it is better for the peasants not to have their own land'. Serfs could not have their own land because it was the property of the nobility. Should the nobles be compelled to give to the peasants lands which had been bought, granted, or bequeathed, when

[1] Romanovich-Slavatinskii, *Dvorianstvo*, pp. 384–6.

they did not want to, and should the peasantry be granted the hitherto exclusive right of the nobility to land ownership? What would
become of the noble when the peasants and the land were no longer
his? Peasant freedom and property rights would not only be harmful to society, but even fatal.[1]

Elsewhere, Sumarokov described in more detail the consequences
likely to follow on the abolition of serfdom. The cost of servants
would rise, and poor noblemen would be without a coachman and a
lackey as well as a cook. More seriously, there would be terrible
disagreement between the landlords and their former serfs, and
many regiments would be necessary to pacify them. As things were,
the landlords and their peasants had a considerable love for each
other, he asserted. This love would be destroyed, and the landlords
would be terrified to live in the provinces, if serfdom were abolished.[2]

Partly because he was such a defender of serfdom, partly because
he was under the influence of current ideas in favour of agriculture,
Sumarokov was against the development of industry, which he saw as
a threat to both serfdom and agriculture. Agriculture generally was
more profitable an occupation than large-scale industry, which could
thrive only where there was a lack of land and a superfluity of peasants, he asserted. Sumarokov was even against the development of
industry on the estates of the noble landlords, as well as in the factories of the bourgeoisie.[3] Another threat to serfdom besides industry
was competition in trade, thought Sumarokov, who was for fixed
prices in the internal market, as well as for external trade with eastern
'savages' rather than with the civilized countries of western Europe,
which would reduce the risk of competition, he believed, and give
Russians an advantageous bargaining position.[4]

Another passionately negative response to the prize essay question
was given by Prince M. M. Shcherbatov, historian, essayist and
strong supporter of the rights of the Russian nobility. To the suggestions of serf property, Shcherbatov said, 'No, no, I run a long way
away from these ideas, and whatever natural law says, let us better
leave the peasants in Russia in that state, in which they have been
during the course of several centuries.' Shcherbatov also demurred to
the adoption of France as a model for Russia that some people had

---

[1] A. I. Hodnev, *Istoriia*, pp. 24–5.
[2] *SIRIO*, x, 82–7.
[3] Sumarokov, 'O domostroitel'stve', Kokorev, *Hrestomatiia*, pp. 223–4.
[4] Pashkov, *Istoriia*, I, 462.

97

been recommending. The payments which the nobles would receive from a régime that might be *ancien* for France but would be *nouveau* for Russia would never equal their present income, Shcherbatov claimed. Not only that, Shcherbatov asserted that the French peasants were dissatisfied, and the Russian peasants content.[1]

Having discussed the entries of the winner of the prize essay competition and of the runner-up, both of which advocated moderate change and the three entries opposed to any change whatsoever, I shall now draw your attention to two essays of a more progressive nature. The first of these, submitted by one Aleksandrov, was drawn up in the shape of theses accompanied by aphorisms drawn from religious writings. Aleksandrov divided the peasants into three groups, farmers, craftsmen and traders, all of whom, he implied, were servants of the state rather than of the noble landlords. The first of these groups should be given property rights, and, while its members were still to pay dues to the lord and the state, those to the state were to be of greater importance. Moreover, dues were to be scaled according to the price of produce rather than its quantity. Thus, the money economy would be encouraged, and the *barshchina* labour services probably doomed.[2]

The anonymous author of entry number 71, who, a Soviet historian has suggested, might well have been A. N. Radishchev, one of the first radical opponents of the Russian autocracy, expressed the view that society consisted of many people living under one authority 'for the mutual relief of their wants', and that 'the mutual help of people living in society, consists for the most part of the exchange among themselves of the fruits accruing from work...' Making the distinction between physical and mental labour, the anonymous essayist went on to say that, just as books were necessary for the second type of labour, so land was necessary for the first. Moreover, property had its origins in the beginnings of civil society, and, therefore, human society could not continue to exist if property rights were taken away from its members. Nothing would so encourage a man to be useful to society as the hope for property, and a peasant with property would concern himself with agriculture, with the raising of livestock by which he would enrich himself and society also. Not only this, natural law made the peasant free and gave him rights

[1] Shcherbatov, *Neizdannye sochineniia*, pp. 8, 12.
[2] Oreshkin, *Vol'noe ekonomicheskoe obshchestvo*, pp. 71-3.

equal to those of others, including rights to land. Wrote number 71:

In each society, the land must be divided so that it can be given to the inhabitants as property, according to the quantity of the inhabitants and the quantity of the profit brought to society by each individual...and each must have social or civil right to his share.

The serfs were to have rights to movable as well as to immovable property. Dues were to be paid, but, it would seem, to the state as a 'social debt' rather than to the landlords as a feudal rent. While not openly condemning serfdom, this competitor made enough proposals to destroy its foundations, arguing that 'all people in society are naturally similar to one another, and try to have equal and, at least, similar pleasures', and that it was extremely unjust for equality of rights not to exist. The changes that he envisaged could be introduced by law, thought number 71. If this were done, it would not be impossible for them to become a regular feature of Russian life.[1]

Less optimistically, two other competitors, the father and son Euler, immigrants from Germany, thought that it was much easier to answer questions about serf property theoretically than in practice, for the nobility would not accept any diminution in their power or income without a struggle.[2] The accuracy of this assertion could be more easily calculated after the views of the nobility as a whole were made known through the Legislative Commission. Even though most of the entries to the prize essay competition were not published, the Empress and her advisers had given members of the nobility fair warning of their belief that some changes in serfdom needed to be at least discussed by subjecting the institution to its first public scrutiny.

A. T. Bolotov, the middle-class noble whose early life and education have been described in the introductory chapter, was visiting Moscow in 1766, when he came across the first number of the *Works of the Free Economic Society*. Bolotov later wrote of this discovery:

As I already had a certain understanding of economic societies in other countries and of all their institutions, I almost jumped with joy, and when I saw from this book that the same kind of thing had been set up in our country, and even named and taken into her particular patronage by the

[1] *Ibid.* pp. 73–7.
[2] *Ibid.* pp. 70–1. Because the accounts of some of these entries to the prize essay competition are taken from the works of Soviet historians, whose point of view differs from that of most western historians, there is some risk that these accounts might seem distorted to western historians fortunate enough to read the entries in the original.

Empress herself, I almost jumped with joy, and began to read everything in it with great enthusiasm and attention. And my satisfaction grew even greater when I saw that, following foreign example, all nobles living in the provinces had been invited to communicate their economic observations to the Society, along with other people of every rank, and that to pave the way for this, sixty-five questions were appended at the end of this book, of such a kind and concerning such matters, to which it could not be complicated or difficult for anybody to answer, provided that he understood something of provincial life and agriculture, and knew how to write and possessed a pen.[1]

Having lived for several years in the provinces, Bolotov was well qualified to answer the questionnaire, and submitted a complete and detailed reply that was published in the second number of the *Works*.

Describing the situation in the Kashira district of Moscow province, Bolotov wrote that he considered the worst hindrance to advancement in agriculture to be the confused division of the fields. He nowhere found that the peasant had all his land together next to his home and vegetable patch, or even near it: everywhere it was distributed among all the fields belonging to the local village. This disorder was common to the peasants of the state, of the church, and of the nobility. As far as the third of these groups was concerned, even where the noble was the sole and continuous landlord, the peasants' land would generally be cut up into strips, and scattered among several fields, while the noble's land might be consolidated. But there would not be many villages belonging only to one landlord: most would be divided among several landlords. These landlords would usually come from one family, and might own woods and meadows and other appendages in common. There would often be arguments between them concerning the extent of their rights to the appendages, and the serfs would often bicker about them, too. Even if there were little disagreement, many disadvantages resulted from the mere facts of piecemeal land distribution, and multiplicity of landlords. It was impossible to manure or plough the land properly. Nobody could do all his sowing at the optimum time. Growing crops could not be adequately looked after, or protected from the incursions of animals, and many difficulties arose at harvest time.[2]

In his memoirs covering the period at which he submitted his reply to the Free Economic Society's questionnaire, Bolotov described how he tried to persuade his neighbours to agree on some

[1] Bolotov, *Zhizn'*, II, 318.   [2] *TVEO*, II, 162–3, 165–7.

joint action to bring order into their local situation, but without success.[1] For all this, however, he claimed in one of his answers that a general improvement was noticeable in the economic condition of the provinces. 'Estate and household management flourish from hour to hour, particularly with the landlords,' he wrote, 'undoubtedly because many landlords, enlightening themselves with the sciences, and seeing various foreign places, are adopting several new things and institutions as much as possible.'[2] Unfortunately, neither Bolotov nor the others who replied to the Free Economic Society's questionnaire provided much evidence that this was indeed the case. For example, the Society was interested in the extension of the cultivation of wheat and potatoes. From the replies to the questionnaire it was evident that wheat was very little grown, and potatoes sometimes even unheard of. The Society also asked, 'Whither is the surplus grain crop transported to be sold?' The replies indicated that surpluses were rare or sold locally for the most part.[3]

Two correspondents pointed out that a handbook distributed by the Senate had been efficacious in curtailing cattle plague.[4] Apart from this, the replies to the questionnaire do not provide much evidence to support the optimism of Bolotov or that of a contributor to the *Works* in 1767 who declared that science was beginning to show the way and reason to conquer all.[5] Much more representative of the feelings of writers with actual experience of Russian agriculture was Brigadier Olishev's complaint that the three-field system was not being introduced in his Vologda district of Archangel province because of peasant idleness and ignorance, as well as lack of time due to the heavy burdens placed upon their peasants by the landlords.[6] The accent of most correspondents, of course, would be on the faults of the peasants rather than on the shortcomings of the landlords,[7] although there were several who praised peasant diligence.[8]

Some contributors to the *Works* believed that the principal threat to Russian agriculture came from another source, the movement of

[1] Bolotov, *Zhizn'*, II, 184. [2] *TVEO*, II, 184.
[3] These replies, taken from the first few numbers of *TVEO*, were sent from Orenburg and Slobodsko-Ukraina. Nearer the capitals, surpluses were transported thither. Soviet historians have, of course, recently argued with some force the case for talking of an all-Russian market in grains and other crops during the eighteenth century. See, for example, N. L. Rubinshtein, *Sel'skoe hoziaistvo Rossii vo vtoroi polovine XVIII v.*
[4] *TVEO*, VII, 50; X, 50. [5] *TVEO*, VI, 3–4.
[6] *TVEO*, II, 109–10. [7] See, for example, *TVEO*, VIII, 158–9, 218–20.
[8] See, for example, *TVEO*, II, 216–19; VII, 81–2, 109–10.

the peasants from the rural areas to the towns and factories. In his 'Notes on former and contemporary agriculture', 'R' argued that the number of people engaged in agriculture was half what it had previously been. To indicate the great changes that had occurred, he considered it enough to refer to those working in Moscow and St Petersburg as cabmen, tavern-keepers, butchers, hawkers of haberdashery, pancakes, pastries and kvass, and many others working in food shops, to those keeping up kitchen gardens and peddling roots and herbs for cooking, of whom at most a tenth were in such occupations twenty years before. Continued 'R':

> I can boldly say that in both capitals there are up to fifty thousand, if not more; not to mention the great number of stone-masons, carpenters and others occupied in various trades. In similar large towns the same thing is to be found. From the number of farming peasants, all those who are healthy, young and almost the best people do not only do no farming for society, but feed themselves on cereals bought from those remaining in the countryside, and, to the great detriment of agriculture, raise the price of grains.

'R' also complained of the attraction of mines and factories, which, he asserted, lured peasants from the land as did the towns.

Admitting that it was not his business to discuss the leading members of society, 'R' had some criticism to make of officers of middle and low rank now retired and living in the provinces, particularly the younger men. They built themselves large homes, furnished them richly, possessed several officials and liveried servants, and a smart pair of horses for travelling, or even a troika. Twenty or so years before, their fathers had moderate-sized homes, two or three servants in simple but clean clothing, and much less ostentatious arrangements for travelling. The luxurious living of the younger generation was a further cause of detriment to agriculture. The interest of both people and landlords in it must be revived, concluded 'R'.[1]

Top people took the *Works of the Free Economic Society*, and there can be no doubt that this organ of the Russian establishment demonstrated a considerable bias towards agriculture, like the writings of

---

[1] *TVEO*, VI, 59–68. Lyashchenko, *History*, p. 273, points out that, in fact, the urban population of Russia increased from 300,000, or 2·3 per cent of the population, in 1722 to 1,300,000, or 3·6 per cent of a larger population, in 1796. Many of the people referred to by 'R' would be part of a floating population inhabiting the towns seasonally, and not included in the governmental statistics on which the above figures are based.

the Empress and other leading members of society. While this bias was encouraged by physiocratic and other theory, it had strong roots in Russian tradition, and, as far as we know, poorly educated nobles unfamiliar with the *Works* would share the prejudices of most of the contributors to that journal and its patron.[1]

At the same time, many nobles were not averse to making money out of mines and manufactures. While the nobility dominated agriculture, it also had a considerable interest in industry. According to official statistics collected by M. D. Chulkov, the production of state metalworks in 1767 reached a value of something over 250,000 roubles, non-noble private metallurgical output totalled an amount valued at just over 730,000 roubles, and nobles earned more than 1,500,000 roubles from their metal interests. The leading noble metallurgical industrialists were the Stroganovs and the Demidovs, who, between them, earned more than a half of the income of their class from this source.[2] The total value of large-scale cloth production at about the same time was just over a million roubles, according to Chulkov's statistics, of which the share of the nobility was a little more than half, with the distribution among individual nobles being considerably wider than in the case of the metallurgical industry. Nobles participated in a by no means negligible, although nowhere so dominant, manner in the minor manufacturing industries of silk, linen and paper.[3] Moreover, nobles would be closely connected with some peasant small-scale manufacturing not included in official statistics.

In contemporary Russian economic theory, writers from the nobility showed less interest in industry than in agriculture. It is noteworthy that a noble in favour of industrial development, such as was P. I. Rychkov, was still concerned that this development should not take place at the expense of agriculture. 'For society as a whole,' he wrote, 'no trade and no handicraft can be as advantageous as agriculture.'[4] Factory workers should be selected from those who had

---

[1] See Michael Confino, *Domaines et seigneurs en Russie vers la fin du XVIII e siècle*, p. 38.

[2] From 'Vedomost'...o...kazennyh i partikuliarnyh zheleznyh, mednyh i mineral'-nyh zavodah...', published by M. D. Chulkov, *Istoricheskoe opisanie rossiiskoi kommertsii*, VI, Book 2, 547–615.

[3] From 'Vedomost'...skol'ko fabrik...', in Chulkov, *Istoricheskoe opisanie*, VI, Book 3, 591–605. Soviet historians, who have been very interested in the question of Russia's industrial growth in the eighteenth century, attribute a smaller share in this process to the nobility. See, for example, I. S. Golubnichii, etc., *Ekonomicheskaia istoriia SSSR*, pp. 120–5.　　　　[4] P. I. Rychkov, 'Nakaz dlia upravitelia...', *TVEO*, XVI, 35.

not previously worked on the land, wrote Rychkov, because it was harmful to take people away from the land for the benefit of industry.[1] Of the two kinds of service performed by the serfs for their masters, Rychkov preferred the actual labour of *barshchina* to the commutative *obrok*, thus further protecting agriculture.[2]

As far as trade was concerned, writers interested in this aspect of Russia's commercial development would, on the whole, be happy to see a continuance of the trend that had caused Russian exports to rise from a total value of 4,567,422 roubles in 1742 to 12,762,492 roubles in 1762.[3] Thus, in 1762, B. M. Vorontsov wrote of the desirability of Russia getting its hands on the monopoly of trade in the Black Sea and with the countries of southern Europe,[4] and, at about the same time, there was agitation for a Russian port on the Sea of Azov to help Russia secure a firm grasp on trade between Europe and Asia.[5] For all these ideas of promoting Russia's trade in other areas, 85 per cent of it was still with western Europe, trade with Britain, and, to a lesser extent, Holland, continuing to predominate.[6] As in industry, so in trade, an agricultural complex was very influential in pertinent speculation. In an article in the first number of the *Works*, T. Von Klingshtet argued that, while factories were perhaps the basis of prosperity in England, France and Holland, agriculture was golden in a country as vast as Russia. Already hemp was the country's most important export, if she developed her other agricultural products, she could become the grain basket of Europe. Wheat in particular should be grown for export. (Russians generally preferred rye, and white bread was as unnecessary a luxury for the lower orders as were champagne and burgundy for the upper class, claimed Von Klingshtet.)[7] With the nobles dominant in farming for profit, they would obviously play an important part in the trade that Von Klingshtet envisaged.[8]

[1] Rychkov, 'O manufakturah iz hlopchatoi bumagi i iz verbliuzhnei shersti', *TVEO*, VII, 20.　　　　[2] Rychkov, 'Nakaz', *TVEO*, XVI, for example.
[3] H. F. Von Storch, *Historisch-statistisches Gemälde des russischen Reichs am Ende des Achtzehnten Jahrhunderts, Supplementband*, s. i. The bulk of the export trade was still in raw materials and agricultural produce, the fruit of a 'feudal' economy. See A. I. Baranovich, etc. (eds.), *Ocherki istorii SSSR, Period feodalizma, Rossiia vo vtoroi polovine XVIII v.*, p. 127.
[4] *Arhiv Vorontsova*, XXV, 301–2.
[5] N. N. Firsov, *Pravitel'stvo i obshchestvo v ih otnosheniiah k vneshnei torgovle Rossii*, pp. 45–6.
[6] Pashkov, *Istoriia*, I, 437; D. Gerhard, *England und der Aufsteig Russlands*, p. 39.
[7] *TVEO*, I, 160–78.
[8] A. I. Baranovich, etc. (eds.), *Ocherki istorii SSSR, Period feodalizma, Rossiia vo vtoroi polovine XVIII v.*, pp. 41–5.

Kommertsiia, or commerce, could mean to these eighteenth-century writers not only industry and trade, but transport and communications, credit and monetary exchange as well. On the whole, these writers appear to have concentrated on industry and trade rather than on the other branches of *kommertsia,* although they were by no means unaware of the importance of the latter in the economic development of their country.[1]

CATHERINE'S EARLY ECONOMIC POLICY

Actions speak louder than words, and it is therefore important to consider the policy of Catherine's government in practice as well as in theory during the first five years of her reign. When A. A. Kizevetter wrote on this theme in 1929, he said that the then generally accepted picture of the period could be described as follows. Catherine came to power with many ideas for reform, and, to begin with, tried to put some of them into effect. However, she discovered in 1767 that the nobility was opposed to most of the innovations that she was attempting to introduce, and decided to change her policy to accommodate its prejudices. Kizevetter argued that there was in fact little difference between Catherine's policy after 1767 and her previous policy and that, beneath a veneer of liberal intentions, there was a hard core of conservative legislation right from the start. In most respects, Kizevetter's case is irrefutable, although it could be stated in a manner rather less damaging to Catherine's reputation as a progressive ruler, perhaps. In other words, the Empress was an expert politician as well as a capable thinker, and was treading warily at every moment, even going at times in the opposite direction to the one she would have preferred.[2]

Thus, while anxious to do something about serfdom and to make provision for its eventual abolition, Catherine actually took steps to protect the institution soon after her accession to power. Peter III's emancipation of the nobility had aroused rumours among the serfs of the imminence of their own emancipation, and these contributed to the outbreak of a series of popular uprisings. These made a great impact on the new Empress,[3] who found herself bound to support the existence of serfdom and to introduce laws directed towards that end.

[1] See, for example, Pashkov, *Istoriia,* I, 483; Shcherbatov, *Neizdannye sochineniia,* p. 134.
[2] Kizevetter, in *Sbornik statei Miliukovu,* pp. 309-25.   [3] *SIRIO,* x, 381.

'We are resolved to preserve inviolate the estates and possessions of the landlords and to maintain the peasants in their dutiful obedience to them', declared an imperial decree in July 1762.[1] In 1763 it was decreed that the peasants who had participated in revolts would be forced to pay the costs of their pacification.[2] Two years later, the nobility was empowered to send troublesome serfs into exile for penal servitude, and this right was soon extended.[3] Serfdom was further protected in 1767, when the serfs were denied their chief means of seeking peaceful redress for their grievances, the right of petition. In the decree announcing this prohibition, it was explained that disobedience of their landlords by the serfs stemmed largely from the rumours spread around by wicked people about changes in the laws, thus demonstrating that news of the Legislative Commission, like that of the emancipation of the nobility, had an unsettling effect on the peasantry.[4] It was also almost certainly more than coincidental that a few months before the enactment of this decree, on her return from a trip along the Volga, Catherine told the Senate that she had been given over six hundred petitions during her journey, mostly peasant complaints about the exactions of the landlords.[5] At the same time as she was inviting representatives of several classes to participate in her Great Commission, the Empress was, albeit advisedly, turning a deaf ear to the spokesmen of nearly half her people.

Maternal concern for the peasantry was by no means entirely absent from the legislation of Catherine's first five years. For example, a decree of November 1767 confirmed an earlier imperial command of 1761 that the landlords should arrange for the welfare of their serfs at times of poor harvest by setting up grain stores, or by buying grain.[6] In this measure, too, the government was showing a protective attitude towards agriculture as well as towards the peasants, although such an attitude was more clearly demonstrated by the institution of

---

[1] *PSZ*, xvi, 10–11, no. 11,593, 3 July 1762.

[2] *PSZ*, xvi, 309–10, no. 11,875, 11 July 1763.

[3] *PSZ*, xvii, 10, no. 12,311, 17 January 1765; xvii, 545–6, no. 12,556, 28 January 1766. According to the terms of the second decree, some of the troublesome serfs were to go into the army.

[4] *PSZ*, xviii, 334–6, no. 12,966, 22 August 1767.

[5] Solov'ev, *Istoriia*, vi, 331. For other anti-serf measures of the first years of Catherine's reign, see Beliavskii, 'Vopros', *Vestnik moskovskogo universiteta*, ix (1963), no. 6, 49–52.

[6] *PSZ*, xviii, 392, no. 13,017, 26 November 1767. An element of maternal concern for the peasantry is also detectable in the decree of 1766 prohibiting the sale of adult serfs for three months before a recruit levy, and the acceptance of purchased serfs as recruits. See *PSZ*, xvii, 997–1015, no. 12,748, 29 September 1766.

the Free Economic Society and by decrees encouraging the immigration of foreign colonists and the cultivation of potatoes.[1]

In the major industrial laws of her first five years, Catherine would appear to have protected and enlarged the privileges of the nobility. Thus, she was quick to confirm Peter III's prohibition of purchase of serfs for employment in bourgeois factories, obliging the middle-class factory owners to use hired labour and reserving the use of servile labour to the dvorianstvo.[2] In 1765 the nobility was guaranteed exclusive control over the private preparation of alcoholic liquors.[3] Far from promoting the interests of the nobility in her industrial and commercial policies, Sacke has argued, in spite of these acts, Catherine was primarily anxious to foster the growth of Russia's nascent bourgeoisie, which was now closely linked with some members of the aristocracy who were more interested in their trading associates than in the other nobles. Sacke considered that Catherine's policies were favourable to the bourgeoisie and its influential allies, in their removal of restrictions on internal trade, their promotion of exports and regulation of imports, their encouragement of industrial growth, their construction of new harbours and attempts to arrange new depots for Russian goods, their improvement of land and water communications, and their development of credit facilities.[4] While it is obvious that such measures as these would be welcomed by the merchants and other groups within the loose framework of Russia's bourgeoisie, it is difficult to see why they would be unacceptable to the nobility as a whole, too, even though some nobles looked down upon trade and industry and wanted to have nothing to do with these activities. However, such nobles would be from the very aristocracy that Sacke says was providing allies for the bourgeoisie. Moreover, the Catherine who was encouraging the alliance, according to Sacke, had shown disapproval for the participation of nobles in trade in her Instruction, and no enthusiasm for their industrial activities.[5] Again, some nobles might not be able to

[1] See *PSZ*, XVI, 126–7, no. 11,720, 4 December 1762, which encouraged the immigration of foreigners, except Jews, and the return of *émigrés*; XVII, 141–8, no. 12,406, 31 May 1765, which recommended the cultivation of potatoes where nothing else would grow. Various decrees connected with the execution of the survey would also tend to foster agriculture. See, for example, *PSZ*, XVII, 329–39, no. 12,474, 19 September 1765.
[2] *PSZ*, XVI, 47–8, no. 11,638, 8 August 1762.
[3] *PSZ*, XVII, 208–16, no. 12,448, 9 August 1765.
[4] G. Sacke, 'Adel und Burgertum in Der Regierungszeit Katharinas II von Russland', *Revue Belge de Philologie et d'Histoire*, XVII, 815–52.   [5] Reddaway, *Documents*, p. 267.

appreciate the advantages to them of a thriving foreign trade, short-sighted and introverted as their economic attitudes were, but few revealed a rooted opposition to commercial development during Catherine's first quinquennium. It is very difficult, then, to concur with Sacke's view that the Empress pursued economic policies in favour of the bourgeoisie and its aristocratic allies at the expense of the rest of the nobility. To take further examples, when, in December 1762, Catherine talked with her Senate about setting up consulates in western European countries and a trade bank in Russia, curtailing luxury imports and removing some restrictions from the merchant class,[1] she was not necessarily thinking of undermining the prosperity of the nobility. Indeed, the execution of the suggestion of closest interest to the dvorianstvo, the reduction of luxury imports, would strengthen rather than weaken the economic position of the class. Similarly, when, after an examination of the trade question, begun in July 1762 and completed in December 1763, it was decided to set up a new trade commission to replace that of Peter III (which, like the Emperor himself was defunct), the interests of the large mass of the nobility were not directly hurt.[2] Much the same might be said of Catherine's support for the extension of Russian trade in the Middle East,[3] the renewal of the Anglo-Russian Treaty of 1734 with minor changes in 1766,[4] and the introduction of a moderately protective tariff in the same year. (Compared with the previous tariff of 1757, the 1766 rate, both import and export, was lower for raw materials but higher for manufactured goods.)[5]

While it would seem to be incorrect to attribute to Catherine a conscious policy of encouraging the bourgeoisie at the expense of the majority of the noble class, there is a somewhat stronger case for arguing that in her attack on monopoly and her move away from mercantilism, she was giving a considerable boost to the development of trade and industry and thus accelerating the breakdown of the feudal economy, and in the long run, of the noble landlords. Such a

[1] Bil'basov, *Istoriia*, II, 525–6.
[2] *PSZ*, XVI, 31–8, no. 11,630, 31 July 1762; XVI, 452–3, no. 11,985, 8 December 1763. For a general description of the Trade Commission's institution and activities, which were to include promotion of technological improvements in agriculture and of growth in the number of farmers, see A. Lappo-Danilevskii, 'Die russische Handelskommission von 1763–1796', *Beiträge zur russischen Geschichte*, Otto Hötzsch (ed.), pp. 176–213.
[3] Solov'ev, *Istoriia*, VI, 20, 308.
[4] Pashkov, *Istoriia*, I, 437; Gerhard, *England und der Aufsteig Russlands*, p. 39.
[5] S. A. Pokrovskii, *Vneshniaia torgovlia i vneshniaia torgovaia politika Rossii*, p. 114.

tendency would be encouraged by such decrees as that of 1762 abolishing special concessions in, among others, the fish, seal and tobacco trades, and allowing free enterprise to peasants as well as others in, for example, the cotton-print industry; another decree of 1762 permitted people of every rank to establish factories in all towns and districts except Moscow and St Petersburg; that of 1763 abolished the monopoly in the manufacture of gold and silver leaf and other luxury goods.[1] Of wider importance, perhaps, was the decree of 17 April 1767, ordering 'no trade and handicraft, by which town inhabitants can make themselves an honest living, to be forbidden and everything taken from the so-called unlawful factories to be returned to their owners'.[2] A further contribution to the decline of the closed feudal economy was Catherine's considerable expenditure on roads and canals.[3]

Of central importance for all Catherine's economic policies was her handling of money and finance. In her letter to Viazemskii on his appointment to the post of Procurator-General in 1764, Catherine remarked that there was a great need for an increase in the circulation of money. The money department of the Mines College had calculated that there were only 80 million silver roubles in circulation, or less than four per head of the population, and for this reason it had been necessary to introduce copper coinage. As much silver as possible must be attracted into the country, by the grain trade, for example, for which the trade commission had already been ordered to make arrangements.[4] A drastic step to improve circulation, and also to bridge a budgetary gap, was taken at the end of 1768 with the establishment of state banks for the issue of assignats.[5]

As far as the finances of the nobility in particular were concerned, the State Nobility Bank was flourishing during the early years of Catherine's reign, and a list of some of the nobles who owed it money in 1767 demonstrates that those able to provide security in land and serfs were taking full advantage of its credit facilities.[6] However, with 100 roubles the minimum amount for a loan, and two serfs or the guarantee of a wealthy or prominent noble the minimum security,

---

[1] *PSZ*, xvi, 31–8, no. 11,630, 31 July 1762; xvi, 88, no. 11,689, 23 October 1762; xvi, 163–4, 18 February 1763.

[2] *PSZ*, xviii, 85, no. 12,872.   [3] Pashkov, *Istoriia*, i, 438.

[4] Chechulin, etc. (eds.), *Istoriia senata*, ii, Appendix xvi, point 5.

[5] *PSZ*, xviii, 787–92, no. 13,219, 29 December 1768.

[6] *Vedomost' kontory sanktpeterburgskogo banka, 1767.*

the facilities of the bank would be beyond the reach of many lower-class nobles.[1]

Generally, the state budget at this time could be said to have been arranged in favour of the nobility, from the point of view of both income and expenditure. Of a total income of 24·1 million roubles in 1769, over 40 per cent came from direct taxation, principally the poll tax, and more than another 40 per cent from indirect taxes, mainly on trade, drink and salt, all of which were extremely burdensome for the peasantry. Of a total expenditure of 23·3 million roubles in 1767, nearly 50 per cent went on the army and the navy, nearly 25 per cent on the central and local government, over 10 per cent on the court, and much of the remainder on tax collection.[2] Catherine's profligate distribution of money and serfs to her followers is notorious, commencing with her generous rewards to the participants in the palace revolution of 1762.[3] This most obviously reflected the general tenor of her financial policies.

THE LEGISLATIVE COMMISSION AND THE ECONOMY

The moderately progressive views on the reform of serfdom expressed by Catherine herself are almost the only source of information for an evaluation of governmental opinion on this vexed question during the first years of her reign. Little more clarification can be gained from a scrutiny of the instructions of the Senate, colleges, and other government departments.

The Senate wanted peasants in general to be allowed to carry on commercial transactions with other classes. It also suggested a consideration of the treatment to be accorded to serf families if they were doomed to separation as a result of arrangements made for a noblewoman's dowry.[4] These were the sole references to serfdom by Russia's chief executive department.

Another aspect of serfdom was more fully discussed by the State Road Construction Chancellery, which recommended that forced labour be replaced by hired workers on projects connected with the repair or improvement of the Empire's communications. Many

[1] Romanovich-Slavatinskii, *Dvorianstvo*, pp. 343–4.

[2] S. M. Troitskii, 'Finansovaia politika russkogo absoliutizma vo vtoroi polovine XVII i XVIII vv.', Druzhinin, etc. (eds.), *Absoliutizm v Rossii*, pp. 303, 310.

[3] V. I. Semevskii, *Pozhalovaniia naselennyh imenii v tsarstvovanie Ekateriny II-oi*, pp. 12; *SIRIO*, VII, 108–19.   [4] *SIRIO*, XLIII, 19, 26.

state roads, the Chancellery pointed out (even though it was not sure which were state roads and which were not), had been renovated by unfortunate serfs and other peasants taken from the land, of whom the majority had been sent indiscriminately and without proper arrangements to uninhabited regions far away from home, where they suffered anxiety, hunger and ill-health. Sometimes they died, and to no purpose, for they were never able to carry out their appointed tasks. Meanwhile, their domestic circumstances deteriorated. Because of all this, the Chancellery recommended that hired labour be used on the roads, and the peasants who had been compelled to work on the roads could then work on the land or at other tasks, using their time usefully for themselves and their lords.[1]

As far as the treatment of the serfs by their masters was concerned, the Justice College pointed out that there was no exact legislation for cases where serfs had died after harsh punishment, although their lords had not been guilty of malicious intent. The Chief Police Department was in favour of some limitations on the powers of the landlords over their serfs, saying that if it ever came to the department's attention that any noble was repeatedly punishing or crippling his charges for minor offences, a report on the matter would be made to Her Majesty. A less humane suggestion came from the Confiscation Chancellery, that household and other serfs on confiscated estates be sold separately from the estates by auction.[2]

The Senate, colleges, and other government departments, thus put forward no proposals for any significant reform of serfdom. Such changes in the institution as they discussed in their instructions were aimed either at eradicating the more flagrant abuses or increasing the efficiency of the system. Even in the instructions of the various classes of the Russian Empire, there was little more of a direct attack on this problem. This was because these instructions concentrated on class and local needs, and the only group everywhere directly affected by serfdom was the serf mass itself, which, of course, had no voice at the Legislative Commission, and if these peasants were aware of the Commission's existence, they expected nothing from it. A contemporary serf poet well expressed the feelings of his class in 'The Slave's Lament'. 'They are changing the laws to their own advantage,' the anonymous author wrote, 'They are not electing slaves as deputies, for

[1] *SIRIO*, XLIII, 390–2. Of course, the Chancellery did not attempt to apply its evaluation of the comparative merits of forced and hired labour to anything but road construction.
[2] *SIRIO*, XLIII, 171, 349–50, 381–2.

what could slaves say there? They would give themselves liberty to torture us to death.'[1]

The free rural inhabitants had little to say in their instructions about the plight of the serfs. Some groups among them requested guarantees of the right to serf ownership that had conditionally been given them, the Tartars and similar tribesmen made comparable requests, and other peasant groups sought permission to buy serfs, at least as recruit replacements. That was as far as the interest of most of the free rural inhabitants in the institution of serfdom went.[2]

The instructions of the town inhabitants made many references to the serfs, but these fell into two main categories, complaints about serf interference in the bourgeois preserve, trade, and requests that the bourgeoisie be allowed to purchase and possess serfs. The merchants, the principal group of town inhabitants, had recently completely lost their rights to the purchase of serfs,[3] and were anxious to regain them, not to emulate the nobles, they argued, but to carry out their various tasks efficiently. So many were the town duties of the burghers that serf assistance was absolutely necessary, they claimed, hired labour being unreliable. Hired labour was an inefficient source of factory labour, too, since it was difficult to obtain during the summer months. The bad effects on their prosperity of the recruit levies could be avoided if they were allowed to purchase serfs for this purpose, or pay money instead. The merchants reasoned that both the state and the nobility would benefit if the right of serf purchase were extended to their class, the state gaining income from a tax on bills of sale and raised rates of poll tax, and the nobility from the higher prices which its human possessions would fetch in the conditions of greater demand which were bound to ensue.[4]

As most of the free rural and town inhabitants viewed it, the existence of serfdom did not arouse any doubt of its lawfulness or expediency. They accepted the institution as a fact and a law which presented all those who could take advantage of it with great benefits, and attempted to include themselves among their number.[5] The nobility was more intimately connected with serfdom than either of the other principal classes represented at the Legislative Commission,

[1] Kokorev, *Hrestomatiia*, p. 258.
[2] Florovskii, *Vopros*, pp. 26–31. Semevskii, *Krest'iane*, I, 5, points out that the *odnodvortsy*, one of the groups of free peasants, had some rights to serf possession.
[3] *PSZ*, xv, 966, no. 11,490, 29 March 1762.
[4] Florovskii, *Vopros*, pp. 32–9.   [5] *Ibid.* p. 39.

and was therefore certain to have more to say on the subject. This was expected by the government to some extent,[1] and recognized by some of the instructions of the nobility. For example, the Mihailov nobles considered it necessary 'to use this God-given, memorable occasion to look after the separate wants of us nobles and our peasants', while Shcherbatov's Iaroslavl' assembly thought that 'the nobles, being the possessors of land and villages, must activate their concern...for the peasants, subjects of the same Sovereign and subordinated to them'.[2] However, in general, the nobility was less interested in the internal than the external aspects of serfdom. That is, like the other classes, it accepted the existence of the institution as incontrovertible fact and law, believed the care and regulation of its human property to be its own affair, and applied itself principally to a consideration of the relationship between this private domain and the state and the other classes in the state, particularly the merchant class.

At the time of the convocation of the Legislative Commission, the nobility had the almost exclusive right to purchase and possess serfs, and it wished to consolidate this virtual monopoly. 'To people of every kind, to the nobility and the merchant class, similarly to other ranks,' said the Kashin instruction, 'general privileges have been granted, so that each kind might have its own advantages, and one would not trespass on the prerogatives of another, and each use that with which it had been privileged.'[3] The possession of populated villages had been an exclusive privilege of the nobility since ancient times, said the electors of the Pereiaslavl'-Zalesskii district, and it was necessary to confirm it 'so that the rank of dvorianin be raised to its former level of advantages'.[4] Nobody of whatever rank should be allowed to purchase villages unless he had received the diploma of dvorianstvo from the monarch, it was argued. They claimed that if such purchase rights were allowed to all and sundry, many slights would be suffered by the nobles and their purses would be hit as well as their pride, for competition would produce a rise in prices, and the number of villages possessed by noble families would inevitably decline.[5]

[1] See, for example, Markevich, *Zap. imp. od. ob.* xx, 18.
[2] *SIRIO*, iv, 272; 309. Both from Moscow.
[3] *SIRIO*, iv, 460. Kashin was in Moscow. See also Shuia, Moscow, iv, 395–6; and Bolhov, Belgorod, lxviii, 493.
[4] *SIRIO*, viii, 495. Pereiaslavl'-Zalesskii was in Moscow. See also, for example, Mihailov Moscow, iv, 276–7; Vologda, Archangel, xiv, 462; and Viaz'ma, Smolensk, xiv, 452.
[5] See, for example, Romanov, Moscow, *SIRIO*, viii, 458; Zaraisk, Moscow, iv, 345; and Pustorzheva, Novgorod, xiv, 314.

Concerning the merchant class specifically, the complaints of the nobility, particularly in the central industrial region, were directed at the purchase by this class of populated estates for industrial purposes. It was sometimes conceded that merchants should be allowed to rent noble property,[1] but almost never to buy it. If the merchants were to get their hands on a large number of villages, it was argued, trade and agriculture would decline.[2] Shcherbatov's Iaroslavl' assembly thought that merchants underpaid serfs, and tortured them with overwork, with the result that there were many serf revolts.[3] As a whole, the nobility thought it necessary for the merchants to return what factory villages they still possessed to the state, or to sell them at reasonable rates to the nobility.[4]

While some instructions conceded that factory owners should be allowed to possess skilled workers,[5] the consensus was that the bulk of the labour force should be hired. Thus, idle people would find work, and the families of the workers would receive more money. Moreover, as a result of money earned in the factories by the serfs during the agricultural off-season, the nobles would benefit from the increased circulation of money in their districts. If their recommendations were carried out, the nobles submitted, the factories would never be short of hands. If a shortage were to arise somewhere, the Klin instruction suggested that the local marshal of the nobility should try to remedy the deficiency by finding suitable workers in the surrounding districts.[6]

Some rather exceptional ideas of the ownership of serfs by the merchant class were put forward by the nobles of Krapivna, Vologda and Mihailov. The first assembly wanted to allow the merchants a conditional right to the possession of serfs. It pointed out that, although the merchants owned a considerable number of serfs, they were not able to compete with foreign manufacturers because of the low level of their production. These factory-owners had already received back what they had paid for the serfs, and now lived in luxury and idleness. If in the future they did not produce such items

[1] See, for example, Viaz'ma, Smolensk, *SIRIO*, xiv, 452.
[2] See, for example, Shuia, Moscow, *SIRIO*, iv, 395.
[3] *SIRIO*, iv, 300.
[4] For return to state, Klin, Moscow, *SIRIO*, iv, 260–1; for sale to nobility, Luh, Moscow, viii, 483.
[5] Kashin, Moscow, *SIRIO*, iv, 465; Kerensk, Voronezh, lxviii, 439.
[6] Klin, *SIRIO*, iv, 260–1; Iaroslavl', iv, 301; Luh, viii, 483; Shuia, iv, 396; Tula, iv, 413. All from Moscow.

as scythes, which had to be bought at high prices from abroad, their villages should be confiscated by the state. The Vologda electors wanted merchants to be allowed to buy recruits, recognizing that they suffered through losing their servants to the army. While arguing that the prohibition of serf ownership should be enforced on the merchants, since these temporary owners knew that they would not permanently possess their serfs and therefore did not try to look after them properly, the Mihailov nobles said that the alternative hire of workers would reduce the number of farmers but increase the quantity of consumers. So, heathen foreigners should be imported as a labour force, and these should all be freed from the factories after twenty to thirty years.[1]

These untypical suggestions made very little inroad into the solid front presented by the nobility on the subject of its exclusive right to serf ownership. This was defended by some assemblies to such an extent that they wanted the property of a noblewoman to remain with her family if she deserted her class for a commoner husband, or at least to return to the family after her death.[2] Anybody who tried to introduce the idea of restrictions on the nobility's exclusive right met with no success whatsoever, even if he were Gregory Orlov. According to his son, the Marshal of the Legislative Commission, Alexander Bibikov, suggested the institution of a class of free farmers at the local election that he attended, but met with a negative response from his fellow nobles in Kostroma. Solov'ev wrote that the marshal of the Chernigov nobility, A. Bezborodko, could not persuade his fellows to insert in their instruction the comparatively mild request that limits be put to the authority of the landlords over their serfs.[3]

While no attention was paid to those who wanted even mild restrictions on serfdom, those who suggested an extension of the rights of the nobility in this sphere, or an increase in the number of serfs, were supported with enthusiasm. For example, some instructions asked for changes in the punishments for bootlegging, since those serfs sent into the army or exile for this offence often used their punishment as a stepping-stone to liberty.[4] The Kerensk and Krapivna nobles wanted the church peasants to be sold to their class, the

---

[1] Krapivna, Moscow, *SIRIO*, viii, 562–3; Vologda, Archangel, xiv, 462–4; Mihailov, Moscow, iv, 276–7.   [2] Belgorod district, *SIRIO*, lxviii, 660; Odoev, Moscow, viii, 492.
[3] Florovskii, *Vopros*, pp. 45–6; Bibikov, *Zapiski*, p. 41.
[4] Viaz'ma, Smolensk, *SIRIO*, xiv, 452–4; Kolomna, Moscow, iv, 337; Voronezh district, lxviii, 357.

former suggesting that each purchaser be limited to a thousand souls, and the latter that male serfs be sold at thirty roubles a head, by which the exchequer and society as a whole would benefit.[1]

In their consideration of the exclusive right to serf ownership, its extension and protection from outside interference, the nobles were obviously concentrating on the external rather than the internal aspects of serfdom. Such a concentration is also clearly visible in the remarks made by the nobles of the western provinces on the important question of serf flight.

The number of runaways was so great, said the Opochka instruction, that the Polish nobility, which welcomed them, had no more room for them on its estates unless it moved its own peasants further away from the border.[2] /The prosperity of the Russian landlords obviously suffered a great blow from their loss of a large number of serfs, and several of their instructions expressed the fear that they might be ruined and the security of the state threatened by peasant flight.[3] The seriousness of this problem had a considerable effect on the deliberations of the landlords, therefore, and forced them to make a detailed diagnosis of it and several suggestions for its cure. Yet, while the Empress had considered the exactions of the landlords to be a significant contribution to serf flight,[4] they themselves could not agree with her. For example, the Roslavl' electors requested that runaways be excluded from tax apportionment calculations, so that landowners might not lose their estates 'guiltlessly' through the payment of the taxes of the runaways, because the landowners were guilty of 'no error' in these cases.[5] According to the nobility, the main reasons for serf flight were recruit levies; the poll tax, the system for the collection of which was burdensome for both peasants and lords alike, it was argued, and state taxes; state work, carried on for the most part without pay, such as road construction; the arrangements for the sale of salt; and the restrictions on alcoholic liquors, which, according to the Pskov instruction, were necessary to make life bearable for the serfs.[6]

---

[1] Kerensk, Voronezh, *SIRIO*, LXVIII, 443–4; Krapivna, Moscow, VIII, 559.

[2] Opochka, Novgorod, *SIRIO*, XIV, 267. The Opochka nobles also blamed the Jews for the flight of their serfs.

[3] See, for example, Velikie Luki, *SIRIO*, XIV, 365; Pskov, XIV, 384. Both from Novgorod. See also Roslavl', Smolensk, XIV, 425.

[4] Reddaway, *Documents*, p. 258.   [5] Roslavl', Smolensk, *SIRIO*, XIV, 426.

[6] Opochka, *SIRIO*, XIV, 266; Pustorzheva, XIV, 296–303; Pskov, XIV, 381–4. All from Novgorod. Roslavl', Smolensk, XIV, 426.

Peter Panin also thought that some of these were responsible for serf flight, but he added to them the limitless power of the lord over his peasants.[1] The nobles, for their part, added the attractions of the freedoms of Poland; poor harvests and lack of food; arguments, and other troubles with peasant neighbours; and crimes of various kinds. Sometimes, serf wives ran away from their husbands, or vice versa, making arrangements with members of the appropriate opposite sex. The nobility also made accusations of enticement and concealment against the Polish nobles, and schismatics. Troop movement, quartering and victualling, were both blamed for peasant flight by the western nobility, and generally complained of throughout the Empire.[2]

Unfortunately, such was man's ingratitude that runaway serfs gathered together in bands of brigands and singled out the landlords, who considered themselves in no way responsible for peasant flight or any of the vexations helping to cause it, as the particular objects of their attacks. 'They particularly kill the nobility', complained the Penza instruction, echoed by several others.[3] Perhaps disillusioned by these 'groundless' attacks upon them, some assemblies of nobles looked on the serfs as a whole as inherently wicked, or as enemies of the state.[4] To look at peasant flight from a more objective viewpoint, the landlords were themselves to a large extent responsible for it, and might well have curtailed it by setting their own house in order, as well as by suggesting more strongly fortified frontiers and the reduction of state taxes and services.

In their consideration of their exclusive ownership of serfs, and threats to it, in their analysis of serf flight, too, a certain ambiguity is evident in the remarks of the nobles. As S. Briullov put it, the attitude of the landlord to the serf differs:

according to whether he is considering him from the point of view of his possession, a part of his immovable property; or from the point of view of

[1] Solov'ev, *RV*, xxxv, 314–17.
[2] Pustorzheva, *SIRIO*, xiv, 295; Velikie Luki, xiv, 366; Opochka, xiv, 266. All from Novgorod. Viaz'ma, xiv, 454; Dorogobuzh, xiv, 435; Smolensk district, xiv, 421. All from Smolensk province. Chuhloma, Archangel, xiv, 476; Kolomna, Moscow, iv, 336. On troop movement, quartering and victualling, see, for example, Lihvin, Moscow, *SIRIO*, viii, 443–4; Shliussel'burg, St Petersburg, xiv, 246; Obonezhskaia Piatina, Novgorod, xiv, 330; Pereiaslavl', Little Russia, lxviii, 152; Har'kov, Slobodsko-Ukraina, lxviii, 267; Kadom, Voronezh, lxviii, 327–8.
[3] Penza, Kazan', *SIRIO*, lxviii, 13. See also Pskov, xiv, 383; Ostrov, xiv, 277; Toropets and Holm, xiv, 402.
[4] Pereiaslavl'-Zalesskii, Moscow, *SIRIO*, viii, 498; Pustorzheva, Novgorod, xiv, 299.

a human individual, asserting a right to a more or less free existence; in the first case he conserves the physical and financial power of the being subjected to him from the predatoriness of the merchant and the state official, attempting to keep these powers for himself; in the second case, where the question of the regulation of free peasant labour crops up, of measures against peasant flights, the lord behaves towards the *muzhik*, not with tenderness and concern, but, on the contrary, with cruelty.[1]

Similarly, while the nobles requested lower state taxes and fewer state services, very few of them wanted any regulation of the money paid to them and the labour performed for them by their serfs, although, in this second case, a matter of internal rather than external policy, it is their silent acceptance of the existing situation rather than violent protest against it that indicates the majority view of the assemblies of the nobility.

Only a handful of instructions proposed any change at all in *obrok* payment or *barshchina* work. As far as *obrok* was concerned, the Vereia and Shatsk assemblies suggested that the rates be kept at a moderate level so that the serfs could avoid extreme poverty. The Iamburg nobility wanted to prohibit *obrok*, because of its deleterious effect on agriculture, for 'in the *obrok* villages there is neither reserve nor seed grain for either the landlords or the peasants'. The Rostov instruction stated that the prosperity of the church 'economic' peasants was in decline because of the *obrok* basis of their agriculture.[2] There was even less mention of *barshchina* than of *obrok* in the comments and proposals of the nobility. The Valuiki and Pustorzheva assemblies both considered that two days *barshchina* would be sufficient, agreeing that excessive impositions had contributed to peasant flight.[3] The other assemblies, by saying nothing on the subject of *obrok* or *barshchina*, did not admit their implication in serf flight or any other problem, and gave tacit support to the continuance of both systems on an unregulated basis.[4]

Much the same might be said of the attitude of the bulk of the nobility to the sale of serfs. Very few instructions mentioned the subject, although it had been the source of some controversy during recent years. A decree of 1766 had prohibited the sale of adult serfs

[1] Briullov, *VE*, I (1876), 61.
[2] Vereia, Moscow, *SIRIO*, IV, 371; Shatsk, Voronezh, LXVIII, 459; Iamburg, St Petersburg, XIV, 249; Rostov, Moscow, IV, 354–5.
[3] Valuiki, Belgorod, *SIRIO*, LXVIII, 582; Pustorzheva, Novgorod, XIV, 296.
[4] Semevskii, *Krest'iane*, I, 50, 66, points out that there were no official restrictions on *obrok* or *barshchina*.

for three months before a recruit levy, and the acceptance of purchased serfs as recruits.[1] The Smolensk electors wanted the 1766 law
rescinded to enable them to buy recruits to stop their serfs from
running away to Poland. The Vologda assembly sought the same
repeal, arguing that it would facilitate a firmer discipline in allowing
the landlords to sell the most stubborn and lazy of the serfs and to
retain the better souls among them. More generally, the Sudislavl'
instruction requested that permission be granted for the sale of whole
villages of serfs apart from the land, provided that the local district
officials gave their assent. On the other hand, there were a few
assemblies in favour of restrictions on serf sales. The Kineshma
nobility expressed approval, albeit qualified, of the law of 1766, the
Shliussel'burg electors wanted the local landlords to be restrained
from selling their household servants and peasants to Great Russia so
that the local economy would not be threatened. Similarly, the
Mihailov group pointed out that it was necessary to encourage farmers to stay put and to care for their land with more enthusiasm and
diligence, to conserve their woods, and to keep their whole economy
on a firm basis. Therefore, serfs should not be sold apart from the
land, at least not for export from their own district. Another assembly
from Tambov was concerned about how serfs should be sold after the
death of their masters.[2] Most instructions concerning the death of the
landlords were more interested in the welfare of their heirs than that
of their serfs, however.[3] This is a further illustration of the attitude
of the nobility as a whole to questions affecting the internal relations
of the class with their human property.

Serfdom, of course, overshadowed all other economic questions
discussed by the nobility in their instructions, agriculture, industry
and trade, and others. Nevertheless, some individual discussion of the
above questions is advisable, although, before this is attempted,
consideration must be given to the references made to serfdom at the
general assembly of the Legislative Commission by the deputies of the
nobility. These references fall into three main categories, the causes
of serf flight, the disadvantages of allowing commoners to possess

[1] *PSZ*, xvii, 997–1015, no. 12,748, 29 September 1766.
[2] Smolensk district, *SIRIO*, xiv, 421; Vologda, Archangel, xiv, 463–4; Sudislavl',
Moscow, iv, 285; Kineshma, Moscow, iv, 420; Shliussel'burg, St Petersburg, xiv, 246;
Mihailov, Moscow, iv, 276; Tambov, Voronezh, lxviii, 330.
[3] Sudislavl', Moscow, *SIRIO*, iv, 283; Maloiaroslavets, Moscow, iv, 326; Galich,
Archangel, xiv, 494; and Simbirsk, Kazan', lxviii, 7–8; and others.

serfs, and the advisability of freeing the serfs. Two preliminary points need to be made before examining these references. First, the deputies would not necessarily be reflecting the views of many of their fellow nobles, and their statements on the serf question are a less valuable indication of the thinking of the class as a whole than the instructions. Secondly, there is some evidence, although by no means conclusive, that Catherine was responsible for bringing up the question of serf freedom and for introducing into the Commission at least one of the two noble deputies who made most of the progressive remarks concerning serfdom, G. Korob'in and Ia. P. Kozel'skii. Once again, she may have been launching a trial balloon to test the reactions of the assembly to sentiments that she herself was too careful to utter.[1]

Entering the debate on serf flight on 5 May 1768, and answering a commoner's charge that serfs ran away because of the oppressions of the landlords, I. Vyrodov, representing the Belgorod nobility, maintained that the motives of the runaways stemmed rather from the burdens of state construction and transport duties, and their own negligence and idleness. P. Stepanov, the noble deputy from the Vereia district, echoed this last remark, adding drunkenness as a serf vice, although conceding that there were some cruel landlords who contributed to the defection of their serfs.

Speaking after Vyrodov and Stepanov, G. Korob'in, representing officially the Kozlov nobility and unofficially, perhaps, the Empress, set the cat among the pigeons by attributing the responsibility for serf flight largely to the landlords. Some of them, declared Korob'in, asked for more than the usual payments from their serfs; there were others who, having contracted considerable debts, took their peasants away from agriculture and home, and sent them off to work to repay the annual interest on their loans. A larger group of landlords than either of the first two seized the small surpluses that their serfs had been able to build up through hard work, and this practice constituted a considerable threat to the security not only of the landlords but of the whole state. Korob'in suggested that limits be placed on the power of the landlords; that the serfs be given some property rights, as suggested in the Instruction; and that fixed rates be arranged for serf payments to their lords.

---

[1] Brikner, *Istoriia*, v, 572; Miliukov, *Ocherki*, iii, 326. Both Brikner and Miliukov say that Korob'in was given the job of defending the draft of the Rights of the Nobles by Catherine.

The Legislative Commission and the economy

Korob'in's analysis of the serf flight problem, and his suggested remedy for it, were attacked by several deputies from the nobility. On 12 May 1768, A. Opochinin, representing the Uglich assembly, first of all exaggerated the arguments of Korob'in, and then went on to attack them. If the proprietors were to have nothing to do with the estates of their subordinates, and did not fully own their serfs, said Opochinin, the sole result would be hate between masters and subjects. If there were bad and depraved landlords, then a law introducing trusteeship of their estates would take care of them. No *obrok* village was ever ruined by the levies of its lord, but always by poor harvests and other accidents, claimed Opochinin. The relations between masters and serfs should remain on their former basis, he concluded. M. Kondyrov, the noble deputy from Zaraisk, also argued that the *status quo* be maintained. If limits were placed on the power of the landlords, he warned, abuses and ruin would result. Korob'in was young, reasoned the Oboian nobility's M. Glazov, he had not spent much time in the provinces, and was not fully acquainted with the rural economy. Several of the retorts to Korob'in were based on arguments first advanced before he had spoken, serf flight being again attributed by various deputies to 'depraved morals', 'idleness and negligence', and 'drunkenness'. A. Pohvisnev, representing the Kromy nobility, the deputy who attributed serf flight to drunkenness, went on to say that the serfs already had the right to surplus produce, and, if Korob'in were referring to immovable property, chaos would result from such a concession. As far as restrictions on the power of the landlords were concerned, the degree of freedom enjoyed by any people must correspond to the state of its morals, and the inferior morals of Russian tillers of the soil necessitated a strict supervision over them. Rather ironically, Pohvisnev declared that the restrictions suggested by Korob'in were insufficient to guard against the baseness of which the human soul was capable, and, therefore, trusteeship would be a more secure guarantee against evil landlords. After I. Zherebtsov, a soldier-farmer delegate from Nizhnii Novgorod, had praised Korob'in, arguing that the inordinate level of impositions, stemming from the luxurious living of the landlords and the insatiable greed of their stewards, was the main cause of peasant flight, Pohvisnev returned to the attack, indignation and imagination flaring. 'The Russian Empire is completely happy,' he declared, 'and is not only secure, but is terrible to its enemies, and fruitful—one does not hear (as in other European countries) of revolts, of riots caused by hunger...'[1]

Perhaps it was the patent falseness of this declaration that stirred Korob'in to speak again, although he actually concentrated on defending himself against the allegations of Glazov that he knew nothing of provincial life, and refuting some misrepresentations of his first speech. After Korob'in's second speech came the most important attack on his views, by Shcherbatov, and the most important defence and development of them. by Ia. P. Kozel'skii. Far be it from him, said Shcherbatov, speaking on 22 May 1768, to defend cruel and inhuman landlords, but they were by no means the sole cause of peasant flight. The size of the Russian Empire, including eight of the world's climates, forced many to seek the most suitable region to live in, and the varying quality of the land and its insufficient quantity in some areas had the same effect. The inconstancy and poor morals of the peasants also contributed to their mobility. If Korob'in were correct, asked Shcherbatov, and high taxes caused the peasants to run away, why did not all the peasants, instead of only some, desert their masters? He unwittingly answered this question to some extent himself, by saying that the situation varied from place to place, although the conclusion that he drew from this state of affairs was that it was impossible to fix general limits on taxes and services. Continuing his arguments, Shcherbatov asked, did Korob'in want his serfs to have immovable property? If so, where did he think it would come from? Would it not have to come from the landlords? Addressing himself to the deputies of the free rural inhabitants, and forgetting, perhaps, that most of them were not sympathetic to the plight of the serfs anyway, Shcherbatov declared:

Did our fathers, who had the honour to marshal their services against common enemies and to defend the Orthodox faith, aspire to receive rewards so that now their heirs would be compared to tyrants? Will such be your reward for the salvation of you and your souls?

Did they not realize that in receiving land they would be burdened with all kinds of lawsuits? It would be far better, Shcherbatov concluded, to leave things as they were, and have local government officials from the nobility keep their eyes open for abuses by the landlords.[2]

[1] *SIRIO*, xxxii, 53–5, 60–1, 65–6, 70–1, 77–80.   [2] *SIRIO*, xxxii, 83–5.

The Legislative Commission and the economy

Delivering his speech the day after Shcherbatov, Ia. P. Kozel'skii, the deputy of the nobility of the Dnepr Hussar Regiment from New Russia, and, possibly, like Korob'in, the emissary of Catherine, expressed the opinion that it was feasible to fix standards for *barshchina* and *obrok*, even when variations in climate and fertility had been taken into account. For the fertile areas remote from towns, Kozel'skii proposed a *barshchina* of two days work for the lord, two for the state, two for the serf himself, and a Sunday free from labour. In less fertile areas, and those nearer the capitals and other towns, where the commutative *obrok* predominated, Kozel'skii wanted to introduce a money rate comparable to the value of the energy expended on the *barshchina*, which he thought would entitle the lord to twenty kopecks a week from each serf, or ten roubles a year. Beyond these fixed service limits, and payment rates, Kozel'skii wanted the serfs to enjoy the right to guaranteed hereditary possession of movable and immovable property, with the reservations that they could not sell or mortgage immovable property without their lords' permission. Generally, Kozel'skii considered, the predicament of the serf could be compared to the situation of the industrious bee, which did not always work for itself, but looked on what it obtained as its own property, and defended it, and bit and stung for it, and even died, when a man or animal came up to its hive. If the peasant drank, it was not from laziness, but from depression caused by his realization that he possessed nothing.[1]

In the second subject of discussion concerning serfdom at the general assembly, the rights of commoners to serf possession, there was considerable repetition of arguments advanced in the instructions. Shcherbatov, as in many other debates, led the way in this, and the argument that he propounded on 15 October 1767 was perhaps the most explicit against serf possession by the chief non-noble aspirant to the right, the merchant class. The merchants, Shcherbatov pointed out, had argued that serf hire was an unsatisfactory means of acquiring labour, that hired workers were not as reliable as those who were owned by their masters. This appeared to Shcherbatov to be the same as arguing that somebody who did something involuntarily was more enthusiastic than somebody who applied himself to work through his own choice. Moreover, the whole of Europe showed that nobody could possess unfree men, and the merchants would therefore

[1] *SIRIO*, xxxii, 87–9.

have to hire their labour. (In Shcherbatov's view, it seems, Russian serfs were voluntarily tied to their landlords, if this is to understand him aright.) The state, as well as the merchants, would suffer from the latter's serf possession. At the time he spoke, Shcherbatov calculated that there were 17,000,000 Russians and 3,300,000 farmers in the Empire. Each farmer, then, had to produce for over five people. If the merchants were allowed to possess slaves, each farmer would have to feed more mouths, and Russia's food position would become more serious.[1]

The third question concerned with serfdom during the deliberations of the general assembly arose during the consideration of a rather mystifying section in the draft of the rights of the nobles, apparently stating that nobles could emancipate their villages if they so desired. Shcherbatov did not like this idea at all. To give somebody freedom, he said (17 September 1768), would be harmful to the general welfare, and would lead finally to the destruction of the state, and what was potentially injurious to the state was impossible for a noble to contemplate. The very name of freedom could be harmful for an unenlightened people, continued Shcherbatov. A proof of this, he considered, was that, just as heat was opposite to cold, so diversity was to uniformity. As soon as the chain legally binding the state together began to be destroyed, thoughts of freedom would be prompted. Before it was too late, and Russia embarked on a course of action that would be unalterable, Shcherbatov adjured his countrymen to recall the unhappy events of the Time of Troubles at the beginning of the seventeenth century.[2]

In reply to Shcherbatov, Korob'in said that, as soon as the authority for freeing villages was given, if it were observed that the freedom of a village were in any way harmful, the right could be curtailed. The name of freedom was by no means harmful. It could be an inducement to the peasants that would be useful for the state and for the landlords. The view of Shcherbatov was also attacked by L. Tatishchev of the Izium nobility, who commenced his speech with the bold, categorical assertion that it was the will of the Empress that the serfs be emancipated. This was too strong a statement for Marshal Bibikov to take, and he interrupted Tatishchev to observe that this was not the subject of the discussion, and that deputies had no power to talk about the desires of the Empress. Unabashed, Tatishchev went

[1] *SIRIO*, viii, 108–10.   [2] *SIRIO*, xxxvi, 26–7.

on to declare that it was the wish of Her Majesty to inculcate the idea of freedom into everybody, for which she must be praised. No harm would come to agriculture if the noble dealt with his peasants as subjects rather than as slaves. Finally, as an example of this point, Tatishchev cited England, which caused the Marshal again to break in, this time to remind the speaker that the subject for debate was the Russian situation, not the English. Returning to the offensive, Shcherbatov protested that he was not speaking for himself or his class, but for the good of the state, and went on to assert that the idea of freedom would be harmful to agriculture, because Russia was a northern state and a cold one, in which, consequently, it was necessary to force peasants to work. The state could not conduct the complete supervision of such a vast realm, and, therefore, the nobles carried out the supervision of the peasants in their possession. As far as England was concerned, it had to be made known that the freedom of that country had cost the blood of thousands and the misfortunes of many virtuous and just monarchs. Shcherbatov again referred to the Time of Troubles, which he thought had made clear the fact that what was advantageous to one country could be harmful for another.[1] For him, as for many of his peers, the introduction of freedom to Russia would be greatly to the national detriment.

While serfdom permeated all other economic questions discussed in connection with the Legislative Commission, these must be examined to some extent separately, in particular agriculture, industry, trade, communications and finance. Russian bias towards agriculture, it has been pointed out, was influenced both by ancient native tradition and contemporary, mainly foreign, theory. There is not much evidence of theoretical influence in the instructions of the nobility, except in some from the central Moscow province, into which the enlightened ideas of the Empress and her entourage would be most likely to have penetrated. The Dmitrov electors suggested that, at the end of their biennial election of a district marshal:

the nobility cannot find a more useful exercise for itself than to communicate generally their domestic provisions for the advantage of the rural economy. They can tell each other of their various experiments carried out in agriculture; of institutions to the rural benefit and successes achieved; they can encourage each other to develop agriculture and to

[1] *SIRIO*, xxxvi, 27–9.

Serfdom and the economy

set up more experiments of various kinds...and...they should agree on as much as possible, so that they may, in view of the general good and for correspondence to the maternal aspirations of the Most Gracious Sovereign, not refuse to sacrifice some time and effort on this.[1]

More briefly, the Kostroma assembly wanted landlords to discuss improvements in the rural economy and to make a record of them at their electoral meetings, and the Ruza landlords proposed that foreign colonists be introduced into the crown lands to give good examples of husbandry and household management to the local peasantry. Few such sentiments were uttered in other provinces, although, for example, the Opochka, Novgorod, instruction wanted a local 'guardian' to have among his many duties the collection of statistics on local production, including superfluities and dearths.[2]

At the general assembly Baron Ash, the deputy of the Medicine College, suggested that more potatoes should be grown where the soil was poor, and Baron F. Wolff of the Iamburg nobility argued that poor harvests resulted from the use of the harrow rather than the plough, but a more representative expression of the attitude of the class as a whole would probably be the remarks of I. Stepanov, from the Vereia district, that peasants were idle and stubborn and in need of closer supervision. The views of many rural inhabitants, including, no doubt, some landlords, are summarized by I. Chuprov, the deputy of an Archangel group of peasants, who observed that 'decrease and increase are under the authority of Almighty God'.[3]

Although there are few signs of science beginning to show the way and reason conquering all in those materials of the Legislative Commission concerning agriculture, the more down-to-earth traditional bias towards this aspect of the rural economy can readily be detected in the instructions of the nobility, and, while there was little abstract realization of how an improvement in agriculture could be achieved, three fairly widespread concrete requests would certainly tend to stimulate it. These were for the execution of a survey, the decentralization of the Estates College, and the institution of local grain stores.

A general survey had been announced in 1754, and again in 1765,[4] but it was apparent from the instructions that such a survey had not been widely carried out. Only one county from the central province,

[1] *SIRIO*, VIII, 505.   [2] *SIRIO*, IV, 249, 315; XIV, 273.
[3] *SIRIO*, IV, 76–7.
[4] *PSZ*, XIV, 104–61, no. 10,237, 13 May 1754; XVII, 329–39, no. 12,474, 19 September 1765.

126

Moscow, had been surveyed, said the Vladimir nobility, and there had been many arguments there as a consequence of this. The delay in the survey, the Senate instruction said, was due to these arguments, which were caused by the excessive subdivision of the estates. The Senate's view was that in order to expedite the survey, as well as to encourage the nobility to remain in service, this subdivision must be avoided. Several instructions from the nobility turned the Senate's argument upside down, asserting that the survey would help to eradicate the subdivision of the estates. The Serpuhov assembly requested that a detailed survey be carried out at the expense of joint owners to ensure that each received his share of land held in common with other landlords. The Arzamas nobility wanted the state survey to divide appendages among those landowners with rights to them, so that large landowners bent on improvements would not be impeded by small landowners, who restricted the attempts of their more progressive neighbours at wood conservation and mill construction. On the other hand, the Vereia instruction thought that a detailed state survey would help those poor landlords who could not afford lawsuits to protect their rights to land and various appurtenances, and the Venev electors were probably thinking along the same lines when they requested that those whom the survey revealed as expropriators of the lands of others be punished.[1] In order that arguments might be settled quickly, several instructions requested that survey records be kept locally, or that local officials, the *voevoda*, commissars elected by the nobility, or specially appointed surveyors, be put in charge of the survey.[2]

This tendency towards provincialization of state institutions was more marked in another widespread request of the instructions aimed, to some extent at least, at the improvement of agriculture, namely the decentralization of the Estates College. As the Kostroma electors pointed out, if land sales and mortgages and other affairs could be arranged without trips to Moscow or St Petersburg, expenses would be reduced and arrangements completed more quickly.

[1] The Senate's remarks, *SIRIO*, XLIII, 19. Vladimir, VIII, 549–51; Serpuhov, Moscow, IV, 364; Arzamas, Nizhnii Novgorod, LXVIII, 106–7; Vereia, Moscow, IV, 377–9; Venev, Moscow, IV, 342. See also, for example, Mihailov, Moscow, IV, 275–6; Shatsk, Voronezh, LXVIII, 458–9.

[2] For local preservation of survey records, Nizhnii Novgorod district, *SIRIO*, LXVIII, 100–2; Kurmysh, Nizhnii Novgorod, LXVIII, 122–3; Kaluga and Medyn', Moscow, IV, 293. For control by local officials, Mtsensk, Belgorod, LXVIII, 620; Kashin, Moscow, IV, 467–8.

Similar requests were made by many other assemblies from all quarters of the Russian Empire, some of them adding that records, if kept locally, would assist in the settlement and avoidance of disputes. Several assemblies asked for the construction of stone archives to ensure the preservation of these records.[1]

A third general request potentially conducive to an improvement in agriculture was for the institution of local grain stores. This was probably prompted less by the concern of the landlords for their peasants than by state legislation, for it had been decreed in 1761, and confirmed in 1767, that the landlords should arrange for the welfare of their peasants at times of poor harvest by setting up grain stores, or by purchasing grain, inevitably, of course, at high prices.[2] Thus, some assemblies argued that state stores were necessary since the noble landlords themselves suffered too much at times of poor harvest to worry about their serfs.[3] Generally, noble instructions proposed that the stores should be set up or subsidized by the state to distribute grain in times of scarcity to the landlords and their peasants, although there was considerable variation among them as to the operation of these stores. Suggestions were put forward that the stores be subject to the control of commissars from the nobility, that they cater for the army as well as for other civil classes, and that they assist in the arrangement of more equitable buying and selling. Only one assembly, from Zubtsov in Novgorod, seems to have wanted the nobility to carry out its statutory obligations, and pay for the stores itself, along with contributions from the peasantry. The Zubtsov assembly also maintained that, human weakness being what it was, it was too much to hope that the stores would be set up without compulsion.[4]

Apart from these three proposals, which came from all sections of the Russian Empire, concerning the survey, decentralization of the Estates College and grain stores, there were some others, to varying extents less widespread, in the instructions of the nobility tending

[1] Kostroma, Moscow, *SIRIO*, IV, 250–1. Similar, Iaroslavl', Moscow, IV, 305; Dorogobuzh, Smolensk, XIV, 437; Chuhloma, Archangel, XIV, 476–8; Karachev, Belgorod, LXVIII, 531–2; Ufa, Orenburg, XCIII, 10; Rzhev-Volodimirov, Novgorod, XIV, 282–5. For stone archives, Penza, Kazan', LXVIII, 20–1; Orel, Belgorod, LXVIII, 511–13.
[2] *PSZ*, xv, 648–9, no. 11,203, 14 February 1761; XVIII, 392, no. 13,017, 26 November 1767.
[3] For example, Mozhaisk, Moscow, *SIRIO*, VIII, 546; Pustorzheva, Novgorod, XIV, 307–8.
[4] See, for example, Bezhetsk, Moscow, *SIRIO*, IV, 384; Ustiuzhna, Novgorod, XIV, 322–3; Karachev, Belgorod, LXVIII, 531. For commissar control, Kashin, Moscow, IV, 463–5; for army provision, Shelonskaia Piatina, Novgorod, XIV, 345; for assistance in trade, Mtsensk, Belgorod, LXVIII, 619–20. Zubtsov, Novgorod, XIV, 316–17.

towards the improvement of agriculture. The one most generally put forward was for the conservation and protection of forests. Of course, in this and the other requests, the desire to protect the interests of the nobility was more obviously influential than any altruistic concern for the welfare or advancement of agriculture. Rather than talking of the necessity for forest conservation, the instructions of the nobility expressed the desire that the rights to forests of other orders of men be restricted. They asked that contractors should not receive advantages as far as forests were concerned, that government 'woodmasters' be kept out of them, and that military and naval tree-felling be restricted. The Bolhov electors wanted a local forest reserved for the Tula arms factory, which they had been obliged to guard at considerable expense, to be sold to them.[1]

A few assemblies from Moscow province wanted hunting on their land to be curtailed,[2] and others, mostly from Moscow, sought a change in the date for meadow closure.[3] However, the principal aim of the nobility connected with agriculture, as yet unmentioned, was the exclusive possession of land. This point has been examined during the discussion of serfdom, but there were other groups besides those wishing to own serfs with whom the nobility clashed over the question of land possession, and the nobility was naturally anxious to establish its dominance over these upstarts too. Thus, several Moscow assemblies wanted some free farmers to be sent off to Little Russia, Voronezh and Belgorod because of local land shortages: Little Russians, in their turn, were not happy in their land relations with the Cossacks, Voronezh landlords with theirs to the Tartars and free farmers, and Belgorod electors wanted the land of local free farmers to be transferred to the nobility because of local land confusion and shortage. Landlords from Orenburg thought that there was too much land at the disposal of the Cossacks and that surpluses should be sold to them themselves, and that Bashkirs and Tartars should be sent off elsewhere when their encroachments proved too irksome.[4]

[1] Obonezhskaia Piatina, Novgorod, *SIRIO*, xiv, 330; Arzamas, Nizhnii Novgorod, lxviii, 107; Penza, Kazan', lxviii, 16–17. Bolhov, Belgorod, lxviii, 500.

[2] Serpuhov, *SIRIO*, iv, 365; Romanov, viii, 457; Uglich, viii, 475–6; Aleksin, viii, 452.

[3] Kostroma, *SIRIO*, iv, 253; Romanov, viii, 455. Both from Moscow. See also Vologda, Archangel, xiv, 464–5.

[4] Venev, Moscow, *SIRIO*, iv, 342–3; Krapivna, Moscow, viii, 556; Nezhin and Baturin, Little Russia, lxviii, 137–8; Kasimov, Voronezh, lxviii, 447; Efremov, Voronezh, lxviii, 463–4; Karachev, Belgorod, lxviii, 529–30; Kursk, Belgorod, lxviii, 545–8; Orenburg district, xciii, 4–6; Ufa, Orenburg, xciii, 8–10.

Serfdom and the economy

The nobility's desire for dominance in land possession was equally to be found in areas where land was scarce, and where it was in plentiful supply. In the central regions of the Russian Empire, where land was scarce, the nobility sought permission to buy land in the steppe, and from the recently nationalized monastic lands. In Voronezh and Orenburg, where there was a plentiful supply, the landlords wanted to be allowed to buy surpluses cheaply, and, as just indicated, to have the land for themselves rather than letting it go to Cossacks, Bashkirs and Tartars. The New Russian nobility also requested that land surpluses be sold to them.[1]

At the sessions of the general assembly of the Legislative Commission, several deputies spoke of the need for reservation of the rights of land possession to the nobility. Noble representatives from Central Russia, from Orenburg, from Slobodsko-Ukraina, from Little Russia and the Baltic provinces all declared that it was necessary to stop members of other classes from trespassing on this preserve of the nobility.[2]

Many of the other remarks made by deputies at the general assembly echoed points made by the instructions concerning division of estates, forest conservation, hunting and fishing rights, and grain stores, for example. There were, however, a few new ideas. Outstanding among these was perhaps Kozel'skii's proposal for a government department of agriculture. This department, thought Kozel'skii, should be given annual information by each landlord on how much cereal had been sown and harvested, and the information could be used for the benefit of the state, the landlords and the peasants alike.[3]

Like the Empress, the government departments considered that agriculture was Russia's most important economic pursuit, the Senate's view in deciding which branches of industry were most

[1] Zaraisk, Moscow, *SIRIO*, IV, 346; Krapivna, Moscow, VIII, 559; Verhnii Lomov, Voronezh, LXVIII, 434–5; Elizavetgrad Hussar Regiment Officers, New Russia, XCIII, 28.
[2] See, for example, *SIRIO*, IV, 209–10, where I. Ignat'ev, the deputy from the Rzhev-Volodimirov district of Novgorod, argued that all those who had reached the appropriate civil rank should be forbidden to purchase land if they had not definitely been made nobles; XXXII, 79, where E. Tihanovskii, of the Ufa, Orenburg, nobility, requested that his local assembly's land possessions be kept secure from the encroachments of the Bashkirs, Chuvashes and other tribesmen; VIII, 296, where A. Kondrat'ev, representing the Sumy, Slobodsko-Ukraina, district, defended his electors against the pretensions of the Cossacks; XXXII, 314, where G. Poletika, from Lubny, Little Russia, requested the confirmation of the land rights of the Ukrainian nobility; and VIII, 348–9, where A. Vil'boa, of the Estinskoe *rytsarstvo*, Livonia, made the same request on behalf of his peers in the Baltic provinces.   [3] *SIRIO*, XXXII, 88.

worthy of encouragement being that an evaluation of the relative impact of their development on agriculture should be of the greatest weight.[1] The College of Manufactures agreed with the Senate that agriculture was of paramount importance in the economy, although its instruction also claimed that manufactures were indispensable in the simplest rural life, that the middle section of the state's inhabitants had a need for more manufactures, and that the nobility required them to an even greater extent. Moreover, claimed this college, the army and navy could not continue without manufactures, and towns and trade could not develop. Continuing its examination of that sphere of the economy under its jurisdiction, the College of Manufactures went on to give a general consideration to the question of manufacturing development in Russia. Peter the Great, the College thought, must be given credit for having given the first real impetus to the growth of industry, but, because the needs of the state had been pressing in his time, it had been necessary for him to disregard the confusion and inconsistency of some aspects of this development. So, just as Peter was responsible for the commencement of manufacturing, it would be the task of Catherine II to eradicate abuses, establish order, and reconcile all branches of industry to one general aim. The abolition of monopolies was necessary, so was a change in the attitude of the merchant class, and the nobility, too, had to be called to order. During the reign of Peter the Great, all and sundry had been granted the right to set up factories in an effort to accelerate industrialization, and nobles in particular had been sent abroad to learn applicable techniques. But the noble manufacturers, however useful in their day, had produced confusion in service and ranks that had wrought a great deal of harm. Only now, under the wise and firm Empress, could this fault be corrected. Progress could be certain if each class stuck to its job, and did not try to encroach on that of another class.[2]

The instructions of the College of Mines and the Commerce College, the other government departments principally concerned with Russia's industrial development, were briefer and vaguer than that of the College of Manufactures, and add very little to our knowledge of official thinking on this question. However, the deputy of the Commerce College, S. Mezheninov, had some interesting remarks to make at the General Assembly on 3 October 1767. He said, for

[1] *SIRIO*, XLIII, 14.   [2] *SIRIO*, XLIII, 206–10.

instance, that he thought that the argument about whether or not industry should be developed by the merchant class or the nobility was rather lame. He declared:

Let everybody seek their own advantage, there is no shame in this for anybody. Only would that they did not interfere with each other. It would be best of all if the nobles set up such factories as did not already exist in Russia; but our Russian people is in this case similar to birds, which, finding a piece of bread, snatch it from one another until, crumbling it into the smallest fragments, mix them up with dust or earth and completely lose them.

Mezheninov went on to describe how the nobility had been particularly at fault in the past. Some twenty or so years ago, he claimed, seeing the great profits accruing from the manufacture of sailcloth, and not realizing that many factories had been built for this purpose already, the nobility had set up many more, creating a glut and not spotting its mistake until too late. It was not advisable, thought Mezheninov, to allow nobles to construct factories and works, lest they ruin themselves and other industrialists by their immoderate production, and desert agriculture, which was more necessary than any factory. Russia already had enough ironworks. Why add more when there were already sufficient, so that their descendants would have to use straw rather than timber as a fuel? Glassworks, like ironworks, used up a great deal of wood, and the crockery and bottles produced by them were not found in the homes of the aristocrats or even of the middle class, but in the huts of the lower orders, in which wooden or earthenware containers could suffice as they always had done. So glassworks were dispensable. And was it a good thing to set up factories for which Russia had no raw materials, such as sugar factories and the like? For a pie could not be called your own, if you bought wheat at a market, ground it at somebody else's mill, asked for yeast from your neighbour, and engaged another person's cook to do your baking for you.[1] Mezheninov, then, seemed to share the contemporary inclination towards agriculture and away from general development of industry, particularly by the nobility, and the outlook of the College of Manufactures was broadly similar to his.

Several of the noble instructions agreed that unrestricted industrial development was most inadvisable, and, like Mezheninov, they showed a particular interest in timber conservation. Quite a few of

[1] *SIRIO*, VIII, 50–2.

the assemblies in the central industrial region complained about the exhaustion of local wood supplies. The Iaroslavl' electors were disturbed by the shortage of building timber in their locality, and requested that none be used for factory construction in the future; the landlords of Kaluga and Medyn' wanted a similar ban introduced, particularly near the capitals; and the Tula district asked that all factories within 200 versts of Moscow be destroyed. Most detailed in its plaint was the Aleksin instruction, which lamented the fact that there were thirty factories in the neighbourhood, all at a short distance from each other and from Moscow. These factories used up so much wood that it was scarce and high-priced, and the peasants could not afford to buy any, and consequently lived in very poor conditions. The local Gzhatskaia Wharf could not be maintained properly because of the lack of timber, communications with the capital might be affected, and grain prices there might shoot up. The Aleksin nobles requested that the factories be moved off to Siberia, or, as their Tula peers had asked, that such establishments at least be banned within a 200 verst radius of Moscow.[1] In other parts of the Empire, the Voronezh assembly, echoing a point made by Mezheninov, thought that iron and glass factories should be prohibited in their district and local needs supplied by Siberian works, and the Usman' instruction also sought a prohibition of local factories, arguing that they used up timber supplies without any advantage accruing to the landowners.[2]

For all these requests that factories be banished from certain areas, only one noble instruction appears to have concurred with the view of the College of Manufactures and Mezheninov that the industrial activities of the nobility should be curtailed. This was the Shuia instruction, which wanted the nobles not to own factories, and the middle class not to possess villages, with the labour requirements of the latter being satisfied by serfs with temporary passports. Most assemblies considering the question, who should be allowed to have factories, claimed that right for the nobility. The Viaz'ma landlords said that they should certainly be allowed factories, while the mer-

---

[1] *SIRIO*, IV, 312, 292–3, 407–8; VIII, 540–1. All from Moscow. Metalworks had been forbidden within a 200 verst radius of Moscow by decrees of 1753 and 1754, but with the consequent decline of the metal industry, the decrees were rescinded. See A. I. Baranovich, etc. (eds.), *Ocherki istorii SSSR, Period feodalizma, Rossiia vo vtoroi polovine XVIII v.*, p. 104. The Gzhatskaia Wharf was an important transit centre for the grain trade. See *ibid.* p. 30.

[2] Voronezh district, *SIRIO*, LXVIII, 357; Usman', Voronezh, LXVIII, 370–1.

chants should equally definitely be forbidden villages. The Ustiuzhna electors asked that, if landlords found ore or minerals on their estates, they be permitted to exploit them without seeking the assent of the College of Mines. Similarly, the nobles of Serpuhov, Tarusa and Obolensk wished to start factories without petitioning the College of Manufactures or Mines, and to sell their products wherever they liked. Finally, the Pskov district complained that many nobles freed from service had no means of making a living, and therefore needed the right to set up factories. Incidentally, the Pskov lords revealed the degree of their spirit of enterprise by requesting the state to establish flax factories in their neighbourhood, so that peasants could be employed, and foreign merchants be prevented from exploiting them.[1]

Evidence of their rivalry with merchant industrialists, as well as of their desire for governmental decentralization, can be seen in the requests of several assemblies of nobles that departments of the Colleges of Mines and Manufactures be introduced into the provinces. The principal motive for these petitions was the reluctance of the landlords to go to the central Colleges to seek redress for their grievances against middle-class factory owners. The Serpeisk electors wanted such industrialists to be tried locally for concealment of runaway serfs, illegal felling of trees, and encroachments on the lands of others; and another Moscow district, Pronsk, wanted to be able to get their runaway serfs back from the industrialists without having to go to the capitals.[2] Other requests for the decentralization of the Colleges of Mines and Manufactures to allow local trials of bourgeois factory owners came from nobles in the provinces of Voronezh and Belgorod.[3]

At the general assembly of the Legislative Commission, several deputies from the nobility examined the question considered in some instructions, who should own factories? Just as only one instruction from the class seems to have considered that it should be expressly forbidden factory ownership, so only one noble deputy appears to have thought similarly on the subject. This was F. Iazikov, representing the Rostov district, who, like some government departments and, albeit in a different context, most of his peers, wanted all classes to keep to their individual functions, and thought that factory pos-

---

[1] Shuia, Moscow, *SIRIO*, IV, 395–6; Viaz'ma, Smolensk, XIV, 452; Ustiuzhna, Novgorod, XIV, 323; Serpuhov, Tarusa and Obolensk, Moscow, IV, 363; Pskov, Novgorod, XIV, 375–6, 392.　　[2] *SIRIO*, VIII, 513; IV, 387.

[3] Voronezh district, *SIRIO*, LXVIII, 362–3; Kerensk, LXVIII, 438–9; Shatsk, LXVIII, 457–8. All from Voronezh. Belev, Belgorod, LXVIII, 613–14.

session by the nobility was deleterious to the common good, since noble industrialists used their own serfs rather than hired labourers, and worried about their factories rather than about agriculture. Commenting on this opinion, O. Kozhin, from the Kashin assembly, conceded that there was something in Iazikov's argument, and proposed that only *retired* nobles manage factories. If this were decided upon, serfs could be kept busy in the winter, theft would be reduced, and many other beneficial consequences would follow.[1]

Kozhin's moderate suggestion was not enough for some deputies. At the opposite end of the range of opinion to him and Iazikov was Prince Shcherbatov, who, speaking on 8 October 1767, argued very positively in favour of the nobility's right to full participation in Russia's industry. As far as metalworks were concerned, declared Shcherbatov, the ores, which were the reason for their existence, were to be found in the ground, which, in turn, was the property of the nobility alone. In like manner, the timber that was a prerequisite for smelting was one of the other fruits of this monopolistic possession. Other types of factory could easily be set up by the landlords, since they processed raw materials produced on the estates. If nobles maintained factories, they would contribute to the prosperity of agriculture by increasing the demand for the necessary raw materials, and would also keep the serfs occupied at all times of the year, while a monopoly of industry by the merchants would harm agriculture and could not result in such a firm control of the serfs. Shcherbatov refused to consider that the industrial rights of the mainstay of autocracy might be reduced. 'God keep me even from thinking', he exclaimed, 'that at such a time, when goodness and justice reign on the throne, the nobility, instead of acquiring certain rights, might lose some of them.' Shcherbatov would rather contemplate the rosy future bound to follow on the acceptance of his proposals. The landlords with their own factories on their estates, would produce for the wholesale market in the winter only, and would concentrate on agriculture in the summer. Acquiring money for their manufactured goods, they would buy more cattle. Having more horses, they could farm more intensively, and their cultivated produce would become more abundant as their ploughing profited from their industry.[2]

The other important industrial question aired by noble deputies at the general assembly was peasant manufacturing, which had recently

---

[1] *SIRIO*, IV, 163–4, 191–2.   [2] *SIRIO*, VIII, 58–63.

been growing in size and importance. Here, the dvorianstvo was on the defensive, protecting the activities of its serfs from the attacks of the middle class. Some merchants demanded that the peasant handicraft industry be completely prohibited, and that all craftsmen be enrolled in town guilds on a permanent basis. A reply to this demand that met with the approval of over twenty noble deputies was given by M. Retkin, representing the Pereiaslavl'-Riazan district. In the first place, argued Retkin, agriculture would suffer if the basic crafts were removed from the countryside and concentrated in towns alone. The farmer would be obliged to leave his work and go to towns, hundreds of versts from home, for nothing more than to get his plough or wheels repaired. On the other hand, the bourgeois craftsmen would not be able to carry out all the necessary work by themselves. They could not even provide a sufficient number of stonemasons and carpenters for the capitals. It was indisputable that enthusiasm for handicrafts must be aroused, as indicated by the Empress in many parts of the Instruction, but it should also be borne in mind that each incentive to the craftsmen should not cause any constriction on members of other classes. Experience had shown that many nobles were prepared to spend considerable sums of money on the education of their serfs, improving many crafts to the desirable quality. What justice would there be if these craftsmen were taken from their masters and enrolled in urban guilds? Moreover, the laws must comply with the climate of each country. Therefore, in Russia, where the ground was covered with snow for more than six months each year, leaving the people idle, it was necessary to use this time for peasant handicraft work, so that they would not become accustomed to unemployment. Apart from this, it could be said that the Russian army benefited from peasant handicrafts, since, when peasants became recruits, they were already trained in certain useful skills. Retkin did not deny that guilds had their uses, but considered that the basic trades should be permitted to the peasants, without them joining the guilds but without excluding other classes from the trades. Other crafts, too, should be open to everybody, but those who wanted to practise them on a commercial basis should be obliged to join the guilds. Craftsmen should not be taken from their lords, but if a landowner taught his serf a trade and did not allow him to join a guild, then this worker should be able to work for his master only.[1]

[1] *SIRIO*, IV, 126–7.

Before examining the attitude of the nobility to trade, I shall comment briefly on the other sides to the questions of manufacturing and trade, in particular the merchant class attitudes to them. Some of the merchants argued in a similar manner to many nobles and government departments that all classes should keep to their own spheres of activity, the merchants, however, often interpreting this argument to imply, as did A. Bekishev of Tara town, that the merchants should have the exclusive right to own factories. In greater detail, A. Popov, representing the burghers of the Rybnaia Sloboda, complained that the nobility had been given emancipation and special protection, and now invaded the rights of the bourgeoisie to factory ownership and trade, neither of which should be allowed it. The merchant class should have the permanent right to the exclusive ownership of works and factories, and to the purchase of the necessary land and serfs, it should be permitted to keep distilleries and to own shops and inns in the towns without paying state *obrok* on them. As for the peasants, they should be prohibited from trespassing on the bourgeoisie's trading activities and could sell their surpluses wholesale at a reasonable price to the merchants. The consequences of peasants taking up trade were darkly painted by Popov, who asserted:

Now in Russia many farmers completely leave agriculture and enter trading affairs, instead of resigning themselves to their lot and developing agriculture, from which...advantages accrue to the whole of society and income to the state. Because of their ignorance of the subtlety of commercial relations many of these farmers trade themselves out of business and into bankruptcy, without paying the merchants the money for the goods which they have obtained from them, and hiding themselves away from the towns but without resuming agriculture. The evil results from this that the farmers remaining in the villages where the said tradesmen were inscribed in the census, pay their poll tax and *obrok* for them, and because of this decline into poverty.

The peasants should not be denied the right to sell their products in the towns and villages, continued Popov, but the sales must be retail, at moderate prices, and of the seller's own cultivation. He was also in favour of the extension and strict enforcement of guild membership, and argued that, if nobles joined guilds, they should receive no special privileges.[1]

The question of peasant trade was discussed in some depth by the general assembly of the Legislative Commission from the end of

---

[1] *SIRIO*, viii, 48, 42–3.

September to the end of November 1767, during a consideration of the rights of the merchant class. In this case, the merchants were the plaintiffs, charging that the peasants were encroaching on their preserves, and a few members of the nobility acted as counsel for the defence. Several of his fellows went further than Popov and wanted all peasant produce to be sold to them, denying the peasants even the right to sell their grains or vegetables locally on a retail basis. The peasants' rejoinders to these demands varied as did the demands themselves. Some protested that the towns were so remote from the villages that the costs of the journeys from one to the other and back again were not covered by the sales of their surpluses to the merchants. The merchants claimed that they or their assistants went round the villages buying up the surpluses of the peasant farmers: the latter counter-claimed that this happened rarely, at the wrong time, or not at all. The peasants also pointed out that they needed money at particular times of the year, when, for example, they had to pay state taxes or other dues. The necessary cash could be raised only on the spot in many cases, and the merchants took advantage of the peasants' predicament, also offering very low prices to the peasants in the towns when they knew that the villagers would not want to return home without a sale. All these arguments by the peasants concealed the fact that there was a growing number of entrepreneurs from their class whose development constituted a real threat to the prosperity of the merchant class. Peasant trade of any description, by the free groups represented in the commission or the serfs, did not worry the bulk of the nobility, which was inclined to plead for the rural inhabitants rather than for those of the towns.[1]

The acerbity of the debate on peasant trade reached a climax on 30 October 1767, when A. Blaznov, from the town of Vologda, declared that the peasants, forgetting the fear of God and the laws of the state, were trading like actual merchants and had dared to cause commerce to be undermined, the predicament of the legitimate merchants reaching such a point that they had been forced to go away to other countries. Making one of his rare interventions into the proceedings of the general assembly, Marshal Bibikov said that he found Blaznov's last remark shameful, that no such assertion could be made about *all* merchants, that it was not possible for *all* of them to leave the country without their supervisory bodies noticing the drift

---

[1] *SIRIO*, VIII, xxiii–xxvi, from the foreword by D. Polenov.

and stopping it. The general pitch of the debate seldom reached such a shrill tone as this, the nobles in particular being moderate in their approach, probably because their vital interests were not directly affected here. Thus, while E. Ofrosimov of the Livny district described the evils resulting from the merchants' monopoly of trade in an unequivocal manner, Iu. Lermontov, representing the Galich assembly, conceded that much harm was done the merchant class by peasant trade in expensive articles of non-handicraft manufacture such as silks and brocades, and that something should be done to restrict this type of commerce. Similarly, during later discussions on the rights of the nobles, while it emerged that there were several nobles in favour of wide trading rights for their class, a few of them suggested various limits on noble activity in this field.[1]

A small number of statements advocating trade rights for the peasants and the nobles were to be found in the instructions of the dvorianstvo. The Mihailov assembly requested that both serfs and masters be allowed to sell both wholesale and retail all day long in all towns, although it thought that the merchants should continue to manage internal and external trade as a whole. While the Shuia electors wanted the serfs to be allowed to traffic in cloth and food-stuffs, the Romanov dvoriane sought an extension in the selling rights of all provincial inhabitants, and the Pskov landowners considered it desirable that everybody have freedom of disposal for his products so that merchants would not have unfair advantages. Other proposals came from the Iaroslavl' district, which was in favour of restrictions on the rights of the merchant class, and from the Kashin assembly, which thought that trade in all commodities should be the monopoly of their growers or manufacturers, and that, in addition, the landlords should be allowed to trade in salt in their own villages.[2]

As far as foreign trade was concerned, the government departments were not happy with the situation. The Senate said, 'it is indisputable that commerce here is still in a poor state', and wanted the merchant class to be given a better education, more credit facilities, and improved rates of exchange. The College of Manufactures, while noting with approval that goods to the value of 881,000 roubles

---

[1] *SIRIO*, vIII, 185, 231–4; 328; xxxII, 262–8. The patent foolishness of Bibikov's remarks is a further indication of his inadequacy for the job of Marshal.

[2] Mihailov, *SIRIO*, IV, 274; Shuia, IV, 392–3; Romanov, vIII, 455–6; Iaroslavl', IV, 301–2; Kashin, IV, 465. All from Moscow. Pskov, Novgorod, xIV, 391–2, 375–6.

of the annual production estimated at a total of 2,790,000 roubles were exported, said that a greater proportion of industrial products should be sold abroad.[1] The instructions of the nobility showed little desire for participation in Russia's export drive: indeed, the instructions that mentioned exports were against them. The Krapivna electors complained that the prices of iron, tallow and leather had risen because of exports, which, they thought, should be restricted in the above commodities and completely forbidden in the cases of grain and timber because of local shortages. The Ostrov assembly requested a ban on timber exports because of a wood dearth in its district, and the Pskov landowners were also in favour of such a ban. One instruction at least revealed a similarly negative attitude towards imports, the Estinskii district wanting them to be generally discouraged, and either forbidden or heavily taxed in the specific case of malt. Little more awareness of the necessity of a thriving foreign trade was demonstrated at the general assembly by the deputies of the nobility, although Shcherbatov at least spoke out strongly on the subject. Shcherbatov thought that the merchants complained too much of competition in internal trade, while they were neglectful of foreign trade. Let them look outward, he declared, 'There are the true keys to the wealth of the merchants! Let them turn to them, and then they will see that the real advantages of society are linked with their prosperity'. Shcherbatov also said that the nobles would assist the merchants by selling them their products for export, although the goods would be sold to foreigners if the Russian merchants did not offer a just price for them.[2]

To establish an opinion of the attitude of the noble class as a whole towards the important question of trade, an interpretation has to be made of the silence of most of the instructions and deputies on this subject. As in several other cases, silence probably meant apathy, and an inability to look beyond the most selfish needs of a backward feudal economy. Their reticence on the topic of trade makes a strange contrast with the relative verbosity of the nobility on the problem of alcoholic liquor, which was perhaps more widely discussed in the instructions than any other and often given particular emphasis. For example, the nobles meeting at Kadyi lamented the fact that

[1] *SIRIO*, XLIII, 16–17, 208.
[2] Krapivna, Moscow, *SIRIO*, VIII, 557–8; Ostrov, Novgorod, XIV, 278; Pskov, Novgorod, XIV, 394–5; Estinskii district, Livonia, LXVIII, 73. Shcherbatov, VIII, 65, 138.

they could not have any home-produced alcoholic drinks with them, and had therefore been compelled to buy them from the local drinking houses. The liquor that they had purchased had a disgusting aroma, they claimed, and therefore they requested a revision of the law of 1765 which had guaranteed the nobility a monopoly of private distillation but forbidden landlords to have this process carried on in their absence, or to transport the end product to the towns even for their own consumption. Apart from this request, and one or two others of an even less significant nature, the Kadyi dvoriane thought that a consideration of more general questions was best left to their deputy.[1]

No other assembly gave the drink question as much of its attention as did that meeting at Kadyi, but a great number of them from all quarters of the Russian Empire had something to say on the subject, advancing a considerable range of arguments for changes in the 1765 law. If it were not amended, poverty would result for the nobility, and agriculture and cattle-raising would suffer, it was claimed. If the suggested changes were made in the law, bootlegging and brigandage would be reduced and the state's income would be much larger.[2] The nobles generally wanted to be allowed unrestricted manufacture of alcoholic liquors on their estates, whether they were living on them or not, and a free right of transport of these commodities to the towns for their own use.[3] There was a less widespread proposal that the nobility be given wide rights to trade in drink, the Krapivna electors, for example, wanting this trade to be taken from the lease-holders and given to retired officers.[4] Shcherbatov echoed this idea to some extent in one of the few references to the drink question at the general assembly.[5]

Two related sets of topics have still to be dealt with in this survey of the principal economic questions discussed by the instructions and deputies of the nobility: communications and transport; and finance and taxes. Communications and transport have already been mentioned to some extent during the examination of the serf problem, the nobles' attitude to them being that the state's requisitions of serf

---

[1] Kadyi, Moscow, *SIRIO*, IV, 351.

[2] See, for example, Vereia, Moscow, *SIRIO*, IV, 381–2; Shliussel'burg, St Petersburg, XIV, 245–6; Krapivna, Moscow, VIII, 559–60.

[3] See, for example, Shuia, Moscow, *SIRIO*, IV, 396; Tula, Moscow, IV, 409; Priluki, Little Russia, LXVIII, 228.

[4] Krapivna, Moscow, *SIRIO*, VIII, 559–60.   [5] *SIRIO*, XXXII, 310.

labour for construction and repair of communications and of serf horses and carts for transport purposes were too onerous. Suggestions were therefore made that the state should pay for the necessary labour, horses and carts out of its own revenues or by a special tax, or that it should distribute its requisitions more equitably among all residents of the relevant districts.[1] There was no denial of the necessity for state communications and transport on the part of the nobility, but, on the other hand, no widespread realization of their great importance.

While the noble deputies showed little more awareness of the significance of the communications and transport problem, the government departments, too, of whom more might have been expected, were not very conscious of it. The Senate said that roads were in a terrible condition and that water communications needed improvement, but had nothing to offer in amelioration of either predicament. The Post-Chancellery thought that the work and wages of its charges should be regulated, and that they should be given some of the recently nationalized church lands, and the State Road Construction Chancellery wanted hired labour to replace the former requisition system, but none of these proposals went very far towards the solution of the problem as a whole.[2]

Much the same might be said of the statements by the government departments concerning the Empire's finances. The Senate considered that the sources and collecting methods for the state's revenues needed to be better organized, since 'the state returns are so confused and mixed up that it has hardly yet been possible to find out about their actual names', but, once again, it put forward no idea about how this rationalization could actually be achieved. The Finance College, for its part, confessed that its accounts were 6,000,000 roubles in arrears and that 96,000 matters were still awaiting its decision. Not surprisingly, perhaps, in such circumstances as these, it did not know how to clear up the mess.[3]

Far from showing any interest in the welfare of the state's finances, the nobles in their instructions were more concerned about the reduction of their contributions to them. Three sources of state *obrok* to which they were liable for payment came under their particular fire.

---

[1] For state support, Opochka, Novgorod, *SIRIO*, xiv, 269; for special tax, Roslavl', Smolensk, xiv, 426–7; for more equitable distribution of requisitions, Uglich, Moscow, viii, 473–4.

[2] *SIRIO*, xliii, 8, 363–70, 390–3. [3] *SIRIO*, xliii, 9, 148.

These were levies on baths, fishing and mills. The Mihailov assembly was opposed to paying all three of them, the Serpeisk electors were against the first and second, and the Nizhnii Novgorod landlords took particular exception to the second and third. Three Novgorod districts disliked the bath tax specifically, as did Bezhetsk and Uglich. Kolomna was against paying *obrok* for fishing in ponds which froze or dried up, and Vereia did not want to pay for disused mills.[1] To help themselves and their peasants, several assemblies desired a cut in the current price for salt, which they thought was too high at forty kopecks a pound, and a few suggested the replacement of the poll tax by something which they could consider more equitable.[2] It would also help them and their peasants, some of the nobility claimed, if prices were regulated. The Bezhetsk assembly wanted a noble commissar to work with the *voevoda* to try to establish fair grain prices, the Shuia electors wanted the state to set legal limits on the price of cereals and other foodstuffs, and the Tula landlords wanted monthly victual price limits to be set by the state.[3] Connected with this request was a common suggestion for regulation of weights and measures.[4] At the general assembly, during the discussion of the draft Rights of the Nobles, several noble deputies were insistent that no tax ever was or could be levied on them, and others subscribed to the proposals for price, weight and measure control.[5]

At the same time that they sought the restriction of levies, taxes and prices, the nobles were interested in the extension of credit facilities for their class. Instructions from all quarters of the Empire, from Moscow, Smolensk, Archangel, Kazan', Belgorod and Little Russia, wanted banks to be set up for this purpose in the provinces.[6] There were suggestions that these banks should cater for loans smaller than the 100 rouble minimum set by the central Nobility Bank, that

[1] Mihailov, Moscow, *SIRIO*, IV, 274–5; Serpeisk, Moscow, VIII, 516; Nizhnii Novgorod district, LXVIII, 102–3; Obonezhskaia Piatina, Shelonskaia Piatina, Bezhetskaia Piatina, Novgorod, XIV, 335, 346, 358; Bezhetsk, Moscow, IV, 385; Uglich, Moscow, VIII, 474; Kolomna, Moscow, IV, 338; Vereia, Moscow, IV, 368.

[2] For lower salt price, Kolomna, *SIRIO*, IV, 338; Gorohovets, VIII, 460; Krapivna, VIII, 557. All from Moscow. For poll tax replacement, Klin, Moscow, *SIRIO*, IV, 264–5; Venev, Moscow, IV, 344.

[3] Bezhetsk, Moscow, *SIRIO*, IV, 383; Shuia, Moscow, IV, 395; Tula, Moscow, IV, 409.

[4] See, for example, Kostroma, Moscow, *SIRIO*, IV, 246; Penza, Kazan', LXVIII, 17–18; Novosil', Belgorod, LXVIII, 491.

[5] See, for example, *SIRIO*, XXXII, 223.

[6] Kashira, Moscow, *SIRIO*, VIII, 486; Smolensk district, XIV, 422; Vologda, Archangel, XIV, 461–2; Kazan' district, LXVIII, 32; Orel, Belgorod, LXVIII, 526–7; Pereiaslavl', Little Russia, LXVIII, 154.

profits from them should go towards the upkeep of local schools, and that they should particularly help those poor nobles in danger of losing their estates through poverty.[1]

The bank question was examined in considerable depth at the general assembly by G. Brovtsyn of the Trubchev district, who argued that, since banking arrangements as they stood tended to be to the disadvantage of the poorer nobles, separate arrangements should be made for their loans and separate sums reserved for them only to draw on. Iu. Lermontov, from Galich, supported by V. Katenin, from Chuhloma, thought that state banks were insufficient for the needs of his class, and wanted private banks to be set up as well.[2] Another financial question discussed at some length by the deputies of the nobility was that of the arrangements for bills of exchange. Here, as throughout their scrutiny of the various aspects of the national economy, the nobles revealed a marked class interest and a desire for the provincialization of government departments.[3]

[1] Dmitrov, Moscow, *SIRIO*, VIII, 510; Chernigov, Little Russia, LXVIII, 244; Starodub, Little Russsia, LXVIII, 199–200.

[2] *SIRIO*, IV, 202–3.

[3] *SIRIO*, VIII, 234–5, 243, 256–7, 285–9, 306, 325.

4

SOCIAL AND POLITICAL ATTITUDES

QUALIFICATIONS FOR NOBILITY

Who was a dvorianin? If anybody definitely knew the answer to this important question in 1767, it should have been the Heraldmaster. But his office confessed in its instruction that it was not certain what the qualifications for dvorianstvo were. On 5 February 1722, about two weeks after the publication of the Table of Ranks, the instruction pointed out, the order had been given that information concerning all Russian nobles should be sent to the Heraldmaster,[1] but, it went on to say, 'up to now accurate information on nobles and their children, in service and retired, also deceased and newly born, has still not been received from all regions'. Particularly, the office possessed no records concerning the Ukraine, Smolensk, Livonia, Estonia and Finland, and foreign nobles in Russian service. Therefore, the instruction lamented, 'a genealogical register of dvoriane, in which all families of Russian nobles would be inscribed, is not at the Heraldmaster's Office'. Moreover, apart from the lack of information, a further impediment to the compilation of a genealogical record was the doubt concerning the qualifications for dvorianstvo. Was this to be proved by service rank, possession of an estate, or both? A more definite ruling was required, the Heraldmaster's Office considered, about the status of those who had received commissioned rank in the army and secretaryship in the civil service.[2]

The Senate, Russia's premier judicial and administrative body, was in a state of doubt similar to that of the Heraldmaster's Office. Since there had not been an exact regulation of the membership of the dvorianstvo, the Senate said in its instruction, many people of various kinds, including some from the low commonalty, had slipped into the nobility on several occasions through their own temerity and under various guises, and had not only taken advantage of this, but sometimes also taken precedence of genuine dvoriane. Thus, some had lost their ambition, and others expected good fortune to come to them, not through their qualities and service, but by impudence. To

---

[1] *PSZ*, vi, 497–9, no. 3896, 5 February 1722.   [2] *SIRIO*, xliii, 137–41.

put a stop to this, the Senate considered it necessary to establish, first, who could be a noble, and, secondly, if somebody were not born into the nobility, but distinguished himself by his services and qualities, when and how could he ask for ennoblement?[1]

Neither of the government departments which would be expected to answer the question, who was a dvorianin, could do so. Nor was much light thrown on the subject by the Empress in her Instruction, for her remarks in this connection were, as so often, rather vague, and her exact meaning, therefore, elusive. Wrote Catherine:

Virtue with *Merit raises* People to the *Rank of Nobility*...There are few Ways which lead so directly to the Attainment of Honours, as the military Service. To defend their Country, and to conquer its Enemies, is the first Duty, and Proper Employment of the Nobility. But though the military Art is the most ancient Way of attaining the Rank of Nobility; and though the military Virtues are essentially necessary for the Existence and Support of the State; Yet still Justice is no less required in Time of Peace than in War; and the State would be destroyed without it: And from hence it proceeds, that this Dignity is not attached solely to the Nobility; but may be acquired by the *civil* Virtues, as well as by the *military*.[2]

Such a description of the qualifications for nobility would appear to constitute a defence of Peter the Great's Table of Ranks, although the Empress made no actual reference in her Instruction to this decree, so often cited as the definitive statement of the demarcation of the Russian nobility from the other classes.

Certainly, many assemblies of the dvorianstvo itself discussed the Table of Ranks, but often only to reject it as for the most part out of date and inapplicable to Russian circumstances in the second half of the eighteenth century. The strongest opposition to Peter the Great's command that everybody reaching the top eight ranks of the service hierarchy or becoming commissioned officers should enter the hereditary nobility came from the old centre of the Empire, Moscow. Many instructions from Moscow province argued that such a degree could be attained only by direct, personal grant of the monarch, several of them claiming that this was exactly what was stated in section 16 of the Table of Ranks.[3] (Such an argument can certainly be drawn from the first part of section 16, but the section later unequivocally gives the order 'to give coats of arms to those, Russian or foreign, as

---

[1] *SIRIO*, XLIII, 15.   [2] Reddaway, *Documents*, 273–4.
[3] *SIRIO*, IV, 245–6, Kostroma; 457–8, Peremyshl' and Vorotynsk; 287–8, Kaluga and Medyn'.

from the dvorianstvo, so also not from the dvorianstvo, who have served up to commissioned rank'.[1]) Interpreting section 16 of the Table of Ranks in a manner similar to the other Moscow assemblies, Shcherbatov and his associates in Iaroslavl' went on to propose the compilation of lists of accredited families of nobles. The electors of Luh and Serpeisk, particularly the latter, were anxious that the old families should not be swamped by new creations.[2]

Several assemblies from other provinces agreed with the attitude of the Moscow province nobility to the question, who was a dvorianin? The Pustorzheva, Novgorod, instruction demonstrates that the antipathy of the nobility towards the Table of Ranks was partly inspired by its growing acquaintance with the western European situation. It requested:

As in all European states, non-nobles reaching the top ranks cannot without a grant of a diploma of nobility ascribe to themselves Von, De, Don and similar nobility; in like manner we also most humbly ask that the ancient dvorianstvo...be distinguished...from non-dvoriane...[3]

While the Simbirsk, Kazan', electors echoed the Muscovite request that staff and commissioned officers should not automatically become ennobled, the Kerensk, Voronezh, assembly did not want non-dvoriane to be allowed to become officers. The Riazhsk district, also from Voronezh, complained that commoners of various kinds, clerks and Cossacks, had assumed the title of dvorianin without the approval of the Heraldmaster's Office, and Belev, Belgorod, asserted that there were all kinds of upstarts claiming dvorianstvo, including some who based their claim on nothing more than that their names were the same as those of genuine members of the upper class. Other Belgorod groups, from Staryi Oskol, Mtsensk and Ryl'sk, like those from Moscow, were in favour of a dvorianstvo created through grant of a diploma alone.[4]

If several instructions from other provinces supported the attack of the Moscow dvorianstvo on the traditional interpretation of the Table of Ranks, there was also a considerable number of others coming to the defence of Peter the Great's renowned decree. Understandably enough, those who approved of the uncomplicated process of officers becoming nobles would not be members of the older

[1] *PSZ*, no. 3890, section 16.
[2] *SIRIO*, IV, 298–9; VIII, 477–9, 512–13.   [3] *SIRIO*, XIV, 314.
[4] *SIRIO*, LXVIII, 7, 443, 384–5, 611, 608–9, 619, 622–3.

Russian noble families, and would tend, therefore, to come from the
newer outlying provinces to the south, Slobodsko-Ukraina and New
Russia, where there was no indigenous nobility. Thus, the instruction
from Sumy, Slobodsko-Ukraina, requested that the Cossack elders
and all others who reached commissioned rank become dvoriane as
prescribed in the Table of Ranks, and the Izium assembly from the
same province argued along similar lines, comparing the local situation to that in the Baltic provinces, where the nobility also appeared
to be experiencing difficulty in getting its status confirmed.[1] From
New Russia, the officers of the Yellow, Black and Bahmut Hussar
regiments all declared in favour of the Table of Ranks. As the first of
these assemblies put it: 'We are here, originating from various provinces, and also seconded from Her Imperial Majesty's Army,
foreign and Russian true subjects of Her Imperial Majesty from the
orthodox people...and do not now rank among the Russian
nobility...' This unsatisfactory state of affairs needed rectification,
the Yellow Hussar officers thought.[2]

Defence of the Table of Ranks also came from a Voronezh
assembly and a Belgorod group. The first of these, for example,
asked that officers be given coats of arms in return for their services,
for without them they considered themselves extremely 'discouraged'.[3] As for the nobilities of the Baltic provinces, the Ukraine,
Smolensk and Siberia, they were in the position of having to consider
their relationship to the Russian nobility as a whole, rather than questions, however important, concerning the internal structure of the
class. Their attitudes to the question, who was a dvorianin, will therefore be examined separately.

First, the discussion of this question by the general assembly must
be scrutinized. The opinions of the deputies concerning qualifications
for ennoblement ran through a wide gamut reflecting, but also
elaborating, the pattern established by their instructions. During the
general assembly's first discussion of the Rights of the Nobles, the
main proponent of the exclusivist claims of the party opposed to
the Table of Ranks was, predictably, Prince Shcherbatov. Speaking on
12 September 1767 Shcherbatov expressed the opinion that some of
Peter the Great's legislation might now be out of date and could be
harmful in a changed Russia. It was no longer necessary that officers

[1] *SIRIO*, LXVIII, 280, 308–10.   [2] *SIRIO*, XCIII, 19–20, 32, 53–4.
[3] *SIRIO*, LXVIII, 364, Usman', Voronezh; 576, Valuiki, Belgorod.

should automatically become dvoriane. To be a worthy noble, a man had to show extraordinary virtue and zeal. The name alone and the recollection of the famous deeds of their ancestors were enough to impel people of nobility to all kinds of great exploits. Shcherbatov asserted in support of his argument that outstanding Romans performed so notably because they believed that they were sprung from heroes. Baron Puffendorf was called in for support as well as ancient Romans, Shcherbatov citing the learned opinion of that legal expert that rank alone did not create nobility, but that rather the monarch gave the title of noble to whom he pleased.[1]

While several deputies agreed with Shcherbatov and added to his arguments,[2] there were others ready to come to the defence of the Table of Ranks. For example, speaking on 21 September 1767, Ia. P. Kozel'skii, one of the proponents of liberal views on the serf question, claimed that, if the ancestors of the Russian dvoriane had first received their honours for their loyalty and virtue in service, and not by distinction of birth alone, they could not scorn and belittle those who were now becoming officers for the same reasons. If the ancient dvoriane were alone favoured, and the newly created dvoriane were neglected, then a rift would ensue in state service, for those with no prospect of reward would serve without any zest and love for the fatherland. Superior education was often advanced to support the claims of the exclusivists, but what was the educational status of their predecessors? Newly created dvoriane were accused of trying to increase the size of their estates, but people of this type were surely superior to indolent wastrels. Two final allegations attacked by Kozel'skii were that officers not born into the dvorianstvo were timid before their superiors, which, he claimed, could not be proven, and that some were too poor for their high station, which he considered no fault, for, 'even in our time, in Europe, there are states, in which the most indigent nobility considers itself to be on a level with the rich in its privileges; moreover, poverty accompanied by good morals is not detrimental to honour or achievement'.[3]

Shcherbatov could not listen to such a speech and remain silent. He was astonished that Kozel'skii had, as he put it, reproached ancient Russian families with their base origin, since not only Russia, but the whole world, could be a witness to the contrary, to the fact

---

[1] *SIRIO*, IV, 149–53.
[2] E.g. I. Chaadaev, *SIRIO*, IV, 153–4.   [3] *SIRIO*, IV, 187–9.

that these families stemmed from Riurik and Vladimir and the great servants of the Grand Dukes.[1] Continued Shcherbatov:

How can Russia, gathered together now in the person of its deputies, listen to the imputation of baseness to such families as have given her their services through the unbroken course of many centuries! How can she not recollect the spilt blood of these most worthy men! Be my witness, most precious fatherland, of the services rendered to you by your most precious sons—the dvoriane of the ancient families. You will be my witnesses, those very places where, at the wish of our Monarch, the Mother of the fatherland, we have gathered for our security! Were you not in the power of predatory hands? You holy temples, were you not shamed by heathens? Who gave you the hand of help in your peril, Russia? Your true offspring, the ancient Russian dvorianstvo!

Shcherbatov, the daily journal noted, spoke and concluded 'with an extreme movement of the spirit, which could be observed by the tone of his voice'.[2]

There was little sign of compromise between the two noble points of view of the Table of Ranks during the general assembly's first discussion of the Rights of the Nobles. N. Motonis, from the Ukraine, perhaps came nearest to it in his suggestion that the following questions should be asked. How many dvoriane were there, and how many were necessary to man the various services? How were dvoriane created before Peter the Great's legislation, and had there been more abuses of the past or of the present system? If there were insufficient nobles in Russia, the Petrine system should be retained, thought Motonis, particularly if it were found that it had led to no increase in abuses. If, on the other hand, it were discovered that there was an adequate or even over-abundant supply of dvoriane, or that the present mode of entry into the dvorianstvo led to an inordinate amount of corruption, the assembly should then ask the sovereign to place limits on the numbers of the class.[3]

As for the non-noble deputies, they were staunch defenders of the structure of the dvorianstvo as established by Peter the Great. Indeed, while E. Fedilov, of the Voronezh free farmers, I. Kuznetsov, the town deputy from Menzelinsk, and I. Antonov, the town deputy from Iaransk, expressed their support for the Table of Ranks, I. Smirnov

---

[1] According to the Chronicle, both Riurik and Vladimir inaugurated their reigns by appointing members of their immediate entourage as their representatives in the principal cities. These men were probably the great servants to which Shcherbatov referred. See Florinsky, *Russia*, I, 21.

[2] *SIRIO*, IV, 193. [3] *SIRIO*, IV, 170.

and V. Rozhnov, the town deputies from Ruza and Putivl', appeared to want to make rank even more superior to heredity than Peter had intended.[1]

When the question of qualifications for dvorianstvo was raised at the general assembly during its second discussion of the Rights of the Nobles in July 1768 the two points of view held by deputies from the top class moved closer together. A. Nartov, deputy of the Money Department of the Mines College, suggested on 17 July 1768 that it should be definitely accepted that those 'who by the enactments of the Sovereign Peter the First had received the right and property of dvoriane up to the present time through their...ranks' were dvoriane. About a hundred deputies concurred with Nartov's proposal, including nearly twenty from the nobility, the majority of whom were from the central provinces.[2] Surprisingly, perhaps, none other than Shcherbatov himself agreed with Nartov, although he made the additional suggestion that henceforth nobody call himself dvorianin without the special conferment of the sovereign.[3] A similar proposal to that of Nartov, put forward by I. Viazemskii on 7 August 1768, met with the approval of eighty deputies from the dvorianstvo, with the central provinces again well represented,[4] while a favourable vote was also given to an alternative idea announced by two town deputies that the problem of qualifications for dvorianstvo be made the sole concern of the Heraldmaster or settled according to the Table of Ranks,[5] thus indicating that there was no unanimity of outlook on this question.

Those who attacked the Table of Ranks were often in favour of the recognition of certain gradations among the members of the dvorianstvo and of the registration of them in special lists. There was considerable precedent for both of these partialities. Elizabeth's commission, most recently, had produced a plan of hierarchy for the dvorianstvo comprising five different strata. These were:

1. Ancient aristocratic families from Russia, from Poland or elsewhere.
2. The descendants of all those in service in 1700, whose fathers or ancestors had been made dvoriane, and who, according to governmental records, had been granted an estate, and a charter.

---

[1] *SIRIO*, iv, 214–19.　　　　　　　[2] *SIRIO*, xxxii, 180–2.
[3] *SIRIO*, xxxii, 184.　　　　　　　[4] *SIRIO*, xxxii, 260, 289–90.
[5] *SIRIO*, xxxii, 298.

3. Foreign immigrants of proven nobility.
4. Local people or immigrants of proven nobility in the conquered provinces. These would have to be confirmed as there was a mass of individuals in these provinces who considered themselves nobles, but who had no right to do so.
5. All those who had achieved dvorianstvo through civil or military service as laid down by Peter the Great up to the time of the publication of the projected new law code. After this time, dvoriane of the above type were not to be hereditary, so that their children might have more incentive.[1]

For its part, Catherine's committee on the dvorianstvo had considered, although not definitely recommended, one principal division of the dvorianstvo between the old families, particularly princes, barons and counts, and the new, 'according to the example of other European states'.[2]

While neither the Heraldmaster's office nor any other government department had anything to say on the subject of the graduation of the dvorianstvo in their instructions for Catherine's Legislative Commission, several of the instructions and deputies of the dvorianstvo put forward relevant suggestions. The Kashin, Moscow, instruction proposed a division of the nobility into three classes—ancient, by merit, and by law, while the Iaroslavl' instruction wanted the dvorianstvo to consist of Russian and immigrant princes; certified counts and barons; and nobles who had received diplomas. The Pustorzheva, Novgorod, dvorianstvo sought the recognition of the following distinctions between the ancient and newly created dvorianstvo: first, by rank; secondly, by prohibiting new creations from taking on the titles of ancient families; thirdly, by not attributing noble status, suggesting origin from ancient noble blood, to new creations. Another Novgorod assembly, from Tver', also wanted a clear distinction to be made between old and new dvoriane, with the latter being registered in separate records.[3]

Of those who considered the question of gradations of dvorianstvo at the general assembly, Prince N. Davydov, of the Romanov, Moscow, nobility put forward the most complete and interesting proposals. Various peoples, Davydov pointed out, had developed groups of rights and privileges which had served as the basis for their

---

[1] Latkin, *Zakonodatel'nye kommissii*, I, 159–60.
[2] Kalachov, *Materialy*, II, 20. [3] *SIRIO*, IV, 459, 298–9; XIV, 314, 327.

orders of nobility: for example, the Senators of Rome and the old families of Egypt grew up on such a foundation. Similarly, several of the ancient philosophers had been in favour of the division of the nobility into classes: for example, both Plato and Aristotle had suggested four of them. These systems of antiquity, Davydov claimed, were applicable to Russia. It was also of significance that such an aristocrat as Shcherbatov expressed the opinion that, to avoid bickering and jealousy, princes and counts should enjoy precedence only in their titles and coats-of-arms.[1]

The request for gradations of dvorianstvo was often linked with that for the registration of all members of the class. The Kashin and Iaroslavl' assemblies made both requests, and so did Shcherbatov. If the marshal kept records of all dvoriane in his district and communicated this information to the Heraldmaster, considered Shcherbatov, 'the valuable name of the dvorianstvo, preserved in its purity, and the glory of its ancestors, inspiring everybody to the service of the fatherland and the sovereign, will now obtain new successes for the fatherland'.[2] Requests for official gradations and registration of nobility, and for stricter definition of qualifications for nobility, all to some extent encouraged by a growing awareness of the practices of other European countries, revealed a growing class consciousness on the part of the dvorianstvo.

Many groups of nobles from provinces comparatively recently joined to the Russian Empire were less interested in the Table of Ranks and degrees of nobility than in their traditional rights and privileges. Most prominent among these were the nobles of the Baltic States and the Ukraine, or Little Russia.

The division of the Baltic nobility into an aristocratic *rytsarstvo* and a less exclusive *zemstvo*, already clearly reflected in the preliminaries to the Legislative Commission, was again on prominent display in the instructions. Thus, those from the *rytsarstvo* of four Estonian districts requested the confirmation of their former privileges and elective rights, and the sole instruction from the Vyborg nobility similarly asked for the maintenance of their status as it was in the days of Swedish rule. The Vyborg group also appeared to oppose the Table of Ranks in its request that all nobles families be required to possess a *matrikul*, or diploma, to assist in the preservation of the order from the

---

[1] *SIRIO*, iv, 179–81; xxxvi, 11.   [2] *SIRIO*, iv, 460–1, 298–9, 162.

infiltration of commoners, while the Estonians were insistent that the *rytsarstvo* be kept separate from the *zemstvo*. In like manner, the *rytsarstvo* of two Livonian districts wanted confirmation of their rights and privileges, and one of them expressly sought the purity of their order without any adulteration by outsiders. On the other hand, the Livonian *zemstvo* was very keen to be equated with the *rytsarstvo*, and, in demonstrating this eagerness, indirectly expressed some support for the Table of Ranks. Nobles of the *zemstvo*, whether created by birth, or by diplomas, or by military services, their instruction said, should be considered united with the *rytsarstvo* in one corps.[1]

The attitude of the Ukrainian nobility, or *shliahetstvo*, was comparable to that of the Baltic nobility in its request for the confirmation of former rights and privileges, but differed from its northern counterpart in its additional petition for inclusion in the dvorianstvo on an equal footing with Great Russians. The Gluhov assembly, for example, asked for such confirmation and inclusion, and, with varying emphasis, so did four other Little Russian groups.[2]

The heterogeneous nobility of the new southern provinces, for its part, also sought complete acceptance into the dvorianstvo. From New Russia, the Dnepr Lancer Regiment, inhabiting a county recently detached from the Ukraine, asked for the preservation of their earlier status and for equality with the Great Russian nobility, which had been promised, they maintained, in the decree of 15 April 1763, setting up the province, while the Georgian nobles of the Donets Lancer Regiment requested this equality and the grant of diplomas and coats of arms, property and class rights.[3] From both New Russia and Slobodsko-Ukraina, as pointed out above, came considerable support for the Table of Ranks.

The vast spaces of the east demand little attention here because of the sparseness of their population. However, although the Tobol'sk town instruction pointed out that, apart from those temporarily in service there, 'there is no Russian dvorianstvo' in Siberia, several of the local inhabitants who deemed themselves noble desired to receive the rights possessed by the dvoriane of the central provinces, and wanted local organization to be instituted for the nobility there. Similar requests came from Eniseisk, Iakutsk and Irkutsk.[4]

---

[1] *SIRIO*, LXVIII, 45–6, 86–8, 91–2, 59–60, 66–7, 71–2, 79.
[2] *SIRIO*, LXVIII, 127–8. See also LXVIII, 134–6, Nezhin and Baturin; 147–9, Pereiaslavl'; 174–6, Kiev; 234–6, Chernigov.
[3] *SIRIO*, XCIII, 23, 25, 40–2.　　　　[4] *SIRIO*, CXXXIV, 297, 299, 290, 414, 390–1.

Apart from these points made in the instructions, there was also considerable representation of the views of the nobilities of the outlying provinces in the general assembly of the Legislative Commission. In October 1767 S. Samoilov, deputy of the town Eniseisk, remarked that, during the conquest of Siberia, local nobles had been made dvoriane in some towns in order to carry out certain services. Many of these had acquired land and settled there after completing these tasks, receiving payments in money and kind, and their numbers had been fixed by a decree of 1725. However, continued Samoilov:

The Siberian dvoriane, not possessing equality with the Russian dvoriane in the pay that they received, and not being satisfied with their lands, occupying, moreover, positions which are generally entrusted to staff, or at least commissioned officers, are in a complete decline of spirits and suffer great ruin.

For these reasons, Samoilov urged that Siberian nobles be given unequivocally the status of Russian dvorianstvo.[1]

Some very interesting comments were made on Samoilov's speech by Prince Shcherbatov, whose concern for Siberia may well have partly stemmed from the position on trade routes between Siberia and Moscow of the district that he represented, Iaroslavl'. The Siberian population, declared Shcherbatov, had been formed from Cossacks, runaway serfs, exiled criminals, and merchants. Since North America was not discovered, or at least little known, during the time of this formation, the merchants had sold a significant amount of produce at great profit throughout Europe, and Siberia prospered. But it could not be shown by any of the relevant records that Great Russian dvoriane had been sent there. The Siberian 'dvorianin' was therefore not socially superior, but only possessed rank, and that in a non-hereditary fashion. Neither this, nor the decree of 1725, was enough to link him to the dvorianstvo. Nevertheless, thought Shcherbatov, it would be a good thing to have a nobility in Siberia, because, where there were nobles, there also were their subjects; where there were the subjects of the nobles, there agriculture and manufactures were carried on, and prosperity increased; where there was prosperity, there the arts and the sciences flourished. Therefore, Shcherbatov suggested that the Siberian governor should be empowered to confirm or create local nobles, who would be able to acquire land, although not from Great Rus-

[1] *SIRIO*, IV, 155–7.

sians. A Siberian dvorianin would not be considered the equal of his Great Russian peer, but rather a member of the highest degree of the middle class, and he would also be honoured according to his rank. After Shcherbatov had finished speaking, the deputy of the Vereia dvorianstvo, I. Stepanov, rose to express his partial agreement with him, although rejecting the idea that the Governor be empowered to create nobles. Only the sovereign, Stepanov reminded Shcherbatov, could do this. It is perhaps noteworthy that Shcherbatov, so often considered the representative of the extreme right wing of noble thought, should be criticized for a proposal that one of his fellows looked on as too radical, although Stepanov seems to have mistaken what would merely have been an administrative convenience for an attempt to limit the power of the monarch. For his part, the Siberian Governor himself, D. I. Chicherin, made the observation that there were many families in Siberia originating from the central Russian dvorianstvo, and these should be accorded their full due. As far as others were concerned, they should be made Siberian commissars and given officer's rank when they achieved sufficient status.[1]

Attention was switched to the Baltic provinces in November 1767, after some preliminary remarks and requests concerning their situation in October. On 22 November 1767 N. Tolmachev, of the Liubim dvorianstvo, referring to the plea of the Livonian, Estonian and Finnish nobilities for the maintenance of their former rights, declared that, for the promotion of the general good and the eradication of the confusion produced by the different systems of law, all the peoples of Her Imperial Majesty should be subjected to the same laws. Tolmachev later took the Kiev town deputy to task for arguing that uniform laws would be of no help to his particular region. Replying for his Baltic province, A. Vil'boa said that the Livonian rights and privileges fitted the disposition of the people living under them. Over a long period of time, their correspondence had been demonstrated by the faith, the climate and customs experienced by the local people. This, and the proven voluntary obedience to their laws by the inhabitants of Livonia, led Vil'boa to ask that the rights and the privileges of the local nobility be included in the new code of laws for their permanent preservation. Speaking for the Livonian *zemstvo*, Von Blumen argued that those who sought uniform laws for the whole empire contradicted the wishes of monarchs from Peter the Great

[1] *SIRIO*, IV, 159–61, 204.

onwards, all of whom had confirmed Livonia's peculiar legal system. In similar fashion, although at a somewhat later date, I. Golovkin of the Vyborg nobility expressed the hope that the ancient local privileges, confirmed partly by the decrees of 1727 and 1766, would not be abolished by the new law code.[1]

From the Ukraine, V. Zolotnitskii wanted both the Little Russian and Baltic nobilities to retain their former rights, and to acquire those of Great Russia through service or possession of estates there. As far as discussion of the new provinces to the south was concerned, V. Mihal'ch, representing the Elisavetgrad Lancer Regiment of New Russia, emerged as the principal spokesman, arguing that the Table of Ranks should be maintained to guarantee the rights of Russian and immigrant noblemen, actual and prospective.[2]

The question of the rights and privileges of the outlying provinces came to a climax in September 1768, after the Baltic deputies had reiterated the arguments for their confirmation. After allowing, and indeed encouraging, such statements on previous occasions, Marshal Bibikov now intervened to put a stop to them. Citing the fifteenth section of the commission's rules of procedure, which stated that the composition of a new law code, and that only, was to be discussed, Bibikov went on to point out that, in making their remarks on the draft of the Rights of the Nobles, Baltic, Ukrainian and other deputies had overstepped their terms of reference by asking for the confirmation of their former rights and privileges. The deputies were not allowed to discuss matters concerning government, still less those depending solely on the monarchical authority, declared the Marshal. The requests for confirmation submitted by the deputies would have to be formally rejected. Bibikov also announced a breathing space to allow deputies to prepare for the next discussions.[3] It is probable, of course, that Bibikov had been instructed by the Empress to make this prohibition, since the continued requests for the recognition of their traditional status, actual or imagined, by the deputies of the outlying provinces could only hinder Catherine's plans for their russification.

[1] *SIRIO*, IV, 219–22; VIII, 330–9, 348–9, 350–1; XXXII, 308–9.

[2] *SIRIO*, XXXII, 307–8; IV, 194–5; XXXII, 301–2.

[3] *SIRIO*, XXXII, 323–45; IV, 221; VIII, 321–2; XXXII, 345–6. Besides those nobilities discussed here, another, from Smolensk, emitted a weak dying gasp at the Commission. See Smolensk district instruction, *SIRIO*, XIV, 418, and M. M. Bogoslovskii, 'Smolenskoe shliahetstvo v XVIII veke', *ZMNP*, CCCXXII, 61.

NOBLE RIGHTS AND PRIVILEGES

On the face of it, the most important of the rights and privileges of the dvorianstvo was freedom not to serve. However, not only had this emancipation been granted by Peter III with several reservations, and accepted by Catherine somewhat grudgingly, but the nobles themselves expressed little enthusiasm for it in their instructions. Indeed, at least one assembly, that from Kashin in Moscow Province, sought the return of obligatory service, arguing that:

> Every dvorianin should serve his fatherland ten years without respite, at the end of which he should be discharged if he wants to serve no more, because the first duty of the dvorianin is to demonstrate his merits to his fatherland for all those advantages with which he is endowed by the sovereign...[1]

The question of the freedom of the dvorianstvo was discussed more fully in the general assembly of the Legislative Commission than in the instructions. During the second discussion of the Rights of the Nobles, the question was debated by G. Korob'in, of the Kozlov, Voronezh, dvorianstvo, and I. Vyrodov, representing the Belgorod assembly. Vyrodov declared that the sovereign alone was free, that the freedom of others needed to be limited by the law. The dvorianin should be free solely in the affairs of his own household. As far as service was concerned, the noble should have no freedom, and be bound to serve the fatherland in return for education, and preference before others. If they were allowed to choose to serve or not to serve, many would choose not to serve, either because of thoughtlessness or youth, and the fatherland would not be defended. In answer to Vyrodov, Korob'in stated that by definition a free man could act only in a manner that was not contrary to law. Moreover, he could defend the fatherland without being in service: there was, in fact, a difference between service and defence of the fatherland.[2] Korob'in, it will be recalled, was quite possibly a mouth-piece for the Empress on the subject of the freedom of another class, the serfs, and might well have been speaking for her again on the freedom of the dvorianstvo. If this were so, Catherine was moving towards a more liberal view in this sphere than that which she appears to have held in the first few years of her reign.

In a later debate on the same theme, I. Bantysh-Kamenskii, the

[1] *SIRIO*, iv, 468–9.   [2] *SIRIO*, xxxvi, 13.

deputy of the New Russian Black and Yellow Hussar Regiments, made the point which seems to have been central to the argument of the supporters of obligatory service. Each man was prone to idleness, and therefore compulsion was necessary, he declared. If it were not compulsory for dvoriane to serve, then it should not be compulsory for farmers to till the soil, or for merchants to carry on their affairs for the benefit of the whole of society. Every good without compulsion became an evil, claimed Bantysh-Kamenskii.[1]

Of rather more interest to the dvorianstvo as a whole than the somewhat abstract topic of freedom from service was the very practical question of promotion in service. Before the reign of Catherine, dvoriane enjoyed little official preference in service, whatever many of them managed to secure for themselves in actuality. With the accession of Catherine, edicts granting dvoriane service advantages of various kinds began to appear. Thus, in July 1762 it was ordered that non-commissioned nobles forced to retire from service through illness be given commissions on retirement, 'so that they may have precedence before those non-dvoriane who will be released'.[2] In 1764 instructions given to army colonels required that non-commissioned dvoriane be given precedence in promotion over commoners, and, in 1765, a decree announced that young nobles were to be promoted with 'an advantage over non-dvoriane according to their quality'.[3]

Such concessions as these did not satisfy some assemblies of nobles, who asked for more in the instructions to their deputies. Two Novgorod groups, for example, wanted dvoriane entering service to be cut off for ever and completely from soldiers and N.C.O.s. Kerensk, Voronezh, electors requested that, first, commoners should not be made officers, and that, secondly, retired officers from the nobility with less than thirty souls in their possession be given a state pension.[4] At the general assembly, S. Skrypitsyn, from Kineshma, Moscow, referring to the eighth section of the emancipation decree, asked for an enlargement of the terms of promotion for retiring noble servicemen. M. Glazov, representing the Oboian', Belgorod, assembly,

---

[1] *SIRIO*, xxxvi, 14–16.
[2] *PSZ*, xvi, 20, no. 11,611, 15 July 1762.
[3] *PSZ*, xvi, 972–99, particularly 973, no. 12,289, 8 December 1764; *PSZ*, xvii, 318–19, no. 12,465, 5 September 1765. The second decree refers principally to the civil service.
[4] *SIRIO*, xiv, 275, 346; lxviii, 443, 446. A submission reflecting an opposite viewpoint to that of the Kerensk electors came from those of Valuiki, Belgorod, who sought protection for the rights of non-noble officers (lxviii, 576).

thought it necessary to legislate that only dvoriane be promoted to certain ranks both in the infantry and the cavalry.[1]

A growing consciousness of the exclusiveness of their class, obvious enough in their attitude towards service promotion, was more clearly revealed in the statements of the nobles concerning their rights in the unhappier sphere of corporal and other punishment. This consciousness was particularly pronounced in the instructions from the central Moscow province. While the Kaluga and Medyn' electors wanted dvoriane not to suffer corporal or capital punishment before they had been stripped of their rank, the Iaroslavl' assembly wanted nobles convicted of minor offences to be punished in a manner different from plebeians, because the severe retribution that was usually meted out might deprive young nobles of the high-born thoughts they had been brought up to hold. The Kashin dvoriane wanted members of their class to be free from corporal punishment generally, and, in particular, asked that a dvorianin who struck a priest or officer pay a fine, while somebody of meaner rank should be knouted for striking a noble. Similarly, as a punishment for the concealment of runaway serfs, the Krapivna electors considered that landlords should be fined, and other ranks knouted or sent off to join the army as well as fined, and Pereiaslavl'-Zalesskii dvoriane proposed that criminal members of their class should be punished by a fine applicable solely to them.[2] From outside Moscow, while the Simbirsk, Kazan', instruction made a request similar to that of Kaluga and Medyn', and that from Belgorod wanted young nobles in the army not to undergo corporal punishment, the Kopor'e, St Petersburg, assembly put forward the idea of freedom from arrest for the dvorianstvo, except by the appropriate marshal of the nobility, or his assistants.[3]

The question of the punishment of the dvorianstvo was not aired very much at the general assembly of the Legislative Commission. During the first discussion of the Rights of the Nobles, V. Bibikov, from Elets, Voronezh, echoed the request featured in several instructions that dvoriane should be degraded before receiving corporal punishment, and Shcherbatov also declared that dvoriane should not be exposed to this kind of retribution.[4] During the second discussion

---

[1] *SIRIO*, IV, 203, 213.
[2] *SIRIO*, IV, 288, 302, 462–3, 468; VIII, 560, 495.
[3] *SIRIO*, LXVIII, 7, 657–8; XIV, 243–4.   [4] *SIRIO*, IV, 148–9, 152.

of the Rights of the Nobles, there was a debate on the subject of punishment between S. Domashnev, of the Sumy, Slobodsko-Ukraina, nobility, and V. Vedeneev, of the Tambov, Voronezh, free farmers. To Domashnev's assertion that nobility was an honour that was untouchable, Vedeneev countered with the argument that, 'if there is no punishment for the dvorianstvo, then this will be contrary to holy writ'.[1]

Perhaps the most important rights of the nobility were those connected with property. Bestuzhev-Riumin, in the suggestions that he made as a member of Catherine's committee on the dvorianstvo, had considered that the first and most important privilege of the class was to bequeath its property as it pleased.[2] This view appears to have been shared by several assemblies of nobles, who pressed for freedom of disposal of their property in the instructions. Explaining the motives for this request, the historian Briullov pointed out that Russian society at the higher level had long outgrown family life in the broad sense of the word by the middle of the eighteenth century. Such family ties had been weakening for a long time, wrote Briullov, and ideas about the obligatory distribution of family property among all a noble's children were now thought by many to be a restrictive and an unreasonable anachronism.[3] Therefore, while there were, on the one hand, complaints that family property had been sold to strangers, there were, on the other, numerous demands for unrestricted rights of disposal.[4] At the same time, some assemblies were anxious to avoid the subdivision of property that had brought countless arguments and even ruin to many families,[5] although very few favoured the restoration of Peter the Great's Western-influenced entail law.[6] Other changes sought in the field of inheritance were, first, that parents should be the heirs of deceased childless children, and, secondly, that husbands and wives should have first claim on the property of deceased spouses.[7]

[1] *SIRIO*, xxxvi, 18–19. See also the remarks of M. Glazov, xxxii, 216.
[2] Kalachov, *Materialy*, ii, 32.   [3] Bruillov, *VE*, i (1876), 80.
[4] For example, these requests came from Dmitrov, Moscow; Pskov, Novgorod; Viaz'ma, Smolensk; and Simbirsk, Kazan' (*SIRIO*, viii, 507–9; xiv, 397–8, 446–9; lxviii, 6).
[5] For example, two Moscow groups, Poshehon'e and Luh (*SIRIO*, iv, 423–4; viii, 481–2).
[6] The capital district of Moscow, Pereiaslavl'-Zalesskii, also from Moscow, and Ryl'sk, Belgorod, seem to have been the only groups in favour of the entail law's restoration (*SIRIO*, iv, 228–9; viii, 496; lxviii, 623–5).
[7] See Briullov, *VE*, i (1876), 80; Kazan', *SIRIO*, lxviii, 31; Tambov, Voronezh, lxviii, 330.

If noble requests concerning disposal of property showed a considerable awareness of the rights of the individual dvorianin, their attitudes to the questions of honour and dignity demonstrated a well-developed consciousness of the inviolability of the class as a whole. Here, as elsewhere, the feeling was strongest at the centre of the old Muscovite Empire. Thus, the Pronsk and Tula dvoriane talked of insults to the honour of the class, and suggested fines for them, and the Mozhaisk electors went further in rejecting the idea of monetary retribution for such insults, because, they felt, 'the dvorianstvo does not compare its honour with money'. The Shuia assembly wanted retired dvoriane to wear a special badge in their hats to distinguish them more clearly from other ranks, and, while the Moscow nobles from Serpuhov, Tarusa and Obolensk complained that the dvorianstvo was forced into a crowd with the lower orders at the central Estates College,[1] the Riazhsk, Voronezh, landlords were unhappy at being obliged to mingle with the mean and lowly in the entrance hall to the local *voevoda*'s chambers. 'The commoners', said the Riazhsk instruction, 'commit great discourtesies, and dare to remain in their seats without giving them up, and the dvoriane are forced to stand up and to suffer this offence.'[2]

LOCAL GOVERNMENT AND CLASS ORGANIZATION

The irregular movement of the nobility towards greater class consciousness and fuller participation in provincial affairs during the eighteenth century has been traced in the introductory chapter. Both these developments came to something of a head during the reign of Catherine II, with the active assistance of the Empress herself. First, in ordering the nobility to come together in provincial districts for the election of a marshal and deputy to assist her in her great legislative endeavours, Catherine accelerated the formal organization of the class in the provinces. Once created as 'the first organ of noble class government',[3] the marshal of the dvorianstvo was retained for other purposes unconnected with the affairs of the Legislative Commission, and became the general manager of the business of his class in his locality.[4] This retention was probably fore-

[1] *SIRIO*, IV, 388, 412; VIII, 545; IV, 396–7, 364.
[2] *SIRIO*, LXVIII, 388.
[3] Korf, *Dvorianstvo*, p. 18.   [4] *Ibid*. p. 21.

seen from the beginning, since the decree calling the election of the marshal stipulated that he should remain in office for two years.[1]

Secondly, both the class formation and sphere of activity in the provinces of the dvorianstvo were discussed by the Empress and her advisers during the opening years of her reign. Among the questions addressed to the committee on the dvorianstvo in 1763, for example, was one concerning the differentiation of nobles who had been in service from those who had not. To establish firmly this differentiation, the question was raised of whether it would not be useful to enact as a permanent law 'that the former be not employed in any provincial or town service or levies or duty details, and, on the other hand, that the latter alone bear this burden?' This question appears to have reflected the traditional negative attitude of the nobility towards local service, as did the suggestion of committee-man Nikita Panin that staff-officers and above should be excused such service, which should be confined, moreover, to the affairs of the dvorianstvo alone. A. P. Bestuzhev-Riumin took the opposite view in asking for the expansion of the corporate activity of the class at the local level. So that the nobles freed from service should not live in what he considered to be harmful idleness and irresponsibility, Bestuzhev-Riumin thought that it would be good for the provincial nobles to elect from their number *landraty*, who, on receiving the confirmation of the Senate, would have under their authority all the districts belonging to their assembly, settle arguments between nobles, and carry out other tasks for the state and their class. For example, the *landraty* would be guardians for their assembly wherever necessary, and intercessors at their local courts when dvoriane suffered insults or injuries. In order to keep the emancipated nobles from idleness, they could also be given the opportunity to elect suitable people from their assembly as *voevody* or as assistants to the *voevody* or governors. Thus, thought Bestuzhev-Riumin, not only would government departments be freed from superfluous complaints about the present non-elective local officials, but the new officials would be very much on their guard against causing the nobility any trouble, through the fear that they might lose their job and the respect of their fellows.[2] Both the recommendations of Panin and Bestuzhev-Riumin were absent from the final report of the committee on the dvorian-

[1] *PSZ*, no. 12,801, Letter B, point 11.
[2] Kalachov, *Materialy*, II, 20–1, 36, 31–2.

stvo, which asserted the right of voluntary service at all levels, arguing that this would not cause any reduction in the number of state servants, since 'everybody recognizes it as a favour, when he is allowed into service'.[1] Solov'ev wrote that Catherine was irritated by what he called this obviously untrue representation of the nobility at that time,[2] but Korf rejected Solov'ev's interpretation, declaring that the dreams of the dvorianstvo always culminated in state service, and that Catherine was already thinking of making wider use of these aspirations.[3] To appraise the accuracy of the opinions of these statesmen and historians, the attitude of the nobility as a whole towards service can be established by an examination of their instructions and the speeches of their deputies at the Legislative Commission, and the attitude of Catherine can be established by a glance at her policies and her ideas during the first five years of her reign, and at her reception of proposals offered by her advisers. The latter first:

In May 1763 the Empress took a trip to Rostov and Iaroslavl', along with Ia. P. Shahovskoi and several other members of her entourage, to have a look for herself at local institutions, after a Major Arsen'ev had been sent out on a similar tour in March and April of that year.[4] Also during the first year or so of her reign, Catherine was probably the recipient of some letters written on the subject of provincial judicial procedure by one Vonliarliarskii, who argued that peasant officials enjoyed too much power and should be replaced by commissars elected from the nobility. Vonliarliarskii talked of these commissars carrying out 'most distinguished service', including affairs of such importance that they must be conducted by the 'best dvoriane'. The old, obligatory service as envisaged for the Petrine commissars was giving way, it appears, to a concept of influential, privileged administration by new-style officials.[5] Was Catherine thinking of accepting this novel view, or of retaining the bureaucratic concept of local government as reintroduced at the end of the 1720s?

An answer to this question, as well as an elaboration of it, is to be found in an examination of Catherine's first attempts to reform local government based on the knowledge and understanding that she had gained during the first year or so of her reign. Three main

[1] *SIRIO*, VII, 240.   [2] Solov'ev, *Istoriia*, V, 1470
[3] Korf, *Dvorianstvo*, p. 11.
[4] Got'e, *Istoriia*, II, 161; Shahovskoi, *Zapiski*, pp. 195–201.
[5] Got'e, *Istoriia*, II, 164.

directions have been discerned in the early work of the Empress in the field of provincial administration: towards the quick settlement of actual problems requiring immediate attention; towards the improvement of the moral standards of government officials; and towards the implementation of current rationalistic theory.[1]

The most important move in the first of these three directions was the decree connected with the establishment of local institutions promulgated in December 1763.[2] In attempting to improve the pay and regulate the sphere of duty of her provincial officials, Catherine hoped to reduce the confusion with which she had become well acquainted. At the same time, she was receiving suggestions to clear up the mess more completely from advocates of increased power for the bureaucracy on the one hand, and for the nobility on the other. Thus, while Shahovskoi proposed the introduction of an elective noble element into local government, others recommended detailed 'police' duties for the governors, including the supervision of cultural development and of production expansion in the area assigned to them.[3] In two anonymous memoranda contributing to the preparation of the establishment decree, one on the functions of the governor, and one on those of the *voevoda*, there was an expression of, first, the bureaucratic, and, secondly, the class outlook. The memorandum on the governor said that the dvorianstvo had not yet reached the stage at which each member of the class would be sufficiently acquainted with the law, aware of the good of the Empire and possessed of the power to argue, to stand up to the governor while occupying a minor, temporary position in the administration. When incapable people were appointed to provincial posts, they were always under the control of the governor, who then became unnecessarily dominant. Moreover, even if officials from the nobility were able to resist the strength of the governor, they would be restrained from doing so by the fear of what might happen to themselves and their property in the province subjected to the governor. On the other hand, such officials might exploit their power to oppress their neighbours. The memorandum on the *voevoda* suggested that this official should be chosen from the aristocratic dvorianstvo, from whom underlings would then inevitably learn honesty and a sense

[1] *Ibid.* pp. 164-5.
[2] *PSZ*, xvi, 468, no. 11,991, 15 December 1763. The establishment also changed by *PSZ*, xvi, 27-8, 23 July 1762, no. 11,624; xvi, 457-62, 15 December 1763, no. 11,988.
[3] *SIRIO*, vii, 352-4.

of high purpose: when these virtues had grown, preservation of the law and justice would prevail. Such *voevody* would be respected by the nobility, who would not then be subjected to insult and dishonour, the importance of which low-born people could not understand.[1]

The second objective of Catherine's early work in the field of provincial government, the improvement of administrative morals, was also aimed at by the 1763 establishment decrees. Further moves to this end can be detected in the decree ordering governors to be directly responsible to the Sovereign,[2] and in the instructions to Rumiantsev on his appointment as governor of the Ukraine,[3] and the instructions of 1765 to the governors of Moscow and St Petersburg.[4] Decrees granting permission to buy land in the areas under their supervision to the governors and the *voevody* can be interpreted partly as attempts to remove the temptation or even necessity of land grabbing on the part of these officials.[5] While attempting to promote morality in the administration, the Empress also made energetic attempts to remove immorality from it, fighting a keen battle with the age-old problems of extortion and bribery as well as taking a close interest in the execution of her new policies.[6] During the first year or so of her reign, she arraigned the Smolensk Governor and his assistants for involvement in bribery;[7] prosecuted the Belgorod governor and his assistants for similar offences involving the preparation of alcoholic drinks;[8] brought to trial one administrator for extreme corruption in Irkutsk and another for the same crime in the Serb Colonies of Southern Russia;[9] and instigated many lesser proceedings of a comparable nature.[10] Although not all these cases were brought to a conclusion, and there was a tendency for the most powerful men to receive the least punishment, it is irrefutable that the Empress showed considerable determination in her attempts to track down bribery, extortion and corruption of all kinds, and Pro-

[1] Got'e, *Istoriia*, II, 181–2.   [2] *PSZ*, XVI, 716–20, no. 12,137, 21 April 1764.
[3] *SIRIO*, VII, 388.
[4] *PSZ*, XVII, 5–7, no. 12,306, 12 January 1765.
[5] *PSZ*, XVII, 545, no. 12,554, 27 January 1766; XVI, 799–800, no. 12,181, 13 June 1764.
[6] See chapter 2, pp. 49–50.
[7] *SIRIO*, VII, 224–7, 285, 286; Chechulin, etc., *Istoriia...senata*, II, 609.
[8] *PSZ*, XVII, 1037–45, no. 12,781, 11 November, 1766; Solov'ev, *Istoriia*, VI, 287.
[9] *SIRIO*, I, 215–52; Chechulin, etc., *Istoriia...senata*, II, 627–8; Solov'ev, *Istoriia*, V, 1462–3, 1487.
[10] See, for example, *PSZ*, XVI, 304–5, no. 11,869, 30 June 1763; Chechulin, etc., *Istoriia...senata*, II, 628–9; Solov'ev, *Istoriia*, V, 1461, 1467–8.

curator-General Glebov, the highest official in the land, fell partly because of his implication in the Irkutsk affair.[1]

The third aim of Catherine's early legislation in the field of provincial administration, the realization of contemporary rationalistic ideas, was pursued principally by her decree of 11 October 1764.[2] This was distinguished by its all-embracing scope, its announcement of a broad programme for the future development of local government. While its practical significance may have been small, as Got'e said, 'it is interesting from the theoretical point of view as a concrete structure of legislative thought, and as one of the links in the chain of events which finally led to Catherine's provincial reform of 1775'.[3] Of course, a further, more important link in this chain was the Legislative Commission.

The extent to which new ideas and institutions had been introduced by Catherine by the eve of the assembly of this Commission can be gauged partly by an examination of the arrangements made for the new provinces to the south in 1764 and 1765. New Russia was set up in March 1764 on the basis of a report made by Nikita and Peter Panin: its administration was to consist of two departments, one military, subordinate to the War College, and one civil, under the Senate. Both departments became military in actuality, and, generally, the government of New Russia was influenced by the proximity of Turkey, with whom war could have broken out at any time. There was no sign in the establishment of New Russia of the introduction of the institutions of the empire as a whole, with or without changes or improvements.[4] Slobodsko-Ukraina was similarly military in its constitution, with the local Cossack regiments being organized into districts, and the Cossack elders being appointed as assistants to the Governor and the *voevody*, although the Governor and the *voevody* themselves were to be Great Russians. In like manner, local privileges and charters were confirmed, but general imperial laws and administrative arrangements were also to be adopted.[5] A commission was set up in early 1765 to put these ideas into practice under Major-General E. Shcherbinin, the first Governor of the province,[6] and it soon emerged that this was not entirely possible. Elective

[1] Solov'ev, *Istoriia*, v, 1463.   [2] *PSZ*, xvi, 926–32, no. 12,259.
[3] Got'e, *Istoriia*, ii, 192.
[4] *PSZ*, xvi 657–67, no. 12,099, 22 March 1764; Got'e, *Istoriia*, ii, 251–2.
[5] *PSZ*, xvi, 1003–7, no. 12,293, 16 December 1764.
[6] *PSZ*, xvii, 74–5, no. 12,342, 28 February 1765

Cossack commissars were therefore adapted to fit into the new administration and, since landed property was found to be in a particularly chaotic state, a special department of Estate Affairs was attached to the Governor's Office.[1] Generally speaking, the arrangements made for New Russia and Slobodsko-Ukraina were influenced more by local circumstances than by the form of provincial government operating in the Empire as a whole, and there was hardly any sign of reform or innovation in them. In the formation of Mogilev and Pskov in 1772, there was considerable evidence of such change.[2] Between the middle of the 1760s and the beginning of the 1770s, of course, the Legislative Commission intervened. It would appear that, before she had access to the materials of the Commission, the Empress was making little response to the suggestions put to her on several occasions that a greater class element be infused into provincial administration and was rather adhering to the stronger bureaucratic tradition in this field.

In the Instruction, we get few further clues to the thoughts of Catherine on local government; although she put forward there at great length some sophisticated ideas on law, she said almost nothing of the organs which would administer it in the provinces. As for the instructions of the government departments, they reflected both class ways of thinking and the bureaucratic outlook. The Senate took the former view, arguing in favour of the preservation of the marshals and assemblies of the dvorianstvo. Its instruction considered that, since these class officials and organs had been introduced, it was very necessary that they should be maintained, not only for general discussion and suggestions concerning their local needs, but also so that their legal and other affairs might be better arranged. To alleviate the burdens placed on the courts by the trials of arguments among the dvoriane, to relieve the dvoriane themselves of the inevitable red tape incidental to lawsuits, and, most consequentially, to carry out tasks for the state, such as troop quartering, in conjunction with state departments, it was necessary to decide the permanent form and mode of operation of the assemblies and their officers.[3] While the Little Russian College, like the Senate, wanted to introduce elective duties for the nobility,[4] the opposite bureaucratic ten-

[1] *PSZ*, xvii, 133–6, no. 12,397, 20 May 1765. The commissars were first set up by *PSZ*, ix, 736–7, no. 6,883, 10 February 1736.
[2] Got'e, *Istoriia*, ii, 258–9.
[3] *SIRIO*, xliii, 3–19, particularly 13.　　　　　　　　　[4] *SIRIO*, xliii, 221.

dency was very clear in the instruction of the Chief Police Department, which made suggestions for the regulation of practically everything, in the true tradition of 'police' supervision. For example, the instruction expressed the desire 'to allow the first five classes to cover their rooms with silk hangings, and to forbid the other classes and nobles possessing less than two thousand souls to have their rooms, chairs, canopies, etc., with silk covers, except for bedspreads, under pain of confiscation of the forbidden article.'[1] In a supplementary chapter to her Instruction, entitled 'Of good Order, otherwise termed Police', the Empress did not go so far as her Chief Police Department, but demonstrated a considerable amount of approval for its regulative activities.[2] At the same time, she gave no support to the idea of elective officials from the nobility exercising these or other functions in the administration.

To turn to the instructions of the nobility, although Bibikov had reported in 1764 that the situation in Kazan' was improving as a result of the 1763 establishment decree, it is difficult to see any sign of improvement in the situation in Kazan' or any other province in these instructions. To take Kazan' in particular, while a decree of 4 April 1722 had said that *voevody* should be located in all towns within a radius of 200 versts from the provincial capital,[3] the instruction of the Kazan' nobility revealed that many nobles had to travel to this capital for the settlement of even minor affairs.[4]

Looking at Russia generally, evidence came from provinces in all quarters of the Empire from assemblies of dvorianstvo that there was nearly a complete breakdown in the arrangements for the administration of both civil and criminal law. The principal complaint of the nobility in the civil sphere was that, for various reasons, far too much time was spent on the completion of lawsuits. The Iaroslavl' instruction lamented that:

The existing extension of cases and the loss resulting from it, forcing the landlords or their stewards, and often the tillers of the soil themselves to live in the town during farming time, and also the multiplication of affairs, often unimportant in themselves, cause both the courts and the nobility great inconveniences. Many are forced to leave minor insults caused them alone without any complaint, on account of which the farmer suffers

---

[1] *SIRIO*, XLIII, 314.
[2] Reddaway, *Documents*, p. 297.
[3] Solov'ev, *RV*, xxxv, 314; *PSZ*, VI, 524–5, no. 3,935, 4 April 1722.
[4] *SIRIO*, LXVIII, 27.

losses: the households of the dvorianstvo become hostile to each other, and, finally, frequently repeated insults afford a reason for arguments and killings.[1]

Less eloquently, but perhaps more tellingly, the Iur'ev-Pol'skii electors confessed that, because of their lack of numbers and their stupidity, they could not say very much, except that there was a great delay in the settlement of court cases.[2]

Professor Polenov succinctly described some of the reasons for the slow rotation of the wheels of eighteenth-century Russian justice. First, the rules for judicial procedure, as laid down in Peter the Great's still operative decree of 5 November 1723[3] were to blame. Secondly, judges often caused delays sometimes extending to twenty years through fear of the large fines that they could incur for an incorrect decision. Thirdly, the clumsiness of unskilled plaintiffs and the tactics of clever defendants were also to blame.[4]

The Vereia, Moscow, instruction had something to say on all three of these points, albeit not the same as Professor Polenov. The 1723 decree, it observed, had made it possible for a guilty defendant so to delay the course of a case that a plaintiff of moderate means would be forced to withdraw his suit. If punishments were made more severe, and more expeditious use were made of written evidence, justice, the Vereia dvoriane considered, would be more likely to triumph. Both these suggestions were put forward by many other instructions from Moscow and other provinces.[5] As far as judges and other court officials were concerned, the Vereia nobility suggested that those of them who were found guilty of accepting bribes should be executed without hope of pardon. Poor, ignorant people involved in lawsuits beyond their pockets and comprehension should be assisted by annually elected local legal experts.[6] The Riazhsk, Voronezh, instruction amply demonstrated that corrupt officials could be found in other provinces besides Moscow. Local government officials, it said, were guilty of dishonourable actions and a dissolute way of life; had no fear of their superiors or punishment; and were continually drunk even during official meetings. These men would also carry out no business without a bribe, although, to cover up this fact, they used people of lesser rank as their clerks.[7]

[1] *SIRIO*, IV, 304.   [2] *SIRIO*, IV, 318.
[3] *PSZ*, VII, 147–50, no. 4,344.   [4] *SIRIO*, XIV, xiv–xviii.
[5] See, for example, Rostov, Moscow, *SIRIO*, IV, 356; Ostrov, Novgorod, XIV, 279–80.
[6] *SIRIO*, IV, 371–3, 379.   [7] *SIRIO*, LXVIII, 539.

Criminal affairs, most dvoriane appear to have considered,were in a more serious condition than civil. From the south, the Bahmut, New Russia, electors wrote that some people, insensitive to the humanitarian kindness of Her Imperial Majesty, did not only occupy themselves with the robbery, terrorization and plunder of local inhabitants, but also killed some of their masters 'through spite'. Seeing their own people reaching such a degree of audacity and carrying on a life of drunken disorder, the nobles were forced to remain in a state of continuous alert and to attempt to instil fear into their charges, said the Bahmut instruction, which found the principal cause of this state of affairs in the mildness of current punishments, and called for an increase in their severity. Similarly, the Kursk, Belgorod, nobles complained that robbery had increased not only on the highways but also in the homes of the landlords, where destruction and even murder occurred. The Kursk nobles were unhappy that evildoers could not be more severely punished.[1]

The situation was much the same in Novgorod, to the north-west. Declared the instruction from the Pskov district:

> The dvoriane and people of every rank of Pskov county, suffer extreme ravages from brigands, thieves, robbers and other kinds of criminal, which stops very many of the dvorianstvo from living on their estates, for the protection of their lives from wicked torment; because of this, the economy and close supervision and good order of the lands of the peasants, etc., decline and decrease every moment. Those living in the provinces, either through necessity or lack of other place of refuge, are compelled for the defence and protection of themselves and their homes to keep up three or four times the normal number of household servants.

Those sent out to catch the miscreants worked too slowly, continued the Pskov instruction, and those landlords who caught the criminals for themselves suffered through the premature release of such people from jail. The Pskov recipe for the amelioration of the situation was, as elsewhere, harsher treatment for those malefactors who were caught.[2]

The story told to the east, in Kazan', was little different from that recounted in the north-west. Although there had been many edicts about the eradication of thieves and brigands, theft and brigandage were still very much in existence, asserted the Penza electors. The outlaws invaded the homes of the landlords, tortured them cruelly,

[1] *SIRIO*, xciii, 77; lxviii, 539.   [2] *SIRIO*, xiv, 376–7.

chained them up, cut people into pieces and burnt them in their houses. Many landlords suffered terrible fright, and hid themselves secretly away from their homes at night. For the same troubles as those experienced in other provinces, the Penza dvoriane again had the same cure, stronger repressive measures.[1] Even in the central Moscow province, criminal activity was causing as much alarm as in outlying areas and suggesting equally drastic remedies. To impress the mean and the lowly with the dire consequences of embarking upon such nefarious courses of action, the Krapivna instruction wanted public executions to be held in towns.[2]

From these examples, it is evident that, in seeking changes in the existing local administration, the dvorianstvo was most interested in reducing the violent lawlessness throughout the provinces, but a further wide range of duties beyond the suppression of theft and brigandage was also suggested for the officials of the reformed local government. They were to settle arguments between landlords and peasants, or between individual members of the two groups, concerning ploughing beyond boundaries, illegal wood-cutting, indiscriminate hunting, trespass and damage by cattle. The new officials were also to assist economic improvements by collecting and disseminating useful information and fixing fair grain prices. Suggestions were made, too, that they supervise repayment of peasant debts, use by the peasants of passports, and demands placed upon the peasants for horses, carts and labour. Road, bridge and communications construction and repair in general, troop quartering, victualling and movement, were all put forward as suitable for local supervision, as were arrangements for sales and mortgages, tax collection, the survey, the care of the destitute in general and the estates of orphaned, mad, sick and criminal landlords. It was argued that provincial functionaries should protect the illiterate, too, supervise education as a whole, and assist in the eradication of impiety. Finally, in their most important sphere of duty, the suppression of theft and brigandage, these officials were to manage the local police, have the power to raise posses, and even have military detachments under their control.[3]

In reforming local government, the nobility aimed at a greater control over it: the measure of this control varied, the requests of the

[1] *SIRIO*, LXVIII, 13-14.
[2] *SIRIO*, VIII, 561.
[3] See, for example, the capital district of Moscow, *SIRIO*, IV, 230; Kashin, Moscow, IV, 466-7; Opochka, Novgorod, XIV, 270-3; Riazhsk, Voronezh, LXVIII, 388-400.

noble assemblies falling into three main groups.[1] The first of these wanted to preserve the former system with the *voevoda* playing the key part, but wanted either him or his subordinates, or, in some cases, both of them, to be elected by and from the dvorianstvo.[2] The second group wanted to introduce some new officials into the existing local framework. Some instructions called them rural or district judges, others used the Petrine terms, commissars or *landraty*, a few called them commanders of the dvorianstvo, and one talked of elective mediators.[3] The third group of assemblies sought the institution of local elective collegiate bodies.[4] The duties listed above were variously assigned to these reformed and new officials and organs.

While most of the instructions of the dvorianstvo expressed a desire to use their assemblies as corporate electors in local government, only twenty-three of them, about 14 per cent of the total, wanted to use elective rights as the foundation for an independent organization along class lines. Nine of the twenty-three came from Moscow, the most thorough exposition of its ideas being given by the Klin assembly.

The Klin instruction suggested the triennial election of a commander of the nobility, and the annual election of a noble deputy. The former was to have control over all dvoriane in his district, and was to keep strict account of his charges, to note their movements to the capitals and elsewhere, to register all births, marriages and deaths among them, and to look after the genealogical records of the district. He was to be the sole judge of disputes between serfs and landlords, and appeal against his decision was to be to the Senate only. Other projected duties for the commander were to see that all court

---

[1] This pattern largely adopted from Korf, *Dvorianstvo*, pp. 30 ff.

[2] Among this group were the instructions of Kolomna, Moscow, *SIRIO*, iv, 329; Dedilovo, Moscow, viii, 522; Vologda, Archangel, xiv, 459; Karachev, Belgorod, lxviii, 528. All these instructions wished to elect the *voevoda*. Among those aspiring to the election of his assistants only were Chuhloma, Archangel, xiv, 482; Temnikov Voronezh, lxviii, 451; the capital district of Belgorod, lxviii, 647.

[3] Judges were suggested by Ostrov, Novgorod, *SIRIO*, xiv, 279; Zubtsov, Novgorod, xiv, 318; Chernigov, Little Russia, lxviii, 238; Epifan', Moscow, viii, 452; and Dorogobuzh, Smolensk, xiv, 434. Commissars were proposed by Kostroma, Moscow, iv, 247; Uglich, Moscow, viii, 463; Kazan', lxviii, 26-7; and Kerensk, Voronezh, lxviii, 442. *Landraty* were favoured by Pustorzheva, Novgorod, xiv, 303; Galich, Archangel, xiv, 494; Mtsensk, Belgorod, lxviii, 617; and Simbirsk, Kazan', lxviii, 9. Commanders were the choice of, for example, Toropets and Holm, Novgorod, xiv, 405; and elective mediators were put forward by Novyi Torzhok, Novgorod, xiv, 363.

[4] Among this group were Mihailov, Moscow, *SIRIO*, iv, 272; Kashin, Moscow, iv, 469; Iamburg, St Petersburg, xiv, 249; Smolensk, xiv, 418-19; Voronezh, lxviii, 365-9; and Kursk, Belgorod, lxviii, 535-6.

cases involving dvoriane were justly and expeditiously dealt with; to watch for the lawful, correct collection of the poll tax; and to see that the survey was properly conducted and that boundaries were well kept up. The commander was to be obliged to live in his district and was not to be able to leave it without the permission of his society. Because of his many duties, he was to be exempted from all other forms of service. The deputy of the nobility, as envisaged by the Klin assembly, was to be an intercessor for his local peers with the central government. He, like his commander, was to be released from all other functions, but was nevertheless to receive the advantages of state service, eighth class. The Klin instruction also suggested the institution of a national deputy of the dvorianstvo, with first or second class rank, to represent personally the entire nobility before the Empress.[1]

While some instructions, like that from Klin, gave a detailed description of their picture of class government, those from the Baltic and Little Russian provinces talked of little more than the continuance of the election of a marshal, being primarily interested, of course, in the recognition of their former rights and privileges.[2] Among the others, the Kashin instruction concentrated on the marshal's legal functions, and that from Dmitrov on the functions of the marshal *qua* leader of the assembly of the dvorianstvo.[3]

All of the twenty-three instructions thinking of an independent class government for the dvorianstvo wanted to have their own elective official to which could be entrusted the general care of all members of the order in each district, and they also wanted to achieve active participation in local administration. The desire for participation in provincial government was stronger and more widespread than that for class self-government. For the idea of self-government to develop, a clear distinction had to be recognized between the needs and interests of the state and those of the class, and such a distinction was not fully appreciated by many dvoriane in 1767. The class as a whole was content to concentrate on the domination of the other classes in Russian society by securing a firm grip on the local apparatus of state government.[4]

[1] *SIRIO*, IV, 255–9.
[2] The Iarvskii, Virskii, Vikskii and Garskii instructions from Estonia, *SIRIO*, LXVIII, 53–5; Vyborg, LXVIII, 86–94; Nezhin and Baturin, Pereiaslavl', and Chernigov, Little Russia, LXVIII, 144, 153, 238.
[3] *SIRIO*, IV, 460; VIII, 504–7.   [4] Korf, *Dvorianstvo*, 50–1.

Local government and class organization

It must be pointed out that even this aim was not shared by all members of the dvorianstvo. Several assemblies still retained the traditional negative attitude towards service. Thus, the Har'kov nobility from Slobodsko-Ukraina requested that local retired civil and military officers should not be given missions or duties by the state, since these were too costly for the individuals involved.[1] The Belgi, Smolensk, electors pointed out that, when many of them had retired to busy themselves with the management of their estates, the *voevoda* and his council had made them commissars, whose duties they had been obliged to carry out to the neglect of their estates and at their own expense. The Belgi electors therefore requested that they should not be given such appointments without their consent nor without pay, and that the sphere of activity of the commissar should be widened to include the settlement of arguments between peasants and landlords and similar functions.[2] It could be argued, of course, that the Belgi example indicates that members of the dvorianstvo were opposed only to service in its traditional form, and not to the new form of service promoting class interests.

At the general assembly, those noble deputies who spoke on the subject of local government, like most of their instructions, argued in favour of increased activity for officials chosen from the dvorianstvo. A. Protasov, of the Gorohovets, Moscow, assembly was keen to see the introduction into Russia of an official similar to the English J.P., and several of his peers agreed with him.[3] For her part, Catherine was still not wholly prepared to accede to such requests, and allowed discussions of the problem of local government along traditional 'police' lines after the dispersal of the General Assembly. The sub-committee, On Good Order, continued to talk in such a manner, presumably with the approval of the Empress. On 8 October 1769, for example, the sub-committee members:

continued to read from the report of the deputy and member A. Nartov on the non-use of immoderate expenses at weddings, on the non-use at burials of superfluous ceremonies and deep mourning, on civic condolences, on holiday meetings and festivities, on swings, on the making of ice mountains, on games of skittles...and with a ball, on skating in winter, on dancing and singing, on the baiting of bears, wolves and other beasts.[4]

[1] *SIRIO*, LXVIII, 269–70.
[2] *SIRIO*, XIV, 416–17. See also Roslavl', Smolensk, XIV, 428.
[3] *SIRIO*, XIV, xviii–xix, 82–3, 94.
[4] Got'e, *Istoriia*, II, 230–1.

It was probably not by chance that one of the members of this sub-committee was M. Zybin, from the Chief Police Department, whose instruction these proceedings appear to have so closely resembled, and it was certainly appropriate that the sub-committee should be assisted by the Moscow University Professor, J. G. Von Reichel, author of 'Bermerkungen über den Plan von Stadt-Polizei'.[1]

CENTRAL GOVERNMENT AND THE
ROLE OF THE NOBILITY

While the dvoriane could discuss with some freedom questions concerning provincial administration, they could not begin to discuss matters of importance connected with the central government, unless, of course, they wished to run the risk of further disturbances. For the Empress was convinced that the Russian autocracy was essentially unalterable. 'The Sovereign is absolute;' wrote Catherine at the beginning of her Instruction, 'for there is no other Authority but that which centres in his single Person, that can act with a Vigour proportionate to the Extent of such a vast Dominion.' Towards the end of her Instruction, Catherine wrote:

A Monarchy is destroyed, when the Sovereign imagines, that he displays his Power more by *changing* the Order of Things, than by adhering to it, and when he is more fond of *his own Imaginations* than of *his Will*, from which the Laws proceed and have proceeded.[2]

Catherine's self-portrait of an energetic, but careful, absolute monarch appears to have been quite accurate. She contemplated and effected some changes in the central government, but none of them was sweeping. For example, a structural change in the Senate was considered, and then actually carried out in the decree of 15 December 1763.[3] There was a much lengthier discussion just after Catherine's accession concerning the institution of a new deliberative *Sovet*, or Council. A manifesto on the creation of the Council was signed by the Empress in 1762,[4] but the project outlined therein was not adopted.

Two drafts of this manifesto, as well as a memorandum on the subject of the Council, all the work of Nikita Panin, have been published.[5] There have been two major interpretations of these

---

[1] Got'e, *Istoriia*, II, 231.   [2] Reddaway, *Documents*, pp. 216, 292.
[3] *PSZ*, XVI, 462–8, particularly 463–4, no. 11,989.
[4] Kliuchevskii, *Sochineniia*, V, 115.   [5] *SIRIO*, VII, 200–17.

documents. The first, originated by Solov'ev and continued by historians such as Korf and Shcheglov, was that the Council did not materialize in 1762 because Catherine realized that it would constitute a threat to her supreme power. Korf quoted with approval the remark by Shcheglov that:

The attempt at oligarchy of Panin was the last in a line of political plans of the Russian aristocracy, which for so long possessed the power in the government of the state during nearly all the first half of the eighteenth century... The process of the formation of the supreme government under Catherine II, Paul I and particularly under Alexander I was completed without any influence of aristocratic traditions.[1]

The second interpretation of the Council affair was advanced by Chechulin. The gulf between Catherine and Panin, he argued, was exaggerated by some earlier historians. Close contemporary observers, even the scandalmongers among them, did not describe Panin as a person intent on the limitation of the power of the Empress, and Catherine's delay of the execution of Panin's project did not necessarily mean her disapproval of it, since she always scrutinized such plans at length and in detail. Moreover, declared Chechulin, Panin was in no position to force Catherine into any particular course of action. If he had insisted on the acceptance of his project, its rejection would have meant the loss of his influence, and perhaps even his banishment from the court. Therefore, there would have been no point in Panin pushing his project forward too energetically. And, when just a few years later, in 1768, the Council was actually created, Panin was fully consulted. The gap between 1762 and 1768 was explained by Chechulin with the argument that Catherine wanted to think carefully before taking action, and that, meanwhile, the Council enjoyed a *de facto* existence in the shape of the committee on the dvorianstvo, to which several important questions were referred, and whose personnel was identical to that proposed by Catherine for her council in 1768.[2]

To accept Chechulin's interpretation of the Council affair as the better argued and more fully documented is, of course, not to deny the presence in Russia of a would-be aristocracy, although, again, such a presence was hardly likely to make itself strongly felt at the

[1] Quoted in Korf, *Dvorianstvo*, p. 12.
[2] N. D. Chechulin, 'Proekt imperatorskogo soveta v pervyi god tsarstvovaniia Ekateriny II', *ZMNP*, CCXCII, 74–5, 82–4.

Social and political attitudes

Legislative Commission. No instruction had anything at all to say about the Council project, or any other important organ of the central government, existing or proposed, in a manner implying radical change, and much the same could be said of the speeches of the deputies. The instruction of the Moscow district probably represented the view of many nobles when it said that it was to describe the actual needs of the local dvorianstvo, without:

concerning at all the general state institutions and statutes, which demand common agreement from the various parts of the state government and the various peoples subjected to it, nor the state economy, which, according to the time, circumstances and incidental needs, must always be regulated and controlled by the supreme power.[1]

Apart from this, remarks on the central government at the Commission were confined to requests for minor adjustments or for the decentralization of some of the minor colleges, principally the estates, mines and manufactures colleges.[2]

Many instructions devoted considerable space to attesting the nobles' fidelity to their Sovereign and their indirect approval of the central government. The Iaroslavl' electors, for example, noted that the members of the local assembly, in the event of general disturbances in Russia in ancient and modern times and in former wars, demonstrated their services with the spilling of their blood and the extreme sacrifice of their property. But the spilt blood and the property losses both of themselves and their forefathers were sufficiently rewarded by the honour of serving the fatherland, contributing to its glory and making it pleasing to their sovereigns. Referring to the summons of the Commission, the Iaroslavl' electors declared that 'the present gracious command of Her Imperial Highness not only surpasses the rewards already achieved, but cannot be paid for enough by the spilling of all our blood'.[3] Of many instructions in similar vein, several suggested that some permanent monument, a statue or a building, be erected to commemorate the convocation of the Commission.[4]

This obsequiousness directed at the autocrat was, of course, coupled with an autocratic attitude towards the lesser elements in

[1] *SIRIO*, IV, 227. [2] See chapter 3, pp. 127–8, 134.
[3] *SIRIO*, IV, 297–8.
[4] For example, see Volokolamsk, Moscow, *SIRIO*, IV, 243–4; Simbirsk, Kazan', LXVIII, 6; Dorogobuzh, Smolensk, XIV, 440–1. See also V. N. Bochkarev, *Voprosy politiki v russkom parlamente XVIII veka*, pp. 47–8, 51–2.

Russian society, and, at the same time, the obsequiousness itself was mingled with an implication that the services of the nobility were of vital and far-reaching importance. As Bochkarev put it:

Such were the political and social views of the dvorianstvo in the age of Catherine II. The tsar was the autocrat above, the landlords were the autocrats below, and under them, without rights or voice, was the 'common' people, their subjects. Between the all-Russian and the landed autocrats was a strong and close alliance, defensive and offensive, securing the autocracy of the emperor over Russia, and of the dvoriane—over their subjects, an alliance based on mutual trust. In such a state and social order only the autocrats were free, only they were real people: the all-Russian autocrat was free beyond measure, the freedom of the local small autocrats was limited by the boundaries of their estates and the freedom of the great autocrat, sitting on high. However, in this alliance of the political autocracy of the tsar with the social autocracy of the dvorianstvo, the actual power of many small autocrats aimed at replacing the power of the great autocrat and restricting the limits of his freedom. The dvorianstvo, recognizing itself in words as 'the lowest slaves' of its commander, as a complete nonentity, was at the same time proud of the consciousness that all that was Russia was it, the dvorianstvo, and only it...its blood and wounds had created Russia, it preserved her, gave her power and glory. Servilely declaring itself a nonentity before the boundless power of the all-Russian autocracy, the dvorianstvo was convinced that it alone held on its shoulders both the state and even the very power of the monarch, that only the 'noble' class was able, knew how and was obliged to administer Russia; it had to penetrate into all organs of administration and unremittingly watch over every step of the government. The tsar's protection over the dvorianstvo, and the dvorianstvo's—over all Russia, that is what, after all, the socio-political convictions of the average Russian dvorianin at the moment of the summons of the Legislative Commission of 1767 were leading to.[1]

Not only did the panegyrics to the Empress imply a veiled threat to her monopoly of power, a jealous avowal of the dvorianstvo's omnicompetence in the administration of the empire, they were also no sure guarantee of her position as patron of the dvorianstvo. Only five years before this, paeans of praise were being offered to a Peter III on the point of being the victim of a *coup d'état*. However, evidence of such an attempt upon Catherine during the sessions of the Legislative Commission is not to be found.

More tangibly, in their use of such terms as 'the general good' and 'natural law' in their panegyrics, some dvoriane appear to have been

---

[1] Bochkarev, *Voprosy*, p. 28.

moving towards a more subtle check on the all-Russian autocrat than palace revolution or omnicompetent service, towards the concept of a *Rechtsstaat* that was, albeit somewhat ambiguously, encouraged by the Empress herself. But just as there was a mixture of the old and the new in the instruction, so the thought of the dvorianstvo was influenced by the events of the eighteenth century at the same time as it admitted the contemporary idea of the rule of law. Believing that it had played a key role under the successors of Peter the Great and had limited imperial absolutism to its own advantage, the dvorianstvo tended to view the *Rechtsstaat* in a class light, with a spirit of deep contempt towards the 'rabble'. If there were to be equality before the law, some were to be very much more equal than others. Essentially, the *Rechtsstaat* would protect members of the nobility from the kind of arbitrary interference to which Peter the Great, and, to a lesser extent, his successors, had subjected them.[1]

Such ideas as these would indicate a growing feeling of class solidarity among dvoriane. Concrete indication of links between assemblies of nobles at the time of the Legislative Commission is to be observed in the repetition of sections of instructions, or, in some cases, instructions in their entirety. Wherever these phenomena occurred, there was necessarily some close contact between the assemblies of nobles concerned, or at least members of these assemblies. Consequently, it is not surprising that partial or complete instruction repetition is to be found most frequently among the instructions from the old central province of Moscow, where dvoriane would have been longest settled, and which provides at least ten examples of such phenomena.[2] While it is impossible to be certain in

[1] Bochkarev, *Voprosy*, p. 66.

[2] Liubim very similar to Kostroma except for its introduction and conclusion, *SIRIO*, IV, 295–6, 245–54; Iur'ev-Pol'skii very similar to Shuia in its opening panegyric and a later excerpt, IV, 312, 318, 390, 397; Maloiaroslavets, IV, 321–7, similar to Zaraisk, IV, 345–7, and Pereslavl' Riazan, IV, 348–9, in most points; opening panegyrics of Kashin, IV, 459, and Kolomna, IV, 328–9, similar to that of Moscow, IV, 225–7; remarks of Serpuhov, Tarusa and Obolensk, IV, 360–1, on brigandage similar to those of Venev, IV, 341–2; Tula, IV, 409, points 18 and 19, almost identical to Shuia, IV, 395, point 8, and 396, point 10; Lihvin, VIII, 440–1, points 3–9, almost as in Peremyshl' and Vorotynsk, IV, 426–30, and Lihvin, VIII, 443–4, points 13, 14, 15, similar to Tula, IV, 403–4, points 8, 9, 10; Luh, VIII, 479, point 3, similar to Odoev, VIII, 488–9, point 5, and Luh, VIII, 479–82, points 4, 5, 6, 7, 8, 11, 12, 13, 14, 15, 17, similar to Tula, IV, 398–409, points 4, 5, 1, 2, 16, 6, 8, 9, 10, 11, 18; Odoev, VIII, 487, 488–91, points 1, 2, 4, 7, identical to Tula, IV, 400–1, 403, 407–8, points 4, 5, 8, 17; Aleksin, VIII, 536–8, 542, points 1, 2, 6, 7, 9, 17, 19, and conclusion, similar to Kaluga and Medyn', IV, 287–8, 291–4, introduction and conclusion and points 1, 2, 6, 7, 12, 15, 19.

all of these cases, who was the borrower and who the lender and how the loans were arranged, it is indisputable that there must have been considerable interchange of ideas in the Moscow province. Instances of identical instructions are also to be found in the provinces of Estonia and Archangel, a very close copy was made in New Russia, and individual points were inserted into more than one instruction in Little and New Russia, Novgorod and St Petersburg.[1]

Partial and complete instruction repetition appears to indicate a growing communication between dvoriane in the Russian provinces. Provincial development of the dvorianstvo has already been detected in requests for the decentralization of several colleges, the institution of local agencies and the revision of local government. Did this provincialization result in an increase of the tension between members of the class situated in the capitals and those living outside, between the urban aristocracy and the rural gentry and squirearchy? In fact, as argued previously, the middle and lower dvorianstvo could not muster sufficient concerted strength to shift the top of Russia's social pyramid. On the contrary, many members of the dvorianstvo outside the establishment were devoting much of their energy to joining it. As Romanovich-Slavatinskii lamented:

The middle dvorianstvo was bound by its interests to the people, and by its pretensions to the aristocracy. Its real interests drew it to the rural areas, to agriculture—its artificial needs and its manifold pretensions attracted it to the capital, to the towns, to the promised land of the aristocratic *salons*, and abroad, where spending and idling away their time were the princes and the counts—the descendants of the boyars...That is why it was impossible to form a 'gentry' from our middle dvorianstvo...The middle dvorianstvo tore itself away from its natural *milieu*—from the ancestral fields, the sweet-smelling woods, and the family *muzhiki*. It considered these *muzhiki* people of another flesh and blood, it was ashamed to stretch out its hand to its little brother and thrived on two fingers stretched out by an aristocrat.[2]

---

[1] Identical instructions, Archangel, Sudai, *SIRIO*, xiv, 497–8, and Chuhloma, xiv, 469–82; and Estonia, Virskii, Vikskii, Garskii and Iarvskii, lxviii, 45–54. Similarities between Iamburg and Kopor'e, St Petersburg, xiv, 249, point 5, xiv, 243, point 2; Derevskaia Piatina and Vodskaia Piatina, Novgorod, xiv, 259–60, 262, points 1 and 7, xiv, 253–4, 257, points 1 and 9; Shelonskaia Piatina and Opochka, Novgorod, xiv, 346, point 14, xiv, 275–6, point 12; Bezhetskaia Piatina and Obonezhskaia Piatina, Novgorod, xiv, 351, point 2, xiv, 329, point 2; Pereiaslavl' and Nezhin and Baturin, Little Russia, lxviii, 148–9, 154, points 2 and 9, lxviii, 136, 140–1, points 2 and 9; Black Hussar Regiment and Yellow Hussar Regiment, New Russia, xciii, 32, point 2, and xciii, 19–20, point 1; Donets Lancer Regiment and Little Russian Poltava Regiment and Dnepr Lancer Regiment Georgian Princes and Nobles, New Russia, xciii, 56–61, points 1 and 2, xciii, 43–9, points 1 and 2.   [2] Romanovich-Slavatinskii, *Dvorianstvo*, p. 27.

Some without pretensions, such as Bolotov, could attempt to dispense with patronage. Remembering a celebration that he had attended in Moscow in 1763, Bolotov wrote:

Balls and masquerades were given at the court. . .and not everybody had the entry to that, and there were few places, and only for the upper class; and so we could not participate in all these, but were satisfied by our own private meetings and parties.[1]

Bolotov accepted his lot, and generally preferred to live in the provinces, on his own beloved estate. Although offered a job as assistant to Prince S. V. Gagarin, supervisor of some crown estates, and promised rank and salary if he took it, Bolotov was unwilling to leave the ease and quietness of his home, and after some hesitation, rejected the offer. But even he weakened, and accepted a second proposition soon after turning down the first one.[2]

As for the upper-class dvoriane, they had been developing a sense of exclusiveness throughout the eighteenth century, based partly on Russian tradition, partly on a newer western influence. One of the questions considered by the committee on the dvorianstvo had been:

[would it be] a good thing, according to the examples of other states, for the preservation from decline of the upper-class families in their entirety, to institute several large estates as principalities, counties, baronies and domains on such a basis that, for example, in a principality there should be not less than four or five thousand souls, and in the others in proportion?[3]

The absence from Russia of primogeniture and entail, the effects of *mestnichestvo* and the Table of Ranks, and the heterogeneity of the elements composing the dvorianstvo had so far hindered the development of an aristocracy, which some upper-class dvoriane now sought to introduce.

Shcherbatov appears to have developed the clearest picture of the shape that the Russian aristocracy would assume. As described in his

[1] Bolotov, *Zhizn'*, II, 236.
[2] *Ibid.* III, 76, 118, 139. The stereotype of the provincial dvorianin as a shiftless, ignorant wastrel is difficult to destroy because of lack of evidence about him. On the other hand, the stereotype itself has been composed from little evidence. A more accurate impression could perhaps be created through a thorough survey of memoirs and all other available material. Regional variations would have to be given more consideration than has hitherto been the case. For a similar argument, see Robert Forster, 'The provincial noble: a reappraisal', *The American Historical Review*, LXVIII, no. 3 (1963). Forster attacks the stereotype of the French provincial nobleman.
[3] Kalachov, *Materialy*, II, 22.

speeches at the Legislative Commission, Shcherbatov's ideal society was rigidly stratified, with each class carrying out specific exclusive functions: as ordered in his Utopia, the Land of Ofir, the state was 'a model of an *ordentlicher Polizeistaat*, such as an enlightened Prussian bureaucrat might have dreamt about'.[1] However, if Shcherbatov's aristocracy was essentially subordinated to a 'police' state, so all-embracing and important were to be the functions of the class in the economic, socio-political and cultural spheres that there would be little practical differentiation between the needs of the state and those of the aristocracy. In other words, Shcherbatov's picture of an aristocracy differed little from that which the dvorianstvo had painted of itself at the Legislative Commission.[2]

While no other dvorianin at the Legislative Commission described in such detail as Shcherbatov the shape that a Russian aristocracy should take, there were enough upper-class dvoriane participating in the Commission for a representative view on this question to be given, and, although they could not be expected to have put forward suggestions making for a direct assault on the monarchical power, there is no reason why they should not have expressed themselves freely on some important aspects of it. For example, Peter the Great with his decree of 1714 had given a respectable precedent for the introduction of one of the bases of an aristocracy, a system of entail. Yet only three instructions asked for the return of the *maiorat*.[3] Again, it would not have been too controversial to have taken the attack on the Table of Ranks further than the nobles chose to. Yet those seeking restrictions on this promotion and elevation structure pressed for a form of creation of nobility which would be more rather than less dependent on the monarch. If appearances are not deceptive, then, and laying aside disgruntled complaints that times were not what they had been, the would-be aristocracy at the moment of the Legislative Commission had no strong desire for

---

[1] Marc Raeff, 'State and Nobility in the Ideology of M. M. Shcherbatov', *American Slavic and East European Review*, XIX (1960), 374. For a more detailed discussion of the Land of Ofir, see A. A. Kizevetter, *Istoricheskie ocherki*, and N. D. Chechulin, *Russkii roman XVIIIogo veka: puteshestvie v zemliu ofirskuiu kniazia M. M. Shcherbatova*.

[2] Shcherbatov was never an influential member of Catherine's entourage, and was not on friendly terms with, for example, P. I. Panin and A. P. Shuvalov (V. Fursenko, *Russkii biograficheskii slovar'*, *Shchapov-Iushnevskii*, pp. 109, 114). Interestingly enough, the name, Shcherbatov, was adopted under pressure from Ivan III, who was anxious to erase memories of seniority arrangements preserved in various appanage titles still in existence at his accession (E. P. Karnovich, *Rodovye prozvaniia i tituly*, pp. 52–4).

[3] See chapter 4, p. 161.

anything beyond a moderate reform of the arrangements already in existence.

Acting on most members of the dvorianstvo of whatever stratum was the strong cohesive force of respect for rank, binding the class strongly together. Evidence of this beyond what has already been given can be found in many instructions. Thus, the Tula electors requested that all dvoriane be arranged in groups of ten, with the highest ranking member of each group in charge; the Peremyshl' and Vorotynsk assembly wanted a certain local official to be elected from staff and commissioned officers only; and two Novgorod districts wanted staff officers only to be elected as commissars. A gain in rank was widely considered to be an extremely worthwhile reward, and a loss in rank a most degrading punishment. Several groups considered that top-rank dvoriane were entitled to special privileges.[1]

Rank did not always assist the cohesion of the dvorianstvo, for it also reflected and to some extent encouraged the split between the *noblesse d'épée* on the one hand and the *noblesse de robe* on the other. There was no denial of the validity of either type of dvorianstvo. M. Rykachev, of the Bezhetsk, Moscow, society declared it was still possible to achieve dvorianstvo by entering military service, then defending the fatherland, defeating the enemy and thus distinguishing oneself from people of the middle class. Moreover, said Rykachev, 'this distinction can also be achieved in civil service, particularly in peacetime, by justice, virtue, love for the fatherland and observation of the regulations concerning one's position'.[2] However, military service, which did not always include defending the fatherland or defeating the enemy, possessed considerably more glamour and a higher social rating than civil service, which was inevitably associated with a certain amount of degrading 'penpushing'. The gap between military and civil service in the eyes of the dvorianstvo was not clearly revealed in the instructions or the speeches of the deputies, partly because it was so much a known fact of life that it did not call for comment, and partly because its existence did not cause most

[1] *SIRIO*, IV, 398, 435–6; XIV, 253–4, 341–2. On promotion as a reward, see, for example, Epifan', Moscow, VIII, 452; Kursk, Belgorod, LXVIII, 538. On degradation as a punishment, see, for example, Iaroslavl', Moscow, IV, 304–5; Sudislavl', Moscow, IV, 282–3. Regarding special privileges for top-rank nobles, see, for example, Peremyshl' and Vorotynsk, Moscow, IV, 434–5, which wanted the top three or four ranks to be excused meetings of the district assemblies of the dvorianstvo.
[2] *SIRIO*, IV, 164.

members of the class any anxiety. Why should the defenders of the fatherland worry about the welfare of 'penpushers'?

The instruction of the Senate gave a good description of the condition of the civil service, which would give an additional reason for its unattractiveness to members of the dvorianstvo. The Senate pointed out that imperial archives had so increased in the course of a few years that they filled many rooms: this was the result of the regulation that each paper should be kept regardless of its significance. Moreover, the instruction continued, the present civil service system produced 'only dangerous prolongation and obscurity in affairs', and officials were of inferior quality, many of them being the children of former officials without special training. The best of these people went into military service, said the Senate, because of the greater possibilities there for quick promotion in rank. A partial improvement of the civil service would result from the grant of certain ranks to dvoriane in the service, the instruction concluded. Somewhat similarly, the Heraldmaster's office suggested that seniority in the civil service should be more clearly defined.[1] The latter, rather than the former, proposal was put into effect in 1767 with the introduction of a regulation encouraging mechanical septennial promotion and thus a further bureaucratization of the civil service.[2] Such a regulation would tend to alienate dvoriane still more from this branch of service.

Brief consideration must be given to the external relations of the dvorianstvo with the second most powerful class in the empire, the bourgeoisie. There can be no doubt that the nobility was very much in control of the social situation at the time of the Legislative Commission: a few examples should suffice to prove the point. The Serpuhov instruction well described the vulnerability of that town's inhabitants in making the complaint that:

> Travelling along the highway from Moscow to Kiev and other places and back...staff and commissioned officers and couriers, because of the insufficiency of post horses in the town of Serpuhov, take horses in no small quantity day and night from the Serpuhov merchants...and in taking these horses take the merchants by force as drivers and knock them about moreover.[3]

More succinctly, the Bolhov merchants hopefully asked for a decree forbidding dvoriane to call merchants *muzhiki*.[4] The bourgeoisie did

---

[1] *SIRIO*, XLIII, 10, 143–4.
[2] V. A. Evreinov, *Grazhdanskoe chinoproizvodstvo v Rossii*, p. 40.
[3] *SIRIO*, XCIII, viii-ix, quoted by V. I. Sergeevich.   [4] *SIRIO*, CXLIV, 474.

not seek only to strengthen its defences against attacks from the dvorianstvo: some middle-class assemblies wanted to be allowed to join the noble class and to receive all its privileges. Thus, the Riazhsk burghers wanted all factory owners and traders involved in wholesale and foreign commerce to be granted dvorianstvo, rewarded with villages and freed from all taxes, quartering liabilities and other local obligations.[1] With complaints and requests such as these, there could be little hope for the immediate realization of Catherine's hopes for the development of the Russian bourgeoisie.

Even as far as the Empress was concerned, the middle class in Russia was not to be fostered in order that it could play a political part in the state similar to that of some of the bourgeoisies of western Europe. In her Instruction, she did not envisage the third estate as a counter-balance to the second.[2] Of course, nor did she want the nobility to be politically active, and her remarks concerning this class in the Instruction showed her agreement with the service arrangement of the Table of Ranks.[3] For Catherine, the autocracy was unlimited by any social or political check, the only curb it knew was self-restraint. While her mentor, Montesquieu, identified autocratic monarchy with despotism, and supported the idea of a politically influential nobility, Catherine attempted to reconcile her personal form of government with the principles of law and order, not by the development of the participation in it of her top people, but through the introduction of eight guarantees which would boost these principles without infringing autocracy. These were: division of authority; subjection of all without exception to the same laws; uniformity in application of the law; prohibition of spontaneous interpretation of the law; exact description of the instances on which a citizen could be arrested; partial toleration; freedom of the press with certain limits; punishment for deeds and not for thoughts or intentions.

By division of authority, the Empress meant in no sense limitation of it, but rather division of functions among institutions all subject to the monarch. As she said in her Instruction, 'the intermediate Powers, subordinate and depending, proceed from the supreme Power; as in the very Nature of the Thing the Sovereign is the Source of all imperial and civil Power'.[4] The Senate, the colleges and 'the inferior

---

[1] *SIRIO*, cxliv, 241. For a general description of the town instructions, see S. Voznesenskii, 'Gorodskie deputatskie nakazy v ekaterininskuiu komissiiu 1767 goda', *ŽMNP*, New Series, xxiv.   [2] See Reddaway, *Documents*, pp. 275–8.
[3] *Ibid.* pp. 273–5.   [4] *Ibid.* p. 217.

Courts of Judicature', among which the 'intermediate' authority was to be divided, were to make sure that everybody was equal before the law and that the law was uniformly and consistently applied.[1] For the further promotion of justice, the Instruction proposed:

By making the *penal* Laws always *clearly* intelligible, *Word by Word*, every one may calculate truly, and know exactly the Inconveniences of a bad Action; a Knowledge which is *absolutely* necessary for restraining People from committing it; and the People may enjoy Security, with respect both to their Persons and Property; which ought ever to remain so, because this is the *main Scope* and *Object* of the Laws, and without which the Community would be dissolved.[2]

Another boost to the security of a multi-national empire such as Russia, Catherine considered, would be to allow the profession of different types of religion, provided that they were not repugnant to Orthodoxy. With this prudent degree of toleration, the return of 'wandering Sheep to the true Flock of the Faithful' would be more likely than by any other means.[3] Similarly tolerant in her attitude towards deviations from the norm in the field of literary activity, the Empress observed that satirical writings were prohibited in monarchies, but were looked on as misdemeanours rather than crimes, and, furthermore, that:

great Care ought to be taken, in the Examination of *these Libles*, how we *extend it farther*; representing to ourselves, that Danger of *debasing* the human Mind by *Restraint* and *Oppression*; which can be productive of nothing but *Ignorance*, and must *cramp* and *depress* the *rising Efforts* of Genius, and destroy the *very Will* for Writing.[4]

Preceding these remarks on the advisability of a cautious rather than rigorous censorship was a recommendation of a comparable approach to the question of the distinction between words and deeds as grounds for indictment.[5]

The application of these guarantees of law and order under an autocratic government was to be strengthened by the introduction of a sophisticated system of courts and legal proceedings. A large part of the Instruction is devoted to this question, which is a reflection of the importance that Catherine attached to it. Among her proposals in this field were milder punishments, trial by jury, and courts of equity.[6] Such supports for justice notwithstanding, the dependence

---

[1] *Ibid.* pp. 218–19, 228–9.   [2] *Ibid.* p. 237 (more generally, pp. 283–4).
[3] *Ibid.* p. 289.   [4] *Ibid.* p. 288.
[5] *Ibid.* pp. 287–8.   [6] *Ibid.* pp. 225–55.

of the whole legal structure, like every other aspect of government and administration, on the person of the monarch, made the *Rechts-staat* a somewhat flimsy edifice, even in theory.[1] In fact, of course, Russia was ruled by the Empress and the nobility after 1767 as before, and the impressive recommendations of the Instruction were not to be implemented to any great extent.

[1] Reddaway, *Documents*, pp. 235–6. See also A. A. Kizevetter in *Nauchnye trudy russkogo narodnogo universiteta v Prage*, I, 75–7.

5

EDUCATION AND CULTURE

'Peter gave Russians bodies, and Catherine—souls', wrote the poet Heraskov.[1] Certainly, the Empress was very much occupied with the minds and morals of her people, the improvement of which, she thought, would be the principal means of promoting general welfare in Russia. For her, the rule of law was a *sine qua non*, and, for this reason, it was imperative to obtain better laws. 'In order to introduce better Laws,' she wrote in the Instruction, 'it is essentially necessary to prepare the Minds of the People for their Reception.' But the rule of law, indispensable though it was, was only a means to an end, for, Catherine argued, 'A Book of good Laws is nothing but a Bar to prevent the Licentiousness of injurious Men from doing Mischief to their fellow Creatures.' It was better to prevent crimes than to punish them, and to achieve this prevention, she declared, 'order it so, that the *Light of Knowledge* may be *diffused* among the People'.[2]

During the first five years of her reign, Catherine had industriously applied herself to the task of spreading the light of knowledge among at least some of her people. She had first of all attempted to improve the condition of the educational institutions bequeathed to her. For example, in 1765 the Empress instituted an enquiry into the ailing condition of Moscow University. The Moscow professors testified that there were not enough capable occupants of professorial chairs, that the non-academic director was a harmful influence, and that students were often taken away to service before graduation. The professors also wanted higher salaries, and the recognition of the university examination as a prerequisite of entrance into state service.[3] Such investigations as these led to very little. In any case, the Catherine of the first five years could not think of confining herself to these 'small deeds' of modest reforms of institutions already in existence: imbued with the optimistic spirit of her century, she had grandiose dreams of creating a new breed of human beings through

---

[1] Quoted in Kliuchevskii, *Sochineniia*, IV, 202.
[2] Reddaway, *Documents*, pp. 222, 255.
[3] Miliukov, *Ocherki*, II, 749–50.

the introduction of a new system of complete education. As she was later to put it in the Instruction, adults should attempt to instil into children 'all those Virtues and Qualities, which join to form a good Education; by which, as they grow up, they may prove real Citizens, useful Members of the Community, and Ornaments to their Country'.[1]

To help her carry out her grand design, the Empress gathered together assistants and information. The most important collaborator in Catherine's early school projects was Ivan Betskoi, born in 1704 in Sweden, the illegitimate son of Prince Ivan Trubetskoi, who had been taken prisoner at the battle of Narva. Educated and much travelled in western Europe, Betskoi had visited Madame Geoffrin's Paris *salon*, and was probably acquainted with Rousseau and the Encyclopaedists. Catherine had confirmed his appointment as director of the St Petersburg Cadet Corps and president of the Academy of Arts soon after her accession.[2] Betskoi and the Empress made the first full announcement of their plans in the decree of 12 March 1764.[3] In the same year, a commission was sent to examine British schools and universities and to use their findings as a basis for a report containing suggestions for a new system of education in Russia.[4] As well as Russians going abroad, foreign experts were invited to come to Russia to assist in the great reform.[5]

In the decree of 12 March 1764 two major developments were foreseen: the creation of individual educational establishments in St Petersburg and Moscow; and the institution throughout Russia of a comprehensive network of general schools. Betskoi concentrated on the first and easier of these two developments, taking a leading part in founding schools at the Academy of Arts for noble girls and for orphans.[6] Although Betskoi was probably presented with at least two

[1] Reddaway, *Documents*, pp. 272–3.
[2] *Russkii biograficheskii slovar'*, Betankur-Biakster, pp. 5–12. See generally P. M. Maikov, *I. I. Betskoi: opyt ego biografii*, and A. S. Lappo-Danilevskii, *I. I. Betskoi i ego sistema vospitaniia*. The second work is a critique of the first.
[3] *PSZ*, xvi, 668–71, no. 12,103.
[4] Gladys Scott Thomson, *Catherine the Great*, pp. 258–9.
[5] See, for example, N. Hans, 'Dumaresq, Brown, and Some Early Educational Projects of Catherine II', *SEER*, xl, no. 94, 229–35.
[6] For the foundation of these institutions see respectively: *PSZ*, xvi, 948–60, no. 12,275, 4 November 1764; *PSZ*, xvi, 742–55, no. 12,154, 5 May 1764; *PSZ*, xviii, 290–329, no. 12,957, 11 August 1769. Among other early educational projects of Catherine's reign were: a revised set of rules and regulations for the cadet corps, *PSZ*, xvii, 959–92, no. 12,741, 11 September 1766; and for the engineering and artillery schools, *PSZ*, xvi, 94–102, no. 11,696, 25 October 1762.

plans for fulfilling the wider hopes of the Empress, he did little to put them into practice.[1]

A more positive step along the road in education for all was taken by a cosmopolitan group composed of G. F. Miller, G. N. Teplov, Daniel Dumaresq, Philip Dilthey and Timofei Von Klingshtet.[2] Probably in 1766, this group submitted an unprecedentedly detailed plan for state education, after receiving several suggestions for guidance from the Empress herself. There were to be four categories of gymnasium: advanced, military, civil and commercial (open to all Orthodox people, except serfs, between the ages of five or six and eighteen). Each gymnasium of whatever type was to consist of three classes, each of four years in duration. The first two classes were to be similar in all types of gymnasium, while the top (third) class was to introduce specialized training. To supervise the whole project, some outstanding individual was to be appointed protector and head of a special department of education, assisted by a council of directors who would inspect the schools and discuss the best educational methods. In a separate plan, Miller and his associates recommended a scheme of compulsory elementary education for ordinary people between the ages of six and fourteen. While it is probable that Catherine was acquainted with both these plans, in comparison with which the work of Betskoi seems preparatory and fragmentary, the attitude of the Empress towards the plans and the reasons for their non-implementation are unknown.[3]

In these educational projects of the first five years of Catherine's reign, S. V. Rozhdestvenskii has suggested, were embodied four main principles: the combination of moral training with general and professional teaching; the elimination of the class element from education; the introduction of schools for girls, particularly necessary for a society aiming at the creation of a new order of men; and the strict enforcement of obligatory attendance by all male pupils.[4]

Since, in some respects at least, the first three of these principles were somewhat revolutionary, it is hardly surprising that they were

[1] See S. V. Rozhdestvenskii, 'Proekty uchebnyh reform v tsarstvovanie imperatritsy Ekateriny II do uchrezhdeniia kommissii o narodnyh uchilishchah', *ZMNP*, New Series, XII, 181–3.

[2] Miller was a German historian of Russia; Dr Dumaresq was a British educational theorist; Klingshtet was the editor of the *Works of the Free Economic Society*; Dilthey was a professor at Moscow University; and Teplov had been a member of the committees on trade and the dvorianstvo.

[3] Rozhdestvenskii, *ZMNP*, New Series, XII, 187–92.   [4] *Ibid.* pp. 206–7.

not all rigorously applied in theory, let alone in practice. Moral training, of course, had been a part of Russian education from the beginning, but it was now given unprecedentedly wide emphasis. The decree of 12 March 1764 stressed the importance of moral training, without which it considered that real success would be impossible in the arts and sciences.[1] Miller and his associates declared that 'a learned man with bad morals can cause society more harm...than one who has remained in ignorance with a quiet and mild disposition'. Therefore, morals rather than minds should be concentrated on at the beginning of the educational process, and minds could come more into their own when morals had been properly moulded.[2]

As far as the second innovatory principle was concerned, the state gymnasia plan of Miller and company was particularly directed at poor children, but recommended that 'the young of every rank without differentiation could be accepted'. Nevertheless, rigid adherence to this precept would lead to scholastic chaos, it was believed, so the four types of gymnasium would have to be created. Thus, although parents of young dvoriane would have to sign a declaration that they did not want any advantage for their children in food, clothing, care or any other respect, noble students would have to be separated from their fellows in military training, for example, because of the special preparation that they would require for commissions to be received on graduation. Moreover, special schools were to be created for the poorer members of the tradesman class to be raised from 'coarse ignorance' and taught subjects appropriate to their station in isolation from their social superiors.[3]

While class distinctions were apparent in the state gymnasia plan, they were paramount in the projects for female education, in which noble and middle-class girls were to be catered for in completely segregated institutions and with widely differing curricula. If this class distinction were not a sufficient barrier to the realization of the professed aim of the creation of a new order of men, then the deficiency was rectified by the failure to introduce compulsory female education into the projects for systems of general state education.[4] Although Catherine's hopes for even the two girls schools at Smol'nyi were over-optimistic, and although Shcherbatov wrote that these

[1] See *PSZ*, 12,103 *passim.*
[2] Rozhdestvenskii, *ZMNP*, New Series, XII, 208.
[3] *Ibid.* pp. 216–18.
[4] *Ibid.* pp. 221–4.

institutions produced 'neither learned nor well-behaved young girls', and that 'their education consisted more of how to play comedies, than of the training of their hearts, morals and intellects', Miliukov was surely right in pointing out that many Smol'nyi graduates derived considerable benefit from their schooling and started to bring light and fresh air into the Russian family's traditional atmosphere of blind and stuffy prejudice.[1]

Obligatory education for males, the fourth principle enunciated by educational projects composed during the first five years of Catherine's reign, had been introduced by Peter the Great, along with harsh punishments for defaulters such as prohibition of marriage, fines, corporal punishment and banishment to the army ranks. In wishing to mitigate the severity of Peter's guarantees of diligent attendance at school and attention to lessons, the educational theorists of the Empress found no certain substitute.[2]

Very few of the ideas of the first five years achieved implementation. However, in some cases, the announcement of a principle alone marked a step forward and facilitated the reception of new thinking on education. Two of Betskoi's opinions could be viewed in the same manner. His was one of the first voices raised loudly against corporal punishment, long accepted in Russia as indispensable to moral and intellectual training. Children, declared Betskoi, should almost never be beaten. Not only did whippings cow children and even render them unconscious, they also encouraged servile and vicious thinking, and were without doubt injurious to health.[3] Betskoi was also in the vanguard of those who declared that it was not necessary to begin an education with Church Slavonic and Holy Writ.[4]

As in the first half of the eighteenth century, most Russians receiving an education in the 1760s were under the supervision of tutors or in private schools, and were therefore not directly affected by the theory and practice of state education. Nevertheless, some improvement appears to have occurred in the private as well as the public sector of education by the time of the convocation of the Legislative Commission, partly because the generation receiving its education during or just after the reign of Peter the Great had come to full maturity. For example, Bolotov, whose early schooling has been

---

[1] Miliukov, *Ocherki*, II, 753–4.
[2] Rozhdestvenskii, *ZMNP*, New Series, XII, 227–8.
[3] *PSZ*, 12,741, 982–3.   [4] Chechulin, *Dela i dni*, I, 99–100.

described above, and who had since benefited from a stay in Königsberg during the Seven Years War and a considerable amount of autodidactic study, was now himself a teacher, instructing a neighbour's son in arithmetic and drawing.[1] Danilov, whose youthful education has also been described above, had now retired and was occupying himself with the care of his stepson. Wrote Danilov:

> I did not start to teach him as the clerk Filipp Brudastoi...taught me. I taught my stepson without causing him the slightest boredom in my instruction, allowed him to walk around often, and taught him to sit down for his lessons himself, without any compulsion. When he was ten, then I taught him arithmetic and drawing, for which he had a great passion and aptitude; we sent him off later to a boarding school and to university to learn the French language, mathematics and other subjects...When he was fifteen, he joined the artillery as a sergeant.[2]

The improvement in private education must not be exaggerated, however. Bolotov and Danilov might have been flattering themselves, and, in any case, there were still young boys experiencing much the same schooling as they had suffered. For example, a poor dvorianin, Hvostov, who had been abroad during the Seven Years War, thought it necessary to have his son taught German, but could ill afford a tutor. The German whom the elder Hvostov engaged was obliged to work with his employer on the latter's estate, Hvostov Junior reading passages from a German lexicon to his tutor as threshing was being carried on.[3] Of course, French culture was by this time in the ascendancy over German in Russia,[4] and the majority of foreign tutors were French. French teachers of both sexes were often of bad quality and were some of the chief targets for the satirists of the 1760s.[5]

G. Vinskii, a Little Russian born in 1752, was educated at Chernigov and Kiev, where the schools were reputed to be better than in Great Russia. While he thought that his education was not very good, Vinskii believed that it would be wrong to blame his schools and teachers, since, through no fault of their own, they did not possess the qualities necessary for their respective tasks. The dawn of learning in Russia, thought Vinskii, did not really commence before the 1770s.[6]

---

[1] Bolotov, *Zhizn'*, II, 526.   [2] Danilov, *Zapiski*, pp. 121–2.
[3] Hvostov, 'Zapiski', *RA* (1870), p. 552.
[4] Haumont, *La culture française en Russie*, p. 88.
[5] Afanas'ev, *Russkie satiricheskie zhurnaly*, pp. 185–8.
[6] Vinskii, *Zapiski*, pp. 16–17.

Apart from Little Russia, the Baltic States and the capitals, no other region possessed many schools of any kind at the time of the convocation of the Legislative Commission.[1]

EDUCATION AT THE LEGISLATIVE COMMISSION

Discussing general state needs in its instruction, the Senate observed that good schools for persons of all ranks did not exist in Russia, and that it was particularly necessary to set up schools to teach merchants' children the subjects appropriate to their calling. The Heraldmaster's office suggested that, as an incentive to the education of all ranks, except serfs, and particularly nobles, those who learned foreign languages and other subjects at their own expense, and could demonstrate their proficiency, should be rewarded with commissioned rank in suitable commands of their own choice. The Little Russian College, for its part, considered that, although there were schools in the Ukraine, including the academy in Kiev, and gymnasia at Chernigov and Pereiaslavl', they were by no means based on those rules for the edification of the young that it had pleased Her Imperial Highness to present for the correction of her people. Moreover, not enough was being done for the sick, mad and sinful. Therefore, for the upbringing and schooling of both sexes of the nobility and of orphans, a monastery and convent should be assigned to young males and females, and these institutions should be directed towards pious works.[2]

Not surprisingly, the government department instruction that addressed itself most to educational questions came from the Academy of Sciences. After noting the necessity for an increase in the number of schools so that learning could prosper, the Academy went on to suggest that the principal division of schools should be between gymnasia and universities, and that elementary schools should be located in every town and village. Not so much had been achieved as in other states by the schools so far set up in Russia, the most important reason for this being the small quantity of them. To improve the quality and increase the number of Russian schools, the Academy promised to submit a plan to the Commission, but said that this would take some time to complete.[3]

[1] Chechulin, *Dela i dni*, I, 98–9.   [2] *SIRIO*, XLIII, 6–19, points 8, 46; 142–3; 230.
[3] *SIRIO*, XLIII, 371–2. This plan was probably completed and used by the subcommittee on education. See Rozhdestvenskii, *ZMNP*, New Series, XII, 196–7.

Education and culture

Again not surprisingly, of the classes represented at the Commission, the dvorianstvo gave most attention to educational questions. Dvoriane were, of course, under service obligations to acquire an education, and were also probably influenced by the higher cultural level of countries in which many of them had lived during the Seven Years War. Of the provinces represented at the Commission, those to the south-west and north-west were most concerned with educational questions. These were under the influence of their more cultured neighbours and non-Russian pasts. Generally, however, the deputies' instructions, and even less their speeches, showed little interest in education.[1]

One of the main reasons for this lack of interest was the low educational level of those who signed the instructions and elected the deputies. To take just the highest class, about 13 per cent of the dvoriane whose names were attached to instructions were illiterate, and many of the others spelled poorly or wrote ungrammatically.[2]

Among the instructions of the nobility concerned with the cultural situation, many painted a dark picture of the ignorance and sloth of the young members of the class. The dvoriane of the Smolensk district said that they were too poor to arrange to have their children learn even the subjects prescribed by the state, and admitted that many of the children hardly knew how to read and write. The Parfen'ev, Archangel, and Dorogobuzh, Smolensk, assemblies had much the same story to tell, while the Kursk, Belgorod, electors claimed that they could not afford teachers, which left their sons in the same predicament as the young Smolensk nobles.[3] But perhaps the strongest criticism of the educational situation of the dvorianstvo came from I. Kuznetsov, deputy of the town Menzelinsk. At the general assembly on 2 October 1767 Kuznetsov declared that in the Orenburg county of Ufa:

There are dvoriane, who do not learn any foreign subjects, but only the Russian _gramota_, while dragoon children, living with their fathers and taken to schools have learnt arithmetic also, apart from the Russian _gramota_. Of these Ufa dvoriane... there are quite a few who do not know the _gramota_, hoping that they might obtain release after short service, and, moreover, a reward in rank, through their rank of dvorianstvo.[4]

[1] V. N. Bochkarev, 'Kul'turnye zaprosy', _RS_, CLXI, 68–9. [2] _Ibid._ p. 327.
[3] _SIRIO_, XIV, 422, 489–90, 433; LXVIII, 549.
[4] _SIRIO_, IV, 217. Foreign subjects would be any beyond the _gramota_, that is, reading and writing.

However, both the proud corporate feeling and traditions of state service of the nobility were more honourably demonstrated in their descriptions of their low educational level. The Belgorod assembly described how the poor among them lived idly in their homes without education, and therefore could not be of any use to the state, and the Tver', Novgorod, electors regretted that they could not always afford the education of their children, who therefore sometimes grew up without 'the education prescribed for the noble dvorianstvo'. The Vereia, Moscow, instruction complained that the children of poor dvoriane could not go to school in the capitals, and grew up ignorant, often illiterate, and were forced to enlist in the army as ordinary soldiers. The Kostroma assembly, also from Moscow, after remarking that there was a lack of schools in its district, wrote, 'And so their children grow up in ignorance and idleness, and not only become unfit for service, but do not have the least appearance of a dvorianin in their life and conduct'.[1]

The picture painted by the dvorianstvo of their cultural situation was not uniformly dark. Little Russia, for example, was a comparatively enlightened region. Motonis, one of the Little Russian nobility, said that he knew of many people who brought up their children in exemplary fashion. The instruction of the Chernigov nobility said that many of the local inhabitants sent their children to Moscow, St Petersburg and elsewhere to be educated, and the Gluhov group noted that a great enthusiasm for education was apparent locally, even though those sending away their children to be educated, because of the lack of local facilities, became impoverished. As far as the lack of local facilities was concerned, the Starodub electors pointed out that, although there were educational establishments in Kiev, Chernigov and Pereiaslavl', they concentrated on Latin studies. Echoing the Gluhov group, the Starodub electors complained that they had to send their children away if they wanted them to learn more than Latin, and this led to great and often ruinous expense.[2]

Provincial towns in Great Russia conformed to the generally gloomy rule as far as their cultural position was concerned. Archangel, for example, although a thriving trade centre, was stagnant

[1] *SIRIO*, LXVIII, 658; XIV, 327; IV, 381; IV, 246.
[2] *SIRIO*, IV, 170; LXVIII, 236, 130, 193. Vinskii, *Zapiski*, p. 13, wrote that, after completing his basic education at Chernigov and Kiev, he 'left Kiev completely stupid concerning necessary knowledge to such a point that if a kind man...had not shown me the first rules of arithmetic, I would have been obliged to count on my fingers'.

culturally. Its instruction described how the young townspeople were poorly brought up, and, rather than drinking at the fount of knowledge, spent most of their time at the local taverns. Because of their ignorance and that of their elders, international commerce carried on locally always put Russian merchants at a disadvantage in their relations with more capable foreigners. Russian merchants were like manufacturers who, having good materials but poor tools, could not properly finish the job.[1]

The situation of the peasants was even worse than that of most of the dvoriane and the burghers. The voice of the bulk of the Russian people was, of course, barely heard at the Commission, but their coarseness and barbarity were often referred to. The deputy of the Serpeisk, Moscow, dvorianstvo, Count Stroganov, described the murder of a noble family by its serfs. 'These villains,' he said, 'like wild animals, not only cut up their lord, but also his wife, and even tore her unborn child from her womb.' Stroganov thought that 'if this kind of people were enlightened, then, of course, we would not be witnesses to such bestiality'. The bishop of Rostov and Iaroslavl' pointed out the obvious fact that peasant children grew up illiterate throughout the whole empire. This ignorance was to be found among the state peasants of the north as well as among the serfs. In the instruction of the Archangel Kovskaia Volost', the peasants of the Kol'sk district complained of the hardships of elective service, which were aggravated by the fact that they had to hire people to do their paper work for them, since none of their number could read or write.[2]

Popular and urban education, as with that of the dvorianstvo, was more developed in Little Russia than in Great Russia. The instruction of the Kiev diocese, for example, said that in all regimental towns, as well as in many of the smaller towns and some villages, priests sent out from the Kiev Academy were working on the enlightenment of the ordinary people.[3]

Generally speaking, however, the disease stunting the growth of Russian cultural life in 1767 was ignorance, of which the main symptoms were illiteracy and inadequate upbringing. What were the causes of this disease? How was it to be cured? First of all, the disease was self-perpetuating: badly educated parents had no ability or in-

[1] *SIRIO*, cxxiii, 464.
[2] *SIRIO*, xxxii, 457; xliii, 422; cxxiii, 30.　　　[3] *SIRIO*, xliii, 90–1.

clination to bring up their children in a cultured manner. Secondly, even those parents who wished their children to be educated were often too poor to send their children to a school or to hire a tutor for them. There was, of course, a small group of parents in favour of education and able to afford it. There were schools in Russia, there were tutors, and there was even a whole class, the priesthood, whose duty was to spread enlightenment, albeit with a narrow focus, but the situation with regard to priests, tutors and schools was not satisfactory, and had to be improved before real cultural advances could be made.

Both the Efremov, Voronezh, and the Pskov, Novgorod, dvoriane complained of the ignorance of the priesthood, and of the incompetence of the priests to care for their flocks. The Efremov instruction recommended that priests of whatever rank should be educated. They should set a good example to the people, who would be inspired to raise their own cultural level and to have more respect for the law. The Pskov instruction substantially agreed with this. Well-educated priests should be sent out to every district from the seminaries, it said, for, just as people behaved badly when confronted with bad priests, so would they behave accordingly when cared for by good priests. The situation as it was allowed many great evils to exist in society, 'lying, theft, pillage and murder are not eradicated, because however much they are subjected to the wordly law, people have no fear of God and do not respect the teaching about him'.[1]

As for the tutors, they were attacked from both ecclesiastical and lay quarters, and so were some aspects of the foreign culture that they had brought with them from western Europe. The bishop of Rostov and Iaroslavl' complained that 'many dvoriane and people of other rank, teaching their children different languages and secular subjects, do not try to teach the catechism at all, so that many noble children do not know how to read the church script'. He recommended that, under threat of heavy fine, dvoriane and other members of society should teach their children to read Russian books, particularly church books, so that they could get to know the dogmas of orthodox belief and guard themselves against libertines. For its part, the Academy of Sciences considered that 'the foreign teachers instructing our children in our homes undoubtedly bring us more harm

---

[1] *SIRIO*, LXVIII, 463; XIV, 396–7. Bishop Afanasii of Rostov and Iaroslavl' said that 'only the exceptional peasant has a proper knowledge of God himself' (*SIRIO*, XLIII, 422).

than benefit, because by far the greater part of them are worthless rather than good'. The governesses, the madames and the mademoiselles, were often engaged without references, and many of them behaved dishonourably. The Academy of Sciences therefore proposed that immigrant teachers of both sexes be obliged to bring with them some proof of their qualifications and to present this for examination.[1]

The principal reason for the low level of Russian education in 1767 was not the incompetence of the priests or tutors, but the severe shortage of schools. The deputies to the Legislative Commission and their electors were well aware of this fact, and several of them suggested that schools be set up. Dvoriane took the main initiative in these suggestions, with their class consciousness persuading them to ask for schools on a class basis. The Sumy, Slobodsko-Ukraina, electors requested that schools be set up first for the dvorianstvo and then for the tradesman and other classes, and the Serpuhov, Tarusa and Obolensk electors from Moscow province wanted schools for members of each class, but these were not typical.[2] More representative of the view of the dvorianstvo as a whole would be the Belev, Belgorod, more exclusive request that a school should be set up in the local town, in which noble children alone would receive instruction, lest these children 'be contaminated by the lower orders...'. Similarly, the Kostroma, Moscow, dvorianstvo, after drawing a desolate picture of the way in which noble minors wasted their time, asked that, in order that these young people could devote themselves to the state and Her Majesty's Service, Her Majesty's maternal attention might be directed towards them. For their basic general education and proper upbringing, would the Empress order schools to be instituted in provincial towns?[3]

Although the charity of the dvorianstvo did not usually extend to other classes, several assemblies were concerned with the less affluent members of their own class. The Belgorod assembly, for example, expressed the hope that 'all noble children who cannot be educated at home because of their poverty, and cannot travel to the established educational institutions because of their distance, will learn reading

[1] *SIRIO*, XLIII, 422–3, 372.
[2] *SIRIO*, LXVIII, 276; IV, 363–4.
[3] *SIRIO*, LXVIII, 610–11; IV, 246. Similar requests to be found in the instructions from Kaluga and Medyn', and Vereia, Moscow, Smolensk, and Kursk, Belgorod (*SIRIO*, IV, 289, 381; XIV, 422; LXVIII, 549).

and writing and similar subjects proper for the dvorianstvo in their towns'. Two Novgorod districts wanted food and clothing to be assigned to schools for poor noble students from the great bounty of Her Imperial Majesty, while the Alatyr', Nizhnii Novgorod, electors thought that the projected schools should cater for children whose parents owned not more than a hundred souls.[1]

There was no unanimity on the subject of school financing. Vereia, Moscow, and Pereiaslavl', Little Russia, electors wanted the state to finance education, the capital district of the Moscow province wanted proportionate payments from all dvoriane and additional contributions from the parents of students, and Kashin, Moscow, dvoriane also wanted students to be financially supported by their parents. The Kursk, Belgorod, and Tver', Novgorod, societies thought that teachers should be paid for by the state and pupils by their parents, and Tula and Kaluga and Medyn' dvoriane, all from Moscow, thought that either the state or the dvorianstvo could finance the education of young members of the class.[2]

The state and the nobility were by no means the only sources of educational finance proposed in the instructions of the dvoriane. While the Ahtyrka, Slobodsko-Ukraina, assembly wanted the state to give 3,000 roubles to Har'kov College, it also suggested that local schools and teachers could be paid for from the income of the province. The Kiev, Little Russia, nobility wanted a local university to be supported by customs payments and payments for supplies given to the army during wars against Turkey and Prussia. The Chernigov, Little Russia, assembly thought that educational costs could be covered by the profits of a local bank, while the Dorogobuzh, Smolensk, dvoriane thought that books should be sold to pay for schools. The electors of the three Moscow districts, Serpuhov, Tarusa and Obolensk, wanted scholastic finances to come from court fines.[3]

At the general assembly of the Legislative Commission, O. Kozhin, deputy of the Kashin, Moscow, nobility, suggested that, since the dvorianstvo was indispensable to the state, the upkeep of the noble academies should derive from a general state marriage tax. While agreeing with much that Kozhin said, Count Stroganov

[1] *SIRIO*, LXVIII, 658; XIV, 262, 359; LXVIII, 116.
[2] *SIRIO*, IV, 381; LXVIII, 150–1; IV, 231, 468–9; LXVIII, 549; XIV, 327; IV, 405–6, 289.
[3] *SIRIO*, LXVIII, 257, 176–7, 244; XIV, 433; IV, 360.

thought that such a tax would contravene the Instruction of the Empress, and referred in particular to sections 282 and 288 of that document, which implied that there should be a premium on marriage rather than a tax. Any tax for the education of the dvorianstvo would not have been welcomed by the other classes of Russian society, as was made clear by I. Chuprov, representing the Archangel state peasants. Discussing a relevant item in the Rights of the Nobles in August 1768, Chuprov said that schools must be set up at the expense of those who were to make use of them. Marshal Bibikov interrupted him. Could the dvorianstvo set up schools? That was the question. Replying in the affirmative, Chuprov repeated his first remark that it must be done at the expense of the dvorianstvo.[1]

As far as school administration was concerned, dvoriane usually favoured a local basis. Thus the schools would be in the hands of the provincial government dominated by the dvorianstvo, if their requests in that field were also acted upon. To illustrate this line of thought with instructions from Moscow province, that from Tula proposed that schools be placed in the charge of the noble commander, and that from Kaluga and Medyn' wanted a tribunal of nobles to care for local class education. Serpuhov, Tarusa and Obolensk electors wanted the *voevoda* to be the principal educational official, and, more generally, the Dmitrov assembly considered that marshals and local judges should see to it that every dvorianin in their district was making some arrangements for the education of his children.[2]

Several groups of nobles were agreed that it was necessary to set up schools for young members of their own class, and they had similar attitudes to the question of school administration, if not to that of finance. Two other questions had to be considered by the nobility in the field of education: what were the aims of education, and what form should it take? Whatever the answers to these questions, the mere fact that the desire for adequate local schools was in evidence in many provinces was a new phenomenon, and marked a considerable step forward in the cultural development of Russia. The government had long been forced to use coercion in this field: now, many dvoriane voluntarily and even enthusiastically tried to arrange the education of their children.

[1] *SIRIO*, IV, 173–4, 174–5; XXXII, 300. For sections 282 and 288 of the Instruction, see Reddaway, *Documents*, pp. 260–1.
[2] *SIRIO*, IV, 406, 289, 363–4; VIII, 506.

However, the dvoriane concerning themselves with education were rarely interested in it *per se*. Its primary purpose, they considered, was to instil class pride and patriotism, and to make the young capable of useful service and advancement in service. The Belev, Belgorod, electors thought that schools were necessary so that their children might be more worthy and capable than those of any other class to carry on Her Imperial Majesty's military service. From Moscow, the Kaluga and Medyn' assembly considered it important that, by reading the laws instituted by Her Most High Imperial Majesty for the felicity of her subjects, noble students would be inspired to make themselves worthy of the duties to be imposed upon them concerning the administration of these laws. More generally, the Little Russian group from Gluhov expressed the opinion that 'through enlightenment the local youth could more suitably carry out their service to the state advantage', and the Smolensk group from Dorogobuzh argued that 'the more teaching and books are disseminated, the better condition the dvorianstvo can be in and the fitter for service'.[1]

While the Bahmut Hussar Regiment Officers said that their children should go from New Russia to Moscow University and the cadet corps to be educated 'solely for the good of the fatherland and our society', they were also anxious that these children should be assigned to the most suitable kind of service and receive appropriate advantages. Other groups stressed patriotic motives for education less and selfish motives more. The Opochka, Novgorod, district, for example, requested that students who graduated from their gymnasium or passed a cadet corps examination should be rewarded with commissioned rank.[2] The self-interest of the dvorianstvo in the field of education was made even more apparent by some of their deputies at the general assembly. The Belyi Smolensk, representative, B. Potemkin, pointed out that, while corps graduates were almost certain to become officers after their free education, young dvoriane educated domestically at their parents' expense were obliged to commence their service at the same level as illiterates. Potemkin thought that young dvoriane should therefore be commissioned if they passed an examination in the basic subjects and foreign languages. The Poshehon'e, Moscow, deputy, V. Golenishchev-Kutuzov, went further than Potemkin in expressing the hope that dvoriane educated

---

[1] *SIRIO*, LXVIII, 610; IV, 289; LXVIII, 130; XIV, 433.
[2] *SIRIO*, XCIII, 54; XIV, 275.

at the expense of their own family would have an advantage in service advancement over those educated in state institutions. To avoid confusion, V. Baskakov of the Sudislavl', Moscow, dvorianstvo wanted it definitely to be decided which subjects and to what level should be necessary for the acquisition of officer's rank.[1]

While dvoriane were sometimes very down to earth about the purposes of education, they could also be way up in the clouds. The electors of the Pskov district, as well as requesting that those who received a domestic education be placed on a par with corps graduates, put forward the belief that:

Everywhere in the towns there will be gymnasia kept up by the dvoriane themselves. Each will enthusiastically teach his children, without counting the cost, and all civil and military positions will be filled with good and enlightened people; in Russia everywhere knowledge will develop in a very short time.[2]

The Sumy, Slobodsko-Ukraina, group thought that, after schools had been set up for their children and for those of other ranks, 'a great harvest will accrue to the fatherland, and ignorance, depraved morals, superstition, schisms and everything similarly harmful to the existence of a well-behaved people will be destroyed'.[3]

The final question to be considered, as far as the dvorianstvo's opinion on its own education is concerned, is the actual form that this education was to take, that is, what kind of schools should there be, and what should be taught in them? There was, first of all, some desire for new cadet corps to be instituted. The Chernigov dvorianstvo wanted such a corps to be set up in Little Russia, considering it necessary for the inculcation of proper behaviour and of everything useful for a noble in military and civil service. A cadet corps was also requested by the Little Russian groups from Nezhin and Baturin and Pereiaslavl'. The Starodub assembly indicated a possible reason for the widespread Little Russian desire for a cadet corps. By a decree of 1761 addressed to the Director of the St Petersburg Cadet Corps, the Starodub instruction said, it had been ordered that the young Little

[1] *SIRIO*, IV, 209; XXXII, 213, 213–14. Similar ideas to those of Baskakov to be found in the instruction from Serpuhov, Tarusa and Obolensk, Moscow. This said that, for the glory of the flourishing state, fathers and mothers taught children various subjects and languages. Peter the Great, the instruction said, had declared that arithmetic and engineering were sufficient for commissioned rank, but at the present time, everybody was thrown together without any regularity. Could it therefore be pointed out who was to receive what rank for what knowledge? (*SIRIO*, IV, 362–3).

[2] *SIRIO*, XIV, 401.   [3] *SIRIO*, LXVIII, 276.

Russian nobles could not be considered the equals of the Great Russian dvoriane and should not therefore be admitted to the corps, although young Baltic nobles could be admitted.[1] A similar feeling of under-privilege prompted the Moscow district to ask for the institution of a corps in the old capital. The strong class basis of such a corps was well described by O. Kozhin, the deputy of the Kashin district, who also requested the introduction of the corps to Moscow. The Heraldmaster was to see that young dvoriane only were admitted to the corps, according to Kozhin's proposals, and young dvoriane were to receive their education solely in the corps and the naval and artillery schools.[2]

As well as these class schools of a semi-military type, some groups of dvorianstvo also considered means of arranging a more general education for their children. The Ahtyrka, Slobodsko-Ukraina, electors requested that Har'kov College be ordered to accept the children of local dvoriane for the study of military and non-military subjects, and several Little Russian groups wanted local schools for girls as well as boys, and a university or academy in addition to a corps. The attitude of these groups was well expressed by the instruction of Nezhin and Baturin, which declared that such institutions would be set up 'For the enlightenment of the morals of the people and the eradication of ignorance and in consideration of the fact that, without a good education, it is impossible to be a skilful and brave military leader, a wise state servant, just judge, prudent householder, and a useful citizen of society'. The Nezhin and Baturin nobles thought that the university or academy was particularly necessary 'for instruction of higher subjects and the circulation of / the results of / experiments, with which learned men could serve to the state advantage and to their own in household economy and in everything essential to human life'. From the Baltic area, a Livonian group asked for the reintroduction of the gymnasium that had been there in Swedish times.[3]

As well as occurring in the more cultured provinces to the south-west and north-west, thoughts of a more general education were not entirely absent from the centre. The Moscow district wanted an institution for noble girls, and the Tula nobility wanted a gymnasium

[1] *SIRIO*, LXVIII, 237, 137, 150–1, 190.
[2] *SIRIO*, IV, 172–3; LXVIII, 257.
[3] *SIRIO*, LXVIII, 257; Nezhin and Baturin, LXVIII, 137; Pereiaslavl', LXVIII, 150–1; Chernigov, LXVIII, 236–7; LXVIII, 72.

with a professor and two assistants in at least every county town, where the students could learn enough for the completion of their education at the Imperial University and Academy. With the same end in view, Shcherbatov spoke at the general assembly of the necessity of schools in Siberia, so that 'enlightenment should penetrate as much as possible into this land'.[1]

As far as the general curriculum of the new schools was concerned, class considerations and service traditions were, as elsewhere, influential, and so the Belgorod nobility, for example, asked that students be taught reading and writing and other subjects proper for the dvorianstvo including arithmetic and geometry. The Kashin, Moscow, group was similarly interested in preparing its children for service: its educational programme comprised, 'First, the Christian law; secondly, the French and German languages, drawing, fencing, arithmetic, geometry and trigonometry, artillery and fortification.'[2] Additional subjects suggested by other groups were architecture, engineering and geodesy.[3] Some assemblies talked of other subjects 'concerning society', or for the good of society,[4] but gave no hint of what these might be. Thus in 1767 the views of the dvorianstvo on educational curricula and educational questions of all types appear to have been hardly more sophisticated than their views at the time of Peter the Great. In other words, it had taken nearly fifty years for an appreciable number of dvoriane to come to accept voluntarily what Peter had been attempting to knock into their recalcitrant heads at the beginning of the century.

Russian burghers also took an interest in the development of education in 1767, although to a lesser extent than the nobles. In towns, as in districts, the attitude towards schools was tinged by a class feeling of considerable strength. And so the town electors of Solikamsk in Kazan' wanted schools and orphanages for merchants alone, controlled by the magistrates and nobody else.[5]

Burghers generally agreed that town schools should be supported by the towns themselves: they were not as certain as dvoriane that

[1] *SIRIO*, IV, 231, 405–6, 161.
[2] *SIRIO*, LXVIII, 658; IV, 468.
[3] Belev, Belgorod, *SIRIO*, LXVIII, 610–11; Ahtyrka, Slobodsko-Ukraina, LXVIII, 257.
[4] Dorogobuzh, Smolensk, *SIRIO*, XIV, 433; Vereia, Moscow, IV, 381. Chechulin considered that the infrequency of a definite programme for education in the dvorianstvo's instructions revealed a lack of real interest in the subject (*Dela i dni*, I, 97–8).
[5] *SIRIO*, CVII, 537. Similar views expressed by the inhabitants of Riazhsk, Voronezh, CXLIV, 251.

they should receive subsidies from the state. Viaz'ma, Smolensk, electors thought that the income and economy of its inhabitants would pay for the schools, and so thought Vologda and the capital town from Archangel province.[1] The Archangel, as well as the Solikamsk, instruction proposed that school supervision be local, and, along with those from Vologda and Viaz'ma the Archangel electors considered that supervision should be very firm, with education being made compulsory.[2]

Burghers, like dvoriane, looked upon education from a practical point of view. Just as young nobles were to be taught to carry out their class duties more capably, so were young merchants and tradesmen. The Archangel townsmen put forward the most detailed recommendations for the achievement of this aim: their curriculum would include correct writing and style for commercial letters, arithmetic, knowledge of foreign weights and measures, bookkeeping, mercantile geography, foreign languages, Russian and foreign commercial law, and navigation.[3]

Of the few dvoriane to consider the question of bourgeois education at the general assembly, N. Tolmachev of the Liubim, Moscow, district gave it the closest attention. He thought that schools for tradesmen should be set up everywhere to teach reading and writing and to explain the laws of the state. In large towns, Tolmachev wanted high schools to be set up to teach German and English and navigation in addition to the basic subjects.[4]

The question of popular education was raised both by the deputies and their instructions. Some dvoriane, a few bishops and some representatives of the state peasants all spoke or wrote in favour of schools for the peasants. The Kopor'e, St Petersburg, district, Gregory Orlov's constituency, wanted schools to be arranged in churches for peasant children aged 7 to 12 to be taught reading and writing and the first foundations of law at a moderate fee in wintertime only. In this way, the Kopor'e instruction expected, the morals of children would be corrected, and, although this was not actually mentioned, they would not miss any part of the farming season and the state would not have to pay much of a subsidy for their education. The Krapivna assembly from Moscow wanted priests to teach young

[1] *SIRIO*, cxxxiv, 105; cxxiii, 431, 480–1. The Viaz'ma electors thought that an additional source of educational finance could be court fines.
[2] *SIRIO*, as in two previous footnotes.
[3] *SIRIO*, cxxiii, 464. [4] *SIRIO*, viii, 36–7.

souls from the age of 7 at the expense of their parents. Thus, the lower orders would acquire enlightened reason, and, again, at low cost to the state and the dvorianstvo. The bishop of Rostov and Iaroslavl' also wanted peasant schools introduced, by means of which, he thought, 'knowledge of the Christian law will be inculcated, and the coarseness of their manners will be corrected and various lawless deeds...will be eradicated'.[1]

Similarly, at the general assembly, a suggestion for schools catering for young members of his own class put forward by I. Zherebtsov, of the Nizhnii Novgorod county farmer-soldiers, was welcomed by Count Stroganov. After remarking how useful education was for mankind, and how fatal actions were committed by people who were spoiled by ignorance, Stroganov went on to suggest that Zherebtsov's plan be extended to include all tillers of the soil, who, emerging from the darkness of ignorance, would deserve to possess property and freedom. Peter Orlov, the Klin, Moscow, deputy, expressed his agreement with Stroganov, and went on to observe that enlightened knowledge was most necessary for the spiritual animal that was man, but that this knowledge came only rarely by nature and much more often by instruction, which was to be given by schools. With these thoughts in mind, Orlov said, he had set up an elementary school on his own estate, where those peasants too young to work in the fields were taught. This school had been very successful, since his young serfs now realized far better than before their duties to God, their sovereign, their fatherland, and, last, but probably not least, their landlord.[2]

More down to earth were the assemblies of Dmitrov, Moscow Province, and Pskov, Novgorod, who both saw material benefits accruing from popular education: educated serfs would be more productive, they pointed out. Practically minded, too, were the retired N.C.O.s and soldiers of Menzelinsk, who foresaw a better military career for their children if they were to learn to read and write and know something of military affairs before joining their regiments.[3]

As far as the administration of popular education was concerned, the parochial arrangement of peasant schools was most widely supported, with the peasants themselves making contributions to the

[1] *SIRIO*, xiv, 244; viii, 557; xliii, 422.
[2] *SIRIO*, xxxii, 398, 453, 457, 520–2.
[3] *SIRIO*, viii, 507; xiv, 397; cxv, 216.

upkeep of these church schools.[1] If priests were to be the principal teachers in these schools, it was, of course, necessary that they themselves be better educated, as the Kerensk, Voronezh, group suggested, expressing the hope that the lower orders would thus be enlightened and the schism eradicated. The Sumy, Slobodsko-Ukraina, dvorianstvo hoped that 'the dearth of understanding (the rules belonging to the church service, how to preach the word of God and teach the law to ordinary people) church officials will be corrected in many places' as new schools were set up.[2]

Not everybody wanted popular education to be on a clerical basis: the Dmitrov nobility, for example, wanted individual landlords or groups of them to hire lay teachers, who would instruct the peasants in reading and writing and the simple rules of arithmetic.[3] And some were opposed to popular education in any regular shape or form. M. Glazov, the deputy of the Oboian', Belgorod, district, thought that to waste time on the education of peasant children would ruin agriculture. Landlords could send their serfs to school if they wanted to, but it was much more necessary to ensure that the serfs went to church on Sundays to learn how to avoid criminal and schismatic activities.[4]

A much broader programme for elementary education than any put forward in the general assembly was composed by a subcommittee on schools, which included three dvoriane, and whose plan was entitled 'The institution of lower schools in towns and small towns'. The plan proposed the introduction of compulsory elementary education, with schools staffed by church officials, supervised by the priests under the control of the bishops. The Holy Synod was to arrange the publication of the following books: an ABC-book in church and secular print; a short catechism; and a brief treatise on natural law. The Academy of Sciences would be asked to compose two books: the first concerning simple arithmetic including fractions; the second comprising an atlas, with the four quarters of the earth in separate maps and indications of the location of the most important states and towns. It was hoped that the teachers would find these books easy to understand and to explain to their charges. If the pupils completed the study of all these books, they should be given the New

[1] So thought the Bishop of Rostov and Iaroslavl', the Archbishop of St Petersburg, nd Krapivna, Moscow, for example (*SIRIO*, xliii, 422, 418; viii, 557).
[2] *SIRIO*, lxviii, 436–7, 277.
[3] *SIRIO*, viii, 507.   [4] *SIRIO*, xxxii, 533–4.

Testament to read, and the Instruction of Her Royal Highness, as well as an ancient history and other historical and moral works.

All corporal punishments on the children were to be completely forbidden, and the sub-committee's report specified that the pupils were not to be hit on the face, nor seized by the hair or ears. However, idle and stubborn students were to be forced to remain standing in class, or to sit on a special chair, or to study for an extra hour, or to drop down to a lower class. Parents were to pay for their children's instruction and books, unless they were too poor, in which case, after careful scrutiny of their situation, half the fees would be paid from the school funds. An important lay person was to be appointed Chief Ward of the schools, and he would be consulted by the Synod on educational matters, watch the educational progress of the children and interference of parents or guardians, and report on his findings to the Empress.[1]

THE CHURCH

A considerable degree of the elusiveness of a full understanding of Russian history is perhaps a result of the difficulty of arriving at a satisfactory evaluation of the part played in it by the Church and religion. Little help in the resolution of this difficulty is given by the materials of the Legislative Commission, which did not devote much of its attention to religious questions.

Here as elsewhere, the pattern was to some extent set by the Empress in her Instruction. This document, it is true, is prefaced by an invocation, 'O Lord my God, hearken unto me, and instruct me; that I may administer Judgment unto thy People; as thy sacred Laws direct to judge with Righteousness!' The opening remark of the Instruction itself observes that 'The Christian Law teaches us to do mutual Good to one another, as much as possibly we can'.[2] In the remainder of the Instruction, however, four points only are of a predominantly religious nature. In her discussion 'Of the Laws in particular', declaring that there are four classes of crime, Catherine goes on to assert that the first of these consists of crimes against re-

[1] Solov'ev, *RV*, xxxv, 338–9. The three members of the sub-committee from the dvorianstvo were Klingshtet, Baron Ash, the deputy of the Medicine College, and V. Zolotnitskii, representing the Kiev Regiment nobility. The reading of the Instruction was not encouraged in fact, although copies of the document were ordered to be distributed to local government offices. See *PSZ*, xviii, 348–9, 531–2, nos. 12,977, 13,107, 24 September 1767, 28 April 1768.　　　　[2] Reddaway, *Documents*, p. 215.

ligion such as sacrilege, which should be punished by a temporary or permanent excommunication. Somewhat later, in the chapter entitled 'Of Education', the Empress adjured 'Every Parent...to teach his Children the Fear of God, as the Beginning of all Wisdom, and to inculcate in them all those Duties, which God demands from us in the ten Commandments, and our orthodox Eastern Greek Religion, in its Rules and Traditions'. Thirdly, among 'different Statutes which require Explanation', she expressed the opinion that the peace and security of the citizens of a state such as Russia, containing so many different nations, would be greatly endangered by not allowing them to profess different types of religion. Moreover, a prudent toleration of other religions not repugnant to the Orthodox religion and polity was the most certain means of bringing back wandering sheep to the flock of the faithful. Also, extreme caution should be exercised in the examination of persons accused of witchcraft and heresy, since suspicion born of ignorance could prove dangerous to a citizen of the most exemplary behaviour. Fourthly and finally, in the supplement to the Instruction entitled 'Of good Order, otherwise termed Police', Catherine argued that particular care and attention ought to be given:

Not to allow any Thing which may disturb the Celebration of divine Service in Places appointed for that Purpose, and that *Order*, and proper *Decorum* should be *observed* by the Citizens, at the Time of the *Procession with the Cross*, and such like *Rights* and *Ceremonies*.[1]

These remarks do not add up to much. In the third of them, Catherine's recommendation of toleration was rather bold, perhaps, although not unprecedented; for the most part, she was treading warily on matters of religion in her Instruction, enjoining strict observance to the externals of religious ceremony, and saying nothing about inner questions of faith.

She had taken this course right from the beginning of her reign, well remembering that a careless approach to the Russian Church had been one of the reasons for her predecessor's downfall. As she had put it in the Manifesto of 28 June 1762:

Our Greek Orthodox law first of all felt a shock and the destruction of its church traditions, so that Our Greek Church has been...subject to the ultimate danger by the change of the ancient Orthodoxy in Russia and the adoption of an infidel law.[2]

[1] *Ibid.* pp. 223, 272, 289–90, 297.   [2] *PSZ*, XVI, 3–4, no. 11,582, 28 June 1762.

The manifesto had considered that this was more responsible for Peter III's downfall than his unpopular foreign policy. Although the disaffection of the Guards, not necessarily caused by either of these ill-advised policies, was more serious than both of them for Peter, Catherine was careful not to repeat any of the mistakes made by her husband.

A good example of Catherine's delicate approach to church questions is her handling of the problem of the secularization of ecclesiastical estates, a measure introduced during the short reign of Peter III. First, Catherine rescinded Peter's decree, giving as her principal reason the poor preparation of her husband's action. A few months later, the Empress gave detailed instructions to a commission on church estates, and enrolled army officers to help make a list of them. Next, detailed accounts were ordered to be made of the income from these estates, and then the College of Economy was re-established. The transfer of the church estates to the supervision of this college was made effective by the decree of 26 February 1764. The measure was not unopposed, but opposition was weaker than it might have been if the secularization had been carried out more summarily.[1]

Taking her adopted religion seriously, Catherine made some attempt to improve both the moral and material level of the clergy, but without much success. According to I. Znamenskii, priests of low and high degree took and gave bribes, swore and got drunk. 'Had we been able to disclose all the abnormal phenomena in the existence of the clergy during the eighteenth century,' wrote Znamenskii, 'undoubtedly many of our contemporaries would have believed the realistic exposure to be a libel.'[2] The poor material situation of the ordinary parish priest was described in the notebooks of such a one from the Iaroslavl' region, I. Matusevich,[3] and the Synod instruction also pointed out that many priests were obliged to work their own land because of their poverty.[4]

---

[1] See *PSZ*, xvi, 51–3, no. 11,643, 12 August 1762, for the repeal of Peter III's decree; xvi, 117–24, no. 11,716, 29 November 1762, for Catherine's instructions; xvi, 146–52, no. 11,745, 29 January 1763, for enrolment of army officers; *PSZ*, nos. 11,747, 11,789, 11,791, for instructions concerning the arrangement of the accounts; *PSZ*, xvi, 246–7, no. 11,814, 12 May 1763, for re-establishment of the College of Economy; and xvi, 549–69, no. 12,060, for the transfer of church estates to the College. For information on the leader of the opposition to the measure, see articles by Ikonnikov and Barsov in *RS*, xxiv, xxv, xxvi, xv.

[2] I. Znamenskii, *Polozhenie duhovenstva v tsarstvovanie Ekateriny II i Pavla I*, chapters iii, iv, 161–2, 81.

[3] V. I. Semevskii, 'Sel'skii sviashchennik vo vtoroi polovine xviii veka', *RS*, xix.

[4] *SIRIO*, xliii, 49.

The Church

The attitude of the dvorianstvo towards the clergy was not very solicitous. Generally, Lord Macartney considered, 'The clergy of Russia is the least feared, respected, esteemed, or beloved' in all the world,[1] and the dvorianstvo amply demonstrated such an attitude. In 1769 the Synod reported to the Senate that several noble landlords had beaten up church officials, that these clergymen could get no satisfaction from the civil authorities and were often too poor to contemplate court action. In 1767 the government revealed that landlords were not giving priests their fair share of land during the survey.[2]

The instructions of the dvorianstvo concentrated less on suggestions for the improvement of the clerical class than on complaints concerning their situation as it was and harsh remedies for it. The Pronsk, Moscow, electors asserted that theft was practised in their district mainly by the unemployed children of the clergy, who should be sent off to the army or required to pay poll tax. The Kerensk, Voronezh, instruction echoed these two suggestions, and proposed in addition that surplus clerics be sent to the state factories or Siberia, while the Orel, Belgorod, instruction wanted such people to be attached to the estates of the landlords. The dvoriane from the capital district of Belgorod were also concerned with putting to work idle members of the clerical class 'who fall into various kinds of mischief and theft', but the most thorough indictment came from Belev in the same province. It was apparent from local investigations, said the Belev instruction, that local bands of brigands were mainly composed of priests, deacons and sextons. To eradicate these evil gangs, priests should be closely watched, and church officials found guilty of theft should be sent off to the army or exile.[3]

Apart from members of the clerical class, four other groups identifiable by their religion met with the disapproval of the dvorianstvo. Dvoriane did not like schismatics, and instructions to their deputies suggested that these dissenters be completely wiped out, removed or brought under control, or exiled to Siberia, or some other remote part.[4] Non-Christians were not very charitably regarded by the nobility, the Sviazhsk, Kazan', electors, for example, considering

[1] Macartney, *An Account of Russia*, p. 48.
[2] *PSZ*, xviii, 878, no. 13,286, 15 April 1769; xviii, 156–62, no. 12,925, 2 July 1767.
[3] *SIRIO*, iv, 388; lxviii, 444, 521–2, 658–9, 614.
[4] Vereia, Moscow, *SIRIO*, iv, 375–7; Pogara, Little Russia, lxviii, 209–10; Valuiki, Belgorod, lxviii, 582–3.

that these augmented the number of brigands, and should therefore be severely punished, while the Ufa, Orenburg, electors wanted Tartars and similar groups to be removed from their locality, except those who had freely accepted the Orthodox faith as their own.[1] However, converts generally were not given a warm welcome into the ranks of the faithful by the dvorianstvo. The Penza, Kazan', instruction hoped that those who had recently become Christians would be quickly included in the levies for the army, as did that from Alatyr', Novgorod. The Temnikov, Voronezh, electors hoped that local land surpluses would be given to their peasants rather than to the converts.[2] An equally harsh attitude was shown by the dvorianstvo towards non-Orthodox Christians in the border provinces. One of the complaints against runaway serfs put forward by the Pustorzheva, Novgorod, instruction was that:

Most regrettably of all, they destroy their natural faith of the Greek confession without the smallest fear of God. Observing that the Catholic and Uniate rites are more permissive than ours, they not only accept them enthusiastically themselves, but convert their children also. The Polish Catholic and Uniate priests try to cajole them...and to lure them into a permanent attachment to the / Polish / nobility, which leads to the obvious destruction of our revered faith and to our own extreme ruin and eventual emptying of all our borderlands.[3]

The attitude of the dvoriane towards groups identifiable through their religion appears, then, to have been motivated by feelings of self-interest rather than of faith. It could be argued that the instructions were hardly the medium for avowals of piety, and that many dvoriane were in fact deeply religious in their outlook. This was perhaps so, but evidence for such an argument is hard to find. Moreover, religious faith in Russia in the 1760s was under attack from two quarters, one of recent origin, the other age-old. In the first place, the spirit of Voltaire was spreading throughout the capitals and into the provinces. Znamenskii, for example, considered that this spirit was epidemic.[4] Miliukov, while remarking that the ideas of Voltaire struck the dvorianstvo as did any Parisian fashion and spread as fast as a rumour, did not consider that these ideas penetrated deeply. He wrote:

[1] *SIRIO*, LXVIII, 37–8; XCIII, 9–10.
[2] *SIRIO*, LXVIII, 20, 118, 453–4.
[3] *SIRIO*, XIV, 297.   [4] Znamenskii, *Polozhenie duhovenstva*, pp. 164–5.

The Church

The young provincial nobles, coming to serve in St Petersburg, could not but be impressed by the propaganda of the renowned atheists. But later on, one fine day and without ceremony or compromise, most of them returned to the belief or the spiritual indifference of their fathers.[1]

Secondly, and more seriously, the weight of its pre-Christian past still pressed heavily on Russia: superstition and folk-lore were still powerful influences. In her Instruction, the Empress ordered stricter control over 'Magicians, Fortune-tellers, Prophets, and such like *Impostors*'.[2] In its instruction, the Senate recommended severer punishments for self-styled wizards, witches and *klikushi*, epileptics said to be possessed of the devil. The Chief Police Department and the Holy Synod made similar recommendations.[3] More generally, the satirical journals of the time attacked all relics of bygone cultural eras.[4] While the lower orders were most attached to ancient beliefs and attitudes, the dvorianstvo was by no means completely free from them, Fonvizin's plays, *The Brigadier* and *The Minor*, providing amusing examples of the old dvorianin with outmoded views as well as of the young fop under French influence. Along with the new enlightenment and the older Orthodox faith, then, there was an element of heathen obscurantism in the outlook of Russia's leading class at the time of the Legislative Commission.

RUSSIAN CULTURE

Catherine II was a Westerner: 'Russia,' she averred in the first chapter of her Instruction, 'is an European state'. The proof of this, said Catherine, could be seen in the ease with which Peter the Great had undertaken his alterations. This had been greater than Peter himself expected, 'because the Manners, which prevailed at that Time, and had been introduced amongst us by a Mixture of different Nations, and the Conquest of foreign Territories, were quite unsuitable to the Climate'. According to Reddaway, these remarks are the conclusion of an argument, developed in the opening chapter of the Instruction, and forming the foundation for her general thesis. Reddaway interprets Catherine's preliminary argument in the following manner. Religion inculcates an awareness of mutual good: good comprises patriotism and the rule of law. Law should be

---

[1] Miliukov, *Ocherki*, III, 403.   [2] Reddaway, *Documents*, p. 297.
[3] *SIRIO*, XLIII, 6–19, point 26, 305, 45–6.
[4] Afanas'ev, *Russkie satiricheskie zhurnaly*, pp. 139–44, 149.

natural, and, implied in her use of the word 'citizen', the individual is to be active in the state, not a mere subject. For Russia, 'natural' means 'European', and the way is clear for Catherine and the citizens to do their religious duty by giving Russia the best European laws.[1]

The principal group of citizens, whose contribution to mutual good would be most significant, was the dvorianstvo. Were the dvoriane capable of rendering the assistance that their Empress asked of them? Were they sufficiently aware of the ideas, procedures and practices of western Europe? To answer these very important questions, some recapitulation of previous observations now becomes necessary.

To consider first the economic aspect of the consciousness of the nobility, the Free Economic Society and its Works had combined with the slow, cumulative influence of fresh breezes blowing through Russia since the window on the West had been opened to create, by 1767 at least, a nucleus of dvoriane acquainted with current European theories and techniques. These dvoriane appear to have left their mark on the instructions. Requests for the institution of banks, for example, could not have been entirely indigenous in origin. The desire for periodic exchanges of information and opinion concerning estate management revealed a burgeoning spirit of self-improvement in the attitude of some noble assemblies. At the general assembly of the Commission, deputies from the dvorianstvo like Shcherbatov on the one hand and Korob'in and Kozel'skii on the other demonstrated knowledge and understanding of the European economic situation.

In the social and political outlook of the nobility in 1767, acquaintance with the theory and practice of the West is also discernible. Proposals for changes in the structure of the law and administration, as well as for the development of a class organization and the amendment of the Table of Ranks, were to some extent the result of exposure to western Europe. While some of the noble deputies experienced some difficulty in their handling of such unfamiliar concepts as freedom, the debates at the general assembly were considerably coloured by references to alien societies and political structures.

As for the attitude of the dvorianstvo towards education, the ligh of the West is less apparent than the shadow of Peter the Great, with his strong emphasis on education for service purposes. However, the

[1] Reddaway, *Documents*, pp. 216, 322.

fact that many dvoriane wanted to achieve education rather than having it thrust upon them marked a significant step forward, and a desire for more general enlightenment was at least faintly perceptible. Sympathy for Catherine's moderate support of toleration or any other progressive idea in the field of religion is difficult to find in the views of the nobility as expressed at the Commission. Even in other spheres, it must be stressed, those dvoriane who showed an awareness of the enlightened views that the Empress was attempting to help disseminate were in a small minority.

6

CATHERINE THE GREAT AND THE
RUSSIAN NOBILITY

THE SIGNIFICANCE OF THE LEGISLATIVE COMMISSION

The principal reason for the suspension of the activities of the general assembly of the Legislative Commission was probably the official one, the outbreak of war with Turkey. However, it was not so much the preoccupation of the deputies with the Turkish War as that of the Empress herself that caused the curtailment of the commission, for, while Sergeevich accepted the decree of dissolution at its face value, pointing out the large number of deputies who held military rank,[1] Lipinskii observed that fewer deputies actually left the Commission at the beginning of the war than at the transfer of the Commission from Moscow to St Petersburg, and therefore did not consider the closure of the general assembly a military necessity.[2]

The Commission as a whole was now moribund, although continued appointment and election of deputies to it[3] and reference to it in later legislation[4] reflected some uncertainty on the matter of both people and government. It was not until 1774, however, that a more definite conclusion was given to the Commission with a decree ordering the disbandment of the committees and sub-committees. The explanation put forward on this occasion, to allow deputies to go home to pursue 'useful domestic tasks',[5] strongly suggests that there were reasons for the break-up of the Commission other than those contained in official announcements.

An important unofficial reason for the dispersal of the Commission was almost certainly the fact that it had proved itself incapable of the task for which it had been summoned, the compilation of a new law code. Russia's chief class, the nobility, had failed to produce a sufficient number of legal experts. Bibikov and the other directors of the Commission had been incompetent to make the fullest use of the knowledge and talents that some of the deputies had possessed.[6]

[1] Sergeevich, *VE*, i (1878), 260.   [2] Lipinskii, *ZMNP*, CCLI, 232–3.
[3] Florovskii, *Sostav*, pp. 544–6, 564–6.   [4] Korf, *Dvorianstvo*, p. 91.
[5] Lipinskii, *ZMNP*, CCLI, 233–4.
[6] A. S. Lappo-Danilevskii, 'Sobranie i svod zakonov Rossiiskoi imperii, sostavlennye v tsarstvovanie Imperatritsy Ekateriny II', *ZMNP*, CCCIX, 3–44.

The significance of the Commission

A third possible motive for the abandonment of the great legislative endeavour was Catherine's realization of the search for security that had been one of her aims at the time of the convocation of the Commission. The Empress, it will be remembered, had made arrangements for a confrontation with disaffected elements from the dvorianstvo to coincide with the opening of the general assembly in Moscow. No opposition to the rule of Catherine had dared accept her challenge, and by 20 July 1768, Shirley could write to London, 'The Crown is so firmly settled on her head, that I cannot foresee any accident capable of obliging her to place it on that of her son.'[1]

While her own position had been strengthened by the Commission, that of a class whose growth the Empress had expressed a desire to promote, the bourgeoisie, had not received much of a boost from it. Although the town deputies were superior in number to those representing the nobility, the preponderant power of the nobles in every other respect had quickly revealed itself, and, to nurture the tender bloom of Russia's middle class, Catherine might well have considered it necessary not to expose it to any further assaults from the representatives of the dvorianstvo.

Even the minority representation of the nobility at the Commission, for all the impression it made on a contemporary such as Shcherbatov, for all the influence it has had on historians such as Sacke, and, indeed, for all its undoubted curiosity, was soon rendered meaningless. Dvoriane sent to the Commission by towns, government institutions, peasant groups and nationalities brought the total of noble deputies to 228, well above that of the bourgeois deputies, according to a recent analysis, and nobles dominated the committees, sub-committees and discussions of the general assembly.[2]

The dominance of the dvorianstvo over the Legislative Commission, however, was not complete enough to silence all hostile reference to matters of closest interest to that class. Serfdom, to give the most important example, was attacked fairly strongly by such dvoriane as Korob'in and Kozel'skii, not to mention representatives from other social groups whose arguments have necessarily received less attention in this work. Catherine's attitude to the debate on serfdom is somewhat controversial. Soviet historians, generally un-

[1] *SIRIO*, xii, 335.
[2] M. T. Beliavskii, *Krest'ianskii vopros v Rossii nakanune vosstaniia E. I. Pugacheva*, pp. 75, 84, 178.

sympathetic to the Empress, have maintained that she was strongly averse to any consideration of the subject at the general assembly and even closed the assembly because of anti-feudal speeches made there. It has been suggested by pre-revolutionary Russian historians, and reiterated here, that she was in favour of at least a limited amount of discussion on serfdom at the assembly, possibly as a sequel to the prize essay competition that she had launched.

Of considerable, although not necessarily, crucial importance in this controversy are the cases of Korob'in and the other noble deputies who criticized serfdom at the assembly. Korob'in retired from the Commission altogether after his speech about free villages, even though he had been elected member of a sub-committee. On 23 September 1768 Marshal Bibikov announced that 'Mr Korob'in is not at the Assembly', on the following day, that 'he is not here on account of illness', and on 6 November that he was giving up his post as deputy. A new election was held for his place on the sub-committee on 15 December.[1] All that can be said with confidence here is that Korob'in was important enough a person to merit considerable attention from Bibikov: this could equally well be the result of the support that he had received from Catherine or from fellow deputies opposed to serfdom. Certainly, it was quite a common occurrence for deputies to retire from the Commission, and there is nothing necessarily strange about Korob'in's disappearance, nor that of Kozel'skii and Tatishchev, who, it will be remembered, had asserted that it was the wish of the Empress that the serfs should be freed. Historians would be unwise to go as far as Tatishchev, perhaps, but it can still be maintained that Catherine was in favour of an examination of the serf question at the assembly, which was discussing free villages at the instigation of the government as a clause in the draft of the Rights of the Nobles. How else can this be interpreted than as an official invitation to discuss changes in the structure of serfdom?[2]

Such evidence as this, however, is obviously not enough to negate completely the Soviet assertion that Catherine closed the assembly because of the attacks made on serfdom by Korob'in and other deputies, soon after causing the disappearance of Korob'in and some of

[1] Beliavskii, *Krest'ianskii vopros*, p. 246.
[2] See above, p. 124. For further evidence of Catherine's desire for a full examination of the serf question, see the case of I. Stepanov, *Russkii biograficheskii slovar' Smelovskii-Suvorina*, pp. 387–8.

his fellow progressives. Nevertheless, it is both kinder to Catherine and perhaps more accurate to look at the discussion of serfdom at the assembly from another point of view, and to say that, after the speeches of Shcherbatov and other nobles in favour of the retention and even extension of serfdom, she now had more than enough support for her earlier impression that the bulk of the dvorianstvo would be opposed to any reform of Russia's peculiar institution, and that there was therefore no profit to be gained from subjecting it to any further public scrutiny.

Similar doubts about the usefulness of the continuance of the Commission were probably prompted by a further aspect of Catherine's policy, the russification of the outlying provinces to the south-west and north-west. The assertion of their rights and privileges by the deputies of the Baltic nobility, for example, had reached a climax a few months before the dissolution of the general assembly and had destroyed any hope that the Empress might have been entertaining of the immediate and unquestioning acceptance by the Baltic deputies of the incorporation of their provinces into the general administrative framework of the Empire.

A final subsidiary reason for the closure of the Legislative Commission was its patent failure to fulfil Catherine's wish for an advertisement to Europe of the introduction of the Enlightenment into Russia. As the attitude of the majority of the deputies became known to such questions as serfdom and the punishment of criminals, it was increasingly apparent that the sentiments of the Empress and of the liberal members of her establishment were to be little echoed at the Commission and that the whole project could turn out to be something of an embarrassment. The diplomatic representatives of European powers were ridiculing the proceedings of the general assembly. Wrote Shirley to Weymouth in London, for example:

To give Your Lordship a right idea of this choice collection of men, and their operations, permit me to suppose a certain number of the most ignorant of our petty merchants and shopkeepers in Great Britain and Ireland gathered as the several deputies of those nations in America, who either are subjects, or under the protection of His Majesty, and a few gentlemen unacquainted with the general principles, which constitute the basis of good government; this would be perhaps too favourable a copy of the original, now in possession of what Russia prides herself so much upon.[1]

---

[1] *SIRIO*, XII, 326-7.

221

The pride of Catherine could not have been great as she realized the wide gap that existed between the ideas of Europe that she had imbibed and those of the representatives of even Russia's highest class conditioned largely by their local environment.

The Legislative Commission was not without legislative significance. In the first place, it made a contribution towards a more sophisticated collection and codification of Russia's laws.[1] Secondly, some of the materials that it had gathered together were used by the government during the composition of some of the important laws of the latter part of Catherine's reign. Thirdly, the Empress now had a clearer idea of what needed to be done and what could be done to accelerate the development of her Empire. Acclaimed as the Great by her subjects in the general assembly, she could now set about earning the title from posterity, too.

THE DECREES OF 1775 AND 1785

Two of the most celebrated decrees of Catherine's reign, the reform of the provincial government of 1775, and the Charter of the Nobility of 1785, were to some extent influenced by the information received by the imperial administration from the nobility through the Legislative Commission. To varying degrees, the assemblies of nobles had shown themselves keen to exert control over provincial law and order, particularly at the lower levels, and some of their instructions had also suggested the formation of some kind of local self-government for the dvorianstvo. Besides going a considerable way to meet these desires, the decrees of 1775 and 1785 were also partly a response to other wishes of the nobility expressed in 1767.

In the early years of Catherine's reign, two principal schools of thought had existed as far as local administration was concerned, one favouring bureaucratic control, and the other an increased element of class participation, particularly by the dvorianstvo. The Empress at first favoured the bureaucracy, even after the nobility had strongly pressed its claims at the Commission. However, there is a case for saying that the Commission had made clearer the necessity of a wholesale reform of provincial government and of the incorporation into the new order of a stronger class element. The outbreak of the Pugachev revolt in 1773 removed any doubt that Catherine might

[1] Lappo-Danilevskii, 'Sobranie i svod', *ZMNP*, cccxi, 61–7.

still have entertained as to the advisability of making use of the proposals made by the nobility in 1767.

In her thorough preparation of the reform of 1775, Catherine certainly studied the nobles' proposals.[1] She also received much advice from members of her government, and turned to a new source of inspiration, Blackstone, as well as a new model, the Baltic provinces. Outstanding among her advisers was Ia. E. Sivers, Governor of Novgorod, who experimented successfully in the province under his control with an adaptation of the Baltic system of local administration.[2] Not too much must be made of her use of Blackstone, for, although she wrote to Grimm in August 1776, 'Sir Blackstone, who did not send me his commentaries, [nevertheless] alone enjoys the honour of having been read by Her Majesty during the course of two years; oh, his commentaries and I, we are inseparable,' she continued, 'I do not do anything with what there is in his book, but it is my yarn which I unwind in my own way.'[3] While the Baltic provinces were for Catherine a new model, they had served both Peter the Great and his successors as legislative aids, and had thus already made an impact on the Russian Empire. In general, even in its elective element, the reform of 1775 revealed a continuity with tradition as well as a break from it, particularly in its longest lasting aspects. To illustrate this assertion, it is necessary to take a look at the act itself, particularly as it affected the nobility.

The Empress worked for about five months on this act, according to her own account,[4] and wrote out much of the preparatory material and the final draft in her own hand.[5] In the preamble to the Law on the Administration of the Provinces of the Russian Empire, promulgated on 7 November 1775, Catherine pointed out that internal changes, such as the development of the steppes, had made inevitable an amendment of the administrative order. Moreover, the work of Peter the Great in this sphere needed to be continued. A start had been made on this alteration with the summons of the deputies to the Legislative Commission in 1766, but the Turkish War had inter-

[1] M. P. Pavlova-Sil'vanskaia, 'Sotsial'naia sushchnost' oblastnoi reformy Ekateriny II', Druzhinin, etc., (eds.), *Absoliutizm*, pp. 470–2. Pavlova-Sil'vanskaia makes clear that Catherine read a digest of these proposals rather than the instructions themselves.
[2] Korf, *Dvorianstvo*, p. 99.   [3] *SIRIO*, xxiii, 52.
[4] *SIRIO*, xxvii, 57, Catherine to Voltaire.
[5] V. Grigor'ev, *Reforma mestnogo upravleniia pri Ekaterine II*, pp. 201–2. Grigor'ev for example, found one copy of the act written by Catherine on 240 sheets of various sizes.

vened in 1768, and it had become obligatory for the delegates to take up their time and thoughts 'with a no less important exercise, the defence of the faith and the fatherland from foreign and domestic enemies'. The preamble continued by outlining the principal inadequacies in local government as previously constituted. Because of their large size, the provinces were sometimes insufficiently furnished with offices and personnel. Moreover, administrative, financial, criminal and civil cases were all attended to in the same place: 'in one *voevoda*'s office affairs of all kinds and names are combined'. The results of these circumstances were slowness, delay, red tape, chicanery, wilfulness and incompetence. The new system to be introduced by the reform, concluded the preamble, would make for greater smoothness, and increase 'the general quiet and security'.[1]

How were these aims to be achieved? First of all, by more than doubling the number of provinces;[2] secondly, by dividing the offices of provincial government into departments of police, justice, and finance, as well as others; thirdly, by giving the governor the authority to execute the laws on a basis equal to that of the colleges, the way thus being paved for a decentralization of the administration and the liquidation of the colleges.[3] A fourth provision of the reform of 1775 for the achievement of its aims was the introduction of an elective class element into the framework of local government.

As far as the nobility was concerned, its elective officials were to be introduced where the instructions had most requested them, at the district level. Two such officials, between them, were generally to carry out the orders of the central and provincial government, and particularly to look after roads and bridges, the extirpation of bootlegging and trade in forbidden goods, protection against fire, epidemics and cattle plague, the reception of military detachments and supply to them of quarters, meadows and woods. They were also to carry on the struggle against peasant flight and to quell disorders.[4]

In the new arrangement of the courts, the chief officials were to be appointed by the government and the subordinates by election of the dvorianstvo. Both civil and criminal cases were to be within the competence of the district courts, including all those connected with

[1] *PSZ*, xx, 229–304, no. 14,392, 7 November 1775. Preamble, pp. 229–31.
[2] Grigor'ev, *Reforma*, pp. 310–12, describes how this process was carried out, from 1775 onwards.
[3] *PSZ*, 14,392, clauses 413, 414. Beliavskii, *Istoricheskie nauki* (1960), no. 4, 138.
[4] *PSZ*, 14,392, clauses 224–52.

land possession, composition and registration of bills of sale for land and serfs, and arrangements for inheritance.[1]

These measures of the reform of 1775 put into effect several of the requests that the nobles had included in their instructions. As M. T. Beliavskii well puts it, the reform:

carried out the demand of the instructions of the dvoriane for the creation of the class courts, gave them the possibility of deciding their legal affairs on the spot, freed them from the necessity of making long and costly journeys to the Estates College and the other legal and administrative institutions of the capital and the province.[2]

The new elective officials, however, were to be confirmed in their appointment and controlled by the government. Their subordinate position was further demonstrated by the fact that the ranks to be awarded them were rather modest and lower than those to be given to appointed officials.[3] Another indication of the inferiority of those elected can be seen in the fact that they were to receive pay from the state. While this pay was rather insignificant in amount, putting the representatives of the dvorianstvo in their place in the salary scale as well as the rank ladder, the fact of it alone, as Grigor'ev says:

testifies almost more clearly than anything the attitude to the elective principle which was dominant in Catherine's government. The function of the social groups was purely passive, auxiliary. With the completion of the election of the officials...they became governmental functionaries, receiving a salary from the exchequer and completely subjected to their authorities.[4]

Of course, rank and pay, however low, could be an attraction to some as well as a deterrent to others.

While the reform of the local administration reasserted the dominance of the central bureaucracy over the provincial dvorianstvo, it also reinforced the ascendancy of the dvorianstvo over the other classes in the Russian Empire. Thus, the nobles had not asked for any general participation in the government of the towns, and yet the chief town official in the new arrangement was to be appointed by the Senate from the ranks of retired officers. Similarly, the courts of

[1] *PSZ*, 14,392, clauses 66, 67, 166, 173, 195, 196, 197, 205.
[2] Beliavskii, *Istoricheskie nauki* (1960), no. 4, 140.
[3] *PSZ*, 14,392, clauses 47–53.
[4] Grigor'ev, *Reforma*, p. 333. Grigor'ev, *ibid.* p. 367, also points out the stipulation of uniforms for the new officials as an indication of their subordination.

the state and 'economic' peasants were to be directed by dvoriane. The predicament of the serfs was much as before.[1]

The reform of 1775 was a success to the extent that it recognized the realities of provincial life and the potentialities for development: had it not at least partly fulfilled the requirements of the provinces, it would never have lasted in many of its aspects up to the *zemstvo* reform of the 1860s, and in some aspects up to the Revolution of 1917. Although some of its provisions were too ambitious, such as its adaptation of the English Court of Chancery,[2] although many amendments were necessary to fit the peculiar circumstances of various parts of the Empire,[3] although the costs involved were too high,[4] Catherine struggled for several years to make the reform a success, using the services of some of her closest advisers in the process by giving them the posts of provincial governors.[5] If the principle of the separation of powers was by no means completely established, if abuses of the law were incompletely eradicated, if the idea of class participation went largely unrealized, the alliance between the autocracy and the nobility was more firmly established in law, and this, surely, was a step towards the introduction of the rule of law in general.

A further move in this direction, and a sequel to the reform of 1775 was the Charter of the Rights, Freedoms and Privileges of the Noble Russian Dvorianstvo, published on 21 April 1785, and based partly on the report submitted by Catherine's Committee on the Dvorianstvo, partly on the Draft of the Rights of the Nobles drawn up at the Legislative Commission.[6] Eight hundred years of loyal military and civil service had helped Russia achieve its present vast dimensions, the charter began. In return for such services, noble orders had been instituted and certain rights granted for eternity to the dvorianstvo.

---

[1] Beliavskii, *Istoricheskie nauki* (1960), no. 4, 139, 141. It is difficult to be as confident as Beliavskii appears to be with regard to the influence of the dvorianstvo over the town and peasant administrations as set up by the law of 7 November 1775. However, Beliavskii's description probably fits the actuality, if not the theory, of the situation, particularly with regard to the peasants. As M. P. Pavlova-Sil'vanskaia describes the peasant courts introduced by the reform, 'In the conditions of the preservation and reinforcement of serfdom, the strengthening of the dictatorship of the dvorianstvo in the localities, the decisive role...will belong to the royal dvorianin-judge' ('Sozdanie v 1775 godu soslovnyh sudov dlia krest'ian', *Vestnik moskovskogo universiteta, seriia IX, istoriia*, 1963, no. 3, 73).

[2] See, for example, Vinskii, *Zapiski*, pp. 42–3; Pavlova-Sil'vanskaia in Druzhinin, etc. (eds.), *Absoliutizm*, pp. 485–9. [3] Grigor'ev, *Reforma*, pp. 348–9.

[4] *Ibid.* pp. 319–20. [5] *Ibid.* pp. 350–2.

[6] *SIRIO*, vii, 238–66; N. M. Druzhinin, 'Prosveshchennyi absoliutizm v Rossii', in Druzhinin, etc. (eds.), *Absoliutizm*, p. 448.

The dvorianin communicated his nobility to his wife and children, and would forfeit it for certain kinds of crime only: the breaking of an oath; brigandage or theft; the encouragement of criminal activities by others; and crimes by which, according to law, honour was lost and corporal punishment inflicted—a noble could not be subjected to corporal punishment before degradation. For all the above and other offences, a noble must be tried by his peers, and their verdict must be confirmed by the Empress. The emancipation of 1762 was confirmed by the charter, but, said clause 20, as the title and dignity of dvorianin had been, was and would be in the future obtained through service and labours useful to the Empire and the throne, and, as the actual existence of the nobility depended on the security of the fatherland and the monarchy, therefore:

at every time necessary to the Russian Autocracy, when the service of the dvorianstvo is necessary and needful to the general good, then each noble dvorianin is bound at the first summons from the Autocratic Authority to spare neither labour nor life itself for the service of the State.[1]

As before, in fact, emancipation from service was not granted unreservedly: again, in meeting the wishes of the nobility as expressed in 1767, the Empress was maintaining her grasp on the class at the same time as granting it concessions.

Wide economic as well as social rights for the nobility were listed in the charter of 1785: to buy villages; to sell wholesale what was grown or manufactured on estates; to set up small towns or conduct fairs there, albeit with strict controls; and to possess, build or buy houses in towns, and carry on manufacturing in them, or to use 'town right'.[2] The nobles, according to the charter, could also exploit to the full all contents of the earth and water belonging to them, make full use of their woods, and export their cultivated and manufactured products. Landlords were not to be burdened by troop-quartering or by personal taxes, and were to be guaranteed complete freedom of disposal of their property as well as freedom from arbitrary confiscation of their estates.[3]

[1] *PSZ*, xxii, 344–58, no. 16,187, 21 April 1785, clause 20.
[2] I.e., possibly, to join guilds, although the meaning of 'town right' is not clear. Dvoriane were expressly forbidden to join guilds by a decree of 1790. See Romanovich-Slavatinskii, *Dvorianstvo*, pp. 268–9.
[3] *PSZ*, 16,187, clauses 22, 23, 24. Only a few nobles took advantage of the freedom of property disposal to set up entail on their estates in the last quarter of the eighteenth century. See A. M. Anfimov, 'Maioratnoe zemlevladenie v tsarskoi Rossii', *Istoriia SSSR* (1962), no. 5, pp. 151–2.

Besides granting or confirming these personal rights, the Charter of the Nobility also sought to satisfy the wishes of the class in three other spheres: assemblies of nobles; genealogical registers; and proofs of nobility. As far as the first of these was concerned, the charter said that the assemblies would be convened every three years at provincial and district level. The provincial assembly was to hear suggestions made by the governor and 'elect' a marshal for the province, although this official would actually be chosen from two names submitted by the assembly to the governor. The district assembly elections were to be carried out as described in the reform of 1775. The assemblies of dvorianstvo were given permission to present their general needs and wishes to the governor, and their representatives to take complaints to the Senate and the sovereign. However, the activities of the assemblies would no doubt be restricted by the threat of a fine or other penalty for demands or decisions contravening the laws. Regulations concerning the right to attend and vote at the assemblies and to stand for office there provided that criminal or immoral dvoriane would be excluded altogether; that nobles of less than twenty-five years of age could attend but not vote; and that these young nobles or those with estates bringing in an income of less than 100 roubles a year could not be elected into any position. A further disqualification, stated by clause 64, yet again demonstrated the attitude of the government towards those who had taken full advantage of the 1762 emancipation. Clause 64 said:

In the assembly of the nobility there may be a dvorianin who has not served at all, or, who having been in service did not reach commissioned rank, (even though commissioned rank was given to him on retirement); but he must not sit with those who have been honoured, nor may he have a vote in the assembly of the nobility, nor be eligible to be chosen for those duties, which are filled by the election of the assembly of the nobility.[1]

The assemblies and elected officials of the dvorianstvo were to participate in the compilation of genealogical registers which would contribute to the conservation of each noble house. These registers were to be constructed in six sections consisting of: all families ennobled by Catherine and other monarchs, or with proof of nobility dating back a hundred years or more; all military dvoriane as in the Table of Ranks, i.e. all commissioned officers; all bureaucratic and court dvoriane of the top eight ranks; all foreign noble families who

---

[1] *PSZ*, 16,187, clause 64.

had taken on Russian citizenship; all titled families; and all ancient families a hundred or more years old whose noble origins had been obscured by time.[1] Proof of nobility, the charter of 1785 said, could come from several different sources, for example, a diploma granted by Catherine or another monarch, a coat-of-arms, or an estate granted for service. Civil and court officials of lower rank, and perhaps some military nobles, too, were classed as personal dvoriane, and would not participate in the activities of the assemblies or be included in the registers. However, if three consecutive generations of a family achieved personal dvorianstvo, the third could request the grant of hereditary nobility.[2] While the provisions of the Charter of the Nobility concerning assemblies, genealogical registers and proofs of nobility went a considerable way towards satisfying the requests made by some nobles in 1767, the many references made to the directions of the Table of Ranks and the insistence that the governor should have the ultimate control over the activities of the nobility in the provinces showed clearly that the degree of independence now to be enjoyed by the dvorianstvo would be strictly limited.

With the Charter of the Towns, also announced in 1785, and a charter for the state peasants, drawn up but never published,[3] Catherine hoped to bring the social framework of her state nearer completion. As in the Charter of the Nobility, so in the others, the bureaucracy was to keep in check the organs of class self-government. Neither the burghers nor the peasants would have been as fortunate as the nobles, who were, after all, to be supervised by fellow-members of the dvorianstvo, which dominated the bureaucracy as it did the higher strata of government in the second half of the eighteenth century.

SERFDOM AND THE ECONOMY

After the grand debate of the 1760s, the question of serfdom was not publicly discussed again during the reign of Catherine the Great: nor was the legal position of the serfs changed to any significant degree. Of course, contemporary thinkers continued to consider Russia's 'peculiar institution'. The historian Boltin, for example, contemplated emancipation and rejected it, arguing that 'it is common sense not to give it before they have learned its value and how it

---

[1] *PSZ*, 16,187, clauses 66–82.   [2] *PSZ*, 16,187, clause 92.
[3] Druzhinin, in Druzhinin, etc. (eds.), *Absoliutizm*, pp. 451–2.

should be used; otherwise, instead of benefit to them there will be harm, wrong and disaster'.[1] The anonymous author of a treatise published in 1785 and entitled 'Considerations about the drawbacks of giving freedom to the peasants and servants in Russia, or making property of their possessions', declared that, because of the sanguine and phlegmatic humours of the Russian people, freedom could only drive them into permanent idleness. He continued:

In the former Commission for the Composition of a Law Code, the opinions carelessly suggested by the gentlemen deputies, and particularly by Korob'in, sowed this infection in the hearts of low people there as deputies, and completely in vain did Beardé de l'Abaye compose his intelligent solution to the problem, in vain was the opinion of Mr Korob'in contradicted completely by many of the best sons of the fatherland: the hearts seized by this flattering poison could not taste the medicine offered them and the spirit of...depravity was rooted in the wretched and thoughtless souls, born from various incorrect rumours and from the chatter of peasant...and other low-rank deputies, who, after their dispersal, spread these evil seeds even in the most remote provinces.[2]

And then, on the other hand, there was Radishchev, with his assertion that 'this day on which the shackles of our fellow citizens are broken shall become the most famous day in our annals'.[3]

While the Empress did not care at all for what Radishchev wrote, she took some steps towards the mitigation of the serfs' lot. Although it is difficult to support the claim that she made in 1781, 123 decrees in the nineteen years of her reign 'for the relief of the people',[4] she did order that freed serfs could not be re-attached to noble landlords, that private persons could not take upon themselves the functions of a court and punish serfs for flight, theft and other crimes, for example.[5] Catherine at least considered measures of a more significant nature, too, composing a project for a law by which all serf children born after 1785 would be free.[6] It was perhaps a precursor of this project that was understood by Joseph Marshall, a British traveller in Russia some fifteen years earlier, to have been binding on the dvorianstvo. Wrote Marshall:

Now every nobleman...whose estate consists of a given number of families, is obliged to enfranchise one family every year, and they are directed by the

[1] Romanovich-Slavatinskii, *Dvorianstvo*, pp. 386–7.
[2] *Ibid.* pp. 387–8; Florovskii, *Vopros*, pp. 230–1.
[3] A. N. Radishchev, *A Journey from St. Petersburg to Moscow*, trans. Leo Wiener, p. 154.
[4] *SIRIO*, xxiii, 216.   [5] *PSZ*, xx, 82–6, no. 14,275, 17 March 1775, clause 46.
[6] Romanovich-Slavatinskii, *Dvorianstvo*, pp. 388–9.

Empress to select for this purpose the most industrious family they have: the peasant has a farm assigned to him, and the Empress makes him a present of some implement of the greatest use; but he is by the same edict to pay after three years a rent to the nobleman that is considerable; the design of which is to convince the nobility of the advantage of letting their estates to the peasants to be paid a rent in money: and I was informed that many of them had made a great progress in it, partly from conviction of its expediency, and partly from paying their court to the sovereign.[1]

Marshall's remarks would appear to bear witness to the efficiency of Catherine's public relations department rather than to her firm resolve to commence the gradual emancipation of the serfs. Even the existence of the project for gradual emancipation after 1785 is by no means certain.[2] However, the unpublished charter concerning state peasants, also of 1785, guaranteeing freedom and property rights as well as a measure of self-government, is evidence that the Empress made changes that would affect all peasants in the long run, at least in thought, and arrangements for the province of Ekaterinoslav in 1787 ordered their actual implementation there.[3]

Of course, it is easier to find measures protecting serfdom and even strengthening it than measures bringing relief to the serfs and other peasant groups,[4] and the people at large were under no illusions that their welfare was the constant concern of their sovereign. Indeed, they demonstrated their disapproval of her policies in the most widespread popular disturbance of the pre-revolutionary centuries, the Pugachev Revolt of 1773–5. Starting in the Urals and at first involving Cossacks, Bashkirs, other tribesmen, and factory peasants, the revolt later moved towards the centre and the noble estates. Pugachev, styling himself Peter III, turned to address the serfs of the dvorianstvo. In one of his decrees, dated 31 July 1774, he adjured his followers 'to catch, execute and hang and treat in the same way as they, not having Christianity, have dealt with you, the peasants, those

[1] Joseph Marshall, *Travels through...Russia, The Ukraine, and Poland...*, III, 126.
[2] According to Romanovich-Slavatinskii, *Dvorianstvo*, pp. 388–9, the project was seen by Count Bludov, whose testimony does not appear to be corroborated by others.
[3] *PSZ*, XXII, 974–1008, no. 16,603, no date, 1787.
[4] See, for example, M. T. Beliavskii, *Krest'ianskii vopros*, pp. 266–80. Among the decrees cited by Beliavskii from the years 1767–73 are several concerned with serf flight, exile and other punishments for delinquent serfs, and serf army services. Beliavskii also lists decrees guaranteeing the nobles their exclusive right to serf ownership, although he points out that an exceptional case was made for foreign colonists, and he indicates, too, that no limits were put on serf labour and payments.

who were formerly dvoriane...these opponents of our authority and disturbers of the empire and destroyers of the peasants'.[1]

Andrei Bolotov, already shaken by a revolt that had broken out in Moscow in 1771, well described the feelings of the nobles at the news of the approach of Pugachev and his adherents, declaring:

We were all convinced that the lower orders and the mob, and particularly all the slaves and our servants, were secretly in their hearts, although not outwardly, given to every wickedness, and generally all revolted in their hearts, and were ready at the least spark to make fire and flame. The example of the recent terrible rebellion in Moscow was still fresh in our memories, and we not only feared something similar, but expected it every minute. The stupidity and extreme foolhardiness of our lower classes were too familiar, and in such conditions we could not rely even on the fidelity of our own servants, and still considered them not without foundation our prime and most wicked enemies, and particularly after hearing what they were doing with their masters in the more remote and most unfortunate places, and how they either strangled them themselves or handed them over to the villain Pugachev for execution, we watched and waited for strife and a popular rebellion to burst into flame as he started to approach Moscow.[2]

The conflagration that Bolotov feared did not materialize, partly because of organizational, partly because of ideological, weaknesses: a preposterous pretender, leading what may have been more than a rabble but was less than an army, aiming at the institution of a caricature of the government that he wanted to overthrow, could not hope to hold out against regular detachments of troops. At the same time, there can be no doubt that the Pugachev Revolt shook the upper strata of society from the Empress down to Bolotov and his like, and encouraged them to think of the avoidance of the repetition of such a disturbance. Hence, to some extent at least, the reinforcement of the alliance between the autocrat and the dvorianstvo in the provincial reform of 1775.

In the long run, serfdom would be undermined by a force more relentless than revolt and more difficult to suppress, economic change.[3] During the second half of the eighteenth century, the Russian economy was far from stagnant. Catherine welcomed and encouraged developments making for the greater strength of her state,

[1] L. G. Beskrovnyi, B. B. Kafengauz (eds.), *Hrestomatiia po istorii XVIII v.*, p. 394.
[2] Bolotov, *Zhizn'*, III, 145-6.
[3] Of course, humanitarian and political motives would also contribute to the downfall of serfdom.

the nobility took a similar attitude to those which appeared to increase the wealth of the class. Neither the Empress nor the dvorianstvo, obviously, wanted change if it threatened their social and political pre-eminence, and yet, in a sense, nearly all change tended to constitute such a threat, in the long if not the short run. At the same time, those who swam with the tide survived longer than those who fought against it.

Agriculture was by far the most important economic pursuit in the Russian Empire during the reign of Catherine, and the top members of society wanted to keep things that way. Yet, while most landlords believed in the primacy of agriculture, they were not close to the soil, leaving most of the day-to-day supervision of their estates to stewards. Keen to extract as much income as possible from their estates, they were not, on the whole, prepared to develop a new, more remunerative system of farming, which would entail a rearrangement of their human as well as their financial resources (that is, alterations in serfdom and more capital investment).[1] But the landlords could not hold back the slow but irresistible tide of rural development, could not maintain their closed manorial economy inviolate from the pressures of the growing market and the increasing stratification of the peasantry. While it may be legitimate to believe that Soviet historians have exaggerated the power of these pressures, it is surely wrong to deny their existence. At least partly because of them, the landlords strove to preserve and extend their monopoly of land possession as the Empire expanded, attempted to devise a more efficient system of services as an encouragement to greater and more varied production.[2]

Meanwhile, the Empress continued to show her enthusiasm for agriculture by further patronage of the Free Economic Society, the appointment of a provincial director of the economy in the reform of 1775, and the implementation of requests concerning agriculture made by the dvorianstvo at the Legislative Commission. The nobles had asked for the continuation of the survey: the survey was continued, with the rights of commoners being disregarded in favour of those of the nobles.[3] They had sought the decentralization of the Estates College: already struck a mortal blow by the reform of 1775, this college was abolished along with several others by a decree of

[1] M. Confino, *Domaines et seigneurs en Russie vers la fin du XVIIIe. siècle*, pp. 268–75.
[2] N. L. Rubinshtein, *Sel'skoe hoziaistvo Rossii vo vtoroi polovine XVIII v.*, pp. 73, 129–30.
[3] Beliavskii, *Krest'ianskii vopros*, p. 266.

1780.[1] The landlords had also asked in 1767 for greater rights over timber resources: these were given them.[2] (They had expressed a desire for the institution of state grain stores: these, it would seem, were not set up. Although there is evidence to suggest that some landlords continued to make arrangements for grain stores on their estates,[3] the state did not take over or even share the responsibility of the dvoriane in this aspect of good husbandry as several instructions had proposed. At the same time, however, the government did show some interest in the maintenance of grain stores on private and state lands.)[4]

Of course, the nobility's interest in the Russian economy was by no means confined to agriculture. Few members of the class had shown much sympathy with the view put forward by government officials at the Commission of a nobility participating in industry in a limited manner, and many continued to benefit from their activities in both the large-scale and small-scale sectors of industry. An official report on manufactures composed early in the nineteenth century indicated that 78 per cent of the woollen cloth factories, 64 per cent of the mining enterprises, 60 per cent of the paper mills, 66 per cent of the crystal and glass works, and 80 per cent of the potash works belonged to nobles in an industry which, according to most estimates, had more than doubled in size from the 1760s to the end of the eighteenth century.[5] The extent to which the dvorianstvo benefited from the increase in small-scale industry is immeasurable, but, since the activities of the serfs of the nobility have perhaps been better recorded than those of some other peasant groups, there can be little doubt that they extracted at least their fair share of income from this form of enterprise and passed on a slice of it to their masters.

As for the government's industrial policy, it is possible again to see a response to the instructions and speeches of the dvorianstvo. Government decrees on timber conservation[6] and the decentralization of the activities of the Mines and Manufactures Colleges in 1784

---

[1] *PSZ*, xx, 994–7, no. 15,074, 24 October 1780.

[2] *PSZ*, xxi, 676, no. 15,518, 22 September 1782. These rights were confirmed in the charter of 1785.

[3] Confino, *Domaines et seigneurs*, pp. 60, 88, 148, 151.

[4] See, for example, *PSZ*, xxi, 84–95, no. 15,141, 24 March 1781. Among other duties assigned to him, the provincial director of the economy was to see to it that grain stores were being properly maintained.

[5] Blum, *Lord and Peasant in Russia*, pp. 293–4, 297–8.

[6] Baranovich, etc. (eds.), *Ocherki istorii SSSR, Period feodalizma, Rossiia vo vtoroi polovine XVIII v.*, p. 42.

Serfdom and the economy

and 1780[1] could be seen in this way, as well as certain sections of the Charter of the Nobility. Decrees such as that of 1775 ordering 'that nobody from anywhere be hindered from freely setting up mills of any kind and making on them manufactures of any kind without any permit or order'[2] would promote the industrial activity of both noble and serf, and deny the requests made by merchant representatives at the Commission for exclusive privileges in this field. While such a liberal policy might have been to the detriment of the nobility as well as of the official middle class in the fullness of time, in the second half of the eighteenth century, industrialists firmly believed that the dvorianstvo was the class to belong to.[3] An additional reason for this belief was the monopolistic right, guaranteed to the nobility and extended, of the preparation and supply to the state of alcoholic drinks.[4] The manufacture of grain alcohol increased considerably during the second half of the eighteenth century with the growth of commercial agriculture.[5]

An expanding market brought about an increase in both domestic and foreign trade. The Charter of the Nobility recognized the right of the dvorianstvo to participate in both forms of trade, and peasants were allowed to carry on such activities in rural areas. At the same time, Catherine's government attempted to reserve urban commerce for the merchant class.[6] It is impossible to give figures for internal trade during Catherine's reign, but exports rose from a value of about 12,762,000 roubles in 1762 to approximately 43,266,000 in 1793, and imports from 8,162,000 to 27,886,000. In items of export and import, and in the fluctuating tariff rates, the prosperity of the nobility was indicated and protected. Towards the end of the eighteenth century, just under 45 per cent of Russian exports consisted of metals and textiles, in both of which industries the dvorianstvo had a large share, and much of the rest was made up of the produce of the manorial economy, although grain was only just beginning to foreshadow the pre-eminence that it was to enjoy in the

[1] *Ibid.* pp. 287–8.
[2] *PSZ*, xx, 82–6, no. 14,275, 17 March 1775.
[3] N. I. Pavlenko, 'Odvorianivanie russkoi burzhuazii v xviii v.', *Istoriia SSSR* (1961), no. 2, 71–87.
[4] *PSZ*, xxi, 248–71, no. 15,231, 17 September 1781. Other requests concerning alcoholic drinks made in 1767 were granted by this decree, too. See also Beliavskii, *Krest'-ianskii vopros*, p. 267.
[5] Baranovich, etc. (eds.), *Ocherki istorii SSSR, Period feodalizma, Rossiia vo vtoroi polo-vine XVIII v.*, pp. 32–3. [6] *Ibid.* p. 131.

nineteenth century. The principal imports were sugar, dyestuffs, cotton, silk and other superior kinds of cloth, coffee, wines and fruits, with luxuries for the upper class predominant. Tariffs tended to be low on items in noble demand and of manorial production.[1] While she maintained her aversion to monopoly, the Empress certainly tended towards an exclusivist commercial policy.[2]

Trading figures for Catherine's reign need to be treated with care, not only because of the unreliability of available statistics, but also because of the fact that the rouble was depreciating in value during the period. Similar caution needs to be exercised in an examination of the later financial policies of the Empress. One bold and unreserved assertion can be made here, however: certain specific requests made by the dvorianstvo at the Legislative Commission were met. The state levies on baths, fishing and mills were removed by 1775.[3] The terms for bank loans were relaxed, and bank branches were set up in the provinces.[4]

The state budget was unbalanced towards the end of Catherine's reign, income in 1795 amounting to about 56 million roubles and expenditure in the same year to approximately 79 million. Over 46 per cent of the income came from direct taxes, from which the dvorianstvo was exempt, and over 31 per cent from the levy on the sale of alcoholic drinks to commoner consumers, which was also no concern of the nobility. The principal expenditure was on government, over 36 per cent of the total, a considerable part of which would go on the upkeep of the expensive provincial institutions of 1775. More than 28 per cent of the expenditure in 1795 was on the army, and just under 9 per cent on the navy. The court consumed 13·5 per cent of state expenses, education and welfare less than 1·5 per cent. If Catherine were more concerned with the upkeep of her palaces and estates than with the mental and physical prosperity of her people, her alliance with the dvorianstvo obliged her to give her nobles cake and circuses. This is not to explain away her profligacy

[1] Baranovich, etc. (eds.), *Ocherki istorii SSSR, Period feodalizma Rossiia vo vtoroi polovine XVIII v.*, pp. 126–7, 133.
[2] See, for example, Druzhinin in Druzhinin, etc. (eds.), *Absoliutizm*, pp. 442–4.
[3] *PSZ*, xx, 82–6, no. 14,275, 17 March 1775; Romanovich-Slavatinskii, *Dvorianstvo*, pp. 253–4.
[4] *PSZ*, xx, 327–35, no. 14,414, no date, 1775. This decree set up banks in Orenburg, Kazan' and Nizhnii Novgorod, the provinces most severely hit by the Pugachev Revolt. For the adaptation of the State Dvorianstvo Bank to a State Loan Bank, with favourable terms for nobles, see *PSZ*, xxii, 614–27, no. 16,407, 28 June 1786.

completely, and certainly not to forgive it. Of more practical value to the Russian Empire than the money spent on the court and all its trappings was the 5·2 per cent of the state expenditure devoted to communications.[1]

On the whole, both the Empress and the nobility were able to ride the economic changes that took place in Russia during the last decades of the eighteenth century. The ideas of Catherine as expressed in the Instruction and the desires of the dvorianstvo as represented at the Legislative Commission were both incompletely put into practice, perhaps, and yet the essential interests of the monarch and her top class were well protected by legislation, and, as far as can be seen, not as yet seriously threatened.

GOVERNMENT AND SOCIETY

The desires of the nobility concerning provincial government put forward at the Legislative Commission were, as I have pointed out, satisfied to a considerable extent, if not wholly, by the reform of 1775. The rights and privileges were guaranteed by the Charter of the Nobility in 1785: the charter also went a long way towards clarifying the matter of the definition of nobility, asserting and amplifying the Table of Ranks. A further task of importance to the dvorianstvo that the charter carried out was the more complete incorporation into the class of the nobles of the outlying provinces. This was done tacitly and by implication, as it had been done at the time of the summons of the Legislative Commission: that is, the dvorianstvo was described as the nobility of the Russian Empire without allowance for regional variation.

However, Catherine's attitude towards the outlying provinces continued to be characterized by vacillation and inconsistency, or expediency and cunning. Preparing her provincial reform of 1775, she had written, 'These institutions do not concern those provinces, which have specially confirmed privileges, such as: Little Russia, Livonia, etc., and Siberia.'[2] Then, in 1781, the law of 1775 was applied to the Ukraine, three provinces being set up there, although with the reservation that the relevant administrative departments would, at least for the time being, make use of the local system.[3] In

---

[1] N. D. Chechulin, *Ocherki po istorii russkih finansov v tsarstvovanie Ekateriny II*, pp. 202–5, 314–17.　　[2] Quoted in Grigor'ev, *Reforma*, p. 314.
[3] *PSZ*, xxi, 295–7, no. 15,265, 26 October 1781, set up the provinces of Kiev, Chernigov and Novgorod-Severskoi.

three Baltic provinces formed in 1783 and 1784, Swedish laws were to supplement those of the Empire.[1] Siberia was catered for in a more straightforward arrangement of 1782.[2]

As far as the assimilation of the nobility in particular was concerned, difficulties cropped up in the Ukraine in 1783, when the War College was ordered to regularize the local regiments. Cossack ranks were translated into the Table of Ranks, but unsystematically, with members of the same rank finding themselves translated differently. Local assemblies were empowered to decide questions of qualifications for nobility: this led to much abuse, including a trade in diplomas, and so the Heralds stepped in a few years later, attempting to be stricter about proofs of nobility and to prevent errors.[3] In the last instance, the Ukrainian nobility did not protest at its russification. The Empress had foreseen this, writing earlier to Governor Rumiantsev that the desire for positions and even more for salaries would change the old-fashioned ideas of the Cossack leaders and other Little Russian nobles. An additional encouragement to top Ukrainians was the more complete incorporation of the local lower orders into the Russian Empire by the introduction into Little Russia of the poll tax, and therefore serfdom, in 1783. Of the attitude of these topUkrainians towards their russification, Hrushevsky wrote:

The Ukrainians accepted without protest the final abolition of their social and political system. Some of the changes appealed to the Ukrainian officers, especially the recognition of their rights as nobles and the complete enserfment of the peasants; and many of them grasped eagerly at the new rights and bounties which accompanied the change or sought for appointment to lucrative offices in the new system. Little by little the landowners forgot their Hetman state and thought only of the wealth which they had gained as a result of the new laws regarding serfdom, and even those who looked back with nostalgia to the old order consoled themselves by seeking personal careers under the new government.[4]

In the provinces of the Baltic region, the nobility was to participate in elections of class officials as in Great Russia, and the Empire encroached further on the Baltic with a decree of 1773 ordering local officials to learn the Russian language, and another of 1786 abolish-

---

[1] See *PSZ*, xxi, 967, no. 15,774, 3 July 1783; xxi, 967, no. 15,775, 3 July 1783; xxii, 224–9, no. 16,077, 9 October 1784. These decrees set up the provinces of Revel, Riga and Vyborg.

[2] *PSZ*, xxi, 385, no. 15,327, 19 January 1782, set up the province of Tobol'sk.

[3] Romanovich-Slavatinskii, *Dvorianstvo*, pp. 108–12.

[4] Hrushevsky, *Ukraine*, pp. 451, 460–1.

ing the Swedish-type *landrat* colleges.[1] As in the case of the Ukraine, there was little protest about these changes from the nobility of the Baltic. According to Zutis, the attack by the Great Russian deputies on the Baltic privileges at the general assembly of the Legislative Commission had convinced the aristocratic *rytsarstvo* that Baltic autonomy could exist only under the protection of the autocracy, and for this reason they were quite prepared to become the 'mamelukes' of tsarism. Catherine appreciated and exploited this feeling, and, realizing that the only way of reconciling the various interests of the *rytsarstvo*, the dvorianstvo and the autocracy was to encourage the further entrenchment of serfdom, pursued such a policy throughout the latter part of her reign, introducing the poll tax into the Baltic provinces in 1783 as she had in the Little Russian. Further reasons for the easy assimilation of the Baltic region, considered Zutis, were the support given to the move by land-hungry Russian nobles, the awareness of the *zemstvo* that russification would bring them their long-awaited equality with the *rytsarstvo*, and the attractions of jobs and salaries.[2]

In some of the other outlying provinces, such as Siberia, there were questions of a different nature arising as the reform of 1775 came to be implemented there. One of them concerned the lack of dvorianstvo, not the local peculiarities of nobility as in the Ukrainian and Baltic cases. For example, only six dvoriane could be found in the province of Viatka, and so officials to fill the new administration there had to be seconded from the army.[3] Partly to compensate for such a deficiency, perhaps, leaders of the Don Cossacks and Tartars were introduced into the dvorianstvo during Catherine's reign, although this would seem to be more a further indication of the general policy of russification that the Empress was pursuing.[4] (It needs to be mentioned here that a Soviet historian has recently argued that the government's policy in the second half of the eighteenth century was directed, not at the ennoblement of the leaders of the nationalities, but rather at their reduction to the ranks of the peasantry.)[5]

The life of the dvorianstvo in the provinces towards the end of the

[1] *PSZ*, XIX, 818–19, no. 14,036, 9 September 1773; XXII, 671–2, no. 16,424, 12 August 1786.
[2] Zutis, *Ostseiskii vopros*, pp. 370, 586–7.   [3] Grigor'ev, *Reforma*, pp. 322–3.
[4] Romanovich-Slavatinskii, *Dvorianstvo*, pp. 113–14.
[5] N. G. Apollova, 'K voprosu o politike absoliutizma v natsional'nyh raionah Rossii v XVIII v.', Druzhinin, etc. (eds.), *Absoliutizm*, p. 360.

reign of Catherine is difficult to describe because, with the Empire
ever increasing, the variation of provincial life became greater. However, generally speaking, it can be said that there had been change
and progress since the earlier part of the eighteenth century. There
was still not much sign of luxurious living on the estates of the nobles,
but there were more books in their homes, neighbours were not quite
so remote, and, once the Pugachev revolt was over, a higher degree
of law and order could be observed. Developments such as these
were noted by many contemporary memoirists.[1]

One circumstance at least, however, remained very much the same:
those who wanted to get on in the world still found it necessary to
go to the capitals. No longer was it necessary to travel long distances
to settle estate affairs, perhaps, nor to find redress for petty grievances,
nor even to find a teacher or a doctor, but the principal network of
patronage that held the dvorianstvo together and enabled the ambitious to realize their hopes was still to be found in St Petersburg,
and, to a lesser extent, Moscow. The court and high society were
there, the commanders of the army and the high government
officials, promotion and advancement. There, too, of course, were
still 'ins' and 'outs', and divisions between the top ranks and the
rest, between military and bureaucratic dvoriane. For example,
first, in 1774, occurred Catherine's major governmental change: out
went the Orlovs and their supporters, in came Potemkin and his
followers.[2] The harsh treatment meted out to Radishchev was perhaps prompted to some extent by the fact that his patron, Count
A. R. Vorontsov, was an opponent of Potemkin.[3] Secondly, although
the improvement in provincial life failed to produce a genuine gentry,
it did increase the number of nobles with strong roots in the country,
and encourage the extension of the patronage system beyond the
capitals.[4] Thirdly, the expansion of the bureaucracy in the later part
of the eighteenth century tended to promote an *esprit de corps* that
insulated nobles in the civil service from those in the army and navy.
However, there was still a fairly free transference from one branch of
the service to the other, and the gap between them was by no means
as wide as it became in the nineteenth century.[5]

[1] Chechulin, *Russkoe provintsial'noe obshchestvo*, pp. 68–84.   [2] Miliukov, *Ocherki*, III, 370.
[3] See Lang, *The First Russian Radical*, pp. 193–5, for example.
[4] Chechulin, *Russkoe provintsial'noe obshchestvo*, pp. 85–8.
[5] N. F. Demidova, 'Biurokratizatsiia gosudarstvennogo apparata absoliutizma v
XVII-XVIII vv.', Druzhinin, etc. (eds.), *Absoliutizm*, pp. 238–42.

Government and society

The growth of the bureaucracy was prompted by that of government in general. The reform of 1775 demanded a great increase in the staff of provincial departments. Although, as a consequence of this reform, the majority of the colleges were decentralized or abolished, there was no significant reduction in the numbers of central civil servants.[1] As long as there were jobs to be had, as long as their interests were not directly affected, the nobles as a whole were not bothered about such structural changes in the government. Why run the risk of offending the sensitivities of the Empress about her prerogative as long as her autocracy was a guarantor of their predominance?

EDUCATION AND CULTURE

'Influenced by theories of enlightenment, the Catherine of the sixties could dream of the creation of this new race', wrote Miliukov. 'Cooled down by experience of life and disappointed, the Catherine of the eighties could see how insufficient for the execution of this grand scheme were the means within her hands.' So Catherine dropped the grand idea of moulding young Russians completely, and concentrated on questions concerning their instruction. However, she continued to look at these questions in a different way from Peter the Great, believing that instruction should pursue, not narrow professional, but broader pedagogic, aims.

With her change of tack, the Empress adopted a new model, Austria, and a new principal assistant, F. I. Iankovich de Mirievo. Austrian schools had been reformed in 1774, under the influence of Prussian educational practice; Iankovich, a Serbian graduate in law and economics from the University of Vienna, had constructed schools of a Prussian type in a district of Hungary. He was sent to Russia by Joseph II at Catherine's request, arriving in St Petersburg in September 1782, and was immediately enrolled in a newly created school commission headed by Count Zavadovskii. In 1786, after a considerable amount of preparatory work, including the compilation of twenty-seven manuals and textbooks, mostly translated from the German, Iankovich and his associates produced the Statute of Popular Schools, which was published on 5 August of that year. Although Iankovich was its chief architect, and although the Germanic influence on it was strong, the Statute also reflected to a con-

---

[1] Demidova, Druzhinin, etc. (eds.), *Absoliutizm*, p. 239.

siderable degree the ideas of the plans for education composed during the earlier years of Catherine's reign and that drawn up by the Legislative Commission's sub-committee on schools.[1]

'The education of youth', ran the preamble, 'was respected by all enlightened peoples simply because they considered it the only way to assert the good of civil society.' Education also served, the preamble continued, to produce unswerving loyalty to the sovereign, love for the fatherland, and its citizens, and 'a reasonable understanding of the Creator and His holy law'.[2] These aims were to be pursued in two principal types of school: major, with four classes, in all provincial capitals; minor, with two classes, in both provincial and district towns. The classes of the minor schools were to study the same subjects as the elementary classes of the major schools: reading, writing, catechism, church history, elementary grammar and arithmetic, drawing, and rudimentary civics. In class 3 of the major schools, geography and history were to be added to a curriculum including a more advanced stage of the subjects commenced in the first two classes. Class 4 was to be a continuation of class 3, and to introduce in addition geometry, mechanics, physics, natural history and civil architecture. Provision was also to be made for the teaching in the major schools of Latin for those intending to indulge in higher education, and of a foreign language suitable for the area in which a school was located. A matter of prime importance in the implementation of such a programme was, of course, finance. On this question, the statute said:

As the popular schools, by the authority of the arrangements published for the administration of the provinces, are under the management of the Board of Social Relief, this is not only obliged to supervise with all its strength the execution of this Statute, but to concern itself with the upkeep of them, obtaining for this purpose all useful means.[3]

The Governor-General of each province was to appoint a local director of education, and a central administrative body was to be set up in St Petersburg to watch over the popular schools generally.

Of the several special texts to be used in the schools, one of the more significant, perhaps, was that on civics, 'On the Duties of Man and the Citizen', which encouraged everybody to be content with

[1] Miliukov, *Ocherki*, II, 755–8.
[2] *PSZ*, XXII, 646–9, particularly 646, no. 16,421, 5 August 1786.
[3] Beskrovnyi, Kafengauz (eds.), *Hrestomatiia*, pp. 580–2.

that station in life to which God had called him 'In each rank it is possible to be happy', said this text. 'People often think that tsars, princes, noble and aristocratic individuals alone have a happy life; but this, however, is incorrect. God's goodness does not exclude anybody from contentment. Citizens, tradesmen, settlers, also hired workers and slaves can be happy people.'[1]

Young nobles, it is not too rash to assume, would not be averse to assimilating ideas such as these, and yet no great enthusiasm is apparent in their attitude to the popular schools. At the beginning of the nineteenth century, out of 4,136 pupils attending such schools in St Petersburg province, only 670 were dvoriane: out of 507 in Novgorod, only 67.[2] Even these figures show that the dvorianstvo was represented to a greater degree than its total membership relative to the other classes would strictly warrant, but they could be expected to be higher if they reflected the preponderant part that the dvorianstvo played in education at this time. That these figures are not higher is a consequence of noble attitudes towards educational questions as revealed at the Legislative Commission. Where dvoriane had shown interest in schools, they had mostly wanted them to be arranged on a class basis, and to assist members of the nobility in their quest for advancement in service. The popular schools certainly did not fulfil the first requirement, and gave no clear indication of answering the second. Only a minority of the instructions in 1767, moreover, had demonstrated any concern for education, and many nobles had still to realize its utility. Such a dvorianin, quoted by Miliukov, wrote in an application for a government post towards the end of the eighteenth century, 'I partly know how to write...but am not in a position to go through any more education, and having arrived at a mature age, I already can have no further ideas about it, and therefore I have developed the keen desire to serve.'[3]

There is a brighter side to the implementation of the Statute of Popular Schools, and to progress in education more generally during the reign of Catherine the Great. First, just after the death of the Empress, there were forty-nine major schools in operation, with 269 teachers and 7,001 students, and 239 minor schools, with 491 teachers and 15,209 students.[4] While these numbers amount to little more than a drop in the ocean when compared to the population as a

---

[1] *Ibid.* pp. 582–4.
[2] Miliukov, *Ocherki*, II, 759.
[3] *Ibid.* p. 760.
[4] Beskrovnyi, Kafengauz (eds.), *Hrestomatiia*, p. 585.

whole, they mark a great leap forward from the days of Peter the Great's 'cipher' schools, which, in 1727, had a total enrolment of no more than 2,000.[1] Although she was niggardly from the point of view of financing education, the Empress can perhaps be given a little credit for the interest that she showed in the question of the popular schools.

With regard to other establishments towards the end of the century, their number and attendance respectively were as follows:

Universities and gymnasia	3	1,338
Private boarding schools	48	1,125
Military academies	5	1,980
Noble boarding schools	8	1,360
Church seminaries and schools	66	20,393
Medical schools	3	270
Soldiers' schools	116	12,000
Mining schools	2	167
The Academy of Arts	1	348
Other schools	9	765

Together with the popular schools, these figures produce totals of 549 institutions and 61,966 students.[2] Particularly noteworthy are the important parts played in education at this time by the soldiers' schools and the church schools: it is difficult to make an estimate of the number of dvoriane enrolled in them, but probably very few would be taught in the same place as common soldiers, and rather more along with future priests. The Empress would have no direct connection with either of these two types of school. Another point of interest is that two of the noble boarding schools were probably those set up by local assemblies of dvorianstvo in Tver' and Iaroslavl'.[3]

As in the earlier part of the century, many nobles were receiving at least their first lessons from tutors. Some of these were little better than their earlier counterparts. A certain Protas'ev related that in 1785, when he was 12, his father decided that he should be taught German, and so sent his steward off to Moscow with several cartloads of corn and instructions to sell them and to hire a teacher with the proceeds. The steward returned with a man who was good at binding books and making paper models, but an inadequate linguist. A year later, the young Protas'ev was put in charge of another

[1] Miliukov, *Ocherki*, II, 734.
[2] Beskrovnyi, Kafengauz (eds.), *Hrestomatiia*, p. 586.
[3] Chechulin, *Dela i dni*, I, 97–8.

poor tutor, but good cheese-maker and flute-player. Worse was to come, for his next and final teacher was a coarse and cruel disciplinarian without any redeeming talents.[1] However, as argued previously, there is a fairly strong case for assuming that the general level of private education was no worse towards the end of the eighteenth century than it had been at the beginning of it, and probably better.

Educational progress during the reign of Catherine the Great was both a consequence and a cause of a broader cultural flowering, in which, as usual, the Empress herself had a part of some importance to play. Among more important measures in this aspect of her work were: the institution at the Academy of Sciences of a special Russian Academy for the study of language and literature; the extension of the activities of the Academy of Arts; the development of the Hermitage; the invitation to Russian and foreign architects to carry out many different projects; and the continuation of her correspondence with and patronage of some of the great minds of western Europe. 'Carrying out this programme', notes N. M. Druzhinin, 'Catherine herself appeared in the guise of an anonymous publicist-satirist and the author of literary works, enlisted in the struggle with bigotry, superstition and in addition—with the enemies of absolutism.'[2]

The Statute of Popular Schools was Catherine's last major act in the cultural field. Three years after its publication, the French revolution broke out, and Catherine became an open and complete reactionary, watching the events taking place in the home of the Enlightenment with horror and disgust. In February 1790 she wrote to Grimm, 'As a person ignorant of the facts, I simply ask questions, foreseeing the destruction of everything that has been linked with the system of ideas of the beginning and middle of this century, which brought forth rules and principles without which, however, it is impossible to live one day.'[3] The Empress was particularly shocked by the abolition of the privileges of the French nobility. 'What! Are these families to be deprived of what they have obtained by their labours, their service?', she exclaimed. 'Why, tell me pray, take away advantages and honours from people? What incentive will there be for their further deeds? They must all stay in obscurity.'[4]

[1] *Ibid.* pp. 102–3.
[2] Druzhinin in Druzhinin, etc. (eds.), *Absoliutizm*, p. 454.
[3] *SIRIO*, xxiii, 481.　　　　　　　[4] *SIRIO*, xxiii, 495.

By the beginning of 1794 Catherine's disillusionment with the ideas of the Enlightenment was complete. On 11 February of that year, she wrote to Grimm:

And so, you were right, never expressing the wish to be included among the luminaries, the *illuminés* and the *philosophes*, since experience proves, that all this leads to destruction; but whatever they have said and done, the world will never cease to need an authority...it is better to prefer the foolishness of one, than the madness of many, infecting with fury twenty million people in the name of 'freedom', of which they do not possess even the shadow, after which these madmen rush forward to ensure that it will never be achieved.[1]

Catherine placed her hopes for the survival of France on the emergence of a stern dictator, a Caesar:[2] to ensure the survival of Russia, she behaved in such a manner herself during the last years of her reign.

Before the final reactionary years of Catherine's reign, it was possible for the three principal strands of Russian thought, 'Voltairism', freemasonry and humanism, to develop in an atmosphere of unprecedented freedom,[3] and in a period of publishing activity such as Russia had previously never known. According to figures provided by Miliukov, nine and a half thousand books were issued in Russia during the eighteenth century, with the following distribution among quarters of that century:

1698–1724	561 (6%)
1725–50	357 (4%)
1751–75	2010 (21%)
1776–1800	6585 (69%)[4]

In Catherine's view, before the onset of the French Revolution, 'Voltairism' was not a great battle for reform, but rather a struggle for the victory of healthy thinking over superstition, a non-sectarian purgative for men's minds, and an attack against pedantry. Taking up arms in this struggle, the Empress energetically participated in the publication of satirical journals, a movement that occupied Russian intellectuals at the end of the 1760s and beginning of the 1770s. While these journals engaged in friendly and sometimes hostile banter, their outlooks were broadly similar: arguments were concerned with

---

[1] *SIRIO*, xxiii, 593. [2] *SIRIO*, xxiii, 503.
[3] This atmosphere is well described in K. A. Papmehl, *Freedom of Expression in Russia, 750-1800, The History of the Idea and its practical Application* (London Ph.D. Thesis, 1965). Miliukov, *Ocherki*, iii, 396.

means, not ends. It was agreed that obscurantism, bigotry, corruption pseudo-sophistication and extreme adulation of foreign culture should be expunged from Russian life, but Catherine and her adherents could not be happy at being told, even indirectly, that these vices should primarily be removed from the court and the upper ranks of the dvorianstvo. The chief offender in this regard was N. I. Novikov.[1]

Novikov, a dvorianin, albeit of somewhat humble status, was more seriously to incur the displeasure of the Empress for his later journalistic and philanthropic activities, as well as for his involvement in the masonic movement. Freemasonry gained a considerable following in Russia during the latter part of Catherine's reign, with a considerable number of the members of the nobility turning to it as an answer to their spiritual problems, including a few ex-deputies of the Legislative Commission.[2] Although the impact made by Novikov and his associates in both their publishing and charitable endeavours was quite remarkable, according to Kliuchevskii,[3] their movement, like that of the satirical journals, involved only a small section of the dvorianstvo as a whole.

Much the same can be said for the third of the principal intellectual trends to be observed in the reign of Catherine, that of humanism. A representative of this school of thought in the second half of the eighteenth century was S. E. Desnitskii, 'the founder of Russian legal science'.[4] Desnitskii, of middle-class origin, spent several years at Glasgow University, and soon after his return from there presented to the Legislative Commission his 'Proposals on Founding a Legislative, Judicial and Executive Authority in the Russian Empire' Concerning himself with the kind of question to which Tatishchev, Volynskii and Shuvalov had addressed themselves in the earlier part of the century, Desnitskii demonstrated an insight and a subtlety of an order considerably beyond that of his predecessors.[5]

Desnitskii is significant, too, as a representative of a growing class of commoner intellectuals, which, some Soviet historians have argued, was large enough to make it inaccurate to talk of the culture of the

[1] *Ibid.* pp. 349–60; Afanas'ev, *Russkie satiricheskie zhurnaly*, pp. 21–46.
[2] Miliukov, *Ocherki*, III, 405–10; Pypin, *Russkoe masonstvo*, pp. 169–204.
[3] V. O. Kliuchevskii, 'Vospominanie o N. I. Novikove i ego vremeni', *Sochineniia*, VIII, 247–9.
[4] Pashkov (ed.), *Istoriia*, I, 571.
[5] For excerpts from the 'Proposals', see Beskrovnyi, Kafengauz (eds.), *Hrestomatiia*, pp. 590–3.

reign of Catherine as basically noble.[1] Most western historians would not accept this. One thing is certain, or can at least be stated with more confidence, that the vast majority of the Russian people of all classes at this time were little affected by the new forces of enlightenment, but still finding their ideas and their faith where their ancestors had found them.

CONCLUSION

Towards the end of the eighteenth century, as at the beginning, the dvorianstvo and the autocracy were mutually dependent. In contemporary official Russian theory, it is true, the dvorianstvo was not given the key place in the state structure that Montesquieu had ascribed to the nobility, but, in fact, the dvorianstvo dominated the other classes and closely circumscribed the policies of the autocrat. If 'the nobles of that country seemed in 1785 to want little more than what free men generally possessed in most of the rest of Europe',[2] this was surely because they did not know what freedom was in the abstract and because the concrete situation was already sufficiently to their liking, apart from legal guarantees, which to most of them would have been meaningless. If they could get away with beating up merchants and church officials, not to mention the peasants, dvoriane had no need of law, which could be a restraint on such activities. Of course, it could not have been very pleasant to live in Russia when there was little security even for members of the top class, when the central government was still a matter of 'ins' and 'outs', and ejection from it might mean impoverishment as well as disgrace, when provincial life could be disrupted by violence and even death. Anything that could be done by law to reduce this insecurity was increasingly welcome to the dvorianstvo as a whole, and the Charter of the Nobility of 1785, with such clauses as those on the inviolability of the person and property of the dvorianin, was a step in this direction. Along with the reform of 1775, which institutionalized the dominance of the dvorianstvo over the provinces, the charter put an official seal on the preponderance of the nobility over all the other classes and thus began to pave the way for the introduction of law in a more general sense.

In both 1775 and 1785, it has been pointed out, the government

---

[1] For example, see Shtrange, *Demokraticheskaia intelligentsiia*, pp. 4–6.
[2] Beloff, in Goodwin (ed.), *The European Nobility*, p. 189.

was determined to keep the chains of service on the dvorianstvo at the same time as making the terms of service more agreeable. It is wrong to draw the obvious conclusion from this that there was a clear-cut distinction between government and nobility. After all, the leading members of the government were in service themselves, at the top of the Table of Ranks. If little initiative was allowed the elective officials in the reform of 1775, this was principally because they were seen as lower officers in the military-bureaucratic hierarchy, not as a group apart. Much of the effective legislation introduced by the government during the reign of Catherine favoured the dvorianstvo as a whole, as landlords, as officers and cadets. If top dvoriane were particularly favoured, that was the way of the world: to be part of one of the networks of patronage was to give the individual advantages over nearly all other inhabitants of the Empire and the chance of promotion on both the official and unofficial ladder.

Too much has been made of the lack of aristocratic form in the Russian polity in the eighteenth century, of the subservient position of the dvorianstvo in the state structure, compared to that of the nobilities in contemporary western European countries. If comparisons are to be made, the salient features of the situation of the Russian Empire at that time need to be stressed, particularly its size. Russia was at least as large as the rest of Europe put together. Moreover, its frontiers were, for the most part, far from fixed: its people was scattered, and varied in nationality. Cultural and economic development were retarded by poor communications, which also increased the centrifugal tensions and constant fears of dismemberment aroused by the other peculiarities of the Empire. Russia was at war with its neighbours much of the time, and always faced by the threat of internal disturbances. These are the conditions that moulded the dvorianstvo, that gave it a centralized, military-bureaucratic stamp, and reconciled it to the continued existence of autocracy as the form of government.

Catherine well knew that her maintenance of power was as dependent on the dvorianstvo as her assumption of it. A woman of vision, she could see clearly enough what was desirable for Russia: she was also a politician, and knew what was possible for it, particularly after the educational experience of the Legislative Commission. To take again as an example the most important institutional feature of the Empire, serfdom, she recognized that the vast majority of the members of the nobility was opposed to any radical change in it. What could she do? If she had attempted to bring about such a change, almost certainly she would have caused a palace revolution and would be known to us only as another in the undistinguished line of successors to Peter the Great—historians are not usually sympathetic to failures, however well intentioned.

Realizing the impossibility of immediate change, she did little to abolish serfdom, beyond preparing the ground for it by encouraging the growth of the intelligentsia. It would be going too far, of course, to say that she wanted to produce a Radishchev, it may well rather be that she wanted to bring glory on her name by bringing about the assimilation of the current intellectual fashions of Europe by a limited group of Russians and by proudly communicating this development to her western correspondents. In this manner, she certainly gained a large part of her contemporary and posthumous reputation. It may well be, too, that she was intelligent enough to know that ideas are too dangerous for playthings and realized as she turned more conservative in outlook towards the end of her reign that she had started something that her persecution of Radishchev would not be enough to stop. In any case, if we are to judge her by the results of her policies rather than by their motivation, Catherine undoubtedly accelerated the growth of that Russian intelligentsia which would make emancipation one of its chief goals in the fifty years or so following her death and continue the grand debate that she herself had inaugurated in 1765.

Turning to her other achievements, and leaving aside those in foreign policy, Catherine can be credited with at least the promotion of cultural advancement on many fronts, a rationalization of local government, and the pursuit of an economic policy encouraging growth, the last of which would also have the long-term effect of undermining serfdom and autocracy. To look at the debit side of the balance sheet, she can certainly be charged with such shortcomings as her failure to give more support to popular education, her lack of persistence with reform of central government, and her continuance, even enlargement, of the inequitable taxation policies and spendthrift extravagance of her predecessors. In mitigation of these defects, it can be asserted, first, that it would require much more than the energies of an autocrat to put in order an administration headed by a Senate which confessed in 1767 that it was submerged in paper and including a Finance College which admitted in the same year that its accounts were 6,000,000 roubles in arrears and that 16,000 matters were awaiting its decision. Secondly, Catherine's failures, as well as her successes, must be seen in the context of the necessity of appeasing the desires of the dvorianstvo.

To discuss Catherine more generally, for an obscure German Princess to make herself Empress of All the Russias was no mean achievement, to remain Empress for more than thirty years and to die a natural death was probably a greater one. This is particularly impressive when it is remembered that Catherine did not, like her immediate female predecessors, take little interest in the government of her country, but, on the contrary, personally conducted a vigorous internal, as well as foreign, policy. Historians are therefore obliged to give her the full consideration due to Peter the Great and very few other Romanovs. To describe the environment in which her work was carried out, to notice in particular the limitations imposed upon it by the most powerful class in her Empire, contributes, it is to be hoped, to a fuller understanding of her role in Russian development. If the conditions in which she operated are not sufficiently looked at, it is all too easy to dismiss her as a vainglorious and predatory adventuress. Beyond all reasonable doubt, this may be the truth, even nothing but the truth. But it is not the whole truth.

BIBLIOGRAPHY

Afanas'ev, A. N. *Russkie satiricheskie zhurnaly, 1769–1774.* M., 1859.

Aksakov, S. T. *Chronicles of a Russian Family,* trans. M. C. Beverley, etc. New York, 1924.

Alefirenko, P. K. 'Russkaia obshchestvennaia mysl' pervoi poloviny XVIII stoletiia o sel'skom hoziaistve', *Materialy po istorii zemledeliia SSSR,* I. M., 1952.

Anfimov, A. M. 'Maioratnoe zemlevladenie v tsarskoi Rossii', *Istoriia SSSR* (1962), no. 5.

Arhiv Vorontsova, see Bartenev, P. I.

Arsen'ev, K. *Statisticheskie ocherki Rossii.* SPB., 1848.

Avseenko, V. G. *Malorossiia v 1767 godu. Epizod iz istorii XVIII stoletiia po neizdannym istochnikam.* Kiev, 1864.

Bagalei, D. I. *Ocherki iz russkoi istorii,* 2 vols. Har'kov, 1911, 1913.

Baranovich, A. I., Beskrovnyi, L. G., Zaozerskaia, E. I., Indova, E. I. (eds.). *Ocherki istorii SSSR, period feodalizma, Rossiia vo vtoroi chetverti XVIII v.* M., 1957.

Baranovich, A. I., Kafengauz, B. B., Alefirenko, P. K., Klokman, Iu. P., Kusheva, E. N. (eds.). *Ocherki istorii SSSR, period feodalizma, Rossiia vo vtoroi polovine XVIII v.* M., 1956.

Barsov, N. I. 'A Matseevich, mitropolit rostovskii, i delo ot otobranii v kaznu monastyrskih imenii, 1762–1763', *Russkaia starina,* XV.

Bartenev, P. I. (ed.). *Arhiv kniazia Vorontsova...,* 40 vols. M., 1870–95.

Beliavskii, M. T. *Krest'ianskii vopros v Rossii nakanune vosstaniia E. I. Pugacheva.* M., 1965.

—— 'Trebovaniia dvorian i perestroika organov upravleniia i suda na mestah v 1775', *Istoricheskie nauki* (1960), no. 4.

—— 'Vopros o krepostnom prave i polozhenii krest'ian v "nakaze" Ekateriny II', *Vestnik moskovskogo universiteta,* seriia IX, istoriia (1963), no. 6.

Beskrovnyi, L. G., Kafengauz, B. B. (eds.). *Hrestomatiia po istorii SSSR, XVIII v.* M., 1963.

Bibikov, A. A. *Zapiski o zhizni i sluzhbe A. I. Bibikova.* M., 1817.

Bil'basov, V. A. *Istoriia Ekateriny II-oi,* 2 vols. Berlin, 1900, 1912.

Blum, J. G. *Lord and Peasant in Russia from the Ninth to the Nineteenth Century.* Princeton, 1961.

Bochkarev, V. N. 'Kul'turnye zaprosy russkogo obshchestva nachala tsarstvovaniia Ekateriny II po materialam zakonodatel'noi komissii 1767 goda', *Russkaia starina,* CLXI, CLXII.

—— *Voprosy politiki v russkom parliamente XVIIIogo veka. Opyt izucheniia politicheskoi ideologii XVIIIogo veka po materialam zakonodatel'noi komissii 1767–1768.* Tver', 1923.

Bogoslovskii, M. M. *Byt i nravy russkogo dvorianstva v pervoi polovine XVIII veka.* Petrograd, 1918.
—— *Oblastnaia reforma Petra Velikogo, provintsiia, 1719–1727.* M., 1902.
—— 'Smolenskoe shliahetstvo v XVIII v.', *Zhurnal ministerstva narodnogo prosveshcheniia,* CCCXXII.
Bolotov, A. T. *Zhizn' i prikliucheniia, 1738–1795,* 3 vols. M.-L., 1931. (Also in *Russkaia starina,* I–VIII.)
Brikner, A. G. *Die Europaiserung Russlands, Land und Volk.* Gotha, 1888.
—— *Istoriia Ekateriny Vtoroi,* 5 parts in 3 vols. SPB., 1885.
Briullov, S. 'Obshchestvennye idealy v ekaterininskuiu epohu', *Vestnik Evropy* (1876), I.
Catherine the Great, *Memoirs,* trans. Katharine Anthony. New York, 1935.
Chechulin, N. D., *Ekaterina II v bor'be za prestol,* L., 1924.
—— (ed.). *Nakaz Imperatritsky Ekateriny II-oi.* SPB., 1907
—— 'Ob istochnikah "Nakaza"', *Zhurnal ministerstva narodnogo prosveshcheniia,* CCCXXXX.
—— *Ocherki po istorii russkih finansov v tsarstvovanie Ekateriny II.* SPB., 1906.
—— 'Proekt imperatorskogo soveta v pervyi god tsarstvovaniia Ekateriny II-oi', *Zhurnal ministerstva narodnogo prosveshcheniia,* CCXCII.
—— *Russkii roman XVIIIogo veka: puteshestvie v zemliu ofirskuiu kniazia Shcherbatova.* SPB., 1900.
—— *Russkoe provintsial'noe obshchestvo vo vtoroi polovine XVIII veka.* SPB., 1889.
—— 'Vospitanie i domashnee obuchenie v Rossii v XVIIIom veke', *Dela i dni,* I, III.
Chechulin, N. D. Nol'de, A. E., Polievktov, M. A., Presniakov, A. E. *Istoriia pravitel'stvuiushchego senata za dvesti let, 1711–1911,* 5 vols. SPB., 1911.
Chistovich, I. A. *Istoricheskaia zapiska o sovete v tsarstvovanie Imperatritsy Ekateriny II-oi.* SPB., 1870.
Chulkov, M. D. *Istoricheskoe opisanie rossiiskoi kommertsii,* 7 vols. SPB., 1781–8.
Confino, M. *Domaines et seigneurs en Russie vers la fin du XVIIIe siécle. Étude de structures agraires et de mentalités économiques.* Paris, 1963.
Danilov, M. V. *Zapiski artillerii maiora Mihailova Vasilievicha Danilova.* M., 1842.
Derzhavin, G. R. *Zapiski,* M., 1860.
Dmytryshyn, B. 'Economic content of the 1767 Nakaz of Catherine II', *American Slavic and East European Review* (1960), XIX.
Druzhinin, N. M., Pavlenko, N. I., Cherepnin, L. V. (eds.). *Absoliutizm v Rossii, XVII–XVIII vv., sbornik statei k semidesiatiletiiu so dnia rozhdeniia i sorokapiatiletiiu nauchnoi i pedagogicheskoi deiatel'nosti B. B. Kafengauza.* M., 1964.
Ekaterina II, *Sochineniia,* ed. A. N. Pypin, 12 vols. SPB., 1901–7.
Elagin, I. P. 'Proekt...I.P. Elagina ob opredelenii v neotchemlemoe vladenie dvortsovym krest'ianam zemli i o razdache kazennyh dereven' za izvestnuiu platu, na vremennoe i opredelennoe vladenie vol'nym soderzhateliam', *Sbornik kniazia Obolenskogo,* XII. M., 1859.

Bibliography

Epifanov, P. P. '"Uchenaia druzhina" i prosvetitel'stvo xviii veka', *Voprosy istorii* (1963), no. 3.

Evreinov, B. A., Kizevetter, A. A., Losskii, N. D., Slavik, I., Shmurlo, E. F. (eds.). *Sbornik statei, posviashchennyh Pavlu Nikolaevichu Miliukovu.* Praga, 1929.

Evreinov, G. A. *Proshloe i nastoiashchee znachenie dvorianstva.* SPB., 1898.

Evreinov, V. A. *Grazhdanskoe chinoproizvodstvo v Rossii.* SPB., 1887.

Firsov, N. N. *Pravitel'stvo i obshchestvo v ih otnosheniiah v vneshnei torgovle v tsarstvovanie Imperatritsy Ekateriny II,* Kazan', 1902.

Florinsky, M. T. *Russia, A History and an Interpretation,* 2 vols. New York, 1955.

Florovskii, A. V. *Iz istorii ekaterininskoi zakonodatel'noi komissii, vopros o krepostnom prave.* Odessa, 1910.

—— 'K istorii ekonomicheskih idei v Rossii v xviii veke', *Nauchnye trudy russkogo narodnogo universiteta v Prage,* I.

—— *Sostav zakonodatel'noi komissii.* Odessa, 1915.

Forster, R. 'The provincial noble: a reappraisal', *The American Historical Review,* LXVIII, no. 3.

Gerhard, D. *England und der Aufsteig Russlands... 18j.* München und Berlin, 1933.

Golovachev, P. *Sibir' v ekaterininskoi komissii.* M., 1889.

Gol'tsev, V. A. *Zakonodatel'stvo i nravy v Rossii XVIII veka.* SPB., 1896.

Golubnichii, I. S., Pogrebinskii, A. P., Shemiakin, I. N. (eds.). *Ekonomicheskaia istoriia SSSR.* M., 1963.

Gooch, G. P. *Catherine the Great and Other Studies.* London, 1954.

Goodwin, A. (ed.). *The European Nobility in the Eighteenth Century, Studies of the Nobilities of the Major European States in the pre-Reform Era.* London, 1953.

Got'e, Iu. V. *Istoriia oblastnogo upravleniia v Rossii ot Petra I do Ekateriny II,* 2 vols. M., 1913; M.-L., 1941.

—— *Ocherk istorii zemlevladeniia v Rossii.* Sergiev Posad, 1915.

—— '"Proekt o popravlenii gosudarstvennyh del" Artemiia Petrovicha Volynskogo', *Dela i dni,* III.

Grigor'ev, V. *Reforma mestnogo upravleniia pri Ekaterine II, uchrezhdeniia o guberniiah 7 noiabria 1775.* SPB., 1910.

Hans, N. A. 'Dumaresq, Brown, and some Early Educational Projects of Catherine II', *Slavonic and East European Review,* XL, no. 94.

Hasselblatt, R. 'Die instructionen der baltischen Ritterschaften für die gesetzgebunde Commission von 1767', *Baltische Monatsschrift,* XXXVII.

Haumont, E. *La Culture Française en Russie.* Paris, 1910.

Hodnev, A. I. *Istoriia imperatorskogo vol'nogo ekonomicheskogo obshchestva s 1765 do 1865 goda.* SPB., 1865.

Hötzsch, O. (ed.). *Zum Geburtstag Th. Schiemann.* Berlin, 1907.

Hrushevsky, M. *A History of the Ukraine,* ed. Frederiksen, O. J. New Haven, 1948.

Iablochkov, M. *Istoriia dvorianskogo sosloviia v Rossii.* SPB., 1876.

Bibliography

Ikonnikov, V. S. 'Arsenii Matseevich, istoriko-biograficheskii ocherk', *Russkaia starina*, XXIV, XXV, XXVI.

Kafengauz, B. B. *Ocherki vnutrennego rynka Rossii pervoi poloviny XVIII veka.* M., 1958.

Kalachov, N. (ed.). *Materialy dlia istorii russkogo dvorianstva*, 3 vols. in 1. SPB., 1885.

Karnovich, E. P. *Rodovye prozvaniia i tituly v Rossii i sliianie inorodtsev s russkimi.* SPB., 1886.

Keep, J. L. H. 'The Decline of the Zemsky Sobor', *Slavonic and East European Review*, XXXVI, no. 86.

Kizevetter, A. A. *Istoricheskie ocherki*, M., 1912.

—— 'Kriticheskiia zametki po istorii politicheskih idei v Rossii', *Nauchnye trudy russkogo narodnogo universiteta v Prage*, I.

—— *Mestnoe samoupravlenie v Rossii.* M., 1910.

Kliuchevskii, V. O. *Sochineniia*, 8 vols., including *Kurs russkoi istorii*, I–V. M., 1956–9. (Volume IV translated by Liliana Archibald as Klyuchevsky, V. O., *Peter the Great.* London, 1958. Miss Archibald used an earlier Soviet edition. C. J. Hogarth translated Kliuchevskii's *Kurs russkoi istorii* as Kluchevsky, V. O., *History of Russia*, 5 vols. New York and London, 1911–31. Reprint, New York, 1961.)

K.N.V., 'Dvorianskaia gramota', *Istoricheskii vestnik*, XIX.

Knorring, N. N. 'Ekaterininskaia zakonodatel'naia komissiia 1767 goda v osveshchenii inostrannyh rezidentov pri russkom dvore', *Sbornik statei Miliukovu.*

Kokorev, A. V. *Hrestomatiia po russkoi literature XVIII veka.* M., 1961.

Korf, S. A. *Dvorianstvo i ego soslovnoe upravlenie, 1762–1855.* SPB., 1906.

Korobkov, N. M. (intro. and ed.). *Semiletniaia voina, materialy o deistviiah russkoi armii i flota v 1756–1762 gg.* M., 1948.

Korsakov, D. A. 'A. P. Volynskii i ego "konfidenty"', *Russkaia starina*, XLVIII.

—— *Votsarenie imperatritsy Anny Iuannovny.* Kazan', 1880.

Lang, D. M. *The First Russian Radical, Alexander Radishchev, 1749–1802.* London, 1959.

Lappo-Danilevskii, A. S. *I. I. Betskoi i ego sistema vospitaniia.* SPB., 1904.

—— *Ocherk vnutrennei politiki Imperatritsy Ekateriny II.* SPB., 1904.

—— 'Sobranie i svod zakonov rossiiskoi imperii, sostavlennye v tsarstvovanie Ekateriny II-oi', *Zhurnal ministerstva narodnogo prosveshcheniia*, CCCIX, CCCX, CCCXI, CCCXIV.

Latkin, V. N. *Zakonodatel'nye komissii v Rossii v XVIII st.* SPB., 1887.

Lazarevskii, A. M. *Opisanie staroi Malorossii*, 3 vols. Kiev, 1888–1902.

Lipinskii, M. A. 'Novye dannye dlia istorii ekaterininskoi komissii o sochinenii proekta novogo ulozheniia', *Zhurnal ministerstva narodnogo prosveshcheniia*, CCLI.

Longinov, M. (ed. and intro.). 'Materialy dlia istorii komissii o sochinenii proekta novogo ulozheniia, spisok gospodam deputatam', Appendix to *Russkii vestnik*, XXXVI.

Bibliography

Lyashchenko, P. I. *History of the National Economy of Russia to the 1917 Revolution*, trans. L. M. Herman. New York, 1949.

Macartney, Lord. *An Account of Russia*. London, 1768.

Maikov, P. M. *Ivan Ivanovich Betskoi: opyt ego biografii*. SPB., 1904.

Markevich, A. I. 'Predlozhenie o sozyve komissii dlia sostavleniia proekta novogo ulozheniia', *Zapiski imperatorskogo odesskogo obshchestva istorii i drevnostei*, xx.

Marshall, Joseph. *Travels through Holland, Flanders, Germany, Denmark, Sweden, Lapland, Russia, The Ukraine and Poland in the years 1768, 1769 and 1770*, 3 vols. London, 1772.

Miliukov, P. N. *Ocherki po istorii russkoi kul'tury*, 3 vols. Paris, 1930–7.

—— *Outlines of Russian Culture*, trans. E. Davis and V. Ughet, ed. M. Karpovich, 3 vols. Philadelphia, 1943.

Miller, A. *Essai sur l'histoire des institutions agraires de la Russie centrale du XVIe. au XVIIIe. siècles*. Paris, 1926.

Nisbet Bain, R. *Peter III, Emperor of Russia*. London, 1902.

Oreshkin, V. V. *Vol'noe ekonomicheskoe obshchestvo v Rossii, 1765–1917*. M., 1963.

Papmehl, K. A. *Freedom of Expression in Russia, The History of the Idea and its practical Application*. Unpublished Ph.D. thesis, London University, 1965.

Pashkov, A. I. (ed.). *Istoriia russkoi ekonomicheskoi mysli*, tom I, *epoha feodalizma*, chast' pervaia, *IX–XVIII vv*. M., 1955. (Translated as J. M. Letiche (ed. and intro.). *A History of Russian Economic Thought, Ninth through Eighteenth Centuries*. Berkeley and Los Angeles, 1964.)

Pavlenko, N. I. *Istoriia metallurgii v Rossii XVIII veka, zavody i zavodovladel'tsy*. M., 1962.

—— 'Odvorianivanie russkoi burzhuazii v XVIII v.', *Istoriia SSSR*. (1961), no. 2.

Pavlova-Sil'vanskaia, M. P. 'Sozdanie v 1775 godu soslovnyh sudov dlia krest'ian', *Vestnik moskovskogo universiteta*, seriia IX, istoriia (1963), no. 3.

Pekarskii, P. *Zhizn' i literaturnaia perepiska P.I. Rychkova*. SPB., 1867.

Pipes, R. *Karamzin's Memoir on Ancient and Modern Russia, a Translation and Analysis*. Cambridge, Mass., 1959.

Pokrovskii, I. M. *Ekaterininskaia komissiia i tserkovnye voprosy v nei*, Kazan'. 1910.

Pokrovskii, S. A. *Vneshniaia torgovlia i vneshniaia torgovaia politika Rossii*. M., 1947.

Polenov, D. V. 'A. Ia. Polenov, russkii zakonoved XVIII-ogo veka', *Russkii arhiv* (1865).

Polnoe sobranie zakonov rossiisskoi imperii, 1st series, 1649–1825, 45 vols. SPB., 1830.

Portal. R. *L'Oural au XVIII siècle*. Paris, 1950.

—— 'Manufactures et classes sociales en Russie au XVIIIe siècle', *Revue historique*, CCI, CCII.

Pushkarev, I. *Istoriia imperatorskoi gvardii*, 2 vols. SPB., 1844–5.

Bibliography

Pypin, A. N. 'Do-petrovskoe predanie v xviii-om veke', *Vestnik Evropy* (1886), iii, iv.

—— *Russkoe masonstvo, XVIII i pervaia chetvert' XIX vv.* Petrograd, 1916.

Radishchev, A. N. *A Journey from St Petersburg to Moscow*, trans. Leo Wiener. Cambridge, Mass., 1958.

Raeff, Marc. 'Home, school and service in the life of the 18th century Russian nobleman', *Slavonic and East European Review* (1962), xl.

—— 'L'État, le gouvernment et la tradition politique en Russie impériale avant 1861', *Revue d'histoire moderne et contemporaine* (1962), ix.

—— 'State and nobility in the ideology of M. M. Shcherbatov', *American Slavic and East European Review* (1960), xix.

—— 'Staatsdienst, Aussenpolitik, Ideologien. (Die Rolle der Institutionen in der geistigen Entwicklung des russischen Adels im 18 Jahrhundert.)' *Jahrbücher für Geschichte Osteuropas*, New Series (1959), Band 7, Heft 2.

Reddaway, W. F. (ed.). *Documents of Catherine the Great.* Cambridge, 1931.

Richardson, W. *Anecdotes of the Russian Empire.* London, 1784.

Rogger, Hans. *National Consciousness in Eighteenth-century Russia.* Cambridge, Mass., 1960.

Romanovich-Slavatinskii, A. *Dvorianstvo v Rossii s nachala XVIII veka do otmeny krepostnogo prava.* Kiev, 1912.

Rozhdestvenskii, S. V. 'Proekty uchebnyh reform v tsartstvovanie Imperatritsy Ekateriny II do uchrezhdeniia komissii o narodnyh uchilishchah', *Zhurnal ministerstva narodnogo prosveshcheniia*, New Series, xii.

Rubinshtein, N. L. *Sel'skoe hoziaistvo Rossii vo vtoroi polovine XVIII v.* M., 1957.

Russkii biograficheskii slovar', 25 vols. SPB., Petrograd, 1896–1918.

Sacke, G. 'Adel und Burgertum in der gesetzgebenden Kommission Katharinas II', *Jahrbücher für Geschichte Osteuropas* (1938), iii.

—— 'Adel und Burgertum in der Regierungszeit Katharinas II', *Revue belge de philologie et d'histoire* (1938), xvii.

—— 'Die gesetzgebende Kommission Katharinas II: ein Betrag zur Geschichte des Absolutismus in Russland', *Jahrbücher für Geschichte Osteuropas* (1940), ii.

—— 'Katharina II im Kampf um Thron und Selbstherrschaft', *Archiv für Kulturgeschichte* (1932), xxiii.

—— 'Zur Karakteristik der gesetzgebenden Kommission Katharinas II von Russland', *Archiv für Kulturgeschichte* (1931), xxi.

Sbornik imperatorskogo russkogo istoricheskogo obshchestva, 148 vols. SPB., 1867–1916.

Sbornik statei Grekovu, see Volgin, V. P., etc.

Sbornik statei Miliukovu, see Evreinov, B. A., etc.

Semevskii, V. I. *Krest'iane v tsarstvovanie Imperatritsy Ekateriny II*, 2 vols. SPB., 1901, 1903.

—— *Krest'ianskii vopros v Rossii v XVIII i pervoi polovine XIX veka*, 2 vols. SPB., 1888.

—— *Pozhalovaniia naselennyh imenii v tsarstvovanie Ekateriny II-oi, ocherk iz istorii chastnoi zemel'noi sobstvennosti v Rossii.* SPB., 1906.

Bibliography

Semeveskii, V. I. 'Sel'skii sviashchennik vo vtoroi polovine XVIII veka', *Russkaia starina*, XIX.

Sergeevich, V. I. 'Otkuda neudachi ekaterininskoi zakonodatel'noi komissii?', *Vestnik Evropy* (1878), 1.

Shahovskoi, D. 'Russkii deputat XVIII veka', *Minuvshie gody*, November 1908.

Shahovskoi, Ia. P. *Zapiski kniazia Ia. P. Shahovskogo.* SPB., 1872.

Shashkov, S. S. *Istoricheskie etiudy*, 2 vols. SPB., 1872.

Shcherbatov, M. M. *Neizdannye sochineniia*, eds. P. G. Liubomirov, M. V. Zhizhka, M., 1935.

——— *O povrezhdenii nravov v Rossii. . ., i puteshestvie A. Radishcheva*, preface, Iskander, pseud. A. Herzen. London, 1858.

Shmidt, S. O. (intro. and ed.). 'Proekt P. I. Shuvalova 1754 g. "O raznyh gosudarstvennoi pol'zy sposobah"'. *Istoricheskii arhiv* (1962), no. 6.

Shtrange, M. M. *Demokraticheskaia intelligentsiia Rossii v XVIII veke.* M., 1965.

——— *Russkoe obshchestvo i frantsuzskaia revoliutsiia, 1789–1794 gg.* M., 1956.

Simmons, E. J. *English Literature and Culture in Russia, 1553–1840.* Cambridge, Mass., 1935.

Sivkov, K. V. *Materialy po istorii krest'ianskogo i pomeshchich'ego hoziaistva pervoi chetverti XVIII veka.* M., 1951.

Solov'ev, S. M. *Istoriia Rossii*, Edition—*Obshchestvennaia pol'za*, 6 vols. and an index vol. SPB., no date.

——— 'Rasskazy iz russkoi istorii XVIII veka. 1767 god', *Russkii vestnik*, XXXV.

Spiridinova, E. V. *Ekonomicheskaia politika i ekonomicheskie vzgliady Petra I.* M., 1952.

Storch, H. F. von. *Historisch-statistisches Gemälde des russischen Reichs am Ende des Achzehnten Jahrhunderts*, 6 vols. Riga, Leipzig, 1797–1802.

Sumner, B. H. *Peter the Great and the Emergence of Russia.* London, 1956.

Tatishchev, V. N. 'Proizvol'noe i soglasnoe rassuzhdenie i mnenie sobravshegosia shliahetstva russkogo o pravlenii gosudarstvennom', *Utro, literaturnyi sbornik.* M., 1859.

Tatistcheff, Basil. *The Testament of Basil Tatistcheff*, trans. J. Martinof. Paris, 1860.

Thomson, G. S. *Catherine the Great and the Expansion of Russia.* London, 1955.

Tolstoi, D. A. 'Vzgliad na uchebnuiu chast' v Rossii v XVIII stoletii do 1782 goda', *Sbornik statei akademii nauk*, XXXVIII.

Trudy vol'nogo ekonomicheskogo obshchestva k pooshchreniiu v Rossii zemledeliia i domostroitel'stva. SPB., 1765–75.

Tuchkov, S. A. *Zapiski, 1766–1808.* SPB., 1908.

Vedomost' kontory sanktpeterburgskogo banka, 1767.

Vernadskii, G. V. 'Manifest Petra III o vol'nosti dvorianskoi i zakonodatel'naia komissiia 1754–1766 gg.', *Istoricheskoe obozrenie* (1915), XX.

Vinskii, G. S. *Moe vremia: zapiski.* SPB., 1914.

Volgin, V. P., Novosel'skii, A. A., Tret'iakov, P. N., Budovnits, I. U., Ustiugov, N. V. (eds.). *Sbornik statei akademiku B. D. Grekovu ko dniu semidesiatiletiia*, M., 1952.

Bibliography

Volkov, M. Ia. 'Otmena vnutrennyh tamozhen v Rossii', *Istoriia SSSR* (1957), no. 2.

—— 'Tamozhennaia reforma 1753–1757 gg.', *Istoricheskie zapiski*, LXXI.

Voznesenskii, S. 'Gorodskie deputatskie nakazy v ekaterininskuiu komissiiu 1767 goda', *Zhurnal ministerstva narodnogo prosveshcheniia*, New Series, XXIV.

Zagoskin, N. *Ocherki organizatsii i proishozhdenie sluzhilogo sosloviia v dopetrovskoi Rusi*, Kazan', 1876.

Zenkovsky, V. V. *A History of Russian Philosophy*, trans. G. L. Kline. 2 vols. London, 1953.

Znamenskii, I. *Polozhenie duhovenstva v tsarstvovanie Ekateriny II i Pavla I.* M., 1888.

Zutis, Ia. *Ostseiskii vopros v XVIII veke*. Riga, 1946.

INDEX

Academy of Arts, 27, 190, 244–5
Academy of Sciences, 25–7, 80, 195, 199–200, 209, 245
Ahtyrka district, Slobodsko-Ukraina, 201, 205, 206 n.
Alabushev, teacher, 30
Alatyr' district, Nizhnii Novgorod, 201, 214
alcoholic drinks, 9, 36–7, 107, 116, 140–1, 166, 235, 236
Aleksandrov, essayist, 98
Aleksei Mihailovich, tsar', 6, 32
Aleksin district, Moscow, 129 n., 133, 180 n.
Anna, empress, 1, 4–5, 7, 8 n., 19–20, 22, 35, 40
Antonov, I., deputy, 150
Archangel town, 12, 197–8, 207
Archbishop of St Petersburg, 209 n.
Arsen'ev, major, 164
Arzamas district, Nizhnii Novgorod, 127, 129 n.
Ash, baron, deputy, 126, 210 n.
Astrahan' province, 68
autocracy, 1–3, 34–5, 176, 178–80, 186–8, 248–9
Avseenko, V. G., historian, 61, 66

Bahmut district, New Russia, 171
Bahmut Hussar Regiment, New Russia, 148, 203
Baltic provinces, 32 n., 55, 195, 223, 238–9; *see also* nobility, Estonia, Finland, Livonia
banks, 12, 108, 109–10, 143–4, 201, 216, 236
Bantysh-Kamenskii, I., deputy, 158–9
baron, 2 n., 152, 182
Barshchina, 10, 98, 104, 118, 123, 231 n.
Barsov, professor, 26
Bashkirs, 129–30, 231
Baskakov, V., deputy, 87 n., 204
Beardé de l'Abaye, essayist, 93–5, 230
Beccaria, 56
Bekishev, A., deputy, 137
Belev district, Belgorod, 134 n., 147, 200, 203, 206 n., 213
Belgorod district
on church affairs, 213
on education, 197, 200, 206 n.
on government, 173 n.
on nobility, 160
on serfdom, 115 n.

Beliavskii, M. T., historian, 225, 226 n., 231 n.
Beloff, M., historian, 51
Belyi district, Smolensk, 175, 203
Bestuzhev-Riumin, A. P., count, 161, 163
Betskoi, I. I., educationalist, 190–3
Bezborodko, A., marshal, 73, 115
Bezhetsk district, Moscow, 128 n., 143
Bezhetskaia *piatina*, Novgorod, 143, 181 n.
Bibikov, A. I., Marshal
in Commission, 58, 80, 81, 82–3, 124–5, 138–9, 157, 202, 218, 220
in elections, 70, 78–9, 115
on Kazan', 169
Bibikov, V., deputy, 160
bills of sale, 112, 144, 225
Biron, E. J., 22
Bishop of Rostov and Iaroslavl', 198, 199, 208, 209
Black Hussar Regiment, New Russia, 148, 181 n.
Blackstone, Sir William, 223
Blaznov, A., deputy, 138
Bludov, count, 231 n.
Bochkarev, V. N., historian, 179–80
Bolhov district, Belgorod, 113 n., 129
Bolhov, town, 185
Bolotov, A. T., writer
on education, 28–9, 37, 193–4
on patronage, 24, 182
on Pugachev, 232
on rank, 44
on the economy, 99–101
on the emancipation, 40–1
Boltin, I. N., historian, 229
Botvin'ev, N., criminal, 69
bourgeoisie
and Catherine II, 50, 55, 60–2, 81–2, 92, 107–8, 186, 219
and Charter of Towns, 229
and education, 37 n., 197–8, 206, 207
and industry, 35–6, 107–8, 131–7, 235
and serfdom, 92, 95, 112, 114–15, 123–4
and trade, 35–6, 107–8, 137–40
in Commission, 55, 61–2, 66, 74, 81–2, 219
relations with nobility, 66, 74, 185–6, 225–6, 235
Briansk district, Belgorod, 69
Briullov, S., historian, 117–18, 161
Broun, Iu., governor, 67, 74

Index

Brovtsyn, G., deputy, 144
Brudastoi, teacher, 29–30, 194

Cabinet, 19, 36
Catherine I, empress, 2 n., 7
Catherine II, the Great, empress, 46–51, 249–51
  and bourgeoisie, 50, 55, 107–8, 186, 219, 235
  and Commission, 50–2, 57–85 *passim*, 218–22
  and nobility, 1, 22, 45–6, 50, 53–5, 91, 106–10, 146, 159, 179, 186, 219, 226–9, 248–51
  and outlying provinces, 55–6, 67, 157, 221, 237–9
  and western Europe, 56–7, 215–17, 221–2, 245–8, 250
  on education, 189–93, 241–4
  on government, central, 176–9, 186–8
  on government, local, 162–9, 175, 222–6
  on religion, 210–12
  on serfdom, 87, 105–6, 120, 219–21, 229–31
  on the economy, 86–91, 105–10, 233–7
Chaadaev, I., deputy, 149 n.
Chechulin, N. D., historian, 177, 206 n.
Chernigov district, Ukraine
  election in, 72, 73, 74
  on education, 197, 201, 204, 205 n.
  on government, 173 n., 174 n.
  on nobility, 154 n.
  on the economy, 144 n.
Chernigov province, 237 n.
Chernigov town, 194, 195, 197
Chernyshev, Z. G., deputy, 78–9, 81
Chicherin, D. I., governor, 156
Chief Police Department, 111, 169, 176
Chuhloma district, Archangel, 117, 128 n., 173 n., 181 n.
Chulkov, M. D., writer, 103
Chuprov, I., deputy, 126, 202
Church
  before 1762, 24–5, 30–3, 35–7
  in Commission, 60, 199, 201–11, 213–15
  lands of, 38–9, 60, 212
  schismatics from, 117, 187, 213–14
  Synod of, 60, 61, 209–10, 212, 213, 215
Code of 1649, 6, 36, 52
Colleges, 19, 49, 61, 77, 110–11, 178, 181, 186–7, 224, 238–9, 241
  Commerce, 131
  Economy, 60, 212
  Estates, 126–8, 162, 225, 233
  Finance, 142, 251
  Justice, 111

Little Russian, 66, 168, 195
Manufactures, 8, 60, 89, 131–4, 139, 234
Medicine, 210 n.
Mines, 7, 60, 109, 131, 134, 139, 234
War, 167, 238
communications, 91, 105, 107, 110–11, 116, 141–2, 172, 237, 249
corporal punishment, 5, 6, 31–2, 42, 160–1, 193, 227
Cossacks, 59, 60, 61, 66, 72, 129–30, 147–8, 155, 167–8, 231, 238, 239
Council, 176–8
count, 2 n., 152–3, 182
Courland, 29, 135

Danilov, M. V., writer
  on ancestors, 23
  on education, 29–30, 194
  on *maiorat*, 8 n.
  on patronage, 24
Davydov, N., deputy, 152–3
Dedilovo district, Moscow, 173 n.
Demidov, N. D., industrialist, 2 n.
Demidov, family, industrialists, 103
Derevskaia *piatina*, Novgorod, 181 n.
Derzhavin, G. R., writer, 44
Desnitskii, S. E., writer, 247
Diderot, 33
Dilthey, P., professor, 191
Dmitrii, Metropolitan of Novogorod, 78, 80, 81
Dmitrov district, Moscow
  election in, 70
  on education, 202, 208, 209
  on nobility, 161 n., 174
  on the economy, 125, 144 n.
Dnepr Lancer Regiment, New Russia, 154
Dolgorukii, the brothers, 22
Dolinskii, deputy, 73
Domashnev, S., deputy, 161
Donets Lancer Regiment and Little Russian Poltava Regiment, New Russia, 181 n.
Dorogobuzh district, Smolensk
  on education, 196, 201, 203, 206 n.
  on government, 173 n.
  on nobility, 178 n.
  on serfdom, 117 n.
  on the economy, 128 n.
Druzhinin, N. M., historian, 245
Dumaresq, D., educationalist, 191

education
  administration of, 25–8, 172, 190–1, 202, 206, 208–10, 242
  curricula of, 3, 4, 27, 30–1, 206, 242

262

Index

Index

Kaluga and Medyn' districts, Moscow
  on education, 200 n., 201, 202, 203
  on nobility, 146, 160, 180 n.
  on the economy, 127 n., 133
  others, 11, 64
Karachev district, Belgorod, 128 n., 129 n.,
  173 n.
Kashin district, Moscow
  on education, 201, 206 n.
  on government, 172 n., 173 n.
  on nobility, 152, 158, 160, 174, 180 n.
  on serfdom, 113, 114 n.
  on the economy, 127 n., 128 n., 139
Kashira district, Moscow, 100, 143 n.
Kasimov district, Voronezh, 129 n.
Katenin, V., deputy, 144
Kazan' district, 143 n., 161 n., 169, 173 n.
Kazan' town, 12, 22, 28, 236 n.
Kerensk district, Voronezh
  on education, 209
  on government, 173 n.
  on nobility, 147, 159
  on serfdom, 114 n., 115, 116 n.
  on the church, 213
  on the economy, 134 n.
Kiev district, Ukraine, 154, 201
Kiev town, 194, 195, 197, 198
Kineshma district, Moscow, 119
Kizevetter, A. A., historian, 50 n., 105
Klin district, Moscow, 114 n., 143 n.,
  173-4
Kliuchevskii, V. O., historian
  on Catherine II's Instruction, 56-7
  on her policy, 50
  on emancipation of nobility, 43 n., 45 n.
  on *mestnichestvo*, 21
  on regular army and guards, 3-4
  on Russian disorder, 16
Kniazhnin, Ia., writer, 44
Kochubei, writer, 74
Kolomna district, Moscow, 115 n., 117 n.,
  143, 173 n., 180 n.
Kondrat'ev, A., deputy, 130 n.
Kondyrov, M., deputy, 70, 121
Kopor'e district, St Petersburg, 160, 207
Korf, S. A., historian, 43-4, 45, 164, 177
Korob'in, G., deputy
  connection with Catherine II, 120
  criticism of, 230
  importance of, 216, 219-21, 230
  on emancipation of nobility, 158
  on serfdom, 120-2, 124
Kostroma district, Moscow
  on education, 197, 200
  on government, 173 n.
  on nobility, 146 n., 180 n.

on serfdom, 115
on the economy, 126, 127, 128 n.,
  129 n., 143 n.
others, 11, 70
Kotoshihin, G., writer, 6
Kozel'skii, Ia. P., deputy
  connection with Catherine II, 120
  importance of, 216, 219-21
  on agriculture, 130
  on serfdom, 123
  on the Table of Ranks, 149
Kozhin, O., deputy, 135, 201, 205
Kozitskii, G. V., secretary, 58
Krapivna district, Moscow
  on education, 207 n., 209
  on nobility, 160
  on serfdom, 114, 115, 116
  on the economy, 129 n., 130 n., 140,
    141, 143 n.
Kurakina, E., lady of the court, 39
Kurmysh district, Nizhnii Novgorod,
  127 n.
Kursk district, Belgorod
  on education, 196, 200 n., 201
  on government, 171, 173 n.
  on nobility, 184 n.
  on the economy, 129 n.
  other, 12
Kuznetsov, I., deputy, 150, 196
Kvashnin-Samarin, governor, 65

Lapis, teacher, 29
law
  civil, 19, 169-70, 186-7
  criminal, 171-2, 186-7
  natural, 33, 94, 97, 98, 179, 215-16
  rule of, 180, 186-8, 189, 215
Legislative Commission of 1767
  committees of, 77, 80-4, 218
  opening and agenda of, 76-85
  precedents for, 51-2
  preliminaries of, 57-69
  significance of, 218-22
  sub-committees of, 77, 82, 84, 175-6,
    209-10, 218, 220, 242
Lermontov, Iu., deputy, 139, 144
Lihvin district, Moscow, 117 n., 180 n.
Lipinskii, M. A., historian, 54, 58, 59,
  218
Little Russia, *see* Ukraine
Liubim district, Moscow, 180 n.
Livonian *zemstvo*, 154
Lomonosov, M., savant, 26
Lubny town, Ukraine, 74
Luh district, Moscow, 114 n., 147, 161 n.
  180 n.

Index

L'vov, landowner, 69–70
L'vov, the brothers, landowners, 19

Macartney, Lord, diplomat, 213
maiorat, 7–8, 35–6, 161, 183, 227 n.
Maloiaroslavets district, Moscow, 119, 180 n.
Maria Teresa of Austria, 57
Markevich, A. I., historian, 58
Marshall, J., writer, 230–1
Matusevich, I., priest, 212
Mel'gunov, A. P., statesman, 39, 70
Menshikov, A., statesman, 21–2
Meshchaninov, I., deputy, 81
Mestnichestvo, 21, 182
Mezheninov, S., deputy, 131–3
Miasoedov, S., deputy, 69, 70
Mihailov district, Moscow
 on government, 173 n.
 on serfdom, 113, 114, 115, 119
 on the economy, 127 n., 139, 143
Mihal'ch, V., deputy, 21 n., 157
Miliukov, P. N., historian, 193, 214–15, 241
Miller, G. F., historian, 191–2
Mirovich, V., conspirator, 53
Montesquieu, 33, 56, 91, 186, 248
Mogilev province, 168
Moscow district, 40, 71, 161 n., 172 n., 178, 180 n., 201, 205
Moscow town, 4, 11, 25–30, 54, 127, 219
Motonis, N., deputy, 150, 197
Mozhaisk district, Moscow, 128 n., 162
Mtsensk district, Belgorod, 127 n., 128 n., 147, 173 n.
Murav'ev, N., deputy, 78, 81

Nartov, A., deputy, 151, 175
Nezhin and Baturin districts, Ukraine
 on education, 204, 205
 on nobility, 154, 174 n., 181 n.
 on the economy, 129 n.
 others, 72, 73
Nizhnii Novgorod district, 127 n., 143
Nizhnii Novgorod town, 11, 236 n.
nobility
 and agriculture, 13, 88, 99–104, 124–30, 233–4
 and church, 24–5, 213–15
 and education, 25–30, 35–7, 42–3, 195–210, 216–17, 243–5
 and government, 1–3, 15–18, 35–7, 44, 162–80 *passim*, 184–8, 222–9, *passim*, 237–41
 and industry, 5, 8–9, 14–15, 35–7, 103–4, 107–9, 132–6, 227, 234–5

 and serfdom, 9–13, 15, 17–19, 23, 42, 91–9, 112–25, 219–22, 232
 and trade, 5, 9, 35–7, 91, 104–5, 107–9, 137–41, 227, 235–6
 Charter of, 5, 41, 226–9, 235, 237, 248
 class government of, 43, 162–3, 173–4, 216, 228–9
 cohesion of, 5, 9, 23–5, 71, 76, 162, 180–4, 240
 committee on, 45, 152, 161, 163–4, 177
 deputy of, 62–3, 69, 70, 75–6, 162, 173–4
 divisions of, 21–3, 53–4, 64, 65, 70, 71, 75–6, 151–3, 184–5, 240
 early history of, 20–1
 in Commission, 54–5, 60–2, 63–9, 69–76, 81–2, 218–22
 in outlying provinces, 2, 13, 18, 21 n., 22, 55–6, 61, 64, 66–8, 71–5, 129–30, 145, 147–8, 153–7, 221, 237–9
  Estonia, 59, 61, 64, 68, 74–5, 145, 153–4, 156, 174
  Finland, 59, 74–5, 153–4, 156–7, 174
  Georgia, 154
  Livonia, 59, 61, 64, 67, 74–5, 145, 154, 156–7, 237
  New Russia, 66, 72, 75, 130, 154, 167–8
  Siberia, 148, 154–6, 239
  Slobodsko-Ukraina, 66, 72, 75, 130, 154, 167–8
  Smolensk, 145, 148, 157 n.
  Ukraine, 13, 21 n., 66, 72–4, 75, 129–30, 145, 148, 157, 174, 195, 197, 204–5, 238–9
 in provincial life, 3–4, 18–19, 182, 240
 kinds of aristocracy in, 34, 177, 181, 182–4, 249
 lack of gentry in, 181
 marshal of, 62–3, 69, 70, 75–6, 153, 162–3, 174, 202, 228
 registration of, 21, 23, 35–6, 67, 145, 152, 153, 173, 228–9
 relations with bourgeoisie, 66, 74, 185–6, 225–6, 235
 relations with Catherine II, 50, 54–5, 61–2, 81–2, 107–8, 186, 219–21, 222–9, 237–41, 248–51
 rights and privileges of, 5–9, 10, 27, 83, 158–62, 226–9
Novgorod-Severskoi province, 237 n.
Novikov, N. I., writer, 247
Novosil' district, Belgorod, 143 n.
Novyi Torzhok district, Novgorod, 173 n.

Obonezhskaia *piatina*, Novgorod, 117 n., 129 n., 143, 181 n.

265

Index

Index

Von Blumen, G., deputy, 156
Von Klingshtet, T., deputy and editor, 104, 191, 210 n.
Vonliarliarskii, administrator, 164
Von Reichel, J. G., professor, 176
Voronezh district, 115 n., 133, 134 n., 173 n.
Vorontsov, A. R., patron, 240
Vorontsov, B. M., statesman, 104
Vorontsov, M., statesman, 39
Vorontsov, R. L., deputy and statesman, 39, 81
Vorontsova, E., lady of the court, 39
Vyborg province, 153, 174 n., 238 n.; *see also* nobility, Finland
Vyrodov, I., deputy, 120, 158

western Europe
  influence of, 1–2, 7, 14, 15, 24, 34, 41, 52, 56–7, 92–9, 103, 147, 152–3, 216, 221–2, 249
  Denmark, 2, 47–8, 86
  England, 20, 32, 47, 86, 90, 96, 104, 108, 125, 175, 226
  France, 20, 32, 37, 86, 89, 96, 97–8, 104, 194, 245–6

Germany, 8, 22, 26, 32, 37, 46, 86, 194
Holland, 32, 96, 104
Poland, 20, 32 n., 94, 116, 117, 119, 151, 214
Prussia, 2, 38, 46, 86, 201, 241
Sweden, 32, 86, 238
others, 2 n., 20–1, 86, 241
Weymouth, Lord, statesman, 221
Wolff, F., deputy, 126

Yellow Hussar Regiment, New Russia, 148, 181 n.

Zagoskin, N., historian, 20
Zapozhok district, Moscow, 68
Zaraisk district, Moscow, 70, 113 n., 130 n., 180 n.
Zavadovskii, P., administrator, 241
Zemskii sobor, 52, 64
Zherebtsov, I., deputy, 121, 208
Znamenskii, I., historian, 212, 214
Zolotnitskii, V., deputy, 157, 210 n.
Zubtsov district, Novgorod, 128, 173 n.
Zutis, Ia., historian, 239
Zybin, M., deputy, 176